T0221044

Cover image: The Southern Ring is a planetary nebula showing the remnants of a dying Sun-like star. The nebula, composed of gas and interstellar dust, is located some 2500 light-years from Earth and is nearly half a light-year in diameter. The bright star near the center is a companion of the dead star whose transformation has ejected the nebula's gas and dust shells over thousands of years. The NIRCam instrument onboard NASA's (National Aeronautics and Space Administration) James Webb space telescope obtained this image in 2022 (Image: NASA).

Systems Science

for Engineers and Scholars

Avner Engel

Tel Aviv University
Systems Engineering Research Initiative (TAU-SERI)
Israel

WILEY

Hardback ISBN: 9781394211647

Library of Congress Cataloging-in-Publication Data:
Names: Engel, Avner (Researcher), author.
Title: Systems science for engineers and scholars / Avner Engel.
Description: Hoboken, New Jersey: John Wiley & Sons, Inc., [2024] | Includes bibliographical references and index. | Summary: "This book describes the principles of systems science and how engineers, engineering students, and other scholars can put its concepts into practical use at work and in their personal life. Systems science is an interdisciplinary field that studies the foundation of systems in nature and society. It claims that the universe is composed of systems or systems of systems, all of which possess common intrinsic attributes."—Provided by publisher.
Identifiers: LCCN 2023045491 (print) | LCCN 2023045492 (ebook) | ISBN 9781394211647 (hardback) | ISBN 9781394211654 (adobe pdf) | ISBN 9781394211661 (epub) | ISBN 9781394211678
Subjects: LCSH: System theory. | Systems engineering.
Classification: LCC Q295 .E534 2024 (print) | LCC Q295 (ebook) | DDC 003—dc23/eng/20231025
LC record available at https://lccn.loc.gov/2023045491
LC ebook record available at https://lccn.loc.gov/2023045492

Cover design: Wiley
Credit: © NASA and STScI (public domain)

Set in 9.5/12.5pt STIXTwoText by Lumina Datamatics, Inc.

To my wife Rachel and sons Ofer, Amir, Jonathan, and Michael.

"If you can't explain it to a six-year-old, you don't understand it yourself."

"Imagination is more important than knowledge. Knowledge is limited. Imagination encircles the world."

—*Albert Einstein*

Table of contents

Preface

This book describes the fundamentals of systems science and how engineers, engineering students, and other scholars can put these concepts into practical use at work and in their personal lives. Systems science is an interdisciplinary field that studies the foundation of systems in nature and society. It suggests that the Universe is composed of systems or systems of systems, all of which possess common intrinsic attributes.

Along this line, systems science aims to determine systemic similarities among different disciplines (e.g., engineering, physics, biology, economics, mathematics) and to develop valuable models that apply to many fields of study. The advantage of this approach is that people, and in our case, engineers and scholars, can obtain answers to problems by studying and adopting ideas from different domains.

Engineers often seek speedy solutions to technical problems within a relatively restricted mindset. Under this ethos, engineers can be proud of many achievements throughout history. However, this book provides engineers with powerful means to enhance their professional and personal abilities by utilizing holistic and multidisciplinary elements inherent in systems science theory.

The book identifies 10 fundamental systems science principles that open engineers' horizons to various domains from which they can conclude practical insights about their areas of interest. For example, one systems science fundamental deals with interactions between different systems. Consider an engineer who examines a particular interface within a technical system. He may embrace a holistic view in his system design by adopting biological interactions among species. Biology researchers recognize six relationship types (i.e., competition, predation, herbivory, mutualism, parasitism, and commensalism). Thus, by adopting ideas from biology, this engineer can open his design to many creative alternatives.

In brief, this book expresses complex ideas related to holistic and interdisciplinary learning in a concise and easy-to-grasp manner, with many examples and graphics. As a result, the book opens new perspectives and provides practical guidance to engineers and scholars wishing to implement systems science concepts. The book contains the following four parts:

1. **Part 1: Facets of Systems Science and Engineering.** This part starts with a preface to systems science. It defines 10 fundamental principles of systems science: universal context, boundary, hierarchy, interactions, change, input/output, complexity, control, evolution, and emergence. Multiple examples

illuminate each principle. This part also describes ideas about systems thinking, the philosophy of engineering, and systems engineering. Finally, this part brings forth an analysis of an engineered versus a biological system. This analysis emanates from one of systems science's promises to transcend individual disciplines by obtaining knowledge from well-known domains to elucidate less-known domains.

2. **Part 2: Holistic Systems Design.** This part provides fresh, holistic thinking about the system context, which is, by definition, the environment of a system of interest (SoI). Such a view recognizes that systems' context influences SoI in wide, often unpredictable, and sometimes disastrous ways. This concept is illustrated by an extensive example of an unmanned air vehicle (UAV) system of interest in its all-inclusive context. This system context includes natural systems, social systems, research systems, formation systems, sustainment systems, business systems, commercial systems, financial systems, political systems, legal systems, cultural systems, and biosphere systems. Ultimately, this part intends to motivate engineers and designers to create resilient systems that can withstand their contexts' uncertain behavior.

3. **Part 3: Global Environment and Energy: Crisis and Action Plan.** Today, the global environmental and energy crises seem to be humankind's most challenging, systemic predicaments. This part analyzes the environmental crisis regarding past and present global transformation and its environmental predicament. This part proceeds with a proposed systemic, no-nonsense ecological action plan to sustain the Earth's system and human society. Similarly, the global energy crisis is analyzed, including the current global energy status, energy return on investment (EROI), and the impact of renewable energy systems. Again, this part proceeds with a no-nonsense proposed systemic energy action plan for the global energy crisis. This action plan deals with renewable, fossil, and fission energy. In addition, it describes short-term future energy options, including small modular reactors (SMR), and long-term future energy options, including nuclear fusion.

4. **Part 4: More Systems Science for Engineers and Scholars.** This part contains independent articles showing how engineers can utilize systems science creatively. This part includes (1) engineering and systemic psychology, (2) delivering value and resolving conflicts, (3) multi-objective, multi-agent decision-making, (4) systems engineering using category theory, (5) holistic risk management using systems of systems failures (SOSF) methodology, and (6) systemic accident and mishap analysis.

Acknowledgments

The author seeks to acquaint engineers and scholars with facets of systems science. To achieve this objective, the author has drawn upon his engineering experience, communicated with many people, and synthesized information from many sources such as books, articles, blogs, etc. Several researchers have provided permission to incorporate adapted portions of their writings (e.g., texts, images, and ideas) within this book. The author is deeply indebted to these people and institutions:

- Dr. Ismael Rafols from the University of Sussex, England, for permission to use an image of a global science map. Also, Prof. Eberhard Umbach from the University of Osnabruck, Germany, for permission to use ideas and text on criticism of systems science (Chapter 1).
- Prof. Boris Romashov and Dr. Aleksandr Mishin from Voronezhsky State Nature Biosphere Reserve in Russia for permission to use text and an image of red deer and wolves' interactions (Chapter 2).
- Dr. Louise Kjaer from the Technical University of Denmark for permission to use text and ideas on environmental input/output analysis related to corporations and products. Also, Prof. Steven Frank from the University of California at Irvine for permission to use text pertinent to input/output relations in biological systems. Also, Prof. Olivier de Weck and Dr. Kaushik Sinha from the Massachusetts Institute of Technology (MIT) for permission to use text related to structural complexity (Chapter 3).
- The Royal Academy of Engineering, London, United Kingdom, for permission to reproduce intriguing portions of papers presented during seminars on the philosophy of engineering held at the academy in June 2010. Also, Prof. Len Troncale from California State Polytechnic University for permission to use data on recurring systems engineering human systems pathologies (Chapter 5).
- Prof. David D'Onofrio from the University of Phoenix for permission to use text and ideas on comparative analysis between the structure and function of computer hard drives and DNA (Chapter 6).
- Rick Adcock from Cranfield University in the United Kingdom and his colleagues for providing seed ideas on engineered system context in "Guide to the Systems Engineering Body of Knowledge" (Chapter 7).

- David Climenhaga, Canadian journalist and a blogger at AlbertaPolitics, for permission to use text and ideas about small modular nuclear reactors (SMR), including their advantages and disadvantages (Chapter 14).
- Prof. T.K. Das of the City University of New York for permission to use text and ideas regarding cognitive biases (Chapter 15).
- Dr. Anand Kumar of Tata Research Development & Design Centre, Pune, India, for permission to use text and ideas about a systematic approach to deliver value (Chapter 16).
- Prof. Uri Wilensky from Northwestern University, Chicago, Illinois, for permission to use text, images, and the NetLogo software simulator running the wolf–sheep predation model. Also, Prof. Sean Luke from George Mason University, Fairfax, Virginia, for permission to use text, images, and the MASON software simulator to execute the cooperative multirobot observation of multiple moving targets (CMOMMT) model. Also, Teja Pennada from Blekinge Institute of Technology, Karlskrona, Sweden, for providing text and ideas regarding containers' optimal positions in a seaport terminal yard (Chapter 17).
- Dr. Yaniv Mordecai, from Tel Aviv University, Israel, for authoring the central part of Chapter 18, "Systems Engineering Using Category Theory."
- Prof. Takafumi Nakamura from Daito Bunka University, Japan, for permission to embed texts and graphics from his papers on SOSF methodology (Chapter 19).
- Prof. Nancy Leveson and Joel Parker Henderson for permission to adapt ideas and images on Systems-Theoretic Accident Model and Processes (STAMP) and Causal Analysis System Theory (CAST), and Baktare Kanarit and Dr. Daniel Hartmann for permission to adapt ideas and images from their presentation on the Israeli Air Force (IAF) CH-53 aviation disaster of 1997 (Chapter 20).
- Prof. Len Troncale from California State Polytechnic University for permission to use ideas and text on distinguished systems science researchers (Appendix A) and systems thinking researchers (Appendix B).
- Sarah Wales-McGrath, the book's copy editor, for diligent efforts to enhance the manuscript as well as Wiley's editors team, Brett Kurzman, Becky Cowan, Vishal Paduchuru, and Rajeev Kumar, who helped make and shape this book.
- Colleagues at work, Dr. Amit Teller and Shalom Shachar, as well as founding members of the Tel-Aviv University – Systems Engineering Research Initiative (TAU-SERI): Prof. Yoram Reich, Dr. Miri Sitton, Uzi Orion, and Ami Danielli.
- My wife, Rachel, and my sons, Ofer, Amir, Jonathan, and Michael, for supporting and encouraging my book efforts with advice, patience, and love.

Avner Engel
Tel Aviv, Israel

Part I

Facets of Systems Science and Engineering

1

Introduction to Systems Science

1.1 Foreword

1.1.1 The Book

This book describes the fundamental principles of systems science and how engineers, engineering students, and other scholars can put its concepts into practical use at work and in their personal lives. Systems science[1] is an interdisciplinary field that studies the foundation of systems in nature and society. It suggests that the universe is composed of systems or systems of systems, all of which possess common intrinsic attributes.

Along this line, systems science aims to determine systemic similarities among different disciplines (e.g., engineering, physics, biology, economics, mathematics) and to develop valuable models that apply to many fields of study. The advantage of this approach is that people, and in our case, engineers, can obtain answers to problems by studying and adopting ideas from different domains.

Engineers often seek speedy solutions to technical problems within a relatively restricted mindset. Under this ethos, engineers can be proud of many achievements throughout history. However, this book provides engineers with powerful means to enhance their professional and personal abilities by utilizing holistic and multidisciplinary elements inherent in systems science theory.

---

1 A system is: "an arrangement of parts or elements that together exhibit behavior or meaning that the individual constituents do not." Sources: Systems Engineering and System Definitions, ISO/IEC/IEEE 15288:2015.

Science is: "the systematic study of the structure and behavior of the physical and natural world through observation, experimentation, and the testing of theories against the evidence obtained." *The Dictionary.*

Systems Science for Engineers and Scholars, First Edition. Edited by Avner Engel.
© 2024 John Wiley & Sons, Ltd. Published 2024 by John Wiley & Sons, Ltd.

The book identifies 10 fundamental systems science principles that open engineers' horizons to various domains from which they can conclude practical insights about their areas of interest. For example, one systems science fundamental principle deals with interactions between different systems. Consider an engineer who examines a particular interface within a technical system. He may embrace a holistic view in his system design by adopting biological interactions among species. Researchers in biology recognize six types of relationships (i.e., competition, predation, herbivory, mutualism, parasitism, and commensalism). Thus, by adopting ideas from biology, this engineer can open his design to many creative opportunities.

In brief, this book expresses complex ideas related to holistic and interdisciplinary learning in a concise and easy-to-grasp manner with many examples and graphics. As a result, the book opens new perspectives and provides practical guidance to engineers and scholars wishing to implement systems science concepts.

1.1.2 The Overall Structure of the Book

Figure 1.1 depicts the book's overall structure, consisting of the front matter, the main book's body, and the back matter.

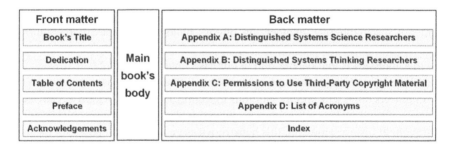

Figure 1.1 Overall structure of the book.

1.1.3 The Structure of the Book's Main Body

Figure 1.2 depicts the structure of the main body of the book. It is divided into four parts as follows:

- Part 1: Facets of Systems Science and Engineering
- Part 2: Holistic Systems Design
- Part 3: Global Environment and Energy: Crisis and Action Plan
- Part 4: More Systems Science for Engineers and Scholars

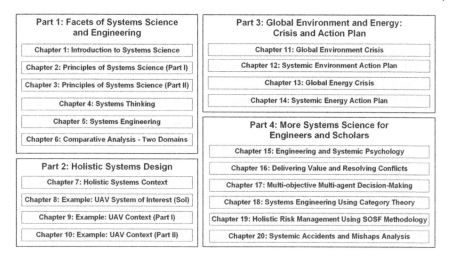

Part 1: Facets of Systems Science and Engineering	Part 3: Global Environment and Energy: Crisis and Action Plan
Chapter 1: Introduction to Systems Science	Chapter 11: Global Environment Crisis
Chapter 2: Principles of Systems Science (Part I)	Chapter 12: Systemic Environment Action Plan
Chapter 3: Principles of Systems Science (Part II)	Chapter 13: Global Energy Crisis
Chapter 4: Systems Thinking	Chapter 14: Systemic Energy Action Plan
Chapter 5: Systems Engineering	Part 4: More Systems Science for Engineers and Scholars
Chapter 6: Comparative Analysis - Two Domains	Chapter 15: Engineering and Systemic Psychology
Part 2: Holistic Systems Design	Chapter 16: Delivering Value and Resolving Conflicts
Chapter 7: Holistic Systems Context	Chapter 17: Multi-objective Multi-agent Decision-Making
Chapter 8: Example: UAV System of Interest (SoI)	Chapter 18: Systems Engineering Using Category Theory
Chapter 9: Example: UAV Context (Part I)	Chapter 19: Holistic Risk Management Using SOSF Methodology
Chapter 10: Example: UAV Context (Part II)	Chapter 20: Systemic Accidents and Mishaps Analysis

Figure 1.2 Structure of the book's main body.

1.1.3.1 Part 1: Facets of Systems Science and Engineering

- **Chapter 1: Introduction to Systems Science.** This chapter provides a preface to the book, followed by a discussion of humanity's challenges. It then briefly encapsulates systems science and describes early systems pioneers. Finally, this chapter presents some criticisms of systems science and relevant responses.
- **Chapter 2: Principles of Systems Science (Part I).** This chapter and the next one define the 10 fundamental systems science principles. For clarity, these principles are presented in two chapters. This chapter describes the following principles: (1) universal context, (2) boundary, (3) hierarchy, (4) interactions, and (5) change. Numerous examples describe each principle.
- **Chapter 3: Principles of Systems Science (Part II).** This chapter describes the following principles: (6) input/output, (7) complexity, (8) control, (9) evolution, and (10) emergence. Again, numerous examples describe each principle.
- **Chapter 4: Systems Thinking.** This chapter discusses the fundamental concepts of systems thinking and the iceberg model of systems thinking. It then explores systems thinking as a system in its own right. Finally, the chapter elaborates on various barriers to systems thinking and describes early systems thinking pioneers.
- **Chapter 5: Systems Engineering.** This chapter brings forth illuminating ideas on the philosophy of engineering. It then describes systems engineering concepts, culminating in systems engineering deficiencies, systems' pathologies, and infamous engineered systems failures and disasters.

- **Chapter 6: Comparative Analysis - Two Domains.** This chapter presents a comparative analysis of biological versus engineered systems. The analysis emanates from one of systems science's promises to transcend disciplines by obtaining knowledge about less-known domains utilizing analogies from well-known domains.

1.1.3.2   Part 2: Holistic Systems Design

- **Chapter 7: Holistic Systems Context.** This chapter provides a holistic description of the systems context, which is, by definition, the environment of a system of interest (SoI). A more holistic view of systems contexts recognizes that the broad environment of SOIs has myriad and settled influences over SOIs. Many spectacular engineering failures can be traced to systems whose designers ignored such consequences. Thus, this chapter covers renewed thinking about the systems context and its components.
- **Chapter 8: Example: UAV System of Interest (SoI).** This chapter and the following two chapters elucidate the concept of holistic systems contexts. This chapter provides a compressive example of an unmanned air vehicle (UAV) system of interest (SoI). The UAV description focuses on the 10 systems science fundamental principles: universal context, boundary, hierarchy, interactions, change, input/output, complexity, control, evolution, and emergence.
- **Chapter 9: Example: UAV Context (Part I).** This chapter illuminates the holistic nature of SoI context issues through the UAV system described earlier. Specific topics related to the UAV systems context are presented in two chapters. First, this chapter describes the following UAV system contexts: (1) natural systems, (2) social systems, (3) research systems, (4) formation systems, (5) sustainment systems, (6) business systems, and (7) commercial systems.
- **Chapter 10: Example: UAV Context (Part II).** This chapter continues to illuminate the holistic nature of SoI context issues through the UAV system described earlier. This chapter describes the following UAV system contexts: (8) financial systems, (9) political systems, (10) legal systems, (11) cultural systems, and (12) biosphere systems.

1.1.3.1   Part 3: Global Environment and Energy: Crisis and Action Plan

- **Chapter 11: Global Environment Crisis.** Nowadays, humanity faces many global predicaments. One of the most challenging, systemic global issues is the environmental crisis. This chapter describes and systemically analyzes it. This analysis includes past and present global transformation and the crisis' environmental predicament.
- **Chapter 12: Systemic Environment Action Plan.** Currently, little is being done about the environmental problem. However, this indifferent attitude will change drastically as life on this planet becomes more and more unbearable for more and more people. Then governments, environmental scientists, engineers, and the public will unite in carrying out measures to combat global

environmental threats to the human species. This chapter provides a systemic action plan for this massive ecological threat to humankind. This plan includes sustaining the Earth's system and sustaining human society.

- **Chapter 13: Global Energy Crisis.** As mentioned before, humanity faces many global predicaments. The second most challenging systemic global issue is the global energy crisis. This chapter describes and systemically analyzes the global energy crisis. This description includes the current global energy status, energy return on investment (EROI), and the effect of renewable energy systems.
- **Chapter 14: Systemic Energy Action Plan.** This chapter provides a systemic action plan for the global energy crisis. This description includes a discussion regarding the global energy dilemma and what can be done about renewable energy, fossil energy, and fission reaction energy. In addition, the chapter describes short-term future energy, including small modular reactors (SMR), and long-term future energy, including nuclear fusion.

1.1.3.2 Part 4: More Systems Science for Engineers and Scholars

- **Chapter 15: Engineering and Systemic Psychology.** This chapter provides systemic links between key psychological features in systems engineering. In particular, it describes schema theory and cognitive biases, which sometimes lead to failed design, building, or systems operations. This linkage is illustrated by several spectacular systems failures, including the Bay of Pigs fiasco (1961), the disastrous 747 collision at Tenerife (1977), the space shuttle *Columbia* disaster (2003), BP's *Deepwater Horizon* oil spill (2010), and the collapse of the Morandi Bridge in Genoa (2018). The chapter then covers ways to undertake cognitive debiasing.
- **Chapter 16: Delivering Value and Resolving Conflicts.** Systems must sustain their ability to deliver value to stakeholders throughout their life. Therefore, delivering systems value requires identifying those things that enhance value to all stakeholders. Likewise, conflicts among developers and builders of systems and their resolutions have been the subjects of many studies and other research. This chapter systematically analyzes two related topics: (1) delivering systems value and (2) conflict analysis and resolution.
- **Chapter 17: Multi-objective, Multi-agent Decision-Making.** Multi-objective, multi-agent (MOMA) decision-making aims to optimize the policies of individual stakeholders concerning multiple objectives within the multistakeholder environment. These decisions should consider the possible trade-offs between conflicting objective functions and stakeholders' desires. The chapter includes the following issues: (1) multi-objective multi-agents, (2) representation of systems activities, (3) key types of systems activities, and (4) three illustrative examples.

- **Chapter 18: Systems Engineering Using Category Theory.** Systems engineers own systems components' conceptual, logical, and physical integration throughout engineered projects. Therefore, adopting a collaborative mindset is crucial because integration occurs first and foremost among people and only afterward among systems and technologies. This chapter describes systems engineering using category theory. It includes the following elements: (1) defining the problem, (2) brief background on category theory and systems engineering, (3) an example of designing an electric vehicle, (4) category theory as a systems specification language, (5) categorical multidisciplinary collaborative design, and (6) the categorical design processes.
- **Chapter 19: Holistic Risk Management Using SOSF Methodology.** The predominant worldview on risk management in current engineering practice is that system failure risks should be addressed during the design phase. However, such an approach excludes proactive handling of emerging risks throughout the systems' life, leading to repeated failures. This chapter uses a systems of systems failures (SOSF) methodology to describe systemic risk management. It includes the following elements: (1) limitations of current risk management practices, (2) features of SOSF, (3) an example of holistic risk management and failure classes, and (4) an example of a synthetic SOSF risk management.
- **Chapter 20: Systemic Accidents and Mishaps Analyses.** This chapter describes different accident causation models, which explain how accidents happen. Based on systems theory, one systemic accident model that reflects the current complex sociotechnical environment is the systems-theoretic accident model and processes (STAMP). The chapter explains the systemic nature of the STAMP accidents and mishaps model. It includes the following elements: (1) basic accident and mishap concepts; (2) classification of accident causation models; (3) the STAMP model, sociotechnical failure mechanisms, and procedures; and (4) causal analysis system theory (CAST) procedures and an example of CAST analysis involving the collision of two CH-53 helicopters.

1.1.4 Disclaimer

The author seeks to acquaint engineers, systems engineers, and other scholars with reasonably acceptable facets of systems science. To achieve this objective, the author drew on his engineering experience; communicated with many people; and synthesized information from many sources, including books, articles, blogs, and the like (giving credit where credit is due). In addition, a bibliography is placed at the end of each chapter covering invaluable sources for a deeper understanding of the various issues discussed in this book. The author gained much knowledge from these resources and is indebted to the individuals, researchers, and experts who created them. Readers should note that the sources of all third-party images and texts, as well as permissions to use them, are provided in Appendix C: Permissions to Use Third-Party Copyright Material.

1.2 Critical Humanity Challenge

According to Rousseau et al. (2016), the founders of general systems theory (systems science today) were mainly concerned with the far-reaching risks to human civilization of the proliferation of nuclear weapons along with looming environmental issues. In addition, they were worried about losing meaning, value, and purpose in human lives. They maintained that science and philosophy relied unrealistically on simplistic models of reductionism and proposed that a new systems theory would provide a more appropriate and enabling paradigm. Sadly, the approach has made little progress, and human existential problems are more significant than ever.

Nevertheless, many scientists believe systems science methodology offers the best-coordinated opportunity to deal with intractable problems. One such issue relates to the global environmental challenge, which, if left unchecked, threatens the existence of humanity in the not-too-distant future.

In their groundbreaking paper "A Safe Operating Space for Humanity,"[2] published in 2009, some 30 eminent European, American, and Australian researchers tried to identify and quantify nine planetary boundaries that should not be crossed to prevent unacceptable environmental change.

These nine planetary biophysical boundaries are (1) climate change, (2) ocean acidification, (3) stratospheric ozone depletion, (4) biogeochemical flows, (5) global freshwater use, (6) deforestation and other land use changes, (7) biodiversity loss, (8) atmospheric aerosol loading, and (9) chemical pollution.

According to the authors, as of 2009, three of these nine planetary biophysical boundaries had already been breached: (1) climate change, (2) rate of biodiversity loss, and (3) changes to the global nitrogen cycle. These findings could induce disastrous consequences for humanity.

Figure 1.3 depicts the model proposed by the study on a safe operating space for humanity. The inner circle represents a safe operating space for nine planetary systems, and the red wedges represent an estimate of the year 2009 position for each variable.

---

2 Rockstrom J. et al. (2009, Sept.). A safe operating space for humanity. *Nature* 461: 472–475. https://www.nature.com/articles/461472a.pdf. Accessed Jan. 2023.

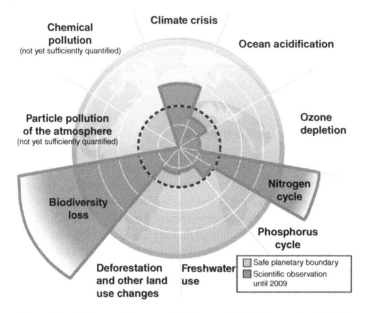

Figure 1.3 Safe operating space for humanity (Rockstrom et al., 2009).

These critical problems require the concerted efforts of governments throughout the world. From a scientific standpoint, systems scientists could provide essential inputs to resolve or mitigate these significant problems. An updated research, "Earth beyond six of nine planetary boundaries" (Richardson et al., 2023), was released recently, indicating a significant deterioration in the current earth's environmental conditions. A description of this new research is discussed in Chapter 11.

1.3 Systems Science in Brief

1.3.1 About Science

According to UNESCO (United Nations Educational, Scientific and Cultural Organization),[3] science is the most significant collective human endeavor. "It contributes to ensuring longer and healthier life, monitors our health, provides

---

3 The 4 Pillars of Education by UNESCO. See The 4 Pillars of Education by UNESCO: You are Mom. https://youaremom.com/parenting/raising-a-child/4-pillars-education-unesco/.Accessed: Jan. 2023.

medicine to cure our diseases, alleviates aches and pains, helps us to provide water for our basic needs—including our food, provides energy, and makes life more fun, including sports, music, entertainment, and the latest communication technology. Last, but not least, it nourishes our spirit. Science provides logical solutions for everyday life and helps us answer the universe's mysteries."

Modern science is typically divided into two major branches: the empirical sciences, which study nature in the broadest sense, and the formal sciences, which study abstract concepts. The empirical sciences are further divided into natural sciences and social sciences. Natural sciences describe, predict, and seek to understand natural phenomena based on empirical evidence from observations and experiments. They may be further divided into two main branches: physical sciences and life sciences. Finally, social sciences are concerned with the relationships among individuals and societies within the human species.

In contrast, formal sciences study formal systems,[4] which are derived by reasoning from self-evident propositions. Applied science, therefore, is the application of scientific knowledge to obtain practical objectives. The relationships between the branches of science are shown in Figure 1.4.

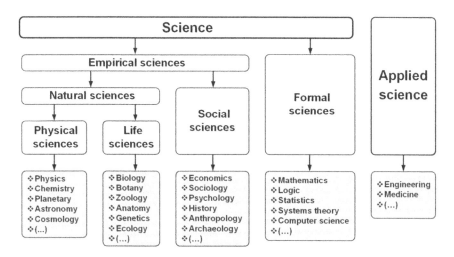

Figure 1.4 Relationships between the branches of science.

Figure 1.5 and Table 1.1 depict some of the most outstanding scientists of antiquity and modern times and their momentous scientific discoveries that have affected much of humanity.

---

4 Derived from https://en.wikipedia.org/wiki/Science. Accessed: Jan. 2023.

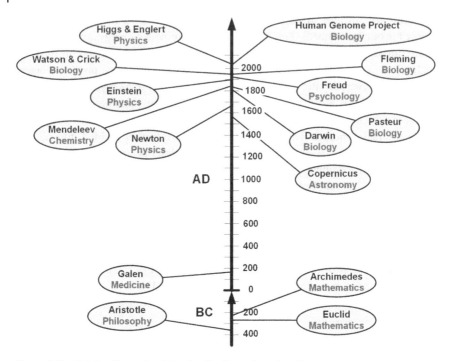

Figure 1.5 Outstanding scientists of antiquity and modern times.

Table 1.1 Momentous scientific discoveries.

Person	Domain	Scientific achievement	Year
Aristotle (384–322 BC)	Philosophy	Philosophical ideas and contributions to physics are still being taught for almost two millennia	350 BC
Euclid (325–270 BC)	Mathematics	Famous mathematical, astronomical, navigation, and other scientific works valid for more than two millennia	300 BC
Archimedes (287–212 BC)	Mathematics	Extensive calculus, statics, hydrostatics, and geometrical theorems valid for more than two millennia	250 BC
Galen (129–216)	Medicine	A flawed medical doctrine that dominated Western and Arab practices for 1500 years	170
Nicolaus Copernicus (1473–1543)	Astronomy	Heliocentrism: the sun is stationary at the center of the solar system, and planets revolve around it	1543

Table 1.1 (Continued)

Person	Domain	Scientific achievement	Year
Isaac Newton (1642–1726)	Physics	Newton's three laws of motion and Newton's law of universal gravitation	1664
Charles Darwin (1809–1882)	Biology	Theory of evolution/natural selection	1859
Dmitry Mendeleev (1834–1907)	Chemistry	Periodic Table of chemical elements	1864
Louis Pasteur (1822–1895)	Biology	Diseases caused by microorganisms that can be killed by heat and disinfectants	1881
Albert Einstein (1879–1955)	Physics	Einstein's special and general relativity theories and Einstein's mass–energy equivalence $E = mc^2$	1905
Sigmund Freud (1858-1939)	Psychology	Freud's psychoanalysis: clinical method for treating psychopathology	1910
Alexander Fleming (1881–1955)	Biology	First antibiotic substance: penicillin	1928
James Watson (1928–) and Francis Crick (1916–2004)	Biology	Double helix structure of the DNA molecule	1953
Human Genome Project (HGP)	Biology	Mapping the human genome	1990–2003
Peter Higgs (1929–) and Francois Englert (1932–)	Physics	Proposing the Higgs boson and its subsequent discovery at the European Council for Nuclear Research (CERN) Large Hadron Collider (LHC)	1960; 2012

1.3.2 Silo Effects

Conventional science adheres to the division of labor by specialization in specific and narrow fields of endeavor. Along this line, academia and other research institutes are organized into discrete faculties and departments, making responsibilities more explicit. For example, the human body is organized into specialized organs.

Accordingly, medical caretakers require specializations, each within a relatively narrow sphere of interest. Furthermore, most scientists are trained to be independent and to focus on precise and focused targets. The great motivation is to stick to a problem and dig deep enough until, eventually, one may find something valuable.

This arrangement often leads academic researchers to ignore relevant research within other scientific domains. As a result, much knowledge is sequestered within individual academic faculties, departments, or small groups of researchers. This type of "silo mentality" tends to create bureaucratic rivalry, tunnel vision, and blind spots, which reduce the potential efficiency of the scientific endeavor. In short, a silo mentality causes excessive compartmentalization, inhibiting communication among domains and stifling innovation (Figure 1.6).

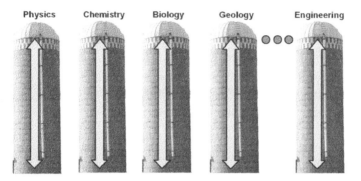

Figure 1.6 Conventional scientific "silo view" (image inspired by Len Troncale's writings).

1.3.3   Systems Science[5]

Systems science is an interdisciplinary field. It studies the essence of systems in nature, society, technology, and science. More specifically, systems science attempts to develop a scientific foundation that applies to all areas of science. This foundation includes the physical sciences (e.g., physics, chemistry), life sciences (e.g., biology, botany), social sciences (e.g., economics, sociology), formal sciences (e.g., mathematics), and applied sciences (e.g., engineering, medicine). In short, systems scientists consider everything in the universe as being composed of systems or systems of systems. Furthermore, all systems share common attributes, characteristics, and organizational and behavioral principles. Therefore, understanding these universal aspects is the basis for understanding the universe. In other words, understanding the principles of systems science can guide the study of any specific kind of system (Figure 1.7).

---

5 Parts of this section were inspired by the writings of George Mobus, Professor Emeritus, School of Engineering & Technology, University of Washington, Tacoma.

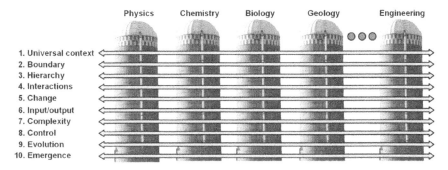

Figure 1.7 Systems science fundamental view (image inspired by Len Troncale's writing).

Table 1.2 defines a set of fundamental principles of systems science that operate overall knowledge domains.

Table 1.2 Systems science fundamental principles.[6]

#	Principle	Short Description
1.	Universal context	The universe is composed of systems and systems of systems.
2.	Boundary	All systems have a boundary that demarcates the system from its context (environment).
3.	Hierarchy	All systems are entities organized in structural and functional hierarchies.
4.	Interactions	All systems contain networks of relations among their components and/or with their context.
5.	Change	All systems change and transform continuously in many dimensions and on multiple time scales.
6.	Input/output	All systems receive information, energy, and/or matter from their context, process it, and then transmit the result to their context.
7.	Complexity	All systems exhibit various kinds and levels of complexity.
8.	Control	All systems have an internal regulatory mechanism to achieve long-term stability or controlled oscillation.
9.	Evolution	Living systems evolve to harmonize with their dynamic context. Inanimate systems are modified to satisfy their dynamic context.
10.	Emergence	All systems exhibit properties or behaviors their parts do not possess.

6 Adapted with modifications from Mobus and Kalton (2015).

1.3.4 Typical Engineered System

There are many definitions of systems. Among them, a broad yet lean and concentrated definition is "A system is a collection of interrelated parts that, by the relationships between them, do things its parts cannot do on their own" (Martin et al., 2019). An example of a simple engineered system in its context (environment) is depicted in Figure 1.8.

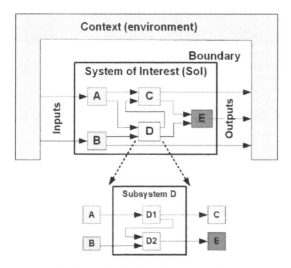

Figure 1.8 Example of a simple engineered system in its context (environment).

1.3.5 The Ad Hoc Collaboration

Shortcomings of silo thinking have been discussed since the term *functional silo syndrome* was coined by Phil Ensor in 1988. One response to this situation involves global scientific collaboration. Researchers collaborate to complement their knowledge and skills and access funding and specialized equipment. In principle, scientists can learn from, work with, and foster global collaborative partnerships with scientists across multiple research disciplines. Also, from a researcher's point of view, collaboration with other scientists combines to create value exceeding the sum of its parts. Mainly, it mitigates the one way of thinking constraint.

For example, let us consider the global environmental challenge. First, there are physical sciences—physics, chemistry, and the like. Second, there are life sciences—biology, botany, ecology, and so on. Third, there are social science—economics, sociology, and the like. How are we going to manage this multidimensional problem? Also, we should consider the engineering aspects: How do we design more efficient and environmentally friendly infrastructure systems? Having collaborating experts from many disciplines means the challenge can be assailed from all sides simultaneously, giving humanity a chance to resolve this problem. A global science map based on citing similarities among SPRU[7] subject categories is depicted in Figure 1.9. Each node represents a discipline, and the connecting lines represent similarities among disciplines.

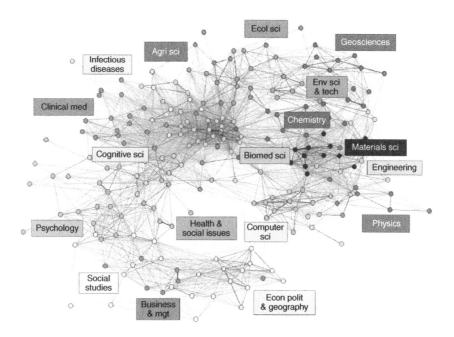

Figure 1.9   Global science map (Rafols et al., 2010).

The fundamental problem with ad hoc collaboration is that it is impromptu, having the character of an improvisation. Often, prospective collaborators know each other or are acquainted through a third party. These relations imply that, by and large, such collaborations do not materialize spontaneously.

Scientific collaboration takes work. First, actively probing for collaborative opportunities and merging skill sets with different researchers takes a lot of work. In addition, authorship issues, project goals mismatch, unclear tasking and responsibilities, different preconceptions about work timeliness (urgency), or—sometimes—incompatible personalities often lead to a failed collaborative effort.

Other problems may arise under a global scientific collaboration regime. Physical distance produces complications. People may be able to meet face-to-face only sometimes. Also, people from different countries operate within various cultures,

---

7 SPRU: Science and Technology Policy Research, University of Sussex, Brighton, England.

speak diverse languages, and conduct business in different time zones. Finally, global scientific collaboration is hindered due to differences in science funding, customs rules, or security and national regulations issues. These elements are particularly true when collaborating with scientists in less industrialized countries where "professional science" is often in the relatively early stages of progression.

1.3.6 Isomorphism

Systems science claims that all systems, regardless of types and domains, share the same broad principles (depicted in Table 1.2). In other words, systems' characteristics in one domain are *isomorphic* to systems' characteristics in other domains. Isomorphism is a mapping between two sets that define a one-to-one correspondence between the components of each set. Therefore, two isomorphic objects have the same properties and may not be distinguished through their structural attributes.

For example, the two words *poppy* and *daddy* are isomorphic because there exists a linear, one-to-one, and onto transformation[8] (T) between these two words (Figure 1.10).

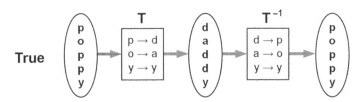

Figure 1.10 Example: two isomorphic words, *poppy* and *daddy*.

On the other hand, the two words *title* and *poppy* are not isomorphic because there exists a linear, one-to-one relationship but not onto transformation (T) between these two words (Figure 1.11).

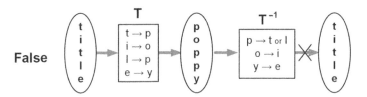

Figure 1.11 Example: two nonisomorphic words, *title* and *poppy*.

---

8 See more: Bijection. https://en.wikipedia.org/wiki/Bijection. Accessed: Jan. 2023.

A mathematical example of isomorphic objects is depicted in Figure 1.12. Let us transform a fourtuple vector of real numbers (R^4) into a 2×2 matrix of real numbers $M_2(R)$ using the transformation T. This relation is a linear, one-to-one, and onto transformation between the two spaces. Therefore, one can say that R^4 is isomorphic to $M_2(R)$.

$$T\ R^4 \longrightarrow M_2(R) \qquad T\begin{pmatrix} a \\ b \\ c \\ d \end{pmatrix} = \begin{pmatrix} a & b \\ c & d \end{pmatrix} \qquad R^4 \cong M_2(R)$$

Figure 1.12 Mathematical isomorphic example.

1.3.7 Overcoming Knowledge Barrier between Domains

Figure 1.13 depicts a general systems science procedure to overcome the knowledge barrier between domains. First, a specific "source" system belonging to a relatively well-known part is analyzed by applying the systems science broad principles described in this figure. The net result of this analysis is a definition of common attributes, properties, and principles of organization and behavior related to the source system. Next, a specific "target" system belonging to a relatively unknown domain is defined based on this information. This definition applies the same methods and broad principles in reverse.

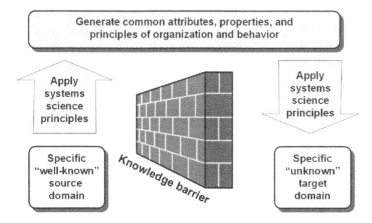

Figure 1.13 A procedure to overcome the knowledge barrier between domains.

1.4 Early Systems Pioneers

Early systems pioneers considered contemporary, twentieth-century science limited by its focus on the discrete parts of reality. They hoped to complement the insulated compartmentalization of the classical science approach with a more holistic approach. In particular, they pursued dialogue, collaboration, and integration between autonomous areas of study. The intent was to model systems' broad behavior and elucidate general principles that can be recognized and applied to other systems in different domains.

Systems science has evolved since the 1950s through many individuals from different natural, social, and formal science disciplines. Two biologists, an economist, a neurophysiologist, a computer scientist, and a mathematical psychologist, all born during the first third of the twentieth century, are widely acknowledged as the founders of systems science.[9] They are discussed in the following sections.

1.4.1 Alexander Aleksandrovich Bogdanov (1873–1928)

Alexander Bogdanov was a Soviet physician, philosopher, science fiction writer, and Bolshevik revolutionary. He proposed unifying all social, biological, and physical sciences, considering them as systems of relationships, and searching the organizational principles that underlie all systems. His pioneering ideas are now regarded as forerunners of systems science theory.

Selected books:

- *Technology Universal Organizational Science/Tektologiya Vseobshchaya Organizatsionnaya Nauka* (Russian), by Alexander Bogdanov, 2003 (revised publication).
- *Bogdanov and His Work: A Guide to the Published and Unpublished Works of Alexander A Bogdanov, 1873–1928*, by John Biggart and Georgii Gloveli, 2017.

1.4.2 Karl Ludwig von Bertalanffy (1901–1972)

Ludwig von Bertalanffy was an Austrian biologist. He grew up in Austria and worked in Vienna, London, Canada, and the United States. He is known as a cofounder of general systems

---

9 For a comprehansive list of distinguished systems science researchers, see Appendix A.

theory (GST) and the von Bertalanffy growth function, a mathematical model of an organism's growth over time.

Selected books:

- *General System Theory: Foundations, Development, Applications*, by Ludwig Von Bertalanffy, 1969 (revised publication).
- *General System Theory: Foundations, Development, Applications*, by Ludwig von Bertalanffy, Wolfgang Hofkirchner et al., 2015 (revised publication).

1.4.3   Kenneth Ewart Boulding (1910–1993)

Kenneth Boulding was an English-born American economist, educator, peace activist, and interdisciplinary philosopher. He is also known as a cofounder of general systems theory. Boulding emphasized that human economics and other behavior are embedded in a more extensive interconnected system.

Selected books:

- *The Organizational Revolution: A Study in the Ethics of Economic Organization*, by Kenneth Ewart Boulding, 1953.
- *Conflict and Defense: A General Theory*, by Kenneth Ewart Boulding, 2018 (revised publication).

1.4.4   James Grier Miller (1916–2002)

James Grier Miller was an American biologist, a pioneer of systems science, and an academic administrator. He established the modern use of the term *behavioral science*.

Selected books:

- *Living Systems*, by James Grier Miller, 1978.

1.4.5   Ralph Waldo Gerard (1900–1974)

Ralph Gerard was an American neurophysiologist and behavioral scientist. He is known for his wide-ranging work on the nervous system, nerve metabolism, psycho-pharmacology, and the biological basis of schizophrenia. In addition, Gerard investigated the biology of language, ethics, biology, cultural evolution, education, and the impact of science on public policies.

Selected books:

- *Mirror to Physiology: A Self-Survey of Physiological Science*, by Ralph Waldo Gerard and Wallace O. Fenn, 2012 (revised publication).

1.4.6 Anatol Rapoport (1911–2007)

Anatol Rapoport was an American mathematical psychologist. He was involved in general systems theory, mathematical biology, and the mathematical modeling of social interaction and stochastic contagion models. In addition, he combined his mathematical expertise with psychological insights to study game theory, social networks, semantics, the psychology of conflict, and international politics.

Selected books:

- *Fights, Games, and Debates*, by Anatol Rapoport, 1974.
- *Decision Theory and Behaviour: Normative and Descriptive Approaches*, by Anatol Rapoport, 1989.
- *Two-Person Game Theory* (Dover Books on Mathematics), by Anatol Rapoport, 1999.

1.4.7 George Jiří Klir (1932–2016)

George Jiri Klir was a Czech American computer scientist and professor of systems sciences at Binghamton University in Binghamton, New York.[10] Klir is known for his research contributions in fuzzy logic, general systems theory, generalized information theory, and interval computations.

Selected books:

- *An Approach to General Systems Theory*, by George J. Klir, 1969.
- *Fuzzy Sets and Fuzzy Logic: Theory and Applications*, by George J. Klir and Bo Yua, 1995.
- *Facets of Systems Science*, IFSR International Series in Systems Science and Systems Engineering, by George J. Klir, 2001.

---

10 The author was privileged to study under Professor Klir in the early 1970s.

1.5 Recommended Books on Systems Science

Many scholars[11] at universities and international organizations[12] continue researching within the various systems science arenas. Interested readers are advised to read the comprehensive, integrative, and balanced volume on systems science written by George Mobus and Michael Kalton: *Principles of Systems Science*, which was issued by Springer in 2015.

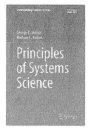  

George Mobus is professor emeritus at the Computing and Software Systems Program, Institute of Technology, at the University of Washington in Tacoma, Washington.

Michael Kalton is professor emeritus of interdisciplinary arts and sciences at the University of Washington in Tacoma, Washington.

Another recommended large and all-inclusive volume on system science, edited by Gary Metcalf, Kyoichi Kijima, and Hiroshi Deguchi, is *Handbook of Systems Sciences*, which was issued by Springer in 2021.

Gary S. Metcalf is a systems theorist and practitioner. He has worked as a family therapist and manager in large corporations. He taught at universities in the United States, Finland, and India for 20 years.

Kyoichi Kijima is a professor emeritus at the Tokyo Institute of Technology; a specially appointed professor at Daito Bunka University; and an adjunct professor at the School of Business Management, Bandung Institute of Technology, Indonesia. He also holds an appointment at the Open University of Japan.

---

11 See List of systems scientists. https://en.wikipedia.org/wiki/List_of_systems_scientists. Accessed: Jan. 2023.

12 See List of systems sciences organizations. https://en.wikipedia.org/wiki/List_of_systems_ sciences_organizations. Accessed: Jan. 2023.

Hiroshi Deguchi is a professor at the Tokyo Institute of Technology, and since 2017, he has been the president of the Japan Association for Social and Economic Systems Studies (JASS).

1.6 Systems Science: Criticisms and Responses[13]

Before proceeding into the rest of the book, readers are invited to examine some criticisms of systems science raised by scientists and laypeople. This section discusses the more relevant ones and responds to them.

1.6.1 Criticisms of Systems Science

Criticisms of systems science are expressed below.

1. **Concepts of systems and models.** Systems science concepts are too general and sometimes too mathematical or too formal. For example, different definitions of *systems* sometimes contradict each other. Also, systems science claims that all aspects of reality are included in its definition of a system. However, this claim leads to the notion that systems science has either an absolute attribute of natural sciences or an absolute attribute of formal sciences. These conflicting attributes make the theory ambiguous.

2. **Structural similarities and integrative concepts**. Systems science aims to identify structural similarities and integrative concepts within different domains. However, empirical studies cannot substantiate this aim, or at least not sufficiently. Conclusions based on analogy could not be considered proof. The use of analogies and the concept of functionalism is not always possible. Also, other interdisciplinary concepts (e.g., open systems, a hierarchy of systems, homeostasis, autopoiesis, control, feedback self-organization, emergence, networks instead of causal chains) are regarded as exaggerated in importance and not belonging exclusively to systems science.

3. **The universal language of science.** Systems science claims to define a universal language of science. Such an objective may be regarded as unattainable. The overwhelming majority of discipline-oriented scientists are made to feel insecure and challenged by such a claim.

4. **Holistic thinking.** Systems science stresses the importance of holistic thinking. This cognitive thinking style focuses on the world, considering its parts as

---

13 This section was partially adapted, with permission, from Professor Eberhard Umbach's paper (Umbach, 2000).

inseparable from the whole and not existing independently. However, the holistic perspective varies across cultures and genders, and thus it is unscientific and not applicable to the scientific method and empirical testing. In addition, holistic thinking makes it hard to determine cause and effect and can become vague, especially when circumstances become more complex.

5. **Quantification and mathematical modeling.** Occasionally, systems science relies on quantification and mathematical modeling. However, by and large, most real issues cannot be treated sensibly with these instruments. For example, quantification can be limited in pursuing concrete, statistical relationships, leading researchers to overlook broader themes and relationships. Quantification often focuses solely on numbers, and researchers risk missing startling information that may have significant value. Furthermore, quantification provides a distorted sense of objectivity by synthetically separating the observer from the observed.

    Mathematical modeling has many benefits that are pertinent to real-world problems. However, its main disadvantage is often derived from its inaccuracy, which, in turn, emanates from oversimplification of the modeling relative to the actual circumstances. As a result, mathematical modeling results must be interpreted by experts. Of course, different people may interpret the results in different ways.

6. **Unified scientific worldview.**[14] Systems science presents a scientific worldview that is based on holism and reductionism. However, systems science does not have a unified and consistent model of the structure and dynamic of its worldview. As a result, different methodologies are not consistent concerning their worldviews. In addition, a specific worldview is often relevant to individuals in a specific domain or a project but not to others. This confusion results in stakeholders establishing different findings based on different worldviews. For example, one may conclude that humankind is in an environmental crisis due to a lack of widely agreed worldview in human thinking.

7. **Different streams of systems science.** Systems science contends with different streams of science. For example, Hieronymi (2013) identifies five significant streams of science fields: (1) physical systems, (2) living systems, (3) cognitive systems, (4) social systems, and (5) technological systems. Systems science is unable to integrate the different streams within its methodology.

---

14 Worldview may be defined as a coherent collection of concepts and theorems that allows a person to construct a global image of the world and thus understand their life experience (Derived from Aerts et al., 1994).

8. **Marginalization of basic research.** Systems science researchers are accused of ignoring and marginalizing basic research. Basic research is scientific research with the aim of improving theories to enhance the understanding and prediction of natural phenomena. At the other end of the spectrum, applied research tends to provide near-term solutions for societal shifts toward sustainability in the face of global change.

1.6.2   Responses to Criticism

Responses to the criticisms of systems science are discussed below.

1. **Concepts of systems and models.** The criticism of the excessive generality of the systems concept is not convincing because creating analytical tools that are applicable as generally as possible is part of the overall scientific methodology. Moreover, the systems concept definition is as general as the notion of the numbers system. As in the case of numbers, the generality of using the systems concept cannot be objected to on epistemological grounds. On the contrary, it is desired to be general.

   The critics' claim that systems science ought to decide unequivocally to be either a formal or a natural science is also not convincing. The importance of systems science has to be seen in its function as a network for the specialized disciplines based on the systems concept. In this function, systems science shares the methods of all specialized disciplines of the empirical sciences, formal sciences, and humanities. Depending on the context, the systems concept has to adapt to different demands. In addition, the rules that are valid in the comparative context should hold for systems-oriented works.

2. **Structural similarities and integrative concepts.** Pure analogies have moved somewhat to the background of systems science because conclusions on that basis cannot be regarded as proofs, and the empirical findings of far-reaching "cross-level hypotheses" have encountered severe difficulties, especially when tried without cooperation with specialized disciplines.

   The conclusion must be that interdisciplinary structural similarities belong to the realm of systems science but only in cooperation with the specialized disciplines. General concepts, like emergence or entropy, yield valid statements in a circumscribed field of science. However, they must be accepted by the responsible specialized science. By this token, these concepts are also part of the specialized sciences and thus are not constitutive of systems science.

3. **The universal language of science.** Many systems scientists view this lofty aim as no longer being a task for systems science. In the inevitable and desired interdisciplinary communication, more and more specialized scientists will favor an interdisciplinary precision of their terms without systems science having to be active in this context.

4. **Holistic thinking.** The concept of the top-down approach and the aim of including as many aspects as possible can be regarded as a provisional explication of holistic thinking. Despite all methodological difficulties, a tendency toward holistic thinking is necessary. This tendency is also true in specialized disciplines. The difficulties, especially in the socioeconomic domain, are considerable. When analyzing the results of holistic thinking, the limits have to be indicated, which unfortunately has not been the case in the past. More research into this aspect is necessary.

5. **Quantification and mathematical modeling.** These methods are not constitutive of systems science but instead of science in general. Nevertheless, they have a firm place in systems science methodology and other specialized disciplines. An inadequate quantification methodology cannot be explicitly attributed to systems science.

6. **Unified scientific worldview.** A unified scientific worldview is based on the idea that every scientific component can be tested with empirical observation and conforms to the highest levels of objectivity. However, many scientific ideas cannot be tested adequately. Also, ethics, an inevitable part of a scientific worldview, cannot be tested.

   Another argument related to the quest for a unified scientific worldview is that science has limits. For example, a few things that science does not do are as follows. (1) Science doesn't make moral judgments, (2) science doesn't make aesthetic judgments, (3) science doesn't tell one how to use scientific knowledge, and (4) science doesn't conclude supernatural phenomena.

   In conclusion, some will say that a unified scientific worldview is not attainable. Others will say that creating a unified scientific worldview is not a part of general criticisms of systems science.

7. **Different streams of systems science.** The existence of different streams within systems science is not an exception in the general context of science. There have also been frequent conflicts about streams and approaches in other disciplines. For example, Newtonian theory maintains that objects fall to the earth because their gravitation pulls them. In contrast, Einsteinian theory maintains that objects move freely along curved spacetime trajectories, and the mass and energy of these objects induce these curvatures.

8. **Marginalization of basic research.** Systems science methods define systems and distinguish them from the environment. They also represent, analyze, and optimize their structure and behavior. An agreed-upon classification of systems science disciplines includes (1) general systems theory, (2) cybernetics, (3) operations research, (4) systems analysis, and (5) systems engineering. The first two classes belong to systems theory, and the other three belong to systems applications. As can be seen from

this classification, systems science engagement in basic research is limited. Therefore, this criticism may be justified, but it is not a decisive argument against systems science in general and its epistemological grounds.

1.7 Bibliography

Aerts, D., Apostel, L., De Moor, B., Hellemans, S., Maex, E., Van Belle, H., and Van Der Veken, J. (1994). *Worldviews: From Fragmentation to Integration,* VUB Press, Brussels. http://pespmc1.vub.ac.be/CLEA/Reports/WorldviewsBook.html. Accessed: Jan. 2023.

Ensor, P.S. (1988). The functional silo syndrome. *AME Target* 16. http://www.ame.org/sites/default/files/documents/88q1a3.pdf. Accessed: Jan. 2023.

Hieronymi, A. (2013). Understanding systems science: A visual and integrative approach. *Systems Research and Behavioral Science* 30 (5): 580–595.

Martin, J. et al. (2019, January 26–29). Redefining "systems engineering" & "system" for the future. Systems Science Working Group, Annual INCOSE International Workshop.

Metcalf, G.S, Kijima, K., and Deguchi, H. (Eds.). (2021). *Handbook of Systems Sciences*. Springer.

Mobus, G.E. The applications of systems science: Understanding how the world works and how you work in it (no date). http://faculty.washington.edu/gmobus/Academics/TINST401/Summer-14/. Accessed: Jan. 2023.

Mobus, G.E. and Kalton, M.C. (2015). *Principles of Systems Science (Understanding Complex Systems)*. Springer.

Rafols, I., Porter, A.L., and Leydesdorff, L. (2010). Science overlay maps: A new tool for research policy and library management. *Journal of the American Society for Information Science and Technology* 61. 10.1002/asi.21368. https://www.researchgate.net/publication/289211064_Science_Overlay_Maps_A_New_Tool_for_Research_Policy_and_Library_Management. Accessed: Jan. 2023.

Richardson K. et al. (2023 Sep.). Earth beyond six of nine planetary boundaries. *Science Advances*, 15; 9 (37). Earth beyond six of nine planetary boundaries - PMC (nih.gov). Accessed: Nov. 2023.

Rockström, J. et al. (2009, September 23). A safe operating space for humanity. *Nature* 461: 472–475. https://www.nature.com/articles/461472a.pdf. Accessed: Jan. 2023.

Rousseau, D., Wilby, J., Billingham, J., and Blachfellner, S. (2016). *Manifesto for General Systems Transdisciplinarity,* Bertalanffy Center for the Study of Systems Science, www.bcsss.org. https://systemeconomics.ru/wp-content/uploads/401-1619-1-PB.pdf.

UNESCO. *Science for society* (No date). https://en.unesco.org/themes/science-society. Accessed: Jan. 2023.

Umbach, E. (2000). The fundamental tasks of systems science. Proceedings of the World Congress of the Systems Sciences and ISSS 2000, International Society for the Systems Sciences, 44th Annual Meeting, Toronto, Canada.

2

Principles of Systems Science (Part I)

2.1 Introduction

Systems science is based on several fundamental principles. A principle is an underlying truth or proposition that is the foundation of a belief or behavior of systems. The 10 fundamental principles of systems science described in this and the next chapter represent the author's top-level worldview on systems science, which emerged through his engineering experience and a synthesis of information from many sources, books, articles, blogs, etc. The material below is presented through multiple examples rather than formal discussions and definitions. The author believes that readers will best comprehend these concepts through such examples.

For readers' convenience, this topic is organized into two parts. This chapter contains the following first set of five systems science principles:

- **Universal context.** Containing the universal dimension and the systems of systems (SoS) dimension.
- **Systems boundary.** Containing notes on the system's boundary, determining the system's boundary, and philosophical analysis of borders.
- **Systems hierarchy.** Containing hierarchy types, an example of the Earth's biological system, and the US Constitution and government.
- **Systems interactions.** Containing types of interactions, causal loop diagram, predators and prey example, and handheld hairdryer example.
- **Systems change.** Containing changes in the Universe system, changes in the Milky Way galaxy system, changes in the solar system, changes in planet Earth, changes in daily objects and systems, and changes in technical systems.

Systems Science for Engineers and Scholars, First Edition. Edited by Avner Engel.
© 2024 John Wiley & Sons, Ltd. Published 2024 by John Wiley & Sons, Ltd.

2.2   Universal Context

The Universal context principle: The Universe is composed of systems and systems of systems.

The Universe may be defined as all of the existing space and time, including planets; stars; galaxies; dark matter; and all other forms of matter, time, and energy. The fundamental principle of systems science is that the entire Universe is comprised of systems and systems of systems (Figure 2.1).

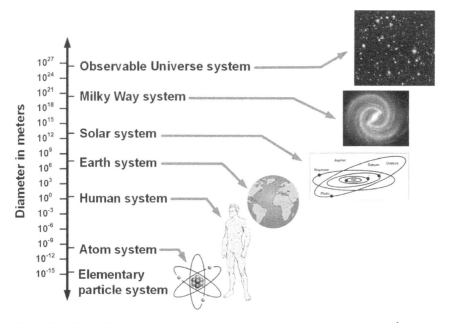

Figure 2.1   The entire Universe is comprised of systems and systems of systems.[1]

2.2.1   The Universal Dimension

Systems and systems of systems are described below.

- **Elementary particle system.** According to current physical theory, this system is comprised of subatomic particles. The set of elementary particle systems includes the fundamental fermions (quarks, leptons, antiquarks, and antileptons). In addition, elementary particle systems include the fundamental bosons (gauge bosons and the Higgs boson).

---

1 Image inspired by: Branches of science. https://en.wikipedia.org/wiki/Branches_of_science. Accessed: Jan. 2023.

- **Atom system.** This system is the smallest unit of matter that constitutes a chemical element. An atom system is comprised of a nucleus of one or more protons and zero or more neutrons. In addition, the atom is composed of one or more electrons. For example, the hydrogen atom (H) is composed of a nucleus containing one proton and no neutrons. In addition, the hydrogen atom contains one electron in its outer layer. The isotopes of hydrogen, deuterium and tritium have one and two neutrons in their nuclei.
- **Human system.** This system is comprised of many different types of cells that create tissues and organs. In addition, the system maintains healthy internal physical and chemical conditions to ensure normal biological processes. In a very simplified manner, the human system is comprised of a head, neck, chest, abdomen, arms, hands, legs, and feet.
- **Earth system.** This system is comprised of four elements.[2] (1) The *lithosphere* is composed of the solid and liquid parts of the Earth's core and the thin crust of the Earth.

  In many places, the geosphere developed a soil layer containing nutrients available to living organisms, thus providing an ecological habitat for many life forms. (2) The *atmosphere* is comprised of a gaseous layer, primarily carbon, nitrogen, oxygen, and hydrogen. The atmosphere receives the Sun energy and vapor from the Earth's surface. The atmosphere then redistributes the heat and moisture across the Earth's surface. (3) The *hydrosphere* consists of water in the Earth's oceans, ice sheets, and glaciers; its lakes, rivers, and moisture found in the soil and within rocks and areas of permafrost, as well as its atmospheric humidity. Finally, (4) the *biosphere* consists of all living organisms. Fundamentally, these organisms require (a) water from the hydrosphere, (b) gases from the atmosphere, and (c) nutrients and minerals from the geosphere. In addition, living organisms are adapted to inhabit one or more of the other three spheres. Humans are part of the biosphere; however, society is becoming the main driver of change within the Earth system.
- **Solar system.** This system is a set of planets and smaller solar objects orbiting the Sun. The most significant elements of the solar system are the eight planets: (1) Mercury, (2) Venus, (3) Earth, (4) Mars, (5) Jupiter, (6) Saturn, (7) Uranus, and (8) Neptune. The other, much smaller, objects include the dwarf planets (i.e., Ceres, Pluto. Eris, Haumea, and Makemake) and thousands of natural satellites, minor planets, and comets.

---

2 See more: https://gml.noaa.gov/education/info_activities/pdfs/TBI_earth_spheres.pdf. Accessed Jan. 2023.

- **Milky Way system.** This system is a spiral galaxy with an estimated diameter of 170,000 to 200,000 light-years. The Milky Way contains approximately 100 billion to 400 billion stars and at least that many planets. In addition, the Milky Way system includes our solar system, which is located about 27,000 light-years from the galactic center.
- **Observable Universe system.** The Universe may be defined as all of space-time and its contents; however, the size of the entire Universe is unknown. In contrast, the observable Universe system is a spherical region with an estimated diameter of 93 billion light-years. This system is comprised of all matter that can currently be observed from Earth or space-based instruments. In addition, scientists estimate that this system contains at least 2 trillion galaxies. However, as the Universe's expansion accelerates, all currently observable objects will eventually appear to freeze in time while emitting progressively redder and fainter light.

2.2.2 Fundamental Types of Systems

One can distinguish between three types of systems: (1) real physical systems, (2) systems in mind, and (3) systems in the abstract (Mobus and Kalton, 2015).

- **Real physical systems.** These types of systems exhibit common (1) patterns, (2) behaviors, and (3) properties that an observer can analyze and use. Patterns are regularities in nature, human-made artifacts, or abstract ideas. Behavior is the interactions among individuals, organisms, or systems with themselves or their environments. Finally, properties are objects that belong to someone or something.
- **Systems in mind.** These systems may be understood and even known but do not necessarily exist. Many theoretical concepts in different fields belong to this category. For example, the theory of evolution regarding the origins of species, proposed by Charles Darwin in 1859, is an example of a system of the mind. Similarly, the general theory of relativity regarding the geometric nature of gravitation, proposed by Albert Einstein in 1915, is an example of a system of the mind.
- **Systems in the abstract.** These types of systems may be described through mathematical or symbolic notations. For example, Mesarovic and Takahara (1989) define a system as "a relation $S \subseteq I \times O$, whereby I and O are sets representing inputs and outputs. Consequently, S may be called an elementary system." This definition reflects a black-box view of a system since its internal structure and internal functions are not represented. Consequently, the above definition deals only with the correlations between inputs and outputs.

Because systems adhere to the same principles, we can say that systems are inherently isomorphic to one another.[3] We can identify a formal mapping between all systems embodying equal principles. Identifying isomorphisms between systems provides a powerful analytical tool by assisting scientists in transforming knowledge from a known system domain to an unknown one.

2.2.3 The Systems of Systems (SoS) Dimension

2.2.3.1 Characteristics of SoS

The term *system of systems (SoS)* has many definitions and interpretations. For example, Maier (1998) posits five characteristics of SoS:

- Operational independence of the constituent systems
- Managerial autonomy of the constituent systems
- Geographical distribution of the constituent systems
- The emergent behavior of the constituent systems
- Evolutionary development of the constituent systems

Geographical distribution may or may not occur (e.g., we may consider equipment and systems within a regular household to be a system of systems). In addition, emergent behavior, as well as evolutionary development, characterizes all systems. Therefore, only the first two characteristics (operational independence and managerial independence) truly represent systems of systems.

Operational independence means that within the SoS, the owners of constituent systems may choose to support a set of SoS functionalities. Furthermore, they may choose to perform specific functions within the SoS as well as outside of the SoS. Similarly, managerial independence means that within the SoS, the managers of constituent systems retain their management independence vis-à-vis the day-to-day operations of their constituent systems.

Many engineers mistakenly consider large and complex systems manufactured by a company that utilizes several contractors and are often distributed over a large geographic area to be systems of systems. For example, let us consider the Airbus A380 passenger aircraft.[4] Airbus's Hamburg (Germany) facility manages the structural assembly and outfitting fuselage sections of the A380. Airbus's Filton's (UK) facility is responsible for wing design; landing gear; and fuel systems' design,

---

3 We take the liberty of slightly expanding the definition of isomorphism: Isomorphism is a formal two-way mapping between differing systems where the two systems embody equal parts, concepts, principles, or patterns.

4 See more: Airbus production. https://www.airbus.com/aircraft/how-is-an-aircraft-built/production.html. Accessed: Jan. 2023.

manufacturing, and testing. Airbus' Broughton (UK) facility assembles the A380 wings, including wing skin milling, stringer manufacture, entire wing equipping, and wing box assembly. Airbus's Saint-Eloi (France) facility delivers equipped and tested engine pylons to Airbus's final assembly lines. Finally, Airbus's Toulouse facility is responsible for engineering (general design, definition of the aircraft structure, systems, integration tests, and more). In addition, the Toulouse facility performs structure testing and materials development of processes, systems organization, flight tests, and the A380's final assembly and preparation for flight.

As discussed above, the A380 is managed, designed, produced, and maintained by individuals working for Airbus. As such, the A380 does not meet constituent systems' operational and managerial independence characteristics and, therefore is not an SoS.

2.2.3.2 Healthcare SoS Example

Healthcare is diagnosing, treating, and preventing human disease, injury, and other physical and mental deterioration. Health practitioners perform it in medicine, nursing, pharmacy, and many other providers. A hypothetical example of a healthcare system of systems, representing a wide variety of healthcare systems worldwide, is described in Figure 2.2 and the following sections.

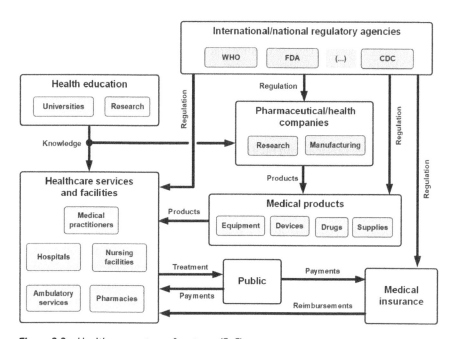

Figure 2.2 Healthcare system of systems (SoS).

The healthcare system of systems is composed of the following independent operational and managerial constituent systems.

1. **Health education systems include:**
   - Medical schools within universities. In general, the mission of most medical universities is to provide healthcare education, advance health knowledge, and provide service to society. In addition, students within medical universities are encouraged to relieve human suffering through a life of service in medicine.
   - Healthcare research within universities. Healthcare research within medical universities focuses on systematically eradicating illnesses through diagnosis and effective treatment. This approach includes scientific studies on patient safety and biomedical and pharmaceutical research.
2. **International/national regulatory agencies systems include:**
   - The World Health Organization (WHO). The WHO is a UN agency headquartered in Geneva, Switzerland. It is responsible for international public health and seeks to attain the highest level of health for all people.
   - The US Food and Drug Administration (FDA). Most countries have regulatory bodies within government health departments. For example, the FDA is a federal agency in the United States responsible for protecting and promoting public health through regulations and supervision related to food safety, tobacco products, dietary supplements, prescription and over-the-counter pharmaceutical drugs, vaccines, biopharmaceuticals, blood transfusions, and medical equipment and devices.
   - The Centers for Disease Control and Prevention (CDC). Another national health organization is the CDC, a US federal agency headquartered in Atlanta, Georgia. The CDC's mission is to protect public health and safety in the United States. This mission is accomplished by, for example, focusing on infectious diseases, food-borne pathogens, environmental health, occupational safety, injury prevention, and educational activities.
3. **Healthcare services and facilities systems include:**
   - Medical practitioners. Healthcare practitioners include physicians, nurses, pharmacists, therapists, rehabilitation specialists, emotional and social support providers, community health workers, and health technologists and technicians.
   - Hospitals. Hospitals deliver healthcare support to their communities. This service typically includes the following services: (1) general medical and surgical, (2) emergency and other outpatient care, (3) psychiatric and substance abuse, (4) family planning and abortion, (5) hospice and palliative care, (6) sleep disorder care, and (7) blood and organ banks.
   - Nursing facilities. Nursing facilities provide residential care combined with nursing and supervisory services. This support typically includes the

following services: (1) home nursing care and other healthcare, (2) mental health care and residential care for people with physical disabilities, and (3) community care for older people.

- Ambulatory service. Ambulatory services provide healthcare services to ambulatory patients (those who are not confined to an institutional bed as inpatients), including (1) outpatient care, (2) medical and diagnostic laboratories, (3) ambulance services, and (4) other ambulatory health care services.

- Pharmacies. Pharmacies are usually retail shops that provide prescription drugs, among other products. Usually, licensed pharmacists oversee the fulfillment of medical prescriptions and provide advice regarding over-the-counter medications.

4. **Pharmaceutical/health companies' systems include:**

- Medical research. Pharmaceutical and healthcare product manufacturers develop new drugs, devices, and equipment and transfer them into clinical trials, leading to scale-up and commercial manufacturing.

- Medical manufacturing. Medical drugs, devices, and equipment manufacturers engage in all aspects of fabrication, from designing specific manufacturing processes to scale-up and ongoing process improvements.

5. **Medical products systems include:**

- Medical equipment. Typical medical equipment includes expensive products such as Computerized tomography (CT) and Magnetic resonance imaging (MRI) machines, electromedical therapeutic apparatuses, irradiation apparatuses, mammography machines, medical laser machines, tomography machines, and robotic surgery equipment.

- Medical devices. Typical medical devices include surgical instruments, ophthalmic goods, vital sign monitors, Transcutaneous electrical nerve stimulation (TENS) machines, nebulizers, endoscopes, venous access devices, glucose meters, and ultrasonic cleaning equipment.

- Drugs. Drug manufacturers may be broken into three groups: (1) biotechnology firms engaging in Research and development (R&D) as well as creating new drugs, equipment, and treatment methods; (2) pharmaceutical firms engaging in research but focusing on manufacturing existing drug portfolios; and (3) makers of generic drugs who specialize in producing and marketing drugs that are identical to name-brand drugs but are not protected under a patent or other legal means.

- Medical supplies. Typical medical supplies include in-vitro diagnostic substances, surgical appliances and supplies, wound care products, Intravenous (IV) solutions, a toxicology laboratory, instrument sterilization products, medical aprons, gloves, and bandages.

6. **Medical insurance systems include:** Medical insurance organizations. Medical insurance parties cover individuals' financial risk related to medical expenses. This funding mechanism spreads the risk to numerous persons. By and large, each country adopts one or a combination of the following financial healthcare schemes: (1) general taxation for the state or county, (2) social health insurance, (3) voluntary or private health insurance, (4) out-of-pocket payments, or (5) donations to health charities.
7. **The public:** Invariably, the public benefits from health systems and bears the costs associated with its health. These costs include health treatment, illness prevention, and protection against various health threats. These expenditures ultimately contribute to a sustainable society.

2.3 Systems Boundary

The boundary principle: All systems have a boundary that demarcates the system from its context (environment).

The Great Wall of China is one of the most remarkable boundary illustrations (Figure 2.3). This monumental undertaking is a system of fortifications built from the seventh century BC to the fourteenth century AD. It was established as a protective boundary between the Chinese empire and the nomadic empires of central and inner Asia.

Figure 2.3 China's Great Wall at Mutianyu, near Beijing.

2.3.1 Notes on Systems Boundary

One of the most critical parts of systems modeling is defining the boundaries between a system and its context. Different definitions of boundaries lead to diverse system models, so choosing an optimal boundary is critical to the systems engineering process. In addition, a system's boundaries determine the scope of responsibility for virtually all aspects of the system's life cycle, from requirement definition; throughout the development process into manufacturing maintenance; and, eventually, disposal.

In addition, the system's boundary identifies a change in control and responsibility. The system's owner is responsible for its behavior and has significant control over it. Beyond the boundary, some other person or organization is responsible, and the system owner has no control over its context. Therefore, the boundary can be designated as the region where the control of the system engineer is terminated.

By and large, the smaller the system, the sharper its boundary. In contrast, large systems and mega-systems often exhibit quite blurred boundaries. So, the decision regarding the system's border is somewhat arbitrary, reflecting the system engineers' point of view. Furthermore, determining the operational limits of a systems of systems (SoS) is particularly difficult because different stakeholders involved in individual systems have varied opinions regarding the boundaries of their systems. Therefore, considering all these views is imperative to an adequate SoS boundary definition (Gorod et al. 2010).

In summary, a system of interest (SoI) is a part of the universe being studied. In contrast, the SoI context lies outside the SoI boundaries but interacts with it. By definition, system engineers and SoI owners may anticipate the type of such interactions, but their span of control is confined within the border of the SoI. Therefore, they cannot affect the context of the SoI.

2.3.2 Determining the System's Boundary

All systems have a boundary that demarcates the system from its context. Often, this boundary is established to undertake a specific analysis of the system. This boundary is located at the confines of the region over which the system's emergent properties are manifested, separating and differentiating a system from its context. The boundary is unique in systems science because it effectively defines and operationalizes the system. In other words, establishing a system's boundary affects the system's internal and external behavior.

Determining where a system's boundary should lie is quite challenging. For example, Open University is the UK's largest academic institution. It is located in Milton Keynes and specializes in distance learning through online teaching.

Does the internet constitute a part of the Open University system or part of its context?

In general, fully establishing a system's boundary requires four steps: (1) defining the system requirements, (2) establishing the physical boundaries, (3) determining the logical boundaries, and (4) documenting the system interconnections and rationale behind those interconnections (Sizemore, 2003).

A simplistic guide for placing a given element inside or outside a system may be defined as follows: Elements needed to fulfill the purpose of the system should constitute a part of the system. Elements that affect or are being affected but cannot be controlled by the system should form a portion of its context. The problem with this definition is that virtually all desired system and context models focus on a limited subset of the abovementioned elements.

The Federal Aviation Administration (FAA DOT/FAA/AR-08/32, 2009) proposed a valuable method to determine a system's boundary by identifying the system's monitored as well as its controlled variables. Monitored variables specify the system inputs to which the system responds. Controlled variables specify the system outputs that affect the context. Therefore, one can identify the appropriate system's desired boundary based on these monitored and controlled variables.

An example of the FAA method for determining a system's boundary is depicted in Figure 2.4. An air conditioning system receives inputs (monitored variables) from the context and produces outputs (controlled variables) into the context.

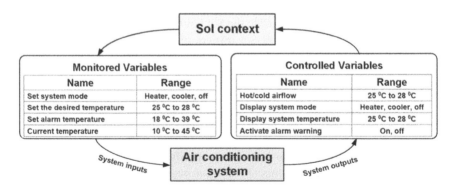

Figure 2.4 Proposed method to determine the system's boundary.

Based on the above analysis, Figure 2.5 depicts the air conditioning system within its boundary, the context of the system, and the interfaces among them. Based on this configuration, the air conditioning system includes the heating/ cooling unit, the temperature sensor, the display/alarm unit, and the control unit.

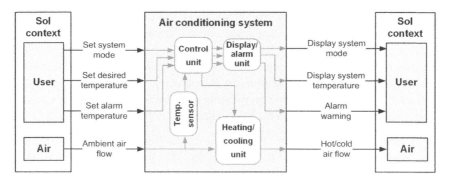

Figure 2.5 The air conditioning system and its boundary, interfaces, and context.

2.3.3 Philosophical Analysis of Boundary

We think of a boundary when considering an entity delimited from its surroundings. For example, the outer surface of a book is the boundary of the book. Similarly, a line (physical or drawn on a map) separating the state of Maryland from the state of Pennsylvania in the United States is the boundary between these two states. Events, too, have temporal boundaries, though they are often quite blurry, like the beginning of the Industrial Revolution. It is also sometimes suggested that even abstract entities, such as a chess game or a set of prime numbers, have boundaries of their own.

Regarding boundary, Aristotle observed, "A boundary is the terminus of each thing, i.e. [1] the primary thing beyond which it is not possible to find anything [of the object], and [2] the primary thing within which everything [of the object] is" (Metaphysics, V.17 1022a4–5, provided in Pfeiffer, 2018).

The *Stanford Encyclopedia of Philosophy* (Varzi, 2013)[5] examines Aristotle's boundary definition, identifying several philosophical puzzles. In particular: (1) One question relates to the intuition that a boundary separates two entities, which are then said to be continuous. As one passes from one entity to the other, we do not pass through the last point directly to the first point in the other entity due to the density of the continuum between the two entities. (2) A second puzzle relates to the fact that Aristotle's definition applies to continuous objects. However, on close inspection, physical objects exhibit a noncontinuous boundary made of swarms of subatomic particles. (3) Aristotle's definition assumes a clear boundary demarcation. This definition leads to a third puzzle associated with the boundary vagueness or fuzziness of many ordinary objects and systems. For example, where exactly is the boundary

─────

5 See more: *Stanford Encyclopedia of Philosophy* (Boundary, 2013). https://plato.stanford.edu/entries/boundary/. Accessed: Jan. 2023.

of Mount Everest? What is the exact boundary of the US air traffic control? What elements are within and what elements are outside the system?

Most philosophers consider boundaries to be parasites to their corresponding entities because the former could not exist without the latter. Along this line, Varzi (2013) provides four philosophical boundary views through examples related to the Mason–Dixon line,[6] constituting the boundary between the states of Maryland and Pennsylvania in the United States.

- **Neither–nor boundary.** The Mason–Dixon line boundary may belong neither to Maryland nor to Pennsylvania. This interpretation implies that contact between Maryland and Pennsylvania may exist even if both are topologically open as long as nothing lies between them. So, according to this view, the states of the union do not use up the whole territory (Figure 2.6).

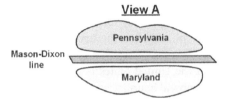

Figure 2.6   Boundary may belong neither to Maryland nor to Pennsylvania.

- **Either–Or boundary.** The boundary belongs either to Maryland or to Pennsylvania, though it may be indeterminate to which of them it belongs. This interpretation implies that contact may exist between the two states only if one is topologically closed while the other is topologically open (Figure 2.7).

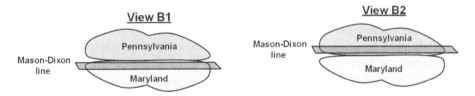

Figure 2.7   Boundary belongs either to Maryland or Pennsylvania.

- **Both boundaries.** The boundary belongs to both Maryland and Pennsylvania. Since limits do not occupy space, we can say that the Mason–Dixon line belongs to Maryland and Pennsylvania (Figure 2.8).

---

6 During the American Civil War (1861–1865), the Mason–Dixon line was considered the boundary between the Northern and the Southern states. Even today, this line divides the North and South both politically and socially.

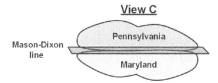

Figure 2.8 Boundary belongs to both Maryland and Pennsylvania.

- **Two boundaries.** There are two boundaries, one belonging to Maryland and one to Pennsylvania. These two boundaries are colocated, that is, they coincide spatially without overlapping. This view enables us to reject the distinction between closed and open entities, treating all extended bodies as closed (Figure 2.9).

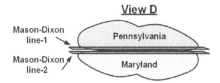

Figure 2.9 There are two boundaries. One belongs to Maryland, and one belongs to Pennsylvania.

2.4 Systems Hierarchy

The hierarchy principle: All systems are entities organized in structural and functional hierarchies.

2.4.1 Types of Hierarchy

All systems are entities organized in structural and functional hierarchies. A hierarchy is an ordered collection of objects inside a whole with asymmetric upward and downward relationships. Thus, each object is located "above," "at the same level as," or "below" some other object. From a hierarchical placement standpoint, an object placed at a higher level is considered superior, and an object placed at a lower level is regarded as a subordinate object.

Objects within a hierarchical structure are linked directly to their immediate vertically upward superior(s) or downward subordinate(s). In such cases, the degree of branching is defined by the number of direct subordinates an object has.

Hierarchy is often used to encapsulate portions of the system (i.e., subsystems) to conceal specific sets of objects and their internal interactions with other things or their context. By and large, ascending the hierarchical structure or function of a system exhibits increased complexity relating to both the design of the system and its functionality. Three basic hierarchy models are standard in higher-level organisms and social systems: centralized, decentralized, and holacratic (Figure 2.10).

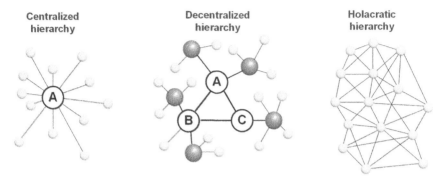

Figure 2.10 Three basic types of hierarchies.

- **Centralized hierarchy.** Under a centralized hierarchy model, one or a few members at the organization's top level handle access to resources and all decision processes. Lower-level members of the social systems are limited in their abilities to access and maintain resources and effect any change within these hierarchical systems. The main benefit of techniques based on a centralized hierarchy is their long-range stability due to each member's fixed and clear role within the hierarchic structure. Within human societies, kings, tzars, emperors, shoguns, and so on had absolute power, and their kingdoms were based on a well-defined centralized hierarchy. For example, Peter the Great (1672–1725) ruled the Russian empire as an absolute monarch and head of a vast centralized bureaucratic order.
- **Decentralized hierarchy.** Under the decentralized hierarchy model, social conduct is governed by delegating decision-making powers and group resources to selected members who are expected to govern according to well-defined norms and official rules. Quite often, these members must be reelected by one means or another to retain their privileged positions. The main benefit of systems based on a decentralized hierarchy is their flexibility and openness to change. Members of the system are free to experiment, innovate, and contribute to the benefit of other members and themselves. In the United States, federal and state governments exemplify a classical decentralized hierarchy model within human societies. The federal government (as well as individual states) is divided into three key branches to ensure no group or individual has too much power. First, the legislative branch (i.e., the Congress, containing the House of Representatives and the Senate) makes laws. The executive branch (i.e., the president, vice president,

cabinet, and most federal agencies) implements the laws. Finally, the judicial branch (i.e., the Supreme and lower-level courts) evaluates rules by interpreting relevant court cases and the Constitution.

- **Holacratic hierarchy.** The holacratic hierarchy model was developed by Brian Robertson and his team in 2007 (Robertson, 2015). Under a holacratic hierarchy, authority and decision-making are distributed throughout the system rather than being vested in a formal management hierarchy. The distributed decision-making structure allows each group member to work on what they like to do or what they do best. An example of a successful mega-project employing a holacratic hierarchical structure is the Human Genome Project (1990–2003). The project aimed to sequence and map our species' (*Homo sapiens*) entire set of genes. The project was run by an international consortium of approximately 30 universities and academic institutes, costing about US$3 billion.

Another way of categorizing hierarchies is based on the maximum number of direct subordinates per single object within a given system. For example, Figure 2.11 depicts five systems, each with one type of hierarchy: linear, flat, branching, overlapping, and inclusion.

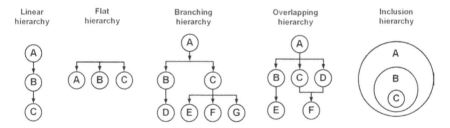

Figure 2.11 Five systems, each with one type of hierarchy.[7]

In a system with a linear hierarchy, the maximum degree of branching is one. So, each object, except the top and bottom, has one direct subordinate and one direct superior object. In a system with a flat hierarchy, the maximum degree of branching is infinity, but none of the objects has a special or a subordinate object. In a system with a branching hierarchy, one or more objects have a degree of branching at level two or more. Also, branching hierarchies are typical and are depicted utilizing tree diagrams. In a system with an overlapping hierarchy, at least one object has two or more superior objects. Finally, in an inclusion hierarchy, each object, except the outer object, is nested (included) within its superior object.

---

7 See more: Hierarchy. https://en.wikipedia.org/wiki/Hierarchy. Accessed: Jan. 2023.

2.4.2 Example of Earth's Biological System

By way of example, Figure 2.12 depicts an inclusive hierarchical model of the Earth's biological system. This hierarchical model consists of objects, starting with atoms and ending with the Earth's biospheres. This complex biological system defines life on Earth, where an increase in organizational complexity accompanies each level in the hierarchy.

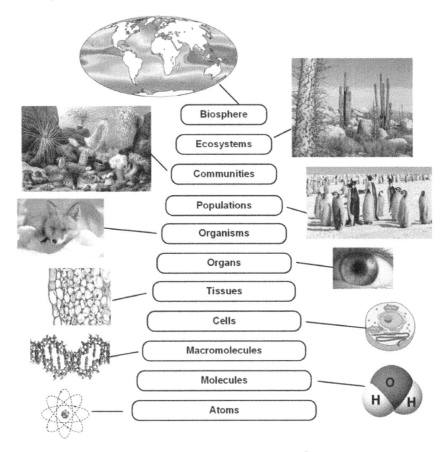

Figure 2.12 Hierarchical model of Earth's biological system.[8]

2.4.3 Example of the US Constitution and Government

Another example of a hierarchy is the US Constitution and government system. The US Constitution is among the most important documents ever created. It was signed at Independence Hall in Philadelphia in 1787 by 39 delegates representing

---

8 Derived from: Biological organization. https://en.wikipedia.org/wiki/Biological_organisation. Accessed: Jan. 2023.

12 states of the fledgling US union. Figure 2.13 depicts this event, with George Washington, Benjamin Franklin, and Alexander Hamilton among the signatories. Howard Chandler Christy painted the scene in April 1940.

Figure 2.13 Signing of the US Constitution.

The US Constitution defines the structure of the federal government and lays out the functionality and interactions among its three branches: legislative, executive, and judicial. Figure 2.14 and the text below describe the hierarchical structure of the US Constitution and government.

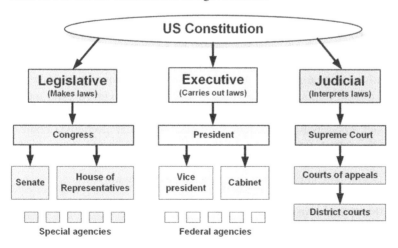

Figure 2.14 The hierarchical structure of the US Constitution and government.

2.4.3.1 The US Constitution

The US Constitution specifies the federal government's division into three branches: (1) the legislative branch, that is, Congress, which is composed of the Senate and the House of Representatives; (2) the executive branch, which is comprised of the president, the vice president, the cabinet, and various federal agencies; and (3) the judicial branch, which is composed of the Supreme Court, courts of appeals, and district courts. The authors of the Constitution intentionally divided the government into three independent branches to ensure that no individual or group would have too much power. In parallel, they provided specific mechanisms whereby each government branch can exert pressure over and influence the other branches (Table 2.1).

Table 2.1 Exerting pressure across US government branches.

Government branch	Cross-government branch responsibilities
Congress	May confirm or reject the president's nominees for the Supreme Court, federal judges, and heads of federal agencies
	Can remove a sitting president from office through a formal impeachment process
President	Can sign or veto legislation created by Congress
	May nominate individuals for the Supreme Court, federal judges, and heads of federal agencies
Supreme Court	Can overturn unconstitutional laws enacted by Congress and overturn unconstitutional executive acts issued by the president

2.4.3.2 The US Legislative Branch

The legislative branch includes Congress, which is comprised of the Senate and House of Representatives. The Senate consists of 100 senators, two from each state of the union. Each US senator is elected for six years, and one-third of the Senate members are elected every two years. In contrast, the House has 435 representatives, who campaign for an equal portion of the US population (slightly over half a million voters per seat). Representatives are elected for two-year terms, and the entire House is elected every two years. American citizens can vote for senators and representatives through free and confidential elections. Congress also includes special agencies and offices that provide support services to the members. In addition to the responsibilities described in Table 2.1, the legislative branch enacts federal laws and has the authority to declare war.

2.4.3.3 The US Executive Branch

The executive branch of the US includes the president, vice president, and cabinet. The president of the United States serves a four-year term and can be elected twice. He leads the country as a commander in chief of the US armed forces. The US vice president assists the president; if the president cannot function, the vice president becomes president. Cabinet members serve as heads of executive departments. The president appoints them, and the US Senate is expected to approve their nomination. The executive branch is comprised of several federal agencies, departments, boards, commissions, and committees. American citizens can vote for the president and vice president via free and confidential elections. In addition to the responsibilities described in Table 2.1, the executive branch carries out and enforces laws through work done by federal agencies, departments, and other groups.

2.4.3.4 The US Judicial Branch

The judicial branch is comprised of the Supreme Court, 13 courts of appeals, and 94 district courts. The Supreme Court includes nine justices and is the highest court in the United States. In addition to the responsibilities described in Table 2.1, the Supreme Court interprets the meaning of the Constitution and applies laws to individual cases. The appellate courts sit below the US Supreme Court, and their task is to review lower trial court decisions. Finally, the district courts sit under the appellate courts, and their task is to conduct legal trials, determine the facts, and issue appropriate rulings.

2.5 Systems Interactions

> The interactions principle: All systems are composed of networks of relations among their components and/or with their context.

Interactions occur when two or more objects have a flow[9] among them or a causality effect upon one another. Therefore, in complex systems, a noticeable impact is often the result of one or multiple causes.

2.5.1 Types of Interactions

By and large, interactions among systems' objects involve the following elements: (1) the internal structure of each object, which contributes to these interactions; (2) the processes and activities within each object related to these interactions; and (3) the flow of material, energy, and information among these objects. Object interactions encompass a broad range of characteristics, including (1) intentionality, (2) directness, (3) explicitness, (4) persistence, and (5) variability. Table 2.2 identifies typical characteristics of objects' interactions.

In addition, interactions within systems are the leading cause of emergent phenomena. For example, Figure 2.15 depicts an example of marine species within their ecological community. An environmental community consists of populations of various species in a given area exhibiting various interactions.

---

9 Flow is customarily composed of one or more of the following interactions: (1) spatial, (2) material, (3) energy, and (4) information.

Table 2.2 Typical characteristics of objects' interactions.[10]

Characteristic	Nature of interactions
Intentionality	Intentionality is the extent to which interactions between two or more objects are intentional. However, exchanges may be anywhere from entirely intentional to completely accidental.
Directness	Directness is the extent to which interactions between two or more objects occur. Exchanges may be anywhere from entirely indirect to fully direct.
Explicitness	Explicitness is how interactions between two or more objects are specified without ambiguous terms. Exchanges may be anywhere from entirely expressed to merely implied.
Persistence	Persistence is how interactions between two or more objects extend over time. Exchanges may be anywhere from transient and short-lived to persistent over a long period.
Variability	Variability is the extent to which interactions between two or more objects occur in random or nonrandom patterns. Such variations bring about uncertainty in the form and magnitude of object interactions.

Figure 2.15 Example: Marine species in an ecological community.

Table 2.3 depicts six main types of interspecies interactions observed in environmental communities.

---

10 Adapted with modifications from Alter (2018).

Table 2.3 Example: Interactions between species in ecological communities.[11]

Interaction type	Description of interaction
Competition	Organisms of two species compete for the same limited resources and often harm one another
Predation	A member of one species (predator) eats members of another species (prey)
Herbivory	A particular case of predation in which the prey species is a plant
Mutualism	A close long-term association between two or more species in which all members benefit
Parasitism	A close long-term association between two or more species in which some benefit and others are harmed
Commensalism	A close long-term association between two or more species in which some species benefit and others are unaffected

2.5.2 Causal Loop Diagram

The dynamics of systems' behavior may be described using a causal loop diagram (CLD). It shows how different elements of biological systems interact with one another. A CLD diagram consists of a set of nodes and edges. Nodes represent system components, and edges represent a relation between them. A link marked (+) indicates positive feedback between the two elements, and a link marked (–) indicates negative feedback. For example, the types of system dynamics between two species in an ecological community, discussed in Table 2.3, are shown in Figure 2.16.

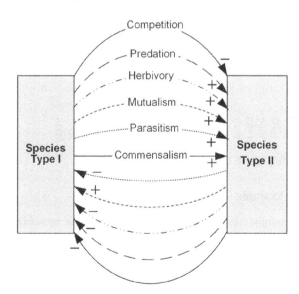

Figure 2.16 Dynamics between two species in an ecological community.

---

11 See Interactions in communities. Khan Academy. Accessed: Jan. 2023.

2.5.3 Predators and Prey Example

A quantitative example of a predatory interaction where members of a predator species eat members of a prey species is available in a study at the Voronezhsky State Nature Biosphere Reserve in Russia (Mishin and Romashov, 2016). The reserve was founded in 1923. It includes 31,000 hectares in Russia, some 450 km southeast of Moscow.

Due to several reasons, including human interference, very few wolves existed in the reserve, and the limited wolf population had minimal influence on the deer population dynamics. However, in early 1970, the wolf population was allowed to grow, leading to a grave crisis in the red deer population.

Besides red deer, wolf nutrition in the Voronezhsky reserve includes hares, beavers, farm animals, and carrions. Nevertheless, in 1973, the red deer population reached a maximum of 1544 individuals. But by early 2000, their number shrank to just a few individuals. After that, the wolf population increased dramatically to about 30 individuals (Figure 2.17).

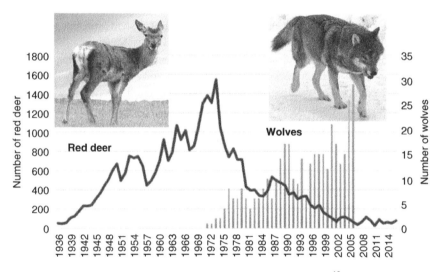

Figure 2.17   Wolves' impact on red deer in the Voronezhsky reserve.[12]

2.5.4 Handheld Hairdryer Example

The following is another example illustrating interactions among a system's components and between a system and its context.[13] A handheld hairdryer is an electromechanical device designed to blow hot air over damp hair to dry it (Figure 2.18). The system is made of the following components: (1) cord,

---

12 Figure derived from Mishin and Romashov (2016).

13 This section was adapted with permission from Engel (2018).

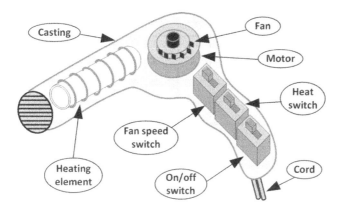

Figure 2.18 Handheld hairdryer and its components.

(2) on/off switch, (3) fan speed switch, (4) motor, (5) fan, (6) heat switch, (7) heating element, and (8) casing. The context of the system is composed of (1) electricity and (2) air.

A design structure matrix (DSM) shows such interactions (Eppinger and Browning, 2012). DSM is a modeling technique that can be used for developing and managing complex systems. It captures the elements of a system and their interactions, as well as the interactions between the system and its context. According to DSM convention, the outputs produced by components are placed along the row of that component. The inputs to a component are placed along the column of that component. In the case of the hairdryer, one can define the following types of interactions: (1) spatial, (2) material, (3) energy, and (4) information.

- **Spatial interactions.** These interactions relate to an object's size, area, shape, position, or orientation relative to other objects in the system's physical space. In this example, spatial refers to the particular physical arrangements of the hairdryer's components.
- **Material interactions.** These interactions relate to transferring material or physical objects among system elements. In this example, the material is air, which interacts with the handheld hairdryer by moving air through it.
- **Energy interactions.** These interactions relate to kinetic, thermal, electrical, chemical, or nuclear energy among system elements. In this example, energy applies to electricity.
- **Information interactions.** These interactions relate to transferring data or other forms of information among system elements. In this example, no interactions associated with information exist.

The resulting DSM is depicted in Figure 2.19. So, for example, the fan speed switch (C) interacts and provides energy (electricity) to the motor (D). Along the same line, the system's context (I) interacts and provides material (air) to the fan (E).

		A	B	C	D	E	F	G	H	I
Cord	A		E						S	
On/off switch	B			E			E		S	
Fan speed switch	C				E				S	
Motor	D					S			S	
Fan	E				S			S, M	S	
Heat switch	F							E	S	
Heating element	G					S			S	M
Casing	H	S	S	S	S	S	S	S		
System's context	I	E				M				

Spatial	S		Material	M		Energy	E		Information	I

Figure 2.19 DSM modeling of the hairdryer components and interactions.

Figure 2.20 depicts the hairdryer's spatial, material, and energy interactions.

The reader should note that input/output between two or more objects constitutes specific interactions between them. For example, the air in the system's context interacts with the fan, which, in turn, transfers air into the heating

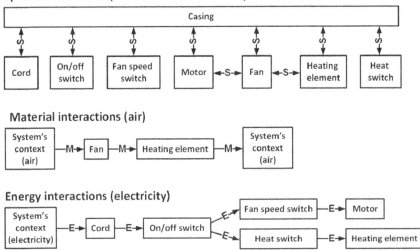

Figure 2.20 Hairdryer interactions: spatial, material, and energy.

element. If the hairdryer operated in a vacuum, the fan would turn but not push air forward, negating its original mission. The air in the system's context interacts with the fan in a particular way.

Such interactions exist throughout the hairdryer's components. Another example could be the casing interacting with the motor by affixing it onto a specific location and orientation within the hairdryer. Without a casing, the motor would drift everywhere and not fulfill its intended role within the hairdryer. In short, the casing interacts with the motor in a particular way.

2.6   Systems Change

> The change principle: All systems change and transform continuously in many dimensions and on multiple time scales.

2.6.1   Systems Change over Time

All systems change and transform[14] continuously in many dimensions and on multiple time scales. Some systems change erratically, that is, with no purposeful course. Other biological and social systems tend to follow adaptation that emphasizes survivability.

The change in the time scale of various systems is a wildly varied phenomenon. For example, electrical changes may occur in micro- or nanoseconds. Chemical reactions may occur in milliseconds or seconds, or more. Similarly, the timescale for microbial reproduction and evolution may be measured in minutes, and social adaptation may take years or decades. For example, consider the social changes during COVID-19, the coronavirus epidemic of 2020. All of these occur at lightning speed relative to geological time scales. For instance, rocks disintegrate and decay over thousands of years due to the impact of mechanical and chemical elements related to atmospheric, hydrologic, and biotic conditions. This process mainly occurs within minerals' nanoscale levels.

2.6.2   Changes in the Universe System

The changes in the Universe offer a spectacular example of change on a cosmological time scale. Throughout history, people held many concepts about the nature of the Universe. However, all of them shared the notion that the stars and the Sun are moving while the Universe, as a whole, is fixed in space.

---

14 We distinguish between *change*, which is a broad term referring to any change or transformation in a system over time, versus *evolution*, which is a directed process whereby a system is adapted to better match its environment or situation.

Only in 1912 did Vesto Melvin Slipher (1875–1969) observe the frequency-shifting of spectral lines of galaxies, indicating that these galaxies are moving relative to the Earth. Later, in 1929, Edwin Hubble (1889–1953) and Milton Humason (1891–1972) proved that the velocity of galaxies increases proportionality to their distances from the Earth, which is the basis for the modern theory of the expanding Universe. The Universe system is all of space-time and its contents. A model of the changing Universe system according to the current cosmological big bang theory is depicted in Figure 2.21.

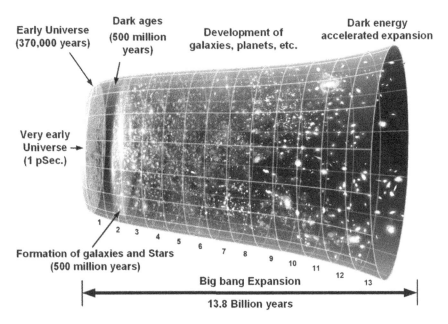

Figure 2.21 Chronology of the Universe (Image: NASA).

According to current cosmological understanding, the Universe system started with the big bang event 13.8 billion years ago.[15] Accordingly, the changing Universe may be chronologically divided into four parts.[16]

---

15 According to prevailing cosmology theory, just before the big bang, all of space-time, all of everything, was concentrated in a small ball with temperatures of over a quadrillion degrees. Why? How does the entire Universe reach this stage? Some scientists suspect that the big bang may have been a big bounce. An older Universe may have existed before ours that after expanding for billions of years, started to collapse in on itself and formed a super-massive black hole, eventually collapsing into a singularity that exploded into our current universe. Some think that this bouncing process will continue forever. But one may ask what the dynamics of the initial bounce are. We may never know. Albert Einstein once said, "Trying to understand what came before the Big Bang is like trying to figure out what is more north than the north pole…"

16 See more in Chronology of the universe. https://en.wikipedia.org/wiki/Chronology_of_the_universe. Accessed: Jan. 2023.

- **The very early Universe.** The very early Universe system lasted about one picosecond (10^{-12} of a second). During this infinitesimal short time, defined as the Planck epoch, the currently understood laws of physics did not apply.
- **The early Universe.** The early Universe lasted approximately 370,000 years. During this time, several cosmological stages occurred, starting with the formation of various subatomic particles at super-high temperatures. Eventually, the Universe becomes cool enough for neutral atoms to form, resulting in the Universe becoming transparent for the first time.
- **The dark ages and formation of galaxies and stars.** This period lasted about a billion years. Initially, the Universe system was transparent and dark, with no light sources except the background cosmic photons released earlier during the Universe's formation. Eventually, clouds of hydrogen slowly collapsed to become stars and galaxies, gradually bringing the Universe system to acquire today's form.
- **The Universe as it appears today.** During this 12.8-billion-year period, galaxies and stars have been born and have died, but the Universe has not changed significantly. And according to current cosmological theory, it is expected to appear very similar for billions of years.

2.6.3 Changes in the Milky Way Galaxy System

Within a few billion years after the big bang, the gases and dust within the interstellar medium gradually collapsed from a roughly spherical shape into a disk-like shape. The early stars in the Milky Way galaxy system were formed in the process. Over time, the Milky Way has grown through galaxy mergers and the annexation of gas and dust from the Galactic halo.[17]

The diameter of the Milky Way galaxy is approximately 200 000 light-years. The galaxy system probably contains some 100 billion to 400 billion stars and roughly the same number of planets. The galaxy system moves at a velocity of about 600 kilometers per second relative to an extragalactic frame of reference.

Scientists claim that our solar system is located about 27,000 light-years from the galactic center, orbiting around the galaxy center at approximately 220 kilometers per second and completing one revolution around the galaxy within 240 million years.

2.6.4 Changes in the Solar System

Our solar system is estimated to have been created some 9.1 billion years after the big bang, that is, 4.7 billion years ago.[18] Scientists think our solar system was

---

17 See more: Milky Way, https://en.wikipedia.org/wiki/Milky_Way. Accessed: Jan. 2023.

18 See more in Formation and evolution of the solar system. https://en.wikipedia.org/wiki/Formation_and_evolution_of_the_Solar_System. Accessed: Jan. 2023.

formed from large rotating interstellar clouds of gas and dust. Gravity caused this mass to collapse as it spun faster and flattened into a disk.

Most of the collapsing mass created the Sun, while the rest formed the eight planets and their moons, asteroids, and other small solar system objects (Figure 2.22). The solar system has changed continuously. Moons have been formed from discs of gas and dust circling their parent planets. Other moons, presumably Earth's moon, are thought to have been created due to collisions with large celestial bodies from within or outside the solar system. Such collisions and occasional asteroid and comet impacts have continued throughout the solar system's history and are expected to continue.

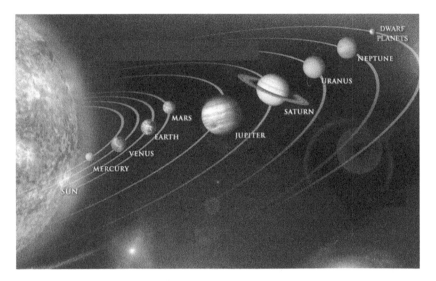

Figure 2.22 The solar system (Image: NASA).

2.6.5 Changes in Planet Earth

Planet Earth was created in conjunction with the formation of the solar system. Volcanic release of hot lava, ash, and gases created the primordial early earth atmosphere. Much of the Earth was molten, and its atmosphere contained almost no oxygen. Over time, the Earth cooled, and a solid crust evolved, supporting the formation of liquid water on the surface.

Continents have formed, disintegrated, floated upon the mantle (i.e., the part of the Earth's interior that lies beneath the crust and above its central core), and collided as the Earth gained a magnetic field that has reversed itself several times over the eons. Earth's surface temperature has fluctuated, leading to rising temperatures due to volcanic outgassing and glaciations due to cosmic events. As time progressed, fluctuating quantities of inorganic compounds such as nitrogen, oxygen, methane, and carbon dioxide dominated the earth's atmosphere.

Figure 2.23 and the text below depict the interactions between the Earth and the biosphere.[19] The bottom of the figure shows four geologic eons, starting 4.5 billion years ago, and some significant geobiological changes during this time.

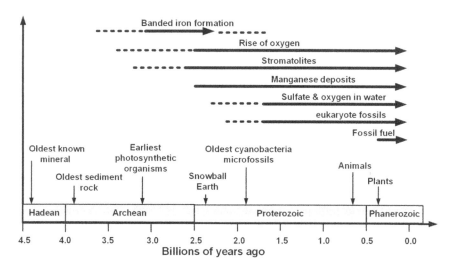

Figure 2.23 Geologic timescale and major geobiological events.

- **Banded iron formation.** These are sedimentary rocks consisting of iron oxides and iron-poor chert. Chert may occur inorganically but often has a biological origin in an oxidizing environment and iron-oxidizing microbes.
- **Rise of oxygen.** The photosynthetic activities of the cyanobacteria introduced oxygen into the Earth's atmosphere. This process profoundly impacted the evolution of the planet and its living organisms.
- **Stromatolites.** These are mounds of layered rock structures initially formed by the cyanobacteria, single-celled photosynthesizing microbes (Figure 2.24).

---

19 See more: Geobiology. https://en.wikipedia.org/wiki/Geobiology. Accessed: Jan. 2023.

Figure 2.24 Living stromatolites in Shark Bay, Western Australia.

- **Manganese deposits.** These deposits are based on chemical compounds, often found in minerals containing iron or oxygen. In terms of abundance, these chemical compounds are widely distributed in the Earth's crust, second only to iron among the transition elements of the Periodic Table.
- **Sulfate and oxygen in the water.** The rise in oxygen, coupled with sulfur isotope fractionation by sulfate-reducing microbes, as well as global glaciations, increased the concentration of sulfate and oxygen in the water. These alterations in ocean surface biogeochemical facilitated the evolution of many diversified organisms.
- **Eukaryote fossils.** The presence of oxygen promoted the rapid evolution of eukaryotes, which are organisms with a cell nucleus enclosed within an external envelope. They also may be multicellular, including many cell types that form different kinds of tissues. This geobiological development subsequently led to the evolution of animals and plants.
- **Fossil fuels.** Fossil fuels include petroleum, coal, and natural gas. These compounds were formed through the anaerobic decomposition of ancient buried organisms.

2.6.6 Changes in Daily Objects and Systems

Another example of change relates to many objects and systems surrounding us daily (to be exact, matter that occupies space and has mass). Fundamentally, objects may undergo two types of changes, physical and chemical. Physical change in an object refers to a change in the properties of matter that does not involve a change in the object's molecular composition. Such properties (e.g., mass, color, weight, volume) are easy to measure without affecting the sample's composition under study. A chemical change in an object refers to creating a chemically different kind of matter with different properties from the original.[20]

For example, the physical heating of a metal beam changes (reduces) its physical strength and ability to carry loads. This behavior is a change in the physical characteristics of the beam. In contrast, chemical change alters the composition of the original matter. For example, the combustion of magnesium metal changes the original magnesium and oxygen substances into magnesium oxide substances (in chemical vocabulary, $2Mg + O_2 \rightarrow 2MgO$).

2.6.6.1 Physical Matter Change Example

A physical change in water (H_2O) is depicted in the semi-log thermodynamic chart in Figure 2.25. The *x-axis* shows a linear temperature range from −200 °C to +400 °C. The *y-axis* shows a logarithmic pressure of 0.01 millibar (i.e., one-thousandth part of normal atmospheric pressure at sea level) to 1 Mbar (i.e., one million times the normal atmospheric pressure at sea level).

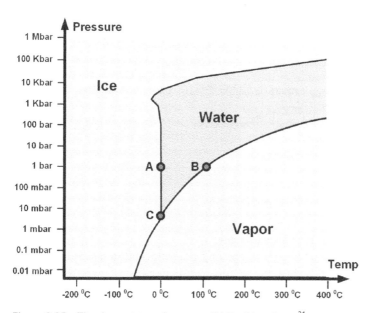

Figure 2.25 The three states of water: solid, liquid, and gas.[21]

---

20 See more: https://opentextbc.ca/chemistry/chapter/physical-and-chemical-properties/. Last accessed: Jan. 2023.

21 Adapted from Phase diagram of water simplified. https://commons.wikimedia.org/wiki/File:Phase_diagram_of_water_simplified.svg. Last accessed: Jan. 2023.

As can be seen, under different conditions of temperatures and pressure, water changes its physical property among the three primary states of solid, liquid, and gas. (1) Solid objects are characterized by their atoms, which are tightly packed together in fixed patterns; (2) liquid objects are characterized by their atoms, which are close together but do not maintain fixed patterns; and (3) gas objects are characterized by their atoms, which are separate and move stochastically in all directions within their boundaries.

The reader should note that (1) point A represents the water freezing point, which occurs at a temperature of 0 °C and pressure of 1 atmosphere; (2) point B represents the water boiling point, which occurs at a temperature of 100 °C and pressure of 1 atmosphere; and (3) point C represents the solid/liquid/gas triple point (i.e., the temperature–pressure point where ice, water, and vapor coexist in equilibrium indefinitely). This phenomenon occurs at a temperature of 0 °C and pressure of 6 mbar (six-thousandths of a nominal atmospheric pressure at sea level). Also note, however, that throughout this temperature–pressure space, the chemical constituents of the water molecules are the same: 11.2% hydrogen and 88.8% oxygen by mass.

State transitions of physical matter are depicted in Figure 2.26. State transition processes in which energy must be supplied are called endothermic. In contrast, processes that release heat are called exothermic.

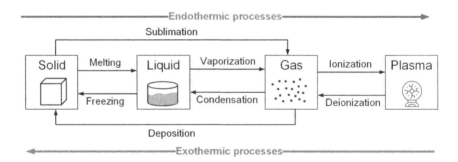

Figure 2.26 State transitions of physical matter.

2.6.6.2 Chemical Matter Change Example

Chemical changes occur when bonds among molecules and atoms are broken and reestablished differently. In other words, one or more substances with certain physical properties (such as specific weight and electrical conductivity) turn into different substances with different physical properties.

For example, Figure 2.27 depicts heavy rust on the links of an anchor chain located near the Golden Gate Bridge in San Francisco. It was exposed to long-term moisture and salt-laden spray, which caused surface breakdown, cracking, and metal flaking.

Figure 2.27   Old rusty anchor chain.

Figure 2.28 depicts a simplified description of iron (Fe) and oxygen (O$_2$), producing a layer of a reddish-brown substance called iron (III) oxide with the common name of hematite and the chemical formula of Fe$_2$O$_3$.

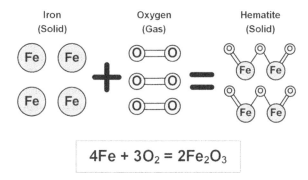

$$4Fe + 3O_2 = 2Fe_2O_3$$

Figure 2.28   Iron and oxygen produce hematite.

The rusting process is substantially more complex because water or moisture in the air acts as a catalyst, accelerating the change process. Furthermore, salt in seawater expedites the rusting process even further due to electrochemical reactions. Therefore, any structure made of iron and exposed to water and oxygen is vulnerable to rust, which consists of several complex chemical compounds like hydrated iron (III) oxides ($Fe_2O_3 \cdot nH_2O$), iron (III) oxide ($FeO(OH)$), and iron (III) hydroxide ($Fe(OH)_3$). Furthermore, surface rust does not protect the underlying iron.

2.6.7 Changes in Technical Systems[22]

Many changes in living systems, as well as technical systems, emanate from aging and decay. For example, the following describes changes in technical systems due to mechanical, electronic, and software aging.

2.6.7.1 Changes in Mechanical Systems
Mechanical systems and components also experience failure modes whose effects accumulate and introduce system failures. Similarly, damage to mechanical systems due to friction or repeated contact between materials is quite common. Corrosion of mechanical systems is a process by which the outer surface of a material undergoes a chemical reaction with its environment. This process leads to a gradual accumulation of damage, often resulting in system failures.

The deposition of materials in pipes causes a reduction of the pipes' cross-sectional areas, leading to flow reduction or the necessity of increasing pressure to maintain the flow level. Therefore, any change in the operating conditions could lead to potential failures such as overheating, reduced flow, or mechanical failure.

Creep is the tendency of matter to deform under stress below its yielding point. Its severity increases when the operating condition is at a temperature close to the material's melting point. For example, a common creep failure involves turbine blades operating at high temperatures. Creep increases the possibility of fatigue failure, and blade elongation reduces blade tip clearance, causing blades to hit the casing (Carter, 2005).

Fatigue is a failure of components caused by the appearance and propagation of small cracks that ultimately break the component. Fatigue occurs due to repeatedly applying cyclic loading, and its damage accumulates according to Miner's law. Many failures are due to fatigue, such as the de Havilland Comet crashes (Withey, 1997).

2.6.7.2 Changes in Electronic Systems
Various electronic analog devices interfacing among digital electronic systems often change their physical characteristics over time. For example, an unmanned air vehicle uses analog sensors to extract airspeed, elevation, and temperature information, affecting various flight parameters.

---

22 Adapted with permission from Engel et al. (2021).

Integrated electronic systems with analog and mixed-signal (AMS) circuits are fabricated using complementary metal oxide semiconductor (CMOS) technology. They are widely used in consumer electronics and life-critical fields like aircraft avionics and pacemakers. However, according to More (2012), the reliability of such AMS circuits manufactured in the deep submicrometer technology is subject to lifetime performance degradation due primarily to aging mechanisms like bias temperature instability (BTI) and hot carrier injection (HCI). Similarly, operational amplifiers (OA), ring oscillators (RO), switched capacitors (SC), successive approximation registers (SAR), and delta-sigma analog-to-digital converters (ADC) are all susceptible to unique aging processes.

Yu's doctoral thesis (2011) discusses the design of reliable nanometric electronic systems under aging conditions. As technology scales further, new reliability problems appear, such as radiation-induced soft errors, fabrication process parameter variations, and circuit aging (degradation). These effects are manifested as the inherent unreliability of the components.

In particular, aged components in sub-65 Nanometer (nm) technologies tend to exhibit timing delays. In other words, a signal of an aged device assumes the correct value but does so more slowly than initially designed. This aging process affects the global timing of the circuit and often produces logic electronic errors on critical paths. In addition, these timing delays may lead to clock skews. They may slow down the system clock, leading to slower system operations and a loss of synchronization with external systems.

Thick-film resistors (TFRs) are also undergoing progressive degradation over time. According to Sinnadurai et al. (1980), the increasing temperature during a standard component's operation or continued storage (before or after manufacturing) induces thermal aging. In addition, humidity, especially at relatively high levels, precipitates severe TFR aging. More specifically, normal life cycle conditions of elevated temperature and humidity tend to increase the resistance of TFRs by as much as an order of magnitude relative to the original design.

Several researchers (e.g., Hossain, 1992) discuss the aging degradation of polymer-based insulation materials used in electronic systems, transformers, capacitors, electrical cables, and so on. This process involves increased absorption leakage currents stemming from the long-term polarization of molecules within the dielectric material. The aging phenomenon accelerates under thermal stress, high humidity levels, and an environment replete with chemical contaminants.

2.6.7.3 Changes in Software Systems

According to Parnas (1994), software products tend to change and invariably exhibit the phenomenon of aging. These changes are essential because computers are changing and becoming obsolete, operating systems and many other software and hardware components are being replaced, and older versions are no longer supported. Further, users often request additional features that only software modifications can fulfill.

Ongoing software maintenance also causes aging. Original designers of software have a specific concept in mind when writing the code. Invariably, modifications are made by people who do not fully understand the original design concept, causing the program's structure to degrade. As a result, changes will be inconsistent with the original concept and sometimes invalidate the original approach. Furthermore, change-induced aging is often exacerbated by the maintainers failing to update the documentation, making future maintenance even more difficult.

Cotroneo et al. (2014) surveyed the current literature on software aging and rejuvenation strategies. Software aging may often be attributed to subtle software faults, which have been introduced during the development or maintenance of the software. Such failures do not immediately cause a software failure but slowly degrade the system performance and eventually cause system failures. This aging process is further exasperated due to software growth in size and complexity.

2.7 Bibliography

Alter, S. (2018). System interaction theory: Describing interactions between work systems. *Communications of the Association for Information Systems*.

Carter, T.J. (2005). Common failures in gas turbine blades. *Engineering Failure Analysis* 12 (2): 237–247.

Cotroneo, D., Natella, R., Pietrantuono, R., and Russo, S. (2014). A software aging and rejuvenation studies survey. ACM Journal on Emerging Technologies in Computing Systems 0 (1): article no. 8.

Engel, A. (2018). Practical Creativity and Innovation in Systems Engineering (Wiley Series in Systems Engineering and Management), Wiley.

Engel, A., Teller, A., Shachar, S., and Reich, Y. (2021, June 21). Robust design under cumulative damage due to dynamic failure mechanisms, *Systems Engineering Journal* 24 (5): 322–338.

Eppinger, S.D. and Browning, T.R. (2012). *Design Structure Matrix Methods, and Applications*. MIT Press.

FAA DOT/FAA/AR-08/32. (2009, June). Requirements Engineering Management Handbook. National Technical Information Service (NTIS). US Department of Transportation Federal Aviation Administration. https://www.faa.gov/aircraft/air_cert/design_approvals/air_software/media/AR-08-32.pdf. Accessed: Jan. 2023.

Gorod, A., Fridman, A., and Sauser, B. (2010). A quantitative approach to analysis of a system of systems operational boundaries. International Congress on Ultra Modern Telecommunications and Control Systems and Workshops (ICUMT), Moscow.

Hossain, M.M. (1992). Effect of humidity and thermal aging on the absorption characteristics in polymer, *Bulletin of Materials Science*, Springer.

Maier, M.W. (1998). Architecting principles for systems-of-systems, *Systems Engineering* 1: 267–284.

Mesarovic, M.D. and Takahara, Y. (1989). *Abstract Systems Theory*, Springer.

Mishin, A., and Romashov, B. (Nov. 2016). Retrospective analysis of the wolf's impact on the number of wild ungulates in the Voronezhsky reserve. *Beiträge zur Jagd-und Wildforschung*. https://www.researchgate.net/publication/321907290_Retrospective_analysis_of_the_wolf%27s_impact_on_the_number_of_wild_ungulates_in_the_Voronezhsky_reserve. Accessed: Jan. 2023.

Mobus, G.E. and Kalton, M.C. (2015). *Principles of Systems Science (Understanding Complex Systems)*. Springer.

More S. (2012). Aging degradation and countermeasures in deep-submicrometer analog and mixed signal integrated circuits. PhD thesis, Technical University of Munich, Germany.

Parnas, D.L. (May 1994) Software aging. *ICSE '94 Proceedings of the 16th International Conference on Software Engineering* (pp. 279–287). IEEE Computer Society Press.

Pfeiffer C. (2018). *Aristotle's Theory of Bodies*. Oxford University Press.

Robertson, B.J. (2015). *Holacracy: The New Management System for a Rapidly Changing World*. Henry Holt and Co.

Sinnadurai, F.N., Spencer, P.E., and Wilson, K.J. (1980). Some observations on the accelerated ageing of thick-film resistors. *Electrocomponent Science and Technology* 6: 241–246.

Sizemore, B. (May 3, 2003). Determining System Boundaries for Federal IT Systems, GIAC Security Essentials Certification Practical Assignment. https://www.giac.org/paper/gsec/2882/determining-system-boundaries-federal-systems/104860. Accessed: Jan. 2023.

Varzi, A. (2004). Boundary. (updated 2013, October 10). *Stanford Encyclopedia of Philosophy*, https://plato.stanford.edu/entries/boundary/. Accessed: Jan. 2023.

Withey, P.A. (1997). Fatigue failure of the de Havilland comet I. *Engineering Failure Analysis* 4 (2): 147–154.

Yu, H. (2011). Low-cost highly-efficient fault tolerant processor design for mitigating the reliability issues in nanometric technologies. PhD thesis, University of Grenoble, France.

3

Principles of Systems Science (Part II)

3.1 Introduction

Systems science is based on several fundamental principles. A principle is an underlying truth or proposition that is the foundation of a belief or behavior of systems. This chapter describes the second set of five fundamental principles of systems science, which, together with the previous chapter, represents the author's top-level worldview on systems science. The material below is presented mostly through multiple examples rather than formal discussions and definitions:

- **Systems input/output.** Containing quantitative model, economic system example, environmental system example, and human body system example.
- **Systems complexity.** Containing definitions of complex systems, feedback loops, the Cynefin framework, and estimating structural complexity (theory and operationalization).
- **Systems control.** Containing simple open and closed-loop control systems, PID control systems, advanced control systems, and biological control in the human body system.
- **Systems evolution.** Containing inanimate and living systems, living systems evolution, *Homo sapiens* example, and homologous example.
- **Systems emergence.** Containing emerging properties, swarming examples, and termite colonies examples.

Systems Science for Engineers and Scholars, First Edition. Edited by Avner Engel.
© 2024 John Wiley & Sons, Ltd. Published 2024 by John Wiley & Sons, Ltd.

3.2 Systems Input/Output

> The input/output principle: All systems receive information, energy, and/or matter from their context, process it, and then transmit the result to their context.

All systems interact with their context through a partially porous boundary that defines and distinguishes the system from its context. So, inputs to the system are whatever flows into it, and outputs are whatever comes out. The distinction between the system and its context embodies the process within the system. Sometimes, systems are defined only through their inputs and outputs. This so-called black-box view of systems confines the analysis of such systems to their stimulus/response behavior.

3.2.1 Quantitative Model

Open systems theory acknowledges that their context strongly influences biological, social, technical, and other systems' parameters. Consequently, these systems can survive only by exchanging matter/energy/information with their contexts. For example, an organization imports raw materials and converts them into end products through various processes. A process is a series of recurrent or periodic activities that interact to achieve results. More specifically, a process consists of a purposeful sequence of tasks that combine resources to produce the desired outcome under a dynamic measure.

The US economist Wassily Leontief developed the first quantitative macroeconomic input/output (IO) model in 1936. The model, depicting linear interindustry relationships within the economy, became widely used and earned Leontief the Nobel Prize in economic sciences in 1973. The model shows how outputs from one or more industrial sectors turn into inputs to one or more other industrial sectors. Therefore, the model depicts the dependent nature of each sector upon every other sector within the economy. Today, almost all countries compile IO tables capturing national product flows between economic sectors.

The model makes the following assumptions: (1) An economy is composed of n sectors, with each one producing x_i units of a specific product; (2) in this process, the j sector uses a_{ij} units from sector i; and (3) each sector may utilize some of its products and delivers them to other sectors as well as to end users e_i.

So, the Leontief IO model may be expressed as follows:

$$x_1 = a_{11}x_1 + a_{12}x_2 + \cdots + a_{1n}x_n + e_1$$
$$x_2 = a_{21}x_1 + a_{22}x_2 + \cdots + a_{2n}x_n + e_2$$
$$\cdots$$
$$x_n = a_{n1}x_1 + a_{n2}x_2 + \cdots + a_{nn}x_n + e_n$$

$$(3.1)$$

Solving the above set of linear equations yields the following matrix operation:

$$X = AX + E \tag{3.2}$$

After some mathematical rearrangements, X can be isolated, yielding:

$$X = (I - A)^{-1}E \tag{3.3}$$

Where:

X is the production-level vector, A is the input/output matrix, and E is the end-user vector.

$$X = \begin{pmatrix} x_1 \\ x_2 \\ \vdots \\ x_n \end{pmatrix} \quad A = \begin{pmatrix} a_{11}, a_{12}, \dots, a_{1n} \\ a_{21}, a_{22}, \dots, a_{2n} \\ \vdots \\ a_{n1}, a_{n2}, \dots, a_{nn} \end{pmatrix} \quad E = \begin{pmatrix} e_1 \\ e_2 \\ \vdots \\ e_n \end{pmatrix} \tag{3.4}$$

3.2.2 Economic System Example

The following example illustrates the Leontief IO model. An economy of a country has three key industrial sectors: mining, building, and steel production. The macroeconomics within the country is expressed below and in Figure 3.1

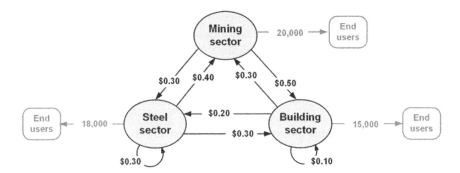

Figure 3.1 A country's economy comprises three key industrial sectors.

1. To produce $1 of output, the mining sector requires $0.30 worth of building products and $0.40 worth of steel products.
2. To produce $1 of output, the building sector requires $0.50 worth of mining products, $0.10 worth of its building products, and $0.30 worth of steel products.
3. To produce $1 of output, the steel sector requires $0.30 worth of mining products, $0.20 worth of building products, and $0.30 worth of steel products.
4. The mining sector delivers $20,000 worth of mining products to end users.

5. The building sector delivers $15,000 worth of building products to end users.
6. The steel sector delivers $18,000 worth of steel products to end users.

The above data yields the three relevant matrices: X is the production level vector, A is the IO matrix, and E is the end-users' vector.

$$X = \begin{pmatrix} x_1 \ (Mining) \\ x_2 \ (Building) \\ x_3 \ (Steel\ ) \end{pmatrix} \qquad A = \begin{pmatrix} \overset{Mining}{0.00} & \overset{Building}{0.50} & \overset{Steel}{0.30} \\ 0.30 & 0.10 & 0.20 \\ 0.40 & 0.30 & 0.30 \end{pmatrix} \qquad E = \begin{pmatrix} 20,000 \\ 15,000 \\ 18,000 \end{pmatrix}$$

Solving this set of system matrices for X using Eq. (3.3) and available computation tools like MATLAB yields the required production levels of the mining, building, and steel sectors:

$$X = \begin{pmatrix} x_1 \ (Mining) & = \$85,034 \\ x_2 \ (Building) = \$68,000 \\ x_3 \ (Steel) & = \$103,448 \end{pmatrix}$$

3.2.3 Environmental System I/O Example

A different IO analysis is provided by Kjær et al. (2015). They use an environmental input/output (EIO) database covering the entire supply chain. In addition, the Danish national IO tables were extended to include emission data for each sector in the economy, making it possible to calculate the environmental life cycle impacts associated with each product output. The reader should note that this research uses the Leontief IO model in its most elementary form regarding the Danish healthcare system as a black box, referring only to the external input and output elements (Figure 3.2).

Figure 3.2 The Danish healthcare system and its input and output.

The Danish healthcare system uses a certain amount of funding (in Danish currency [DKK]) to conduct its mission, generating as byproducts a certain amount of carbon footprint (in carbon dioxide equivalent [CO_2]). The rate of matter/energy/information transferred between the system and its context over time is defined as the system's throughput.

One of the three case studies presented in the Kjær et al. (2015) paper compares the financial spending of healthcare organizations and the relevant corporate carbon footprints. The Danish Healthcare System is responsible for all national healthcare issues in Denmark, primarily providing hospital services.

Figure 3.3 depicts a more detailed set of inputs and outputs of the Danish healthcare system: the financial spending (in Danish currency [DKK]) relative to the carbon footprint (in carbon dioxide equivalent [CO_2]) for the capital region of Denmark in 2011. The figure shows that patient articles, including medicine, were the largest spending category, accounting for 38% of the total spending. However, patient articles accounted for only 19% of the carbon footprint. This ratio is because medicine is relatively expensive, and much money is spent on service-related activities like research and development. In contrast, the category food accounted for only 2% of the total spending, while it accounted for more than 10% of the carbon footprint.

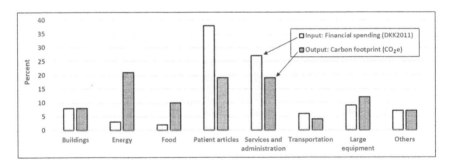

Figure 3.3 Corporate financial spending and carbon footprint: capital region of Denmark.

3.2.4 Human Body System Example

The Leontief IO model may be utilized in many fields beyond economics (e.g., engineering biology, political science). For example, Figure 3.4 and the following text depict a qualitative Leontief IO model of the human body.

The human body is a biological machine consisting of several subsystems. These subsystems are made of organs that interact to sustain life. More specifically, organs are specialized biological structures composed of different tissues that perform specific functions. For example, the cardiovascular subsystem is mainly comprised of the heart, arteries, veins, lymph nodes, blood, etc.

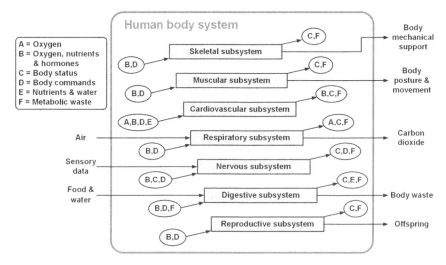

Figure 3.4 The human body IO model.

This human body IO model is composed of the following subsystems[1]:

- **Skeletal subsystem.** The skeletal subsystem consists of bones and cartilage. It gives the body its basic mechanical framework, providing support, structure, and protection for internal organs.
- **Muscular subsystem.** The muscular subsystem consists of the smooth muscles, the cardiac muscles, and the skeletal muscles. Smooth muscles operate within hollow organs such as the intestines and the stomach. Cardiac muscles form the heart, and skeletal muscles are attached to the body's bones, enabling movement and locomotion.
- **Cardiovascular subsystem.** The cardiovascular subsystem consists of the heart and circulatory blood vessels. The latter is a body-wide network of blood, arteries, veins, and lymph, transporting oxygen and nutrients to organs and cells throughout the body and extracting cellular metabolic waste from the body's cells.
- **Respiratory subsystem.** The respiratory subsystem comprises the nasal passage, the windpipe, and the lungs. It promotes the exchange of oxygen and carbon dioxide between the body and the air. This exchange is done by inhaling oxygen-rich air into the lungs and diffusing it into the bloodstream while exhaling removes carbon dioxide.
- **Nervous subsystem.** The nervous subsystem comprises the brain, the spinal cord, and the body-wide nervous structure. It regulates the vital body's

---

1 Several lesser human body subsystems/components are ignored for simplicity's sake.

physiologic functions, such as breathing, heartbeat, and digestion. It also supports perception, comprehension, and responding to the world within and around the body.

- **Digestive subsystem.** The digestive system includes the mouth, stomach, liver, pancreas, kidneys, and intestine. It ends with the anal canal and the male and female urethra. It enables the body to ingest food and convert it into usable nutrients through mechanical and chemical breakdown processes. In addition, it eliminates feces and urine from the body.

- **Reproductive subsystem.** The male reproductive subsystem consists of the penis and the testis. The female reproductive subsystem is comprised of the vagina, cervix, ovaries, uterus, and breasts. The male reproductive subsystem primarily produces, stores, and delivers sperm. The female reproductive subsystem is involved in carrying out pregnancy and childbirth. In sexual reproduction, some distinctive parental traits are transferred from parents to offspring, conserving certain genetic makeups while contributing to the natural selection process of the species.

The qualitative input, internal, and output products of the human body IO model are depicted in Table 3.1. Extending this Leontief IO model to include quantitative data is left to interested readers.

Table 3.1 Class and products of human body IO model.

Class	Products
Input	Air
	Sensory data
	Food and water
Internal	A = Oxygen
	B = Oxygen, nutrients, and hormones
	C = Biological body status
	D = Biological body commands
	E = Nutrients and water
	F = Metabolic waste
Output	Body mechanical support
	Body posture and movement
	Carbon dioxide
	Body waste
	Offspring

3.3   Systems' Complexity

The complexity principle: All systems exhibit various kinds and levels of complexity.

Complexity characterizes the behavior of systems composed of various parts interacting with each other in multiple ways.[2] By and large, the behavior of such systems is intrinsically challenging to model, understand, or deal with—even if complete information about its components and their interrelations is known. This difficulty is due to the numerous elements and relationships between them and the environment. These relationships often exhibit feedback loops, chaotic behavior, nonlinearity, and various dependencies (Bashir and Thomson, 1999, 2001).

3.3.1   Definition of Complex Systems

There are many definitions of complex systems because the precise definition is somewhat tricky. At a minimum, a complex system comprises many components interacting with each other and the environment in many ways. In addition, complex systems generally have distinct properties such as feedback loops and nonlinearity. Observing complexity from a probability and information theory perspective indicates that systems with more parts and interfaces are invariably more complex because of the increased uncertainty of satisfying their requirements.

Consider a bird's flocking or murmuration (see Section 3.6). Scientists understand that the flight behavior of each bird follows a set of simple mathematical rules: (1) keep a minimal distance, (2) fly at the same speed and direction, and (3) avoid collisions with neighboring birds. If the flocking and murmuration system follows a steady, continuous flight pattern, then one could say that this is a simple system. However, the phenomenally elaborated dynamics of flocking and murmuration often seen in nature are so difficult to explain or predict that one is justified in calling this natural system complex.

Different scientists associated with myriad disciplines have studied complex systems from various perspectives. As a result, a wide range of definitions has been developed to define and describe complex systems. For example, some of

---

2 Engineered systems containing both technologies and individuals, communities, or natural elements are often called sociotechnical systems.

them were compiled and later updated by Joseph Sussman in 2000, including the following[3]:

- According to Moses (working paper), a complex system is distinguished by its numerous interconnections between parts and their intricate nature. Although different systems exhibit various levels of complexity, this description is rather vague and does not provide a precise gauge to distinguish between complex and simple systems.
- According to Maier and Rechtin (2000), "A complex system has a set of elements so connected or related as to perform a unique function that is not performable by the elements alone." Acutely, all systems exhibiting emerging properties meet this definition. Therefore, one may reject this definition altogether.
- Sussman (2000) provides a more rigorous definition of a complex system: "A system is complex when it is composed of a group of related units (subsystems), for which the degree and nature of the relationships are imperfectly known."
- Senge (2006) defines complexity in terms of specific dynamic behavior, stating, "A system exhibits dynamic complexity when cause and effect are subtle, over time." And, more precisely, "A system exhibits dynamic complexity when a given action has dramatically different effects in the short run and the long run."

In his PhD thesis, Gutierrez (2012) adopts the following definition of a complex system: "A complex system is, in general, any system comprised of a great number of heterogeneous entities, among which local interactions create multiple levels of collective structure and organization." According to Gutierrez, the above definition centers on three core concepts:

- Complex systems contain a large number of heterogeneous entities.
- Complex systems exhibit emergent behavior due to the interactions among their entities.
- Complex systems exhibit emergent behavior due to multiple levels of organizations and structures.

Gutierrez continues and defines a set of attributes characterizing complex systems (Figure 3.5).

- **Emergence.** Emergent properties of complex systems are not observed within the entities composing the system level but are exhibited at a higher level.
- **Scale.** Complex systems are made of entities interacting at local time and space scales. In contrast, the time and space scales associated with emerging properties of complex systems' interaction are orders of magnitude larger.

---

3 Adapted from: Ferreira, P. (2001, October). Tracing complexity theory: ESD.83. Research Seminar in Engineering Systems. http://web.mit.edu/esd.83/www/notebook/Complexity%20 Theory.ppt. Accessed: Jan. 2023.

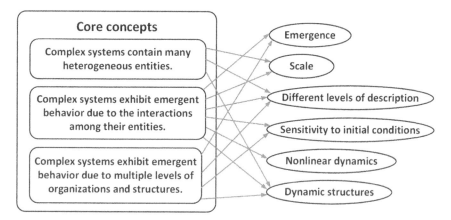

Figure 3.5 Core concepts versus characteristics of complex systems.[4]

- **Different levels of description.** Complex systems may be described at one level by exclusively considering the inherent characteristics of their local entities. Conversely, a complex system may be described by its emerging properties derived from lower-level entities.
- **Sensitivity to initial conditions.** When exposed to minor differences in their initial conditions, complex systems produce significantly different outputs.
- **Nonlinear dynamics.** Complex systems exhibit dynamics and nonlinear behavior. A small perturbation in a system's inputs tends to produce disproportional effects on the system's output.
- **Dynamic structures.** Complex systems exhibit structures that embody the interactions between entities of the system. As these interactions evolve, the behavior of systems evolves, expressing the dynamic structure of systems.

3.3.2 Feedback Loops

Positive or negative feedback loops are virtually always present in complex systems. Under such loops, the output of an element's behavior is fed back into its input, causing either oscillation and instability, or dumping and stability of the output.

Regardless of current technology and computing power, chaotic systems' behavior is nearly impossible to predict. The main reason for this is the sensitive dependence on the initial conditions of each element in the system. A small perturbation in the initial conditions leads to notably different outcomes. So,

---

4 Inspired by Gutierrez (2012). See more: https://theses.hal.science/tel-00758118. Accessed: Jan. 2023.

accurate predictions are difficult even with reasonable knowledge of the relevant equations describing the system's behavior and initial conditions.

Furthermore, in nonlinear systems, a change in the inputs' values does not generate a proportional change in the output. Nonlinear systems may respond in different ways to the same input. For a given change in the input, such systems may generate significantly greater than or less than proportional change in the output, depending on the system's current state.

Dependency is the ability of an element in the system or the environment to influence another element (e.g., its behaviors, characteristics, and properties). Dependencies between two components may be direct or indirect, unidirectional, or bidirectional. See Figure 3.6 and the text below.

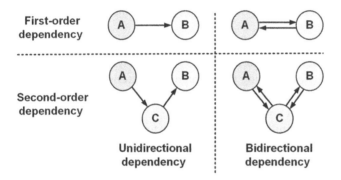

Figure 3.6 Types of systems dependencies.

- **First-order unidirectional dependency.** Element A depends on element B, so variations in element B may influence element A.
- **First-order bidirectional dependency.** Element A depends on element B, and, in addition, element B depends on element A, so variations in each element may influence the other element.
- **Second-order unidirectional dependency.** Element A is directly dependent on element C, which, in turn, is dependent on element B, so variations in B may influence element A.
- **Second-order bidirectional dependency.** Element A is directly dependent on element C, which, in turn, is dependent on element B and vice versa. In that case, variations in each element may influence the other elements.

Another approach to systems' complexity is proposed by Rousseau (2017) and depicted in Figure 3.7. Here, systems embodying increased levels of complexity are depicted hierarchically. Over time, a system at a given level of complexity brings about a system at a higher level.

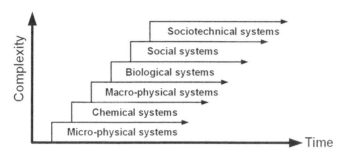

Figure 3.7   Hierarchy of systems' complexities.[5]

3.3.3   The Cynefin Framework

In 1999, Dave Snowden proposed a methodology dubbed the Cynefin framework.[6] This conceptual framework was created to enhance the systemic decision-making process for identifying and selecting a desired alternative from a set of optional choices. The Cynefin framework (Figure 3.8) associates a system's predictability/unpredictability behavior with the most appropriate decision-maker response.

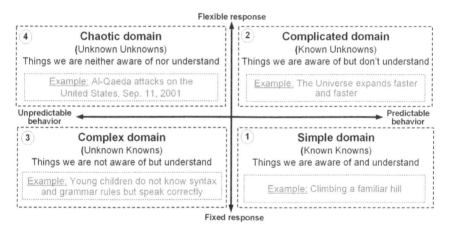

Figure 3.8   Cynefin framework used to aid decision-making.

The horizontal axis describes predictable behavior versus unpredictable behavior. Predictable behavior represents situations, whereby systems embody a high level of cause and effect. The unpredictable behavior represents situations whereby systems embody minimal or no transparent cause-and-effect relationships. The vertical axis describes a range of proposed responses, from flexible to fixed reactions. By and

---

5 Derived from: Rousseau (2017).

6 See more: Cynefin framework, https://en.wikipedia.org/wiki/Cynefin_framework. Last accessed: Jan. 2023.

large, agile/flexible responses to situations vary and depend upon unique circumstances. In contrast, fixed responses to given situations tend to produce the same automatic reactions regardless of the specific circumstances.

Under the Cynefin framework, one assigns a given situation into one of four domains: (1) simple, (2) complicated, (3) complex, or (4) chaotic.

- **Simple domain.** The simple domain represents the *known knowns* syndrome. This syndrome means that the cause-and-effect behavior of the system is apparent, the situation is familiar (e.g., climbing a familiar hill), and a known fixed solution applies to the given situation (e.g., planning the trip up the hill and carrying food, water, maps, communication gear, etc.).
- **Complicated domain.** The complicated domain represents the *known unknowns* syndrome. This syndrome means that the cause-and-effect behavior of the system requires analysis and investigation (e.g., the Universe expands faster and faster). In this case, a range of proper flexible responses must be adapted to the specific nature of the situation (e.g., dark matter theory).
- **Complex domain.** The complex domain represents the *unknown knowns* syndrome. In this context, the cause-and-effect behavior of the system is unknown and could be deduced only in retrospect (e.g., young children talk using proper syntax and grammar). In this case, there is no a priori right or wrong response, so one should develop multiple hypotheses and conduct experiments to identify a viable emergent solution. Here again, the flexible response must be tailored to the specificity of the issue (e.g., create appropriate theories that explain the phenomena).
- **Chaotic domain.** The chaotic domain represents the *unknown unknowns* syndrome. Here too, the cause-and-effect behavior of the system is unknown. However, the system is unstable and often confusing (e.g., Al-Qaeda attacked the United States on September 11, 2001). Therefore, waiting and contemplating is not a viable response. Instead, an urgent and usually fixed response (e.g., saving the lives of as many people as possible) should be carried out.

3.3.4 Estimating Structural Complexity (Theory)

3.3.4.1 Background

Today's large-scale engineered systems are becoming increasingly more complicated and complex. This evolution has led to higher development efforts in realizing such systems, which, in turn, has led many development projects of large systems to fall behind in terms of cost and schedule performance.

Such development cost overruns/failures of systems development projects can largely be attributed to the inability to quantify systems' complexity. The following shows one way to estimate a system's structural complexity. It is based chiefly on Sinha's (2014) PhD dissertation and Sinha and de Weck's (2016) paper.

A key motivation for estimating the structural complexity of a system is to predict, as closely as possible, the development cost of the system. Recently, a focus has been on quantifying structural complexity by developing complexity metrics.

For example, Weyuker (1988) proposed a strict construct validity paradigm for computing the structural complexity of systems. Both Van Wie et al. (2001), dealing with a simple family of electric handheld drills (made by DeWalt), and Wertz and Larson (1996), dealing with the Ørsted satellite system, provide practical information related to the hypothesis that system development cost correlates superlinearly with structural complexity. Finally, Sinha (2014) and Sinha and de Weck (2016) discuss a model for computing structural complexity based on the Hamiltonian system.

1. **Van Wie et al. (2001) research.** This research deals with structural complexities in 14 consumer products. For example, Figure 3.9 depicts an electrical handheld drill system (made by DeWalt). The system is comprised of four modules as well as three internal and several external interfaces.

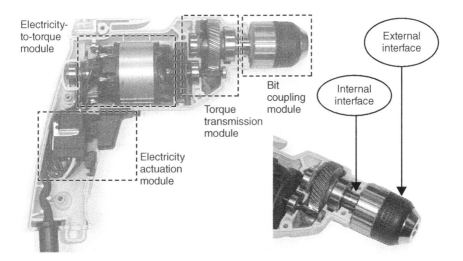

Figure 3.9 Electrical handheld drill (made by DeWalt).

2. **Wertz and Larson's (1996) research.** Wertz and Larson's (1996) research deals with the structural complexity of the Orsted geomagnetic satellite system (Figure 3.10). This satellite was named in honor of the Danish scientist Hans Christian Ørsted (1777–1851), who discovered electromagnetism in 1820.

Ørsted is a low-cost microsatellite built in Denmark. Its mass is 60.7 kg, its boom is 8 m, and its power is 54 W. Ørsted's mission was to (1) measure the geomagnetic field and (2) monitor the high-energy charged particles in the Earth's environment. The satellite was launched in February 1999 on a Delta II rocket from Vandenberg Air Force Base (VAFB), California, with a planned lifetime of one year and, since 2005, Ørsted has measured only the Earth's magnetic field.

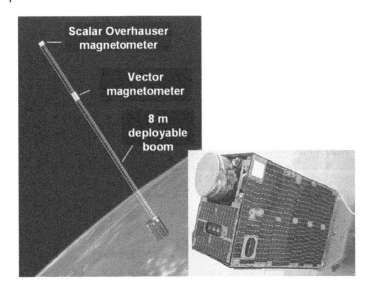

Figure 3.10 The Ørsted geomagnetic satellite system (Source: ESA).

3. **Kaushik Sinha (2014) research.** Sinha (2014) and Sinha and de Weck (2016) discuss a model for computing structural complexity based on the Hamiltonian system. This system is dynamic and is governed by Hamilton's equations. In physics, this system describes the evolution of planetary systems as well as electrons in an electromagnetic field. The model has been adapted for this section.

3.3.4.2 Structural Complexity

Structural systems' complexity is computed based on an analogy with the quantum Hamiltonian complexity (QHC). Within quantum mechanics, the Hamiltonian of a system is a variable characterizing the total energy of that system (including kinetic and potential energy).[7] Each component's complexity is analogous to the self-energy of each atom in isolation. Similarly, the interface complexity is analogous to the interaction energy. Finally, the effect of the network structure among system components acts as a scaling factor upon the interface complexity. Therefore, the following equation defines the structured complexity model of an engineered complex system.

$$Structural\ Complexity\ C = C_1 + C_2 C_3 \tag{3.5}$$

---

7 See Hamiltonian (quantum mechanics), Wikipedia. Accessed: Jan. 2023.

Where:
- C represents the structured complexity of the system.
- C_1 represents the sum of the complexities of individual components alone.
- C_2 represents the sum of the complexities of each pairwise interface.
- C_3 reflects the components arrangement of the system, which is not discernible from the individual components or the pairwise interactions. More specifically, it captures the sum of eigenvalues of the binary adjacency defined as the graph energy $E(A)$. It is computed as follows:

$$C_3 = \frac{E(A)}{n} \qquad (3.6)$$

Where:
A is the connectivity structure represented as a binary adjacency matrix, a variation of the design structure matrix (DSM). This matrix represents the system connectivity structure where the diagonal elements of A are all zeros.

$$A_{ij} = \begin{cases} 1 & \forall[(i,j) \mid (i \neq j) \text{ and } (i,j) \in A] \\ 0 & otherwise \end{cases} \qquad (3.7)$$

$E(A)$ is the matrix energy of the system structure. The energy of a matrix or a graph is calculated by summing the absolute values of the eigenvalues associated with the graph's adjacency matrix.

$$E(A) = \sum_{i=1}^{n} |\lambda_i| \qquad (3.8)$$

n is the number of components in a given system.

In summary, Figure 3.11 depicts the constituents of the system's structural complexity metric.

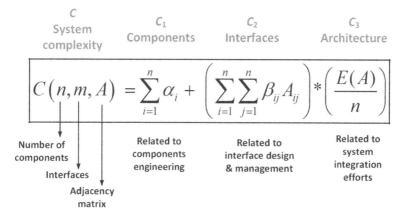

Figure 3.11 Constituents of the system's structural complexity metric.

3.3.4.3 Three General Concepts

This section intends to expand the reader's understanding of three general concepts: the Hamiltonian system, the perception of interfaces, and eigenvectors and eigenvalues.

1. **Hamiltonian system.** Sir William Rowan Hamilton (1805–1865) was an Irish mathematician. He made significant contributions to optics, classical mechanics, and algebra. Among others, he developed Hamiltonian mechanics, which has a close relationship to system geometry and considers the total energy of a system, including kinetic and potential energy. Hamiltonian mechanics is applicable to both classical mechanics and quantum mechanics.

Hamilton

For example, modeling the complexity of the carbon atom under Hamiltonian mechanics:

- Component complexity is equivalent to the self-energy of each atom in isolation ($E = mC^2$).
- Interface complexity is equivalent to the interaction energy of the electrons around the atom ($E = \frac{1}{2}mV^2$).
- Topological complexity captures the sum of eigenvalues associated with a binary adjacency graph energy, $E(A)$.

Carbon atom

2. **Perception of interface.** As in other aspects of systems engineering, the perception of an interface in a given system is often elastic and dependent upon the particular system engineer. It depends on the system's size and the engineer's position within the system hierarchy. For example, referring to Figure 3.12a, one engineer may consider the bolts and the gaskets between the flanges as the interface. Another engineer may consider the six flanges as the interface. Yet another engineer may consider the entire apparatus (i.e., the pipe tee with its six flanges) as the interface.

Analogously, as depicted in Figure 3.12, most of the interface costs will be reduced or nearly eliminated if two or more components are designed and manufactured

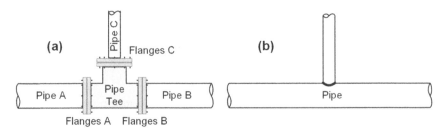

Figure 3.12 Two types of pipe interfaces.

as a single module (of course, the adaptability of this solution is reduced too). Another aspect of interfaces is their fundamental types (Table 3.2).

Table 3.2 Fundamental types of interfaces.

Interface Type	Description
Material	Fluid flow, solid flow, mixture flow, plasma flow
Energy	Mechanical, thermal, hydraulic, pneumatic, electrical, magnetic, electromagnetic, acoustic, chemical, biological, human
Information	Control signals, status signals, data
Spatial	Load transfer, translational, spatial, alignment, positional, proximity

3. **Eigenvectors and eigenvalues.** Eigenvectors representing linear transformations are, by definition, nonzero vectors. That is, changes chiefly by scalar factors when applied. These scalar factors are called eigenvalues, and their corresponding eigenvectors are frequently used when applying linear algebra to various areas of mathematics. For example, finding eigenvalues for the graphic transformation of vector a to vector b is depicted in Figure 3.13.

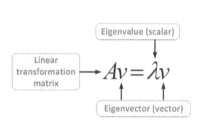

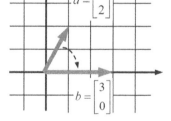

Eigenvector and eigenvalues

Example: transforming vector (a) to vector (b)

Figure 3.13 Linear transformations.

Here are the relevant computations:

Initial vector a and final vector b	$a = \begin{bmatrix} 1 \\ 2 \end{bmatrix}; b = \begin{bmatrix} 3 \\ 0 \end{bmatrix}$
The linear transformation matrix A	$A = \begin{bmatrix} 1 & 3 \\ 2 & 0 \end{bmatrix}$
The basic eigenvalue equation, where A is a linear transformation matrix, v is an eigenvector, and λ is an eigenvalue scalar	$Av = \lambda v$

Insert the identity matrix and equate it to zero $\qquad Av - \lambda IV = 0$

This part must be zero, since the eigenvector v is nonzero $\qquad [A - \lambda I] = 0$

Insert actual values

$$\begin{bmatrix} 1 & 3 \\ 2 & 0 \end{bmatrix} - \begin{bmatrix} \lambda & 0 \\ 0 & \lambda \end{bmatrix} = 0$$

Which is

$$\begin{bmatrix} 1 - \lambda & 3 - 0 \\ 2 - 0 & 0 - \lambda \end{bmatrix} = 0$$

The eigenvalues of this linear transformation are

$$(1 - \lambda)(0 - \lambda) - (3)(2) = 0$$
$$\lambda^2 - \lambda - 6 = 0$$
$$\lambda_{1,2} = \frac{1 \pm \sqrt{1 - 4 * 1 * (-6)}}{2}$$
$$\lambda_1 = \frac{1 + 5}{2} = 3; \ \lambda_2 = \frac{1 - 5}{2} = -2$$

Applying the above linear transformation to an image is depicted in Figure 3.14.

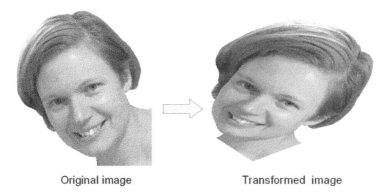

Original image   Transformed image

Figure 3.14 Applying the above linear transformation to an image.

3.3.5 Estimating Structural Complexity (Operationalization)

The following is an operationalization of a structural complexity estimation using the handheld hair dryer system described in Section 2.5.4.

3.3.5.1 Computing Components Complexity (C_1)

The complexity of a system's components is domain dependent. It depends on the technical design and development difficulty related to each component. The following is a list of relevant components complexity characteristics:

1. **Performance tolerance (x_1).** Components with extremely tight performance tolerance requirements tend to have increased complexity.
2. **Performance level (x_2).** A higher component performance level introduces higher complexity levels in its components.

3. **Component size indicator (x_3).** Components that are large in size typically indicate higher complexity. However, this should be taken within the correct context, as hardware and software size–complexity correlations do not necessarily relate.
4. **Number of coupled disciplines (x_4).** If a component involves multiple disciplines, it is typically more complex.
5. **Number of variables and physical processes (x_5).** Increased variables and physical processes typically lead to increased complexity.
6. **Component reliability measure (x_6).** Components with high reliability typically indicate higher complexity.
7. **Lack of existing knowledge of operating principles (x_7).** Lack of existing knowledge about an operating procedure increase complexity.
8. **Difficulty in reusing components (x_8).** Nonreusability of existing components increases the complexity characteristics of those components.

The complexity of each component depends on the component complexity characteristics ($x_1, ..., x_i$) and its cost factor (Cf):

$$C_{Components\,j} = \left(\sum_{i=1}^{n} x_i \right) * Cf; \ 1 \geq x_i \geq 5, \forall_i \tag{3.9}$$

Figure 3.15 depicts the complexity computation of the handheld hairdryer components.

Components complexity											
	Performance tolerance	Performance level	Size indicator	Number of disciplines	Number of processes	Reliability required	Lack of knowledge	Difficulty in reuse	Subtotal	Cost factor Cf	Total
Components	x_1	x_2	x_3	x_4	x_5	x_6	x_7	x_8			
Cord	1	1	1	2	2	4	1	1	13	1	13
On/off switch	3	2	2	2	3	4	1	1	18	3	54
Fan speed switch	2	2	2	2	3	3	1	1	16	3	48
Motor	5	5	4	3	3	5	2	3	30	5	150
Fan	4	3	3	2	2	5	2	3	24	4	96
Heat switch	3	2	2	2	3	4	1	1	18	3	54
Heater	3	3	2	2	3	4	2	3	22	4	88
Casing	4	4	3	2	2	4	3	5	27	5	135
Total	25	22	19	17	21	33	13	18	168		638

Figure 3.15 Hairdryer's components complexity computation.

The hairdryer's components complexity is computed according to the following equation, and its DSM is depicted in Figure 3.16.

$$C_1 = \sum_{j=1}^{m} C_{Components\,j} \tag{3.10}$$

		A	B	C	D	E	F	G	H	I
Cord	A	13								
On/off switch	B		54							
Fan speed switch	C			48						
Motor	D				150					
Fan	E					96				
Heat switch	F						54			
Heating element	G							88		
Casing	H								135	
Environment	I									

Figure 3.16 Hairdryer's components complexity DSM ($C_1 = 638$).

3.3.5.2 Computing Interfaces' Complexity (C_2)

The complexity of the system's interfaces is domain dependent. It depends on the technical design and development difficulty related to each interface. The following is a list of relevant interface complexity characteristics:

1. **Magnitude of entity transfer (y_1).** Interfaces with large entity transfers are typically more complex.
2. **Interface tolerance requirement (y_2).** Interfaces with tighter tolerance requirements tend to have higher complexity.
3. **Unknown interface mechanism (y_3).** Unknown interface mechanisms tend to increase complexity.
4. **Number of disciplines involved (y_4).** Typically, the more disciplines involved in the interface, the higher the complexity.
5. **Interface reliability requirement (y_5).** Interfaces with high reliability are typically more complex.
6. **Difficulty in reusing interface (y_6).** Any limitation of reusability increases complexity.

The complexity of the interface of each pair depends on the interface complexity characteristics ($y_1, ..., y_i$) and its cost factor (Cf):

$$C_{Interface\ type\ j} = \left(\sum_{i=1}^{n} y_i \right) * Cf; \ 1 \geq y_i \geq 5; \forall_i \tag{3.11}$$

Figure 3.17 depicts the complexity computation of the handheld hairdryer pairs interfaces.

	Interface complexity								
Interface types	Magnitude of transfer	Tolerance requirements	Unknown interface mechanism	Number of disciplines	Reliability requirements	Difficulty in reuse	Subtotal	Cost factor Cf	Total
	y_1	y_2	y_3	y_4	y_5	y_6			
Spatial (location, force)	2	3	1	2	3	3	14	1.5	21
Material (air)	3	2	2	2	2	3	14	1	14
Energy (electricity)	2	3	1	3	5	3	17	1	17
Total	7	8	4	7	10	9	45		52

Figure 3.17 Interface complexity computation.

The hairdryer's pairs interface complexity is computed according to the following equation, and its DSM is depicted in Figure 3.18.

$$C_2 = \sum_{i=1}^{n} \sum_{j=1}^{m} C_{Interface\ ij} \qquad (3.12)$$

		A	B	C	D	E	F	G	H	I
Cord	A		17						21	
On/off switch	B			17			17		21	
Fan speed switch	C				17				21	
Motor	D					21			21	
Fan	E				21			21	21	
Heat switch	F							17	21	
Heating element	G				21				21	14
Casing	H	21	21	21	21	21	21	21		
Environment	I	17			14					

Interface type: Spatial | Material | Energy

Figure 3.18 Pairs interfaces complexity DSM (C_2 = 508).

3.3.5.3 Computing Topological Complexity (C_3)

A binary adjacency matrix A is defined as follows:

$$A_{ij} = \begin{cases} 1 & \forall [(i,j) \mid (i \neq j)\ and\ (i,j) \in A] \\ 0 & otherwise \end{cases} \qquad (3.13)$$

Figure 3.19 depicts the hairdryer system's specific binary adjacency matrix A.

$$A = \begin{pmatrix} 0 & 1 & 0 & 0 & 0 & 0 & 0 & 1 & 0 \\ 0 & 0 & 1 & 0 & 0 & 1 & 0 & 1 & 0 \\ 0 & 0 & 0 & 1 & 0 & 0 & 0 & 1 & 0 \\ 0 & 0 & 0 & 0 & 1 & 0 & 0 & 1 & 0 \\ 0 & 0 & 0 & 1 & 0 & 0 & 1 & 1 & 0 \\ 0 & 0 & 0 & 0 & 0 & 0 & 1 & 1 & 0 \\ 0 & 0 & 0 & 0 & 1 & 0 & 0 & 1 & 1 \\ 1 & 1 & 1 & 1 & 1 & 1 & 1 & 0 & 0 \\ 1 & 0 & 0 & 0 & 1 & 0 & 0 & 0 & 0 \end{pmatrix}$$

Figure 3.19 Binary adjacency matrix.

The eigenvalues associated with the hairdryer system's A matrix are depicted in Figure 3.20.[8]

	1	2	3	4	5	6	7	8	9	Total
Real	3.45	-2.09	-0.88	0.00	1.00	0.26	0.26	0.00	0.00	
Imaginary	0.00	0.00	0.00	0.00	0.00	-0.30	0.30	0.00	0.00	
Absolute values	3.45	2.09	0.88	0.00	1.00	0.40	0.40	0.00	0.00	8.21

Figure 3.20 Eigenvalues associated with the A matrix.

The energy of the handheld hairdryer system structure $E(A)$ is the sum of all the absolute values of the eigenvalues of the binary adjacency matrix.
Where:

$$|\lambda| = \sqrt{\lambda_{Real}^2 + \lambda_{Imaginary}^2}$$

and

$$E(A) = \sum_{i=1}^{n} |\lambda_i| = 8.21$$

Therefore, the topological complexity (C_3) for the handheld hairdryer system is as follows:

$$C_3 = \frac{8.21}{9} = 0.91$$

3.3.5.4 Computing the Overall Complexity of the System (C)
Summing up the previous results, the structural complexity of the handheld hairdryer system is

$$C = C_1 + C_2 \times C_3 = 638 + 508 \times 0.91 = 1100.3$$

---

8 Various engines for computing eigenvalues are available on the internet. See https://www. intmath.com/matrices-determinants/eigenvalues-eigenvectors-calculator.php. Last accessed: Jan. 2023.

3.4 Systems Control

> The control principle: All systems have an internal regulatory mechanism to achieve long-term stability or controlled oscillation.

All systems have an internal control mechanism to achieve long-term viability and stability or controlled oscillation. This mechanism is a system element designed to monitor, manage, command, direct, and regulate the behavior and operation of the broader system. In most cases, the primary objective of control systems is to preserve the internal level of order that enables systems to function in a stable equilibrium state and develop over time (Nise, 2015).

3.4.1 Simple Open-Loop Control Systems

At the most basic level, control systems may be classified as open-loop or closed-loop control systems. By and large, open-loop control systems operate manually, whereas closed-loop control systems are generally relatively autonomous.

In open-loop control systems, the control action is independent of the system's output. A manual control system should also be considered an open-loop control system. In addition, the control action is independent of any variations in the input to the system. Many open-loop controls exist, such as the on/off switching of machinery, motors, or heaters. Figure 3.21 shows a typical block diagram of such a system and a water faucet in an open and closed state. Human input is applied to the system (opening or closing the faucet), and the system produces the desired output.

By and large, open-loop control systems are economical, simple to design and build, stable, and easy to operate and maintain. On the other hand, any input fluctuations cannot be corrected automatically.

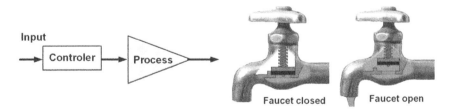

Figure 3.21 Open-loop control system.

3.4.2 Simple Closed-Loop Control Systems

In closed-loop control systems, the actual output value affects the control action. This effect is done by providing a feedback signal interacting with the input, so the control action depends on the desired output. Under negative feedback, the control system compares the output value with the desired value. As a result, an error signal is applied to eliminate the error and stabilize the system. A positive feedback control system is sometimes used to design oscillating systems like electronic clocks, cavity magnetrons, etc.

Figure 3.22 shows a typical negative feedback block diagram of a closed-loop control system. In this example, an unmanned air vehicle (UAV) is tasked to fly to a certain point in space. The UAV continuously monitors its location based on Ground Positioning System (GPS) data and generates corrective navigation commands.

By and large, closed-loop control systems are more accurate, especially under nonlinear conditions. More specifically, the system (in the case of negative feedback) ensures output stability when the input fluctuates. This capability facilitates various degrees of system automation and autonomy. On the other hand, this system is costlier; more complicated; and somewhat challenging to design, build, and maintain. In addition, the systems may reach instability and oscillation due to the unintended presence of positive feedback loops.

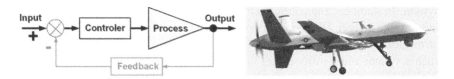

Figure 3.22   Closed-loop control system.

3.4.3   PID Control Systems

Simple feedback control mechanisms exhibit fundamental limitations. First, some feedback loops are not purely positive or negative, primarily when multiple loops exist. In addition, simple feedback is based only on instantaneous residual error data. However, if the processing time is relatively long, the corrected output of the system may be sluggish or even exhibit unwanted oscillations. One solution to these shortcomings is addressed by the PID (proportional, integral, and derivative) control mechanism, which attempts to optimize the system behavior over time by adjusting its control variables (Figure 3.23).

The PID controller implements a second-order transfer function that continuously calculates an error value $e(t)$, which is the difference between the proper value $r(t)$ and the corresponding measured value $y(t)$. Schematically, the PID model contains three elements. First, element P (proportional) generates a signal proportional to the current error value $e(t)$. Element I (integral) generates a

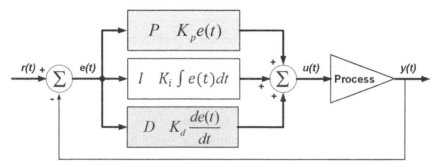

Figure 3.23 PID control mechanism model.[9]

signal proportional to the integrated past values of the error value $e(t)$. Finally, element D (derivative) generates a signal proportional to the best estimate of the future error $e(t)$ trend based on its current rate of change. Figure 3.24 presents two examples of the effects of PID parameters (K_p, K_i, K_d) on systems' step response.

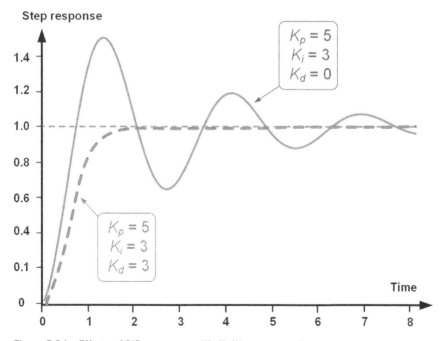

Figure 3.24 Effects of PID parameters (K_p, K_i, K_d) on systems' step response.

9 See PID controller, https://en.wikipedia.org/wiki/PID_controller. Accessed: Jan. 2023.

3.4.4   Advanced Control Systems

All advanced control systems share three sets of essential components: (1) sensors for feeding information into the system, (2) controllers that can process this information and translate input data into output commands, and (3) actuators that can affect the state of the system.

Sensors are system components that are tuned to specific internal or external parameters, encode the information, and transfer it to an appropriate controller. Controllers contain the logic that controls the overall behavior of the system. Controllers act as information-processing units, taking input data, manipulating it, and sending commands to appropriate actuators according to their built-in logic. Actuators are system components that act on the instructions produced by the controllers. They are designed to affect the system that is being regulated so that it conforms to the instructions produced by the controller.

Control theory deals with numerous control system schemes, branches, and subbranches.[10] For example, control theory may be divided into linear and nonlinear control systems. In linear control systems, the output is proportional to the input, whereas in nonlinear control systems, the output is not linear, which is more applicable to real-world systems. The number of inputs and outputs may also categorize control systems. The simplest and most common type is the single-input single-output (SISO) control system, whereas more complex systems utilize the multiple-input multiple-output (MIMO) control system.

Another branch of systems controls deals with centralized versus distributed control systems. By and large, under centralized control, a system is regulated from a single point. On the other hand, a system dispersed over a large geographic area may be controlled by multiple regulation points coordinating their actions through dedicated communication channels. Another branch of systems control deals with deterministic versus stochastic systems control. In general, a deterministic systems control is utilized when the inputs to the system are pretty constant and stable. In contrast, stochastic system control is utilized when the input from the system's context exhibits erratic behavior and random disturbances.

3.4.5   Biological Control Systems in the Human Body

The human body consists of cells, which comprise tissues, which further comprise organs. Additionally, all the metabolic needs of these cells are automated processes that maintain the stability of all biological and social systems. The result of these various processes by which the body controls its internal states is called

---

10 See more: Control theory, https://en.wikipedia.org/wiki/Control_theory. Accessed: Jan. 2023.

homeostasis.[11] Homeostasis requires constant adjustments as conditions inside and outside cells fluctuate over time.

Homeostasis in the human body is achieved through the endocrine system, which acts as a multiple-negative control system (Figure 3.25). In virtually all cases, the endocrine system reverses the direction of change. That is, it keeps things constant and in balance. The endocrine system includes the glands that emit hormones into the bloodstream. Hormones are chemical messenger molecules that cause changes in specific cells and organs. This process regulates the metabolism and development of most body systems through negative and positive feedback mechanisms.

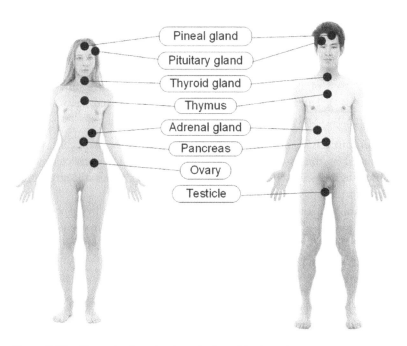

Pineal gland

Pituitary gland

Thyroid gland

Thymus

Adrenal gland

Pancreas

Ovary

Testicle

Figure 3.25 The endocrine glands control most body systems.

For example, when body temperature rises, sensory organs in the skin and the brain detect this change. This detection triggers a command from the brain, making the skin sweat and dilating the blood vessels near the skin's surface, which decreases body temperature. Another example relates to the level of glucose in the blood, which usually increases after a meal. The pancreas releases the hormone insulin, which assists in the delivery of glucose into selected tissues. As a result, glucose concentrations in the blood decrease, so insulin secretion into the blood ceases.

———

11 Homeostasis: The tendency to maintain a stable, relatively constant internal environment.

3.5 Systems Evolution

> The evolution principle: Living systems evolve to harmonize with their dynamic context. Inanimate systems are modified to satisfy their dynamic context.

3.5.1 Inanimate and Living Systems

The evolution principle of systems science distinguishes between living and inanimate systems. Let us dwell on this issue. Living organisms are characterized by their ability to utilize materials for energy and tissue building, grow, reproduce, respond, and adapt to environmental stimuli. In contrast, inanimate systems are modified to satisfy their dynamic context. The word *inanimate* is composed of two Latin roots: *in* means "not," and *animate* means "alive." So, *inanimate* means "not alive."

Erwin Schrödinger[12] (1887-1961) is considered the first modern scientist who addressed the issue of life and genetics from a pure physics point of view (Schrödinger, 1944). Later, James Grier Miller (1978), asserted that all living organisms share and exhibit all the following specific traits:

1. **Arrangement.** Living organisms are comprised of one or more cells, which are regarded as the essential components of life. Inside each cell, atoms combine into molecules, which combine into cell organelles and structures. Similar cells form tissues, and tissues create organs.
2. **Metabolism.** Metabolism is the set of chemical reactions in living organisms that transform inputs (e.g., nutrients, water, air, sunlight) into energy. It is the sum of a living organism's physical or chemical processes through which energy is created and material substance is produced.
3. **Homeostasis.** Homeostasis is the process of living organisms maintaining a stable internal environment when the external environment is altered. For instance, the human heart rate at rest is maintained at about 60 pulses per minute.
4. **Reproduction.** Living organisms reproduce themselves to create new organisms. In unicellular organisms, reproduction occurs by splitting existing cells. In multicellular organisms, two-parent organisms produce sperm and egg cells containing half of their genetic information, and these cells fuse to form a new individual with a complete genetic set.
5. **Response to stimuli.** Living organisms respond to stimuli or changes in their environment. For instance, prey run away from predators, many plants turn toward the sun, and unicellular organisms migrate toward a source of nutrients or away from toxic chemicals.

---

12 Schrödinger was a co-recipient of the 1933 Nobel Prize in Physics for postulating the Schrödinger equation, a mathematical description of quantum mechanics. Schrödinger was also a great thinker whose insights are valued by biologists, philosophers, physicists, and other scientifically curious people.

6. **Development, growth, and death.** Living organisms undergo regulated development, growth, and death. For example, individual cells become bigger in unicellular organisms, while in multicellular organisms, growth occurs through cell division. For example, butterflies develop from eggs that become larvae, fully develop into butterflies, and then die.

7. **Evolution.** Evolution involves natural selection, in which heritable traits, such as brighter fur color, allow organisms to survive and reproduce better in specific environments. Over generations, these traits become more common in a population, making it better suited to its environment.

3.5.1.1 Twenty Critical Subsystems of Living Systems

Living systems theory (LST) is a general theory about all living systems' existence, structure, interaction, behavior, and development. James Grier Miller created this theory as he sought to formalize the concept of "life," which is conveyed in his massive (1100 pages) book *Living Systems* (1978). Living systems are, by definition, open, self-organizing systems that interact with their environment through matter-energy and information exchanges. According to Miller, living systems exist on eight hierarchical levels: cell, organ, organism, group, organization, community, society, and supranational. Each level comprises 20 critical subsystems, which process matter, energy, or information.[13] The first 2 subsystems process energy and information, the next 8 process matter-energy, and the last 10 process information (Figure 3.26).

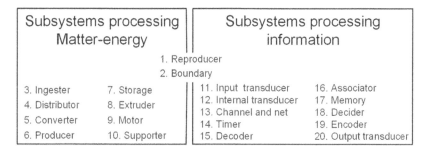

Figure 3.26 Twenty critical subsystems of living systems.

Miller's 20 critical subsystems are described below:

- **Subsystems processing matter-energy and information**
  1. **Reproducer.** This subsystem carries out the instructions in a system's generic information and mobilizes matter, energy, and information to produce one or more replication systems.
  2. **Boundary.** This subsystem holds the system's components together; protects them from environmental harm; and permits or excludes the entry or exit of various types of matter, energy, and information.

---

13 See Living systems, https://en.wikipedia.org/wiki/Living_systems. Accessed: Jan. 2023.

- **Subsystems processing matter–energy**
  3. **Ingester.** This subsystem brings matter–energy across the system boundary from the environment.
  4. **Distributor.** This subsystem transmits matter–energy inputs from the environment and distributes them among various subsystems.
  5. **Converter.** This subsystem changes specific matter–energy inputs into more valuable forms as needed by various subsystems.
  6. **Producer.** This subsystem converts, synthesizes, and integrates matter–energy inputs. The system provides matter–energy output to support growth, repair damage, or replace failing system components. Also, this subsystem provides energy to other subsystems.
  7. **Storage.** This subsystem places matter or energy locally within the system, retains it over time, and retrieves it when needed.
  8. **Extruder.** This subsystem transmits matter–energy out of the system through products or wastes.
  9. **Motor.** This subsystem moves the system or parts of it relative to its environment or its components relative to each other.
  10. **Supporter.** This subsystem maintains the proper spatial relationship among system components so that they interact harmoniously.
- **Subsystems processing information**
  11. **Input transducer.** This subsystem brings information across the system boundary from the environment.
  12. **Internal transducer.** This sensory subsystem receives information from various subsystems within the supersystem and converts it to markers bearing information.
  13. **Channel and net.** This subsystem comprises single or multiple interconnected passages over which markers bearing information are transmitted to all system parts.
  14. **Timer.** This subsystem transmits time-related environmental as well as system-components status to the decider. This information supports the decider in coordinating all dynamic system processes.
  15. **Decoder.** This subsystem converts the markers bearing information obtained from the input and internal transducers into a "private" code that each subsystem can use internally.
  16. **Associator.** This subsystem carries out the first stage of the learning process, forming enduring associations among information items in the system.
  17. **Memory.** This subsystem carries out the second stage of the learning process, storing information in the system and retrieving it when needed.
  18. **Decider.** This executive subsystem receives inputs from all other subsystems and transmits back information outputs for guidance, coordination, and control of all subsystems.

19. **Encoder.** This subsystem converts "private" code used internally by each subsystem into markers bearing information used as "public" code by systems in the environment.

20. **Output transducer.** This subsystem transmits markers bearing information from the system into the environment.

3.5.1.2 Living Species

The term *kingdom* in biology represents the second highest taxonomic rank, just below the domain. Over the years, different researchers have offered different biological kingdom classification schemes. For example, Whittacker (1969), an American ecologist, developed a taxonomy (called Whittaker's Five Kingdom Classification) in which living organisms were classified based on the following criteria:

1. **The complexity of cell structure.** Single-celled organisms have cells with no nucleus (prokaryotic) versus organisms with cells containing a nucleus (eukaryotic).

2. **The complexity of the organism's body.** Unicellular organisms versus multicellular organisms.

3. **Source of energy and nutrients.** Organisms that produce food using sunshine, light, water, and carbon dioxide (autotrophs)[14] versus organisms that eat other plants or animals (heterotrophs).[15]

4. **Evolutionary processes.** Sexual versus asexual biological evolution.

Based on these criteria, Whittaker classified all living organisms into five categories (Figure 3.27 and text below).

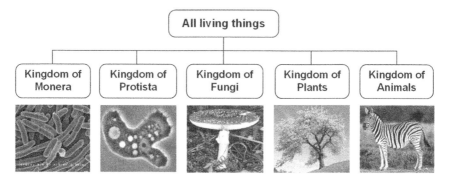

Figure 3.27 Whittaker's five kingdom classification.

---

14 The chemical reaction associated with organisms that produce their food using sunshine energy, water, and carbon dioxide (autotrophs) is $H_2O + CO_2 + Sunshine\ energy \rightarrow CH_2O + O_2$.

15 The chemical reaction associated with organisms that eat other plants or animals (heterotrophs) is $CH_2O + O_2 \rightarrow CO_2 + H_2O + Energy$.

1. **Kingdom of Monera.** The kingdom of Monera is composed of single-celled organisms. They do not have membrane-bound cell organelles or nuclear envelopes. Their energy source and nutrients are based on producing their food using sunshine, water, and carbon dioxide (autotrophs). Also, they replicate by asexual means.

2. **Kingdom of Protista.** The kingdom of Protista comprises organisms with cells having a clearly defined nucleus and nuclear envelopes. They produce food using sunshine, water, and carbon dioxide (autotrophs). By and large, they are unicellular organisms, although some are multicellular organisms like algae and seaweeds.

3. **Kingdom of Fungi.** The kingdom of Fungi comprises organisms that include cells with a clearly defined nucleus (eukaryotic). These cells have nuclear envelopes composed of cellulose and long-chain polymers, a glucose (chitin) derivative. Fungi organisms eat other plants or animals for energy and nutrients (heterotrophic) and reproduce by sexual and asexual means.

4. **Kingdom of Plants.** The kingdom of Plants comprises organisms that include cells characterized by a clearly defined nucleus (eukaryotic) and nuclear envelopes. In addition, all plant organisms contain cells with photosynthetic pigments in their membrane-bound organelle (plastids). Plants can produce food using sunshine, water, and carbon dioxide (autotrophic). However, they are primarily attached to a solid substrate for getting support and, in general, are incapable of moving from one place to another.

5. **Kingdom of Animals.** The kingdom of Animals comprises multicellular organisms, including cells with a clearly defined nucleus (eukaryotic). Animals eat other plants or animals for energy and nutrients (heterotrophic) and, by and large, reproduce through sexual reproduction. However, asexual reproduction is present in some lower forms of animals.

3.5.1.3 Sociology in Living Species

Sociology is a science that focuses on social behavior, tradition, and aspects of culture. Among vertebrate and invertebrate species, processing and transfer of social information have been documented, yet among nonhumans, sustained traditions appear rare, and cultures are rarer still.

In psychology, the term *intelligence* is used with myriad meanings. So, by and large, we may associate intelligence with relatively sophisticated forms of information processing and transfer. Therefore, *social intelligence* may be applied to the social world. According to Whiten and van Schaik (2007), Figure 3.28 and the following text depict an accepted view of the social intelligence pyramid in living species.

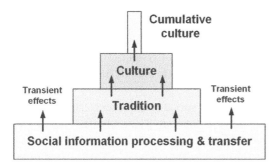

Figure 3.28   Social intelligence pyramid in living species.[16]

1. **Social information processing and transfer (layer one).** Social learning is well established in mammals, birds, and fish, as well as in invertebrates. Much of this learning exploits short-term public information, such as learning about temporarily productive foraging patches or avoiding locations of predators. This sociological phenomenon represents social information processing and transfer among many Animal kingdom organisms.

2. **Tradition (layer two).** Tradition is an inherited, established, or customary action or behavior pattern. It constitutes the second layer of the intelligence pyramid in living species. However, only a subset of such transfer eventuates in tradition because many effects of social learning are often transitory. Tradition may evolve from social learning and short-term functions depending upon different populations of organisms.

3. **Culture (layer three).** Culture is the characteristics of a particular species, encompassing the social behavior, norms, and habits of individuals within the group. Cultures within living species occur when multiple and diverse traditions are followed. The evidence for such cultures indicates that only a small set of relatively highly encapsulated,[17] socially living mammalian taxa show significant cultural complexity.

4. **Cumulative culture (layer four).** Cumulative culture occurs when traditions are gradually modified, elaborated, and improved. Virtually all cumulative cultures reflect human cultures' richness, yet it is minimally evidenced in other species. Cumulative culture is responsible for the complexity of human culture in all its myriad aspects.

---

16 Adapted from: Whiten, A. and van Schaik, C.P. The evolution of animal "cultures" and social intelligence. https://www.ncbi.nlm.nih.gov/pmc/articles/PMC2346520. Last accessed: Jan. 2023.

17 Encephalization refers to the tendency of a species toward larger brains through evolutionary processes.

3.5.2 Living Systems Evolution

Systems related to life and social science adapt themselves to their prevailing context. Adaptability,[18] therefore, is the ability of a system to make, over time, internal or external changes efficiently and quickly to alter its behavior according to changes in its context.

Systems' adaptability time scale is a notably varied phenomenon. The microbial reproduction and evolution time scale is measured in minutes, but social adaptation may take years or decades. For example, consider the relatively quick social evolution during COVID-19, the coronavirus epidemic of 2020. All of these are lightning speeds relative to the evolution of advanced biological systems that adapt and evolve over thousands of years.

All systems within the life and social sciences domains can evolve and learn from experience. By and large, systems aim to adapt to their existing contexts and ensure their survivability. Feedback loops are vital for achieving systems' adaptability within biological and social contexts. Similarly, human-made artificial adaptive systems such as learning machines and robots utilize positive and negative feedback loops to achieve their creators' goals.

The reader should note that adaptation[19] is not synonymous with evolution.[20] Adaptation is a biological mechanism that empowers organisms and societies to adjust and fit into new contexts. By and large, adaptation contributes to the survivability of species and societies, but this is not always the case. In contrast, systems' evolution changes the system, whatever it may be. For example, the planet Earth has evolved continuously from its formation some 4.5 billion years ago to today.

Evolution in biological systems may be defined as "change in the heritable characteristics of biological populations over successive generations."[21] Biological systems evolve through natural selection and genetic drift, increasing the population's pool so that it is favorable to adapting and thriving in the existing context. Therefore, the adaptable organism tends to be resourceful, seek opportunities, think ahead, and be curious.

Fundamentally, there are three types of adaptation: (1) structural, where systems' features adapt to increase chances of existence; (2) physiological, where systems' processes adapt to aid sustainability; and (3) behavioral, where systems' responses adapt to help survival.

---

18 We distinguish between *change*, which is a broad term referring to any change in a system over time, versus *adaptation*, which is a directed process of adjusting a system to better match its environment or situation.

19 See Adaptation, https://en.wikipedia.org/wiki/Adaptation. Accessed: Jan. 2023.

20 See Evolution, https://en.wikipedia.org/wiki/Evolution. Accessed: Jan. 2023.

21 See Evolution Is a Change in the Heritable Characteristics of ... | Bartleby. Accessed Jan. 2023.

3.5.3 *Homo sapiens* **Example**

An alluring example of the adaptability process, covering the three types of adaptation discussed above, is the emergence of *Homo sapiens*, our species, from the lineage of the great apes and, in particular, the gorilla species. According to current genetic research and known fossils research, the lineage that led to humans and gorillas evolved from similar ancestors about 10 million years ago. Then, about 3 to 4 million years ago, variations of the human species appeared, initially in Africa and then throughout the Earth. Scientists believe that all anatomical and cerebral differences between humans and apes are primarily a result of our human ancestors' choice to abandon their forest habitat and adopt terrestrial locomotion using their two legs (i.e., bipedalism).

All in all, the similarities, as well as the differences, between African apes and humans are striking. For example, we share the same internal organs and general bone structure arrangement. In addition, and most importantly, humans and apes have hands with thumbs separated from the other fingers, permitting both species to exercise precision grips.

A comparison of living primate species' DNA sequences shows that humans are closely related to African apes, especially gorillas. Genomic studies show that humans and gorillas share 98% of their DNA material. This similarity means that most human genes are similar or identical to those of the gorillas. Yet, amazingly, this 2% disparity contributes to the differences between the two species in terms of anatomy, intelligence, intellectual accomplishment, and lifestyle. Figure 3.29 and the following text depict the anatomical differences between humans and gorillas.

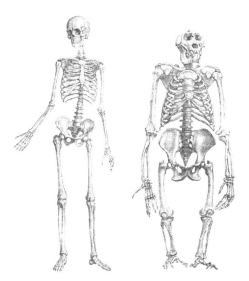

Figure 3.29   Skeleton layout: (L) humans and (R) gorillas.

1. **Body cover.** Gorillas have black to brown-grey hair. In general, hair protects an organism from the sun and cold weather. Gorillas, like other mammals, can release heat only by panting. Humans' adaptability ushered in mostly hairless bodies with large sweat glands that allow humans to remain cooler while running and engaging in other physical activities. These differences provided an essential advantage to our ancestors in the competition for survival in the warm African continent.

2. **Bodyweight.** Gorillas' average weight is approximately 150 to 200 kg. Humans adapted to weigh much less. In European and North American countries, average humans weigh 70 to 80 kg. Globally, the average human weighs just above 60 kg.

3. **Bone structure.** Gorillas' bones are significantly denser than those of their human counterparts. This bone structure must maintain a gorilla's weight and especially its massive volume of muscles. Human adaptability tended to shape humans with lighter and thinner bones, increasing their risk for breaks and fractures but also making humans more agile and quicker, a big plus in the survival game.

4. **Feet.** Gorillas have prehensile (grasping) feet with sideways-facing big toes. These toes are flexible, supporting typical gorilla activities like grasping branches and climbing trees. In contrast, humans adapted short, forward-facing big toes, which provide pushing power for walking and running. In addition, human feet have lengthened, making them better body supports. Finally, human feet act like springs that catapult the body upward during walking and running. However, one byproduct of this adaptability process is that, over the years, human feet lost their ability to grasp and manipulate objects.

5. **Legs and hands.** Gorillas usually move with four limbs on the ground (i.e., quadrupedally). They have relatively long and robust hands that support arboreal locomotion, swinging from one tree limb to another using only their arms (i.e., brachiation). Based on their bone structure, gorillas have a long arm-to-height ratio. For example, when they stand bipedally, their arm span[22] is about 2.5 m, while their height is about 1.8 m. This proportion is approximately 1.4. the arm-span-to-height ratio, which is significantly advantageous to gorillas' climbing and quadrupedal movements.

   Humans walking and especially running bipedally (on two feet) led to the adaptation of long and efficient legs with powerful muscles and springlike tendons. In addition, they did not rely on climbing trees and so adapted relatively short and less powerful hands. The combined result of these processes led humans to acquire an equal arm-span-to-height ratio.

---

22 The physical measurement of the length from one end of an individual's arms to the other when raised parallel to the ground at shoulder height.

6. **Pelvis.** The pelvis of apes is relatively large, extending to the lower back to support the lower body during brachiation through the trees. A gorilla's pelvis is not optimized for upright walking on two legs. Such action requires quite a bit of effort and energy. However, this large pelvis permits the birth of relatively mature offspring, which are neurologically and cognitively more mature than human babies at birth.

   However, to accommodate humans' bipedal locomotion and their adopted terrestrial lifestyle, the pelvis of our ancestors adapted dramatically. The pelvis became shorter, broader and more bowl shaped to better support the organs above. All in all, this evolution provided a sturdy base that supported and balanced the upper body's weight, transferring this weight directly to the legs for efficient and effortless walking and running.

   A downside of this pelvic adaptation in humans was a narrower birth canal in females. Consequently, giving birth became more complicated and riskier than in all other mammals. A partial evolutionary solution to this phenomenon was the birth of fetuses at a less mature stage when their torsos and heads are smaller.

7. **Chest, rib cage, and spinal column.** Gorillas have a round barrel-shaped rib cage and a short and sturdy spinal column. In contrast, humans adapted smaller, flatter chests, pushing the horizontal center of gravity toward the spinal column to stand fully erect. Similarly, the human spinal cord evolved to keep the head and the torso above the vertical center of gravity.

8. **Skull and brain.** Gorillas have substantially larger skulls than humans, but their cranial capacity (the amount of space available for the brain) is only about 500 cubic cm. This limited space is derived from the structure and shape of their skulls. In contrast, humans' skulls adapted to become smaller yet support more room for the brain. As a result, humans' brains become approximately three times the size of gorillas' brains.

3.5.4 Homologous Example

Another example, depicted in Figure 3.30, shows homologous[23] bones in four-limbed animals (tetrapods). The primary bone structure of these animals is the same but has been adapted over time for specific uses. Structurally, the human hand is perfectly adapted to hold different hunting weapons and make primitive tools, thus increasing the chances of survival. Physiologically, four-limbed animals reduce blood flow to their limbs so that significant organs have more blood circulation in winter, protecting them from the cold. Behaviorally, the unique structure of the human hand offers a nearly infinite repertoire of gestures, an early means of communication among individuals and groups of early humans.

---

23 Homology refers to similarities between structures in different species due to shared ancestry.

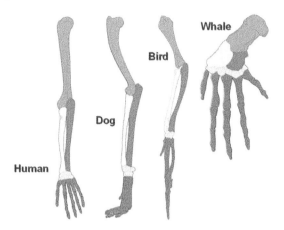

Figure 3.30   Homologous bones in four-limbed animals (tetrapods).

3.6   Systems Emergence

The emergence principle: All systems exhibit properties or behaviors their parts do not possess.

3.6.1   Emerging Properties

All systems exhibit properties or behaviors their parts do not have. Emergence is the appearance of entities "arising out of more fundamental entities and yet are 'novel' or 'irreducible' for them."[24] In layperson's terms, emergent properties or substances emanate from interactions among system parts. Typically, such interactions include feed-forward and feed-backward mechanisms (Figure 3.31).

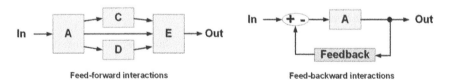

Figure 3.31   Feed-forward and feed-backward mechanisms.

British scientists of the late nineteenth and early twentieth centuries debated whether the constitutive principles and features of classical mechanics and biology were reducible to those of the corresponding "lower-level" sciences of physics and

---

24 See more on emergent properties: *Stanford Encyclopedia of Philosophy*, at https://plato. stanford.edu/entries/properties-emergent. Accessed Jan. 2023.

chemistry. For example, according to John Stuart Mill,[25] all organized bodies (*systems* in current parlance) are composed of parts, but the "phenomena of life, which result from the juxtaposition of those parts in a certain manner, bears no analogy to any of the effects which would be produced by the action of the component substances considered as mere physical agents" (Mill and Killick., 2019).

Mill proposed two modes of conjoint operations in *mechanical* and *chemical* models. In the mechanical model, the emerging properties of several causes acting in concert are identical to the sum effects of each of the causes acting alone. For example, in the mechanical model, the total effect of two forces, F and G, acting in concert on an object p is equivalent to the effect of F acting on p followed by G acting on p.

In contrast, the emerging properties of multiple causes acting in the chemical mode are not the sum effects of the causes had they been acting individually. For example, the chemical reaction between hydrochloric acid (HCl) and sodium hydroxide (NaOH) is sodium chloride (NaCl) or ordinary salt and water (H_2O). Acting individually, one would try to combine, for example, H and Na and Cl and OH. Then one would try to combine the two resultants. However, this two-stage process will rarely work. So, the emerging properties of these reactants are not the sum effects of these reactants had they been acting individually.

3.6.2 Emergent Behavior by Way of Swarming

Swarming dynamics is a prime example of a system-wide emergent behavior exhibited by many living, self-propelled organisms, usually of the same species. Usually, this emergent behavior is characterized by either milling about the same spot or global migration in some direction.

Many different species exhibit this emerging behavior. Consequently, different terminology is usually applied to the different species-based phenomena: Although the term *swarming* is a general one, it is often explicitly applied to insects (e.g., ants, bees, wasps, termites, flies, cockroaches, locusts). The terms *flocking* and *murmuration* refer specifically to swarm behavior in birds. The terms *shoaling* and *schooling* refer specifically to swarm behavior in fish. And the term *herding* refers specifically to swarm behavior in four-legged tetrapods (e.g., caribou, zebras, wildebeest, gazelle). By extension, the term *swarm* is also applied to specialized inanimate objects that exhibit similar behaviors, like robot swarms.

There are both benefits and evolutionary costs to individuals participating in swarming systems. On the benefit side, general biological observations offer

---

25 John Stuart Mill (1806–1873) was a British philosopher, political economist, and civil servant. One of the most influential thinkers in the history of classical liberalism, he contributed widely to social theory, political theory, and political economy. See https://en.wikipedia.org/wiki/John_Stuart_Mill. Accessed: Jan. 2023.

convincing evidence of operational advantages based on distributed control within extensive systems. For example, insect swarming is a survival power multiplier in vital system operations like food foraging, mating opportunities, and defense against predators. On the cost side, swarming, flocking, murmuring, shoaling, schooling, and herding are very noticeable and attract predators.

3.6.2.1 Bee Swarming Example

One scheme of emerging swarming in insects is stigmergy. This phenomenon is a mechanism of indirect coordination between members of the colony system. Here, the hierarchical central control in higher-level biological systems is not present. For example, in a beehive system, the queen does not tell the bees how to forage for food, feed the larvae, maintain the hive, fight intruders, etc. Instead, individual bees communicate with other bees by performing specialized dance choreography or by producing or reacting to chemical scents, stimulating other bees to seek food, nurse larvae, clear waste, fight intruders, split the colony, create a new one, and so on (Figure 3.32).

Figure 3.32 Bees swarming on a tree.

3.6.2.2 Bird Murmuration Example

Another scheme of emerging swarming in higher-level biological systems like birds, fish, and tetrapods follows a relatively simple mathematical model embedded within each member of the swarm system. This model includes adhering to the following three rules: (1) remain close to one's neighbors, (2) avoid collisions with one's neighbors, and (3) move in the same direction and speed as one's neighbors. Under these rules, the swarming system can move uniformly and consistently.

However, quite frequently, one or more individuals within the swarming system (possibly in some leadership position) identify a disruption in the vicinity of the swarming region. Such disruption may include predators, food sources, other birds, high land structures, wind, airplanes, and desired landing and resting sites. Under these circumstances, this individual may violate the above rules and move in an unexpected direction and speed. Since other individuals in the swarming system adhere to the rules, the entire flock abruptly changes its direction and speed in unison. This process creates complex emergent system motions and behavior (Figure 3.33).

Figure 3.33   A flock of murmuring starlings.

3.6.2.3   Bird and Mammal Annual Migrations

Another example of system-wide emergent behavior is revealed in annual bird and mammal migrations due to favorable climate and foraging for food. For example, large birds migrate in a typical V formation. This emerging structure increases the efficiency and range of individual members within the group. In addition, it offers forward and side visibility, enhancing collision avoidance, communication, and predator protection. Similarly, millions of wildebeests, zebras, antelopes, and other herd animals make the annual trek from the Serengeti in Tanzania to the Masai Mara in Kenya and back, seeking wide-open seasonal grasslands (Figure 3.34).

Figure 3.34 Wildebeests engage in the annual great African migration.

3.6.2.4 Fish Schooling Example

Another example of system-wide emergent behavior is revealed in fish shoaling or schooling. Many fish congregate and swim in a large rotating ball, shifting to and fro in a stunning choreography. This emerging behavior allows fish schools to coordinate their motion and shift contour.

Scientists believe such behavior increases shoaling fish's hydrodynamic efficiency by reducing drag, enhancing foraging, and increasing mating probabilities. From a species survival perspective, the emergent advantage of shoaling and schooling is that they improve vigilance against predators and tend to confuse them. In addition, this fast-swirling phenomenon dilutes an individual's risk of being attacked. Figure 3.35 depicts fish schooling, forming a circular ball in defense against two larger butterflyfish.

Figure 3.35 Fish schooling forming a circular ball.

3.6.3 Emergent Behavior by Way of Colony Building

Another type of emergent example relates to termites' colony building. These species create colonies ranging in size from a few hundred to several million individuals within a single mound, and they build one of the most complex structures in the animal world. Their mounds reach a height of 8 to 9 m and consist of chimneys, pinnacles, and ridges (Figure 3.36). Termites' mound-building capability is especially astonishing when one examines their characteristic. Termites exhibit low physiology, biochemistry, biological, and developmental levels. They are usually small, measuring 4 to 15 mm in length, and most workers and soldiers are blind, so communication occurs primarily through chemical, mechanical, and pheromonal cues. On the other hand, termites exhibit a high level of societal organization. Their society is divided into specialized behavioral groups, including caste-like systems composed of kings, queens, soldiers, and workers.

Figure 3.36 Termite mound: an example of emerging social order.

3.7 Bibliography

Bashir, H.A. and Thomson, V. (1999). Estimating design complexity. *Journal of Engineering Design* 10 (3): 247–257.

Bashir, H.A. and Thomson, V. (2001). Models for estimating design effort and time. *Design Studies* 22: 141–155.

Ferreira, P. (2001, October). Tracing Complexity Theory, ESD.83 – Research Seminar in Engineering Systems. See http://web.mit.edu/esd.83/www/notebook/ Complexity%20Theory.ppt. Accessed: Jan. 2023.

Gutierrez, T.N. (2012). A control architecture for complex systems, based on multi-agent simulation (Doctoral dissertation, Université de Lorraine).

Kjaer, L.L., Høst-Madsen, N.K., Schmidt, J. H., & McAloone, T. C. (2015). Application of environmental input-output analysis for corporate and product environmental footprints—Learnings from three cases. *Sustainability* 7(9), 11438–11461.

Maier, M.W. and Rechtin, E. (2000). *The Art of Systems Architecting*, second edition. CRC Press.

Mill, J.S. (1843). *System of Logic*. Longmans, Green, Reader, and Dyer.

Mill, J.S. and Killick, A.H. (2019). *The Student's Handbook, Synoptical and Explanatory, of Mr. J. S. Mill's System of Logic*. Wentworth Press.

Miller, J.G. (1978). *Living Systems*. McGraw-Hill.

Moses, J. Complexity and flexibility (working paper).

Nise, N.S. (2015). *Control Systems Engineering*, seventh edition. Wiley.

Rousseau, D. (2017). Systems research and the quest for scientific systems principles. *Systems* 5: 25.

Schrödinger, E. (1944). What Is Life? The Physical Aspect of the Living Cell, Cambridge University Press.

Senge, P.M. (2006). *The Fifth Discipline: The Art & Practice of The Learning Organization*. Doubleday.

Sinha, K. and de Weck, O. (2016). Empirical validation of structural complexity metric and complexity management for engineering systems. *Systems Engineering* 19: 193–206.

Sinha, K. (2014). Structural complexity and its implications for design of cyber-physical systems. PhD thesis, Massachusetts Institute of Technology (http://dspace.mit.edu/handle/1721.1/89871).

Sussman, J. (2000). *Introduction to Transportation Systems*. Artech House Publishers.

Van Wie, M.J., Greer, J.L., Campbell, M.I., Stone, R. B., & Wood, K.L. (2001, September). Interfaces and product architecture. *In Proceedings of DETC* (Vol. 1, pp. 9–12).

Wertz, J.R. and Larson, W.J. (1996). *Reducing Space Mission Cost*. Springer.

Weyuker, E. (1988). Evaluating software complexity measures. *IEEE Transactions on Software Engineering* 14 (9): 1357–1365.

Whiten, A. and Van Schaik, C.P. (2007). The evolution of animal "cultures" and social intelligence. *Philosophical Transactions of the Royal Society B: Biological Sciences* 362 (1480): 603–620.

Whittaker, R.H. (1969, January 10). New concepts of kingdoms of organisms: Evolutionary relations are better represented by new classifications than by the traditional two kingdoms. *Science* 163 (3863): 150–160.

4

Systems Thinking

4.1 Introduction

Systems thinking is a holistic way to analyze how a system's components interact and how systems work within larger systems over time. Systems thinking contrasts with linear thinking, which studies systems by breaking them into separate components.

Systems thinking has evolved from general systems theory (Bertalanffy and Sutherland, 1974) and has been applied to various fields and disciplines, such as engineering, medicine, the environment, politics, economics, human resources, education, etc.

Systems thinking encourages a shift of perspective that is essential when dealing with the complexities of dynamic systems. It provides a clearer view of the system's components, its interconnected parts, and their relationships. In brief, systems thinking is quite effective for analyzing complex problems, especially problems that are not solvable using conventional reductionist thinking. For example, it can be used to explain dynamic nonlinear behaviors like socioeconomic interactions, behaviors of individuals, internal organization dynamics, and predator–prey relations. In particular, systems thinking expands the range of options for solving problems.

For example, suppose gears in a particular machine often fail for no apparent reason. Instead of replacing the failing gears again and again, a systems thinking approach will look at several possible issues like the (1) gears' design (shape, size), (2) gears' construction (metallurgy, casting, forging), (3) gears' operation (weight, friction, torque, noise), (4) gears' environment (temperature, humidity, vibrations), and (5) gears' maintenance (cleanliness, lubrication). In addition, the systems thinking approach will examine various gears' interconnection factors (gears' interfaces, gears' mechanical loading) that could affect the gears' performance and durability (Figure 4.1).

Systems Science for Engineers and Scholars, First Edition. Edited by Avner Engel.
© 2024 John Wiley & Sons, Ltd. Published 2024 by John Wiley & Sons, Ltd.

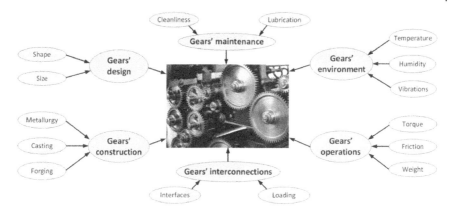

Figure 4.1   Systems thinking example: dealing with gear failures.

4.2   Fundamental Concepts of Systems Thinking[1]

The essential systems thinking concepts are interconnectedness, synthesis, emergence, feedback loops, causality, and systems mapping. These concepts are elaborated upon below.

1. **Interconnectedness.** Systems thinking requires a shift in one's mindset from linear to circular, based on the idea that everything is interconnected. This interconnectedness occurs in both living and inanimate systems. Essentially, everything is dependent upon something else for survival. For example, animals need food, air, and water for sustenance. Plants need carbon dioxide and sunlight to thrive. Everything needs a complex array of other things to survive. Inanimate objects also rely on other things: A car needs gasoline, diesel, or electricity to propel itself. A computer needs electricity distribution to power itself. So, from a system thinking perspective, interconnectedness is a fundamental principle of life. Systems thinking shifts our worldview from a linear, structured view to a dynamic, chaotic, interconnected array of relationships.

2. **Synthesis.** Systems thinking stresses synthesis rather than analysis. Synthesis refers to combining two or more objects to create something new. In contrast, analysis refers to breaking complex objects into simpler components. Analysis fits into a reductionist worldview, that is, dividing systems into parts. Furthermore, nearly all systems are dynamic and often complex, thus

1 Adapted from: Leyla Acaroglu, Tools for Systems Thinkers: The 6 Fundamental Concepts of Systems Thinking, Disruptive Design, Sep 7, 2017. See: https://medium.com/disruptive-design/ tools-for-systems-thinkers-the-6-fundamental-concepts-of-systems-thinking-379cdac3dc6a. Accessed: Jan. 2023.

requiring a more holistic approach. So, synthesis is an appropriate way to grasp the interconnectedness of systems.

3. **Emergence.** Emergence is the outcome synergy of interacting parts. By and large, emergence is expressed as a nonlinear and self-organization of elements within a larger whole. For example, the emerging property of a bicycle is its ability to carry an individual from one place to another. No individual parts, collectively or otherwise, can achieve this outcome unless they are interconnected in a specific manner, for instance, as described in Figure 4.2.

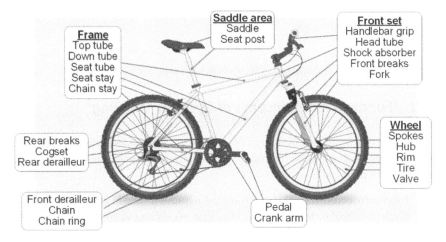

Figure 4.2 A bicycle system and its parts.

4. **Feedback loops.** As mentioned above, systems are interconnected, internally among their components and externally with other systems. This interconnectedness means that individual components affect other components, and systems affect other systems. Generally, this effect may be characterized by a flow or feedback loop of material, energy, or information. Generally, feedback loops consist of positive (reinforcing) and negative (balancing) feedback.

Positive feedback loops tend to reinforce existing phenomena. For example, in nature, typical predator–prey situations occur regularly. For example, wolves kill and eat deer; if there are too many wolves, they decimate most of the deer population and, over time, starve to death. This dynamic leads, eventually, to an increase in the deer population. This oscillating phenomenon is apparent in many systems (e.g., the stock market, soil erosion, etc.) and is heavily exploited in engineering (e.g., electronic oscillators).

On the other hand, negative feedback loops tend to oppose existing phenomena, thus balancing and stabilizing the systems. For example, suppose one drives along a straight road. If the car veers to the right, the driver shifts the steering wheel slightly to the left, and vice versa.

5. **Causality.** Causality is the influence by which one event, process, state, or object contributes to forming another event, process, state, or object. In other words, causality is the connection between a cause and its effect or consequence. However, one should distinguish between correlation and causation. Correlation means a relationship or pattern between the values of two variables.

In contrast, causation means that one event causes another event to occur. However, causation can be determined only from an appropriately designed experiment. For example, in medical research, similar groups receive different medicinal treatments, and the outcomes of each group are analyzed. One can conclude that treatment causes a specific effect only if the groups exhibit noticeably different outcomes. Within systems thinking, causality, as a concept, is deducing how things influence each other. Therefore, the awareness of causality leads to a deeper perspective on connections, relationships, and feedback loops.

6. **Systems mapping.** Systems mapping creates visual depictions of a system, its components, their mutual relationships, and feedback loops. Systems mapping provides a simplified conceptual understanding of a complex system. For example, Figure 4.3 depicts a system mapping showing a system to sustain a healthy public lake.[2] The depicted system contains components as well as positive and negative feedback loops.

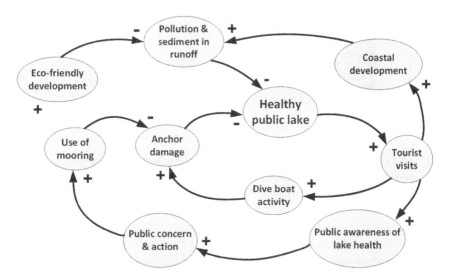

Figure 4.3 System mapping example: sustaining a healthy public lake.

---

2 Adapted from: Steps Towards Systems Mapping, September 16, 2011. See: Steps Towards Systems Mapping | Thinking in Systems in the High School Classroom (wordpress.com). Accessed: Jan. 2023.

4.3 The Iceberg Model of Systems Thinking

It is known that an iceberg has only 10% of its total mass above the water, while 90% is underwater. Along this line, the iceberg model is a valuable systems thinking tool that helps support a deep understanding of problems. Analogically, the iceberg metaphor supports identifying the root causes of problems that are often hidden from view. The iceberg model is comprised of four thinking levels: (1) events, (2) patterns of behavior, (3) underlying structure, and (4) mental models and worldviews. See below and in Figure 4.4.

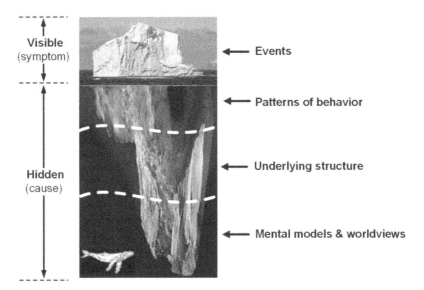

Figure 4.4   Iceberg model of systems thinking.

1. **The event thinking level.** The event thinking level is where one typically perceives the world. For example, envision a person involved in a car accident while driving on the highway. While a problem observed at the event level can often be addressed with a relevant readjustment (e.g., dealing with the individuals involved in the accident and removing the wreckage from the road), the iceberg model encourages one to explore the reasons for the event rather than assume that every problem can be solved by simply treating the symptom or resolving it at the event level.

2. **The pattern thinking level.** Most individual events are part of larger behavior patterns, and similar events tend to occur repeatedly over time. So, exploring below the event level, one often notices patterns, and observing

patterns allows one to forecast and forestall undesired events. So, the systems thinking paradigm encourages one to ask, "Has this event or similar events happened before?" "What are the patterns of occurrences?" "What trends have been seen?" and "Is there a particular situation, environment, or role that experiences this problem?"

In the above example, one may ask, "Are there many car accidents on this stretch of the highway?" "How frequently do such accidents occur?" "Is there a pattern for these accidents along this highway?" "Are the driver's characteristics and driving history relevant to this accident?" and so on.

3. **The underlying structure thinking level.** Below the pattern thinking level lies the structure thinking level. Understanding single or multiple events compels one to see them as part of a larger pattern of behavior that evolves within a particular structure. Structures are relatively permanent. They institutionalize specific behavior, which considerably influences one's behavior. So, the underlying structures of systems generate a specific pattern of behavior. Typically, structures can include the following: (1) physical things like roads, traffic lights, or terrain; (2) organizations like corporations, governments, and schools; (3) policies like laws, regulations, and tax structures; and (4) rituals, which are habitual behaviors so ingrained that they are not conscious.

In the above example, one may ask, "What influences the pattern of car accidents?" "What are the relationships among the highway, automobile traffic, and other physical components underlying the structure?" "What were the conditions of the roads and the pattern of weather?" "What are the rules and regulations governing traffic in this section of the highway?" "Do drivers, in general, habitual behavior contributes to car accidents?" and so on.

4. **The mental model and worldview thinking level.** Below the structure thinking level lies the mental model and worldview thinking level. This mental model and worldview are responsible for one's beliefs and assumptions, which create and shape the system that triggers and causes the problem. Mental models are the attitudes, beliefs, morals, expectations, and values that allow structures to function as they are. One often learns these beliefs subconsciously within their society or family and is likely unaware of them. Typical questions related to mental model and worldview thinking levels are "What assumptions, beliefs, and values do people hold about the system?" "What beliefs keep the system in place?" etc.

In this example, prevalent mental models and assumptions could be the belief of one's invincibility, that is, that one is immune from any catastrophe or mishap; their car is a perfect organ of their body, needing no maintenance or upkeep; and one can disregard traffic regulations at will.

4.4 Exploring Systems Thinking as a System[3]

Systems thinking in and of itself is a system. As such, one can analyze it accordingly. One way to do so is by using systemigrams. These are structured diagrams for visually representing complex systems. They condense rich texts into a single page, providing deeper insights into a system's overall construction and operation. Figure 4.5 depicts a system of systems thinking systemigram, where the thick lines represent strong connections, and thin dotted lines represent weaker, though meaningful, connections.

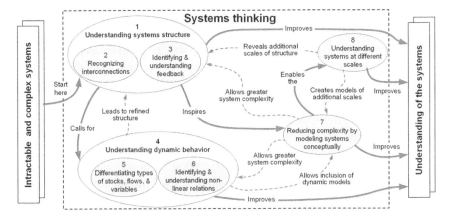

Figure 4.5 System of systems thinking systemigram (Image: Arnold and Wade, 2015).

It is important to note that systems thinking, as depicted in Figure 4.5, operates as a series of continuous feedback loops. The system does not cease to function at the final node. Instead, systems thinking improves continuously as each element is enhanced and improves its connected elements.

1. **Understanding system structure.** This system element aims to promote an understanding of the system structure. System structure consists of elements and interconnections between these elements. Systems thinking expects one to understand this structure and how it facilitates system behavior. Therefore, recognizing interconnections and understanding feedback are keys to understanding systems structures.

2. **Recognizing interconnections.** This element is the base level of systems thinking. This system element aims to promote the identification of all relevant system connections among parts of the system as well as connections between the system and other systems.

---

3 Section adapted with permission from: Arnold and Wade (2015).

3. **Identifying and understanding feedback.** This system element aims to promote the understanding of interconnections that form cause–effect feedback loops. Beyond identifying and understanding these feedback loops, systems thinking expects one to grasp how such loops impact overall system behavior.

4. **Understanding dynamic behavior.** This system element promotes an understanding of the system's dynamic behavior. Interconnections and feedback loops influence the resources, flows, and variables, which, in turn, create dynamic behavior within a system. Such dynamics often reveal themselves as a system-emergent behavior beyond the capability of the system's parts.

5. **Differentiating types of stocks, flows, and variables.** This system element aims to differentiate among types of stocks, flows, and variables. Stocks refer to any pool of a resource in a system. This resource could be physical, like the heat produced by an oven, or emotional, like the level of trust between two persons. Flows are the changes in these levels. Variables are the changeable parts of the system that affect stocks and flows, such as the rate or quantity of stock. Under the systems thinking paradigm, one must differentiate among these elements and recognize how each operates.

6. **Identifying and understanding nonlinear relationships.** This system element aims to promote the identification and understanding of nonlinear relationships. This element is quite similar to the previous system element. However, it refers explicitly to stocks and flows of a nonlinear rather than linear nature.

7. **Reducing complexity by modeling systems conceptually.** This system element aims to promote the different parts of the conceptual model of a system and view it in different ways. This promotion extends beyond the scope of defined system models and enters the sphere of intuitive simplification through various methods, such as reduction, transformation, abstraction, and homogenization. For example, perceptual wholes can reduce the complexity of their parts. This reduction allows the interpretation of greater complexity as the mind holds less detail about each whole.

8. **Understanding systems at different scales.** This system element aims to promote the understanding of systems at different scales. Scale refers to the size of a system that one deals with or the precision of observation or description. The concept of scale is important for understanding many vital concepts of complex systems, such as emergence and complexity profiles.

4.5 Barriers to Systems Thinking

According to Beasley (2012), there are two main streams of systems thinking barriers: the human and the organization/engineering barriers. This section summarizes Beasley's description of the first and the opinion of the author of this book regarding the most significant set of obstacles to systems thinking. Fundamentally, human barriers to systems thinking emanate from the nature of the human mind, which challenges systems thinking. In a nutshell: (1) People avoid deep thinking, (2) people jump to quick conclusions, (3) people disregard and avoid additional information, (4) people are annoyed by dynamics, and (5) people are indifferent and ignorant.

1. **People avoid deep thinking.** Generally, deep thinking is not too typical among many humans. The human mind is oriented to avoid abstract information. One explanation for this mind orientation is that the human limbic system[4] (Figure 4.6), which has sustained the human species for over a million years, stresses our quick action abilities in the face of threat situations rather than our abilities to undertake analysis and deep contemplation.

   This built-in structure of human minds has significant implications in the modern world. First, many people find it difficult to transfer knowledge and sophisticated learning from one situation to another. Second, thinking is often seen as time-consuming and a waste of energy. In contrast to human psychology, systems thinking helps people look beyond the immediacy of emotions toward what is best for themselves.

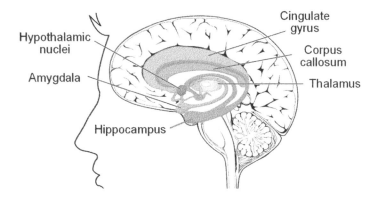

Figure 4.6 Human limbic system.

2. **People jump to quick conclusions.** In a general sense, people often jump to quick conclusions. This response is natural to human behavior because the mind seeks fast and positive progress. In engineering, this is seen in the tendency to adopt and implement the first feasible idea, which creates an illusion of progress.

   So, beyond peoples' tendency to avoid deep thinking, it is intuitive for the human mind to leap to the first feasible solution without contemplating other solutions. This process is compounded because once the mind latches upon a given idea, it will amplify it over all other views. In a broader sense, people

---

4 The limbic system is the part of the brain involved in behavior associated with survival, feeding, reproduction, and caring for offspring.

interpret what they see by what they expect to see, which ultimately tends to blind them to other alternatives.

3. **People disregard and avoid additional information.** Generally, people tend to disregard and avoid readily available information. Typically, one focuses on avoiding problems encountered in the past by ignoring most new issues. But, unfortunately, what one does not know is often more relevant than what one does know. In particular, engineers who ignore vital information cultivate dire future consequences.

   Another aspect of the reluctance of people to obtain more knowledge is that extra information about a problem tends to increase the level of confusion. Increasing confusion can be seen as a worsening situation. So naturally, people tend to avoid adding uncertainty, which would make them more uncomfortable. In contrast, the systems thinking paradigm encourages people to internalize how to act under incomplete information.

4. **People are uncomfortable in dynamic situations.** In a general sense, people are often uncomfortable in dynamic situations. One reason for this phenomenon is that dynamic systems are, by and large, more complex to understand and control relative to static systems. For example, Figure 4.7 depicts a set of gears embedded within a printing press. Comprehending this image is quite natural to most people. However, grasping the dynamics of the printing press system during operation is significantly more demanding (e.g., determining the speed of each gear at any point in time and discerning how power and movement flow within the system).

Figure 4.7   Gears in a printing press (Musee des Arts et Metiers, Paris).

Controlling a dynamic system, where a significant delay exists between an operator action and a system reaction, is challenging. For example, controlling a camera placed on an unmanned air vehicle (UAV) at a great distance is challenging due to the time delay built into the system. In addition, this annoying delay leads to oscillations in the system behavior where the operator tends to overshoot or undershoot the camera's position relative to the target's ground location.

5. **People are indifferent and ignorant.** Finally, sometimes, people are indifferent and occasionally ignorant. The systems thinking concept is abstract. Learning and getting used to thinking in systems is often the most challenging part. This lack of awareness is exacerbated because systems thinking is not taught in schools and is rarely applied across disciplines. Students do not learn about systems, systems principles, mental models, integrative thinking, or synthesis throughout their education. Instead, students are often expected to regurgitate information, much of it of little value.

4.6   Early Systems Thinking Pioneers

Systems thinking originated in the late 1940s, when some key ideas emerged. These ideas included interconnectedness, synthesis emergence, feedback loops, causality, and systems mapping. In addition to the systems pioneers mentioned in Chapter 1, the following describes three eminent systems thinking pioneers.[5]

4.6.1   Norbert Wiener (1894–1964)

Norbert Wiener was an American philosopher and mathematician who taught and researched at the Massachusetts Institute of Technology (MIT). He is regarded as the originator of cybernetics, the science of communication among living organisms and between machines, with broad connections to systems control, engineering, computer science, biology, neuroscience, philosophy, and societal organization.

Wiener is the first researcher to theorize that intelligent behavior results from feedback mechanisms. This concept was an essential early step toward the development of modern artificial intelligence. His most influential book was *Cybernetics or Control and Communication in the Animal and the Machine* (1961).

---

5 For a comprehansive list of distinguished systems thinking researchers, see Appebdix B.

4.6.2 Talcott Parsons (1902–1979)

Talcott Parsons was an American sociologist at Harvard University and one of the most influential figures in twentieth-century sociology.

Parsons analyzed the works of Max Weber, Emile Durkheim, and Vilfredo Pareto, all eminent sociologists of the time. Based on this analysis and additional field data, he proposed his social action theory, the first broad, systematic, and generalizable social systems theory.

4.6.3 Ross Ashby (1903–1972)

Ross Ashby was a British psychiatrist and a pioneer in cybernetics and automatic control systems in machines and living organisms. His two books, *Design for a Brain* and *An Introduction to Cybernetics*, introduced precise and logical thinking into the discipline of cybernetics and were highly influential. These books and his technical contributions solidified Ashby's reputation as a "major theoretician of cybernetics after Wiener." See for example: Ashby (1956)

For more information about distinguished systems thinking researchers, see Appendix B. In addition, a comprehensive biographical history of the 30 most renowned systems thinkers is available at Ramage and Shipp (2020).

4.7 Bibliography

Arnold, R.D. and Wade J.P. (2015). A definition of systems thinking: A systems approach. *Procedia Computer Science* 44: 669–678.

Ashby R. (1956). An Introduction to Cybernetics. Chapman & Hall Ltd, London. See: http://pespmc1.vub.ac.be/books/IntroCyb.pdf. Accessed Jun. 2023.

Beasley, R. (2012, July 9–12). The barriers to systems thinking. *INCOSE International Symposium* (Rome, Italy) 22 (1): 517–531. https://www.researchgate.net/publication/285405766_431_The_Barriers_to_Systems_Thinking. Accessed: Jan. 2023.

Blanchard, B.S. and Fabrycky, W.J. (1990). *Systems Engineering and Analysis* (Vol. 4). Prentice Hall.

Checkland, P. (2018). *Systems Thinking, Systems Practice: Includes a 30-Year Retrospective*. Wiley.

Kossiakoff, A., Sweet, W.N., Seymour, S.J., and Biemer, S.M. (2020). *Systems Engineering Principles and Practice.* John Wiley & Sons. https://courses.minia.edu.eg/Attach/10030systems-engineering-principles-and-practice-2nd-edition.pdf. Accessed: Jan. 2023.

Monat, J.P. and Gannon, T.F. (2015). What is systems thinking? A review of selected literature plus recommendations. *American Journal of Systems Science.* 4 (1): 11–26. https://mycourses.aalto.fi/pluginfile.php/1187882/mod_label/intro/Monat%20%20Gannon_2015_What%20is%20systems%20thinking%20-%20A%20review%20of%20selected%20literature%20plus%20recommendations.pdf. Accessed: Jan. 2023.

Ramage, M. and Shipp, K. (2020). *Systems Thinkers.* Springer.

Senge, P.M. (2006, March 21). *The Fifth Discipline: The Art & Practice of The Learning Organization.* Deckle Edge.

Troncale, L. (2018). *On the Nature of Systems Thinking and Systems Science: Similarities, Differences, and Potential Synergies. Disciplinary Convergence in Systems Engineering Research* (pp. 647–663). Springer International Publishing.

Von Bertalanffy, L. and Sutherland, J.W. (1974). General systems theory: Foundations, developments, applications. *IEEE Transactions on Systems, Man, and Cybernetics 22* (6): 592–592.

Wiener, N. (2019). Cybernetics or Control and Communication in the Animal and the Machine, Reissue of the 1961 edition. MIT Press.

5

Systems Engineering

5.1 Introduction

Systems engineering is an interdisciplinary field within which engineers design, integrate, produce, and manage complex systems. Systems engineering applies systems thinking principles to organize this body of knowledge. The individual result of such efforts, a technical system, could be defined as a set of components that work synergistically to perform desired functions.[1] This chapter describes a top-level, systemic approach to systems engineering. It contains the following elements.

- **Philosophy of engineering.** Including basic systems engineering concepts, engineering and truth, the logic of engineering design, the context and nature of engineering design, roles and rules, the modeling of sociotechnical systems, and engineering as synthesis.
- **Systems engineering concepts.** Including basic systems engineering concepts, organizations, projects, system, life cycles, and processes.
- **Systems engineering deficiencies.** Systems engineering versus other engineering endeavors, systems pathologies, and famous systems failures.

5.2 Philosophy of Engineering

5.2.1 Basic Systems Engineering Concepts

Science and engineering are among the most impressive activities our species has engaged in, so it is well worth a few philosophical thoughts to understand how engineering activities work. Toward this end, the author of this book adapted,

---

1 See Systems Engineering, https://en.wikipedia.org/wiki/Systems_engineering. Accessed: Jan. 2023.

Systems Science for Engineers and Scholars, First Edition. Edited by Avner Engel.

with permission, a condensed and abridged version of five philosophical papers delivered during a chain of seminars at the Royal Academy of Engineering in London in 2010.[2]

5.2.2 Paper 1: Engineering and Truth

This paper aims to explain where the difference between science and engineering makes a difference. That is, where the philosophical issues change if we focus on engineering rather than science. Although there is no clear boundary between science and engineering, accurate and relevant differences between pure and applied work are of philosophical importance. Here are three candidate differences between science and engineering: a difference in output, a difference in knowledge, and a difference in drivers.

The first contrast, as many philosophers of science would have it, is that the ultimate output in science is theory—a set of propositions, equations, and assertions. Perhaps that is a defensible view of science, but it does not seem to do justice to engineering. Of course, one can't do engineering without generating propositions, for example, in specifying a design, but the ultimate output is an artifact, not a statement. It is something physical and manufactured. One certainly would expect this contrast in the ultimate output to make a difference in the form that a proper philosophical analysis should take.

The second contrast concerns knowledge. Epistemologists[3] distinguish between "knowing that" and "knowing how." Knowing that is propositional knowledge—it knows that something is the case. Knowing that a statement is true or a hypothesis is correct. In contrast, knowing how is the ability or skill, for example, how to build a bridge. The contrast between knowing that and knowing how suggests a contrast between science and engineering that parallels the contrast between theory and artifact. Philosophers investigating scientific knowledge have concentrated on the knowledge that. Still, if we want to do justice to engineering, it would appear that philosophers must put considerably more weight on knowing how.

The third contrast has a different character. It is motivated by the thought that the drivers for problem choice in science and engineering tend to differ. In pure

---

2 See *RAENG: Philosophy of Engineering*, Volume 1 of the proceedings of a series of seminars held at The Royal Academy of Engineering, London, June 2010. The authors of the original papers are P. Lipton, T. Hoare, J. Turnbull, M. Franssen, and C. Elliott. Reproduced with permission of the Royal Academy of Engineering, London, UK.

3 *Epistemology*, from Greek, *episteme*, meaning "knowledge," and *logos*, meaning "logical discourse," is the branch of philosophy dealing with the theory of knowledge.

science, the driver is often internal to the scientific community: scientists often get to choose their problems. In engineering, it is more common for the driver to be external to the community of practitioners. As a result, engineers often do not get to choose their problems but have them chosen instead by governments, industries, or other external sources. Here again, we have a difference since the way problems are selected may make a difference in how they are addressed, such that a philosophical account that is more or less suitable to science does not, as it stands, do justice to the realities of engineering practice.

5.2.3   Paper 2: The Logic of Engineering Design

The first question in engineering is: what does the system do? Then, in greater detail: What are its properties and behavior? How does it interact with its users and external environment, i.e., its context? Here, the engineer often answers more technical details than the average system user would be interested in. The answer will likely contain scientific, technical terms, like ohms and farads, which the average user will need help understanding. The engineer who designs and implements a system should find this question trivially easy to answer. Surprisingly, this is different in the case of complex systems like computer programs. Even people who have just finished writing a program are often quite puzzled about what it does: if you ask an awkward question, they will have to experiment, running the program to find out what it does. In the ideal, this should be optional. A program's behavior specification can be written in advance, perhaps at the beginning of the project, and its accuracy should be maintained throughout the design, implementation, manufacturing, and usage.

The second question indeed interests all engineers—it probably was the initial motivation for their choice of engineering as the subject for their study. It is: how does the system work? How does the engine function, and how does it drive the wheels of a car? How does the airplane fly? The answer to this question is usually given by describing the structure of the system and its components. It includes describing how the components are connected and the interaction methods. Again, many sound software engineers are seriously challenged to answer questions like this about their programs. A few weeks after writing a program, they no longer know how it works. This situation causes problems when attempting to diagnose and repair errors that come to light later. It causes even more severe problems when the need arises to produce the next version of their program when needed to make it do something a little different or a little better. The programmers then have to find out, again by experiment, how the program works.

The two questions "what?" and "how?" are equally relevant to pursuing all branches of natural science. For example, a classificatory biologist may enquire, what does a newt or an axolotl[4] do? How does it relate to its environment? And the next question asks how the creature is constructed: what are its limbs and organs, and how do they interact? Unfortunately, sciences that concentrate on these two questions are often characterized as merely descriptive.

5.2.3.1 Basic Questions of Science

The more mature branches of science are indeed based on an extensive foundation of accurate description, but then they address somewhat deeper questions. The first of these is: Why does the system work? What are the fundamental scientific principles, the equations, and the laws of nature on which the system's working depends? So, the aeronautical engineer studies aerodynamics, which makes explicit the laws that explain why an airplane flies. Based on the laws, it is possible to predict how the airplane will respond to its controls; the modern engineer exploits such laws to optimize the quality of systems and reduce their cost.

The final and most distinctive feature of modern science is its pursuit of certainty of knowledge. The scientist aims to assemble a massive body of convincing evidence that the answers to all the previous questions are correct. The engineer uses a wide range of testing before delivering a system to gain confidence that it will meet stakeholders' needs and not fail after delivery. Testing is also used to detect and remove any remaining deficiencies in the product that often appear after implementation. In architecture, this is known as *snagging*.[5] In programming, it is called *debugging*.

5.2.3.2 The Logic of Engineering Design

One may argue that the correctness of a process of rational engineering design follows the same rules of propositional calculus as mathematical proof. However, the individual lines in the proof are much larger than the typical statement of mathematical theorems; each is some engineering description of the system, either in part or as a whole. Moreover, the proof itself is much longer than most mathematical proofs: it consists of the entire collection of engineering documents recording the entire design process for the system. These engineering documents describe the system from different perspectives, for different purposes, and at different levels of detail and abstraction. The most abstract documents are the

---

4 Newt is a small, slender-bodied amphibian with lungs and a well-developed tail, typically spending life on land and returning to water to breed. Axolotl is a small amphibian that never outgrows its larval juvenile stage and can regenerate lost limbs throughout life.

5 Snagging is an inspection process that lists defects or omissions in constructing works for the contractor to rectify.

overall system specifications, answering the question, "What does it do?" regarding the system's properties that interest its users.

5.2.4 Paper 3: The Context and Nature of Engineering Design

The design engineer plays a pivotal role in shaping society and its lifestyle and values, particularly in this modern, technology-driven age that may be associated with the time of Telford.[6] This pivotal role contrasts other well-known engineers like Stephenson[7] and Brunel,[8] who seem to have retreated and become largely anonymous background figures.

5.2.4.1 What Is Engineering?

One definition of engineering is: "Engineering is the knowledge required, and the process applied, to conceive, design, make, build, operate, sustain, recycle or retire, something of significant technical content for a specified purpose—a concept, a model, a product, a device, a process, a system, a technology." This definition is intended to be an all-embracing and comprehensive definition. But its somewhat legalistic approach seems misleading. It describes what many engineers do but masks design's core and fundamental engineering activity.

If we dissect the definition, we can say that "applying knowledge and skill" could refer to any profession. The activities covered by "make, build, operate, sustain" are management activities requiring skilled, well-trained personnel to work according to the designer's recipes and instructions. However, the conception and design of systems are the fundamentals of engineering.

5.2.4.2 What Is "Design"?

According to Webster's Dictionary, design is: "The process of selecting the means and contriving the elements, steps, and procedures for producing what will adequately satisfy some need." However, one can find a fascinating insight into what many people think design is about by listening to intelligent design advocates in their arguments against evolution. This insight is separate from the conclusion that is drawn. The supporters of intelligent design see in the Darwinian concept of natural selection a random, unstructured process in which chance plays a far

---

6 Thomas Telford (1757–1834) was a noted Scottish civil engineer, architect, and stonemason as well as a road, bridge, and canal builder.

7 Robert Stephenson (1803–1859) was a well-known English railway and civil engineer.

8 Isambard Kingdom Brunel (1806–1859) was a famous English mechanical and civil engineer.

more significant role than would be logical to create the dynamic, intricate pieces of life that make up the universe. They fear that this robs human existence of meaning, and they argue that the sheer complexity of the natural world demonstrates, or even proves, the existence of a "designer." Purpose, in their minds, deserves particular emphasis and seems missing from natural selection. They see design as a high-level activity that brings order and meaning to life. Engineers should say Amen to that!

5.2.4.3 Engineering Design Process

The essential nature of design and its phases should be emphasized. These involve intensive two-way dialogue with all sorts of clients.[9] A close fit has to be developed between the client's business plan and risk model and the strategic elements of the proposed design. Both the designer and the clients must agree on the boundaries of the intended system, which must be done in terms of topography and time. "For what period is this system expected to operate?" is a crucial question. Everyone involved must share a standard risk assessment and management process considering the inevitable uncertainties. This understanding is essential regarding the technologies employed and the areas where the design will require creativity and judgment. Finally, it must include a financial model that expresses and tackles the critical economic uncertainties from both the clients' and designers' viewpoints.

In summary, this is the period when the design engineers ensure that there is a clear understanding of the purpose of the system to be delivered by the project and their ability to deliver it. Engineers' failure or success can be estimated between zero and one hundred percent. However, engineers are usually subject to a very transparent and public test. Engineering designers must produce systems and processes that work. Everyone can observe and suffer the consequences if a bridge collapses, an airplane does not fly, and automobiles do not start. The consequences of error are much more evident than in the work of a neurosurgeon, lawyer, or accountant.

5.2.4.4 Societal Risk

Design engineers must take into account not just technology and economics. There are significant nonfinancial benefits and disbenefits to take into account. In addition, engineers must accept that various stakeholders often have different agendas. They may see the boundaries of the system quite differently. This worldview difference was exhibited when Shell planned the decommissioning of

---

9 All the stakeholders.

Brent Spar (Owen and Rice, 1999). Greenpeace had a different plan from Shell's and succeeded in derailing the original Shell design.[10]

5.2.4.5 Aesthetics and Utility

When discussing "design" in the broader community, engineering design does not arise as the first thought or example. One could invite friends to name a designer, and they, most probably, will reply with names like Antoni Gaudi (architect and interior designer, 1852–1926), Christian Dior (fashion designer, 1905–1957), Jonathan Ive (industrial designer, 1967–), and the like.

For example, a bank recently wrote and offered a cash card, which it said had been "designed" by Stella McCartney. The author of this paper was quite impressed to find that a fashion designer had mastered the technology of polymeric materials and their embossing and lamination, not to mention imprinting a magnetic strip, incorporating a chip and the necessary encryption technology. However, on further reading, it was discovered that what the bank meant by "design" was that she had provided a pretty picture to put on the front of the card. Nevertheless, engineers cannot ignore or dismiss this interpretation because pleasing aesthetics are valued and respected. On the other hand, "utility" is taken for granted, mainly because engineers do such a good job. Architects combine utility and aesthetics, but can engineers? And should they? Of course, they should—and often, they do.

5.2.4.6 Engineering and Aesthetics

Automobiles are highly engineered systems, but we know they are bought as much for their appearance and style as for their performance. The Concorde aircraft is a dramatic example of how aesthetically satisfying it can be, even when designing for performance. Even today, one may be astonished at how many people talk about that beautiful, incredible machine in sentimental, nostalgic terms. They say it was such a beautiful airplane, and they appreciate that. But, of course, they also appreciated its performance but emphasized its looks.

Another example is the Viaduct de Millau bridge (Figure 5.1). One may ask his friends who designed it, and they will say it was designed by Norman Foster (1935–). Norman Foster made a magnificent contribution in terms of the outline and shape of the bridge, but the man who ensured that that bridge stood up and could take the traffic and resist the elements was Michel Virlogeux (1946–). Undoubtedly, no one in public at large has ever heard his name.

---

10 Brent Spar was a North Sea oil storage and tanker loading system within the Goose Creek oilfield, operated by Shell UK. By 1991, this facility was considered obsolete, and Shell planned to dispose of it in Atlantic waters about 250 kilometers off the west coast of Scotland at a depth of about 2.5 kilometers. However, Shell abandoned its original plans in the face of the stiff public and political opposition orchestrated, mainly by the Greenpeace organization (Wikipedia).

Figure 5.1   The Viaduct de Millau bridge in southern France.

5.2.4.7   Purpose and Other Values

However, other values appear when reflecting on purpose, apart from utility and making it work and aesthetics. There are ethics, for sure; a social focus because people are concerned with health, education, care for older people, environmental responsibility and sustainable development, and engagement with the developing world.

Fascinatingly, of course, these are issues that are rising on the engineering agenda more and more today. The list is incomplete, but these issues receive engineers' attention worldwide. More reports and studies are being generated to address these values. This trend will help to increase public awareness and appreciation of engineering because it addresses areas that count out there in society. By addressing them, engineers are seen responding to society's broader agenda.

5.2.4.8   Engineering's Social Dimension

The fact of the matter is that engineering should not be technology-driven. Technology is an enabler and a crucial component in the toolkit, but it is not why one is an engineer. The real driver is social because engineers want to increase the quality of life in the community. However, what distinguishes engineering from other equally socially driven professions is its range of activities, ability to combine science with judgment and intuition, and all of this within a disciplined, technical framework. Engineers have the skill and ability to design, according to well-tested rules, complex systems that work. They can combine science-based technologies with social insight to improve the quality of life.

Finally, engineering formation needs to recognize and give much more room for the social skills that a professional engineer needs. For example, to be taught that engineering is 100% technology is a travesty of the truth. Instead, the engineer's mission must surely be to serve the community; to do this, the engineer must have the communication and debate skills to engage the community and address and educate its needs and aspirations.

5.2.5 Paper 4: Roles and Rules and the Modeling of Socio-Technical Systems

The term *system* could be more informative. It was introduced into engineering in the 1940s, leading to the rise of systems engineering in the 1950s and 1960s, but simultaneously obtained a central place in biology and other sciences. The common understanding in the literature is that a system is a complex whole consisting of elements or components related to each other. This understanding makes almost any technical artifact a system.

Since a model of a system should contain all elements that are relevant to the functioning of the system, a model of a socio-technical system must include the operators.

The literature identifies two distinguished approaches to do it. The first is often called hard-systems thinking, and the second is soft-systems thinking. Hard-system thinking was the predominant (in fact, the only) form of systems analysis until the early 1970s. In that period, the emphasis shifted from hard-systems engineering to soft-systems engineering.

Figure 5.2 shows a model of an aircraft system as part of a more extensive air transport system, which is again related to a national transport supersystem. Characterizing the various subsystems that make up the aircraft system does not indicate whether people or machines do some of the operating and controlling. One component of the aircraft system model, the crew, an all-human subsystem, is presented as entirely on par with the other all-hardware subsystems. The air-traffic control system in the enveloping air transport system is operated by people—air-traffic controllers—supported by hardware systems. Still, it cannot be seen from the model that this is so, or that this is so for the air-traffic control system but not for, e.g., the ticketing system, which could be a wholly automated subsystem.

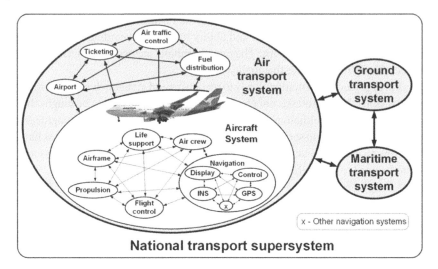

Figure 5.2 Aircraft system embedded in a national transport supersystem.

Especially in the design of socio-technical systems, failing to consider that human beings are fundamentally different from machines may create serious difficulties. The point is not that humans, as biological organisms, are fundamentally different from machines. That remains to be seen. The point is not so much that people make mistakes; they choose the wrong action when a particular condition materializes or fail to recognize where they should take a particular action, which the operator admits.

Due to our incomplete knowledge of nature, hardware malfunctions can never be ruled out. The point is that people can contest a judgment that actual circumstances are or were precisely equal to a specified condition in their list of instructions and can therefore contest whether they should choose or should have chosen a particular course of action. Furthermore, people do not coincide with the roles they fulfill. Instead, they are defined by their individual goals, desires, beliefs, and expectations. Therefore, their judgment will involve a broader range of considerations than any list of instructions. Finally, people are individual persons, part of a social system. They have responsibilities in the roles they fulfill and as individuals, and they are held responsible for their deeds. This responsibility seriously affects which courses of action they will choose. In conclusion:

- Socio-technical systems involve humans both in the role of operators and users. Operators are subsystems of the more extensive system in which they perform their operating work and are included in the system. Users are not part of the system. They are free to use the system or, in the case of a socio-technical system, to participate in it.

- The proper functioning of socio-technical systems requires the coordination of the actions of all people involved, operators, and users. This coordination will usually be accomplished through rules, and the design of such rules is an integral element of designing a system.
- A human decision to follow a particular rule requires an assessment of the situation to justify applying that rule. And even when operators decide that a particular rule applies, they can also be expected to judge whether it is in the person's interest to follow it.
- The history of technology consists, to a large extent, of attempts to remove the "friction" in the system caused by the freedom of operators. Many of these attempts have been successful. One way to decrease such friction is to increase systems' automation and eliminate the operators as much as possible. Unfortunately, operators are everywhere and are continuously being replaced by hardware systems. This option is, of course, no panacea: hardware systems can also fail, even if differently. Additionally, this option has institutional limits, with responsibility, accountability, and liability consequences.
- Finally, regardless of the extent of automation, the friction due to the interpretational and reflective freedom of the system users will remain. One can never automate the users of a system because the system exists to serve its purposes; automated users have no purposes. Although a user cannot be considered part of a system, the person who constitutes the user is often present in the system as an operator, as is the case when an individual driver steers their car along the roads of a traffic network. What one can do is decouple as much as possible the user role and the operator role. The increasing interest in developing fully automated traffic so that, ultimately, the user can sleep his way from A to B is an example of this approach.

5.2.6 Paper 5: Engineering as Synthesis: Doing Right Things and Doing Things Right

5.2.6.1 Engineering as Synthesis

Fundamentally, engineering equals design. Everything else done under engineering is either applied science and technology or is craft—making things. The element that makes engineering different from science and craft is design. That is not popular with university departments, which are often made up of scientists or people trying to pursue the craft of making things. Both groups deserve great respect. Nevertheless, the thesis of this paper remains that engineering is designed.

The notes in the flyer for this philosophy of engineering seminar say that "engineering is primarily a social rather than a technological discipline." This approach is not quite the case. Take an aeronautical example: if you are halfway across the Atlantic, do you want to know that the diameter of the bolt that holds the engine on was calculated? The materials are chosen so that the bolt is sufficiently strong. Or is it there because that is the correct social context? Engineering is about making things that work; if they do not work, people die.

On a lighter note, here is a relevant quotation from one of the leading twentieth-century philosophers of science, Douglas Adams (1952–2001), in a line from "The Restaurant at the End of the Universe," a part of the *Hitch-Hiker's Guide* series. It concerns a party of hairdressers and management consultants who are stranded on prehistoric earth and have formed committees to invent things to make life better. They are having a review of their work: "What about this wheel thingy?" said the captain. "It sounds like an interesting project." "Ah," said the marketing girl, "we have some difficulty there." "Difficulty?" exclaimed Ford, "what do you mean, difficulty? It is the single simplest machine in the entire universe." The marketing girl soured him with a look. "All right, Mr. Wise Guy," she said, "If you're so clever, you tell us what color it should be."

Douglas Adams is funny, but he also makes many perceptive remarks. Getting so obsessed with the "what color should it be?" example, when you miss the point about whether it goes round and carries a load, seems to be a false sense of priorities. Engineering, which is about making things that work, should always maintain sight of the goal.

A popular engineering rule is that "form follows function." Alas, not always—a great example of where function followed form was the design of the Millennium Dome (Figure 5.3). The first decision was how big it would be in square meters, followed by the choice of material to make the roof. Somebody said, "That's pretty good—what shall we do with it?" That is an archetypal example of letting the form dictate the function.

Figure 5.3 The Millennium Dome, London, United Kingdom.

Everyone has their definition of engineering, and the author is "Changing the natural world to make it better meet the needs of mankind." Engineers are about reforming this place from what it was earlier so that it works better to meet the needs of at least a subgroup of humankind. If you want to be biblical, this is a very complex world to design and build in six days, so engineers must finish what God left undone.

This issue brings us to the central message. In practice, engineering is useless unless it is sensitive to what society wants and will use. For example, any wheel is worth having if you are stuck on a prehistoric Earth. However, if you are trying to design a wheel for the next generation of an expensive luxury car, it will only sell if it meets all the needs of prestigious car customers. So engineering design has to be sensitive to the social context of what it is designed for and how it will be built.

5.2.6.2 The Engineering Design Process

Design is the art of compromise. Since it was claimed that engineering equals design, people started to ask whether engineering means compromises. Apparently, yes, because there is rarely a correct answer, a right design because so many stakeholders have conflicting objectives—performance, delivery time, cost, risk, and many others. If the project becomes big enough to have a political dimension, you discuss job security, national pride, and international relations. So many axes are grounded in most engineering projects, and the engineer must consider them all.

One may describe the role of the engineering designer as finding the least bad compromise that all stakeholders can live with. Think of it as plotting their needs on a Venn diagram[11] and trying to find that little blob where they overlap, which everyone can live with. But, of course, almost all real engineering design challenges have no overlapping blob. There is no common ground; the engineers have the diplomatic task of persuading someone to move his position (that is, redefine his needs), or the project needs to be abandoned.

In engineering, there is the principle of iteration—that one puts up an idea and, if it does not fly or if the customer does not like it, one keeps tweaking it and working with all the stakeholders until one comes up with something that can be done. If all else fails, one abandons it—and that is something that engineers are awful at. Engineers persist, even when it does not make sense. The usual problem is that the customer wants a palace until one tells him what it will cost, and then one starts again. This dilemma is especially true of institutional customers. Willy

---

11 See https://en.wikipedia.org/wiki/Venn_diagram. Accessed: Feb. 2018.

Messerschmitt (1898–1978) once said, "We can build any aircraft that the aviation ministry calls for, with any requirement satisfied. But, of course, it will not fly" (see an example of a failed engineering project below). This global problem always arises, with the customer requiring the impossible. The designer is left with trading off a whole load of benefits and constraints to arrive at a compromise that everyone can work with—speed, reliability, maintainability, cost, timescale, mass, comfort, etc.

Engineering design is a mass of disciplines, not all purely technical. Most projects involve various engineering disciplines – mechanics, electrics, electronics, computing, materials, etc. Then there is project management, including planning, construction, testing, operating, and disposing of the system. Finally, we must add many subjective human issues, such as biomechanics, shape, color, and form.

Failed engineering project[12]

Project Pluto was a US government project to develop nuclear-powered ramjet engines for use in supersonic low-altitude cruise missiles. This system would have many advantages over other nuclear weapons delivery systems: operating at Mach 3 and flying as low as 150 meters above ground, it would be invulnerable to interception by contemporary air defenses and carry more and larger nuclear warheads up to 10 megatons of TNT.

The world's first nuclear ramjet engine was run at full power (46 MW) in 1961, and a larger, fully functional ramjet engine ran at full power (461 MW) in 1964, demonstrating the feasibility of a nuclear-powered ramjet engine. However, the ICBM technology reduced the need for cruise missiles. Also, by the early 1960s, there was greater sensitivity to the dangers of radioactive emissions in the atmosphere, and devising an appropriate test plan for the flight tests was intractable. Then, in mid-1964, nearly eight years after its inception, project Pluto was abandoned.

Creativity is not passive; one does not just follow the rules. For example, analysis of the bolt holding the engine in an aircraft must be based on complex calculations, not hand-waving. Also, one cannot look up answers for everything, and, eventually,

---
12 See more: https://en.wikipedia.org/wiki/Project_Pluto. Accessed: Jan. 2023.

one must make a value judgment. Finally, leadership is essential; if the engineer is not going to lead the project, who is? It returns to the marketing people in prehistoric earth; you would not want them leading it. That sets the scene for the six principles related to human as well as technical issues engineers are trying to follow in their design efforts:

1. Debate, define, revise, and pursue the purpose
2. Think holistic
3. Be creative
4. Follow a disciplined procedure
5. Take account of the people
6. Manage the project and the relationships

5.2.6.3 Systems Engineers

People are often held to fall into one of two types, hedgehogs or foxes. Hedgehogs have one trick and do it OK—they have spikes. Foxes have many little tricks, and they are cunning. The popular view is that engineers are hedgehogs and very good at something, while project managers are foxes, being quite good at several things.

Systems engineers, however, must be both; their resume is T-shaped: It has a lot of breadths and at least one deep piece: "There is at least one thing in this project for which I am the expert." If an engineer cannot say that, then apart from anything else, he will not have any credibility with others. Those engineers must be able to do one part of the project in detail and all in outline, setting the agenda for their education. They must know a lot of basic science and engineering—physics, chemistry, and mathematics, the science on which engineering is based.

They also must have an analytical spirit that tries to model problems rather than brainstorm them. They need an awareness of the many disciplines that contribute to the project. Finally, they need to be able to communicate with everybody—from the customer to the technician who assembles their design. The message we are trying to convey to engineering education is, please think about how you form engineers who fit that pattern. This undertaking is challenging and uncomfortable for traditional engineering thinking, but it is crucial to engineering complex systems that work.

That is where we come back to the title of this paper. It started by exploring and doing things right—one does not want the engine to be held on by the goodwill of individuals—but doing the right things is the broader context of engineering systems.

5.3 Basic Systems Engineering Concepts

5.3.1 Systems Engineering Definition

According to the International Council on Systems Engineering (INCOSE), systems engineering[13] is "an interdisciplinary approach and means to enable the realization of successful systems. It focuses on defining customer needs and required functionality early in the development cycle, documenting requirements, and then proceeding with design synthesis and system validation while considering the complete problem."

INCOSE further upholds: "Systems engineering integrates all the disciplines and specialty groups into a team effort forming a structured development process that proceeds from concept to production to operation. Systems engineering considers all customers' business and technical needs to provide a quality product that meets the user needs."

Based on standard 15288, the author considers systems engineering as resting on four fundamental pillars: (1) organization and project concepts, (2) system concepts, (3) life cycle concepts, and (4) process concepts.

5.3.2 Organization and Project Concepts

System engineering is a human-intensive endeavor. Success or failure depends on individual scientists, engineers, managers, and professional staff. Therefore, organizations and project-related processes constitute a significant part of standard 15288. According to the chief information officer (CIO) Wiki, an encyclopedia of information technology management,[14] "An organization is a group of people who work together to achieve common goals and objectives." In general, organizations have management structures that determine the organizations' missions and assign individuals or groups of people to specific roles, responsibilities, and authority to carry out these missions.

A part of an organization (e.g., a department within an organization) as well as a single person within an organization constitute, by definition, an organization. Also, organizations negotiate with other organizations to acquire/supply products or services (Figure 5.4). When an organization enters into such an agreement, it is sometimes called a *party* to the agreement. That responsibility usually refers to a party responsible for a particular aspect of the project. For example, the organization that supplies certain raw materials or subsystems to the project is often called the *supplier*.

---

13 See *INCOSE, What Is Systems Engineering?* https://www.incose.org/systems-engineering. Accessed: Dec. 2022. See also ISO (2015).

14 See: https://cio-wiki.org/wiki/Main_Page. Accessed: Jan. 2023.

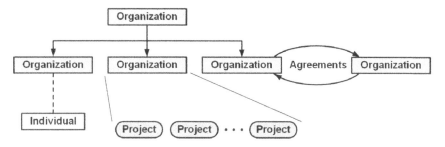

Figure 5.4   Organization and project concepts.

5.3.3   System Concepts

The term *system* in this book refers, in fact, to artificial systems or engineered systems rather than to any system (e.g., the human body). INCOSE adopted Eberhardt Rechtin's system definition: "A system is a construct or collection of different elements that produce results not obtainable by the elements alone. The elements, or parts, can include people, hardware, software, facilities, policies, and documents, all required to produce system-level results. The results include system-level qualities, properties, characteristics, functions, behavior, and performance. The value added by the system as a whole, beyond that contributed independently by the parts, is primarily created by the relationship among the parts; that is, how they are interconnected"[15] (Figure 5.5).

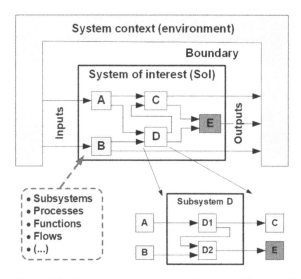

Figure 5.5   Example of an engineered system of interest (SoI) in its context.

───────

15 See Maier and Rechtin (2009).

The following attributes characterize engineered systems:

- Engineered systems (more generically, systems of interest or [SoIs]) exist within a given context with which the system interacts in one way or another. This context could be one or more defined entities like other systems, people, and the like.
- SoIs have boundaries that delineate and separate the system from its context, and systems engineers are expected to define the boundary between a given system and its context.
- A SoI consists of various entities, typically subsystems or parts that carry out processes and functions, and there are specific relations among these systems' entities.
- Entities within SoI have inputs and outputs supporting the internal flow of materials, energy, or information among them. Similarly, virtually all engineered systems have external input and output flow of materials, energy, or information between the system and its context.
- Any entity within an engineered system may comprise a hierarchically structured set of subordinate system entities.

Systems engineers distinguish between operational products and enabling products. Both should be constituents of engineered systems. Unfortunately, many systems engineers consider only the operational product as their SoI, thus missing a large portion of their SoI (Figure 5.6).

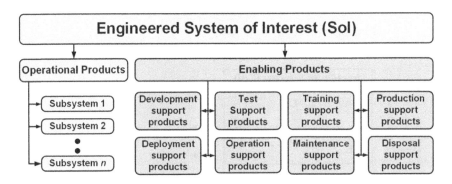

Figure 5.6 Engineered system: example of operational and enabling products.

Operational products are the elements that, in total, perform the operational functionalities of the system. Enabling products do not contribute directly to the operational functioning of the system but provide essential services to the system at different stages of the life cycle, thus facilitating the system's progression toward its designers' goals. Each enabling product plays its role in one or more stages of the system's life cycle. For example, Figure 5.7 depicts wind tunnel testing at NASA's Langley Research Center, supporting preparations for deep space missions of the second-generation Space Launch System (SLS). This activity may occur during the late system design stage, verifying broad system design concepts.

Figure 5.7   Concept testing at NASA's wind tunnel facility (Image: NASA).

5.3.4   Life Cycle Concept

A system life cycle is a structured approach to creating, maintaining, and retiring engineered systems. Many life cycle models have been defined based on analysis of typical tasks undertaken by engineers within different domains. This approach makes those tasks amenable to traditional management planning and control techniques. For example, different organizations such as the US Department of Defense (DoD), the National Aeronautics and Space Administration (NASA), and various industries (e.g., automobile, electronics, telecommunication, and aerospace) define different system life cycle models.

Typically, a life cycle model is composed of stages. Each one represents a significant period in the life of a system. More specifically, a life cycle stage defines its unique contribution to the cradle-to-grave progression of an engineered system. Standard 15288, by the way, does not advocate any particular life cycle model.

Figure 5.8, Table 5.1 and Table 5.2 depict this book's generic life cycle model. This model incorporates the V model proposed by Barry Boehm in the 1970s,

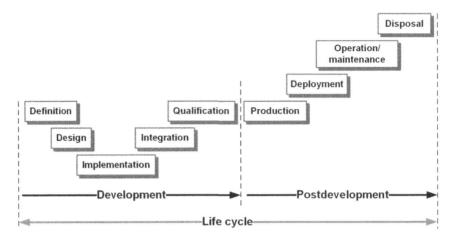

Figure 5.8 Generic system's life cycle model.

Table 5.1 Generic System Life Cycle Model (Development).

	Stage	Purpose
Development	Definition	Formulate the SoI operational concepts and develop the system requirements
	Design	Create a technical concept and architecture for the SoI
	Implementation	Build the components (e.g., subsystems) of the SoI. Each component is built, purchased, and tested to ensure its stand-alone compliance with its allocated requirements.
	Integration	Connect all the system's components into a complete SoI
	Qualification	Perform formal and operational tests on the completed SoI to ensure that it performs its intended functionality and ensures the quality of the SoI as a whole

describing the development portion of the systems' life cycle. In addition, the generic model describes the postdevelopment portion of the life cycle. In brief, the left-hand side of the V model corresponds to satisfying stakeholders' requirements and the design of the desired system and its components. The right-hand side of the V model consists of building the individual components, integrating them, and verifying and validating the system. The postdevelopment portion of the life cycle includes production, deployment, operation/maintenance, and disposal.

Table 5.2 Generic System Life Cycle Model (Postdevelopment).

	Stage	Purpose
Postdevelopment	Production	Produce the SoI in appropriate quantities
	Deployment	Deploy the SoI in its planned contest
	Operation/maintenance	Operate the SoI in its intended context to accomplish the intended functionality; in addition, maintain the SoI, and correct any defects
	Disposal	Properly dispose of the SoI and its elements upon completion of its life

5.3.5 Process Concepts

Standard 15288 defines a process framework that reflects engineered systems' life cycle evolution. More specifically, these processes represent a broad superset providing: (1) organizational context to enable projects, (2) project management processes for any stage in a system's life cycle, as well as (3) all of the technical processes for the entire life cycle of the system. Users (e.g., organizations, projects, etc.) can adapt and apply an appropriate set of processes, defining individualized systems' life cycle practices appropriate to their purpose and doctrine. Each process within standard 15288 is described in terms of the following attributes.

- **Process.** A process is a set of one or more activities that collectively convert inputs into outputs.
- **Title.** A title summarizes the scope of the process as a whole.
- **Purpose.** The purpose describes the high-level objective for performing a given process.
- **Inputs.** Inputs consist of information, artifacts, or services used by processes to generate specified outcomes.
- **Activity.** An activity encapsulates a set of cohesive process tasks.
- **Task.** A task defines a set of requirements, recommendations, or actions intended to contribute to achieving one or more outcomes of a process.
- **Outcome.** An outcome is an observable result emanating from a successful process performance.

Figure 5.9 shows a concept map depicting elements of a standard 15288 process. The image should be "read" as follows: "The standard 15288 process has a title; has a purpose; receives inputs; and is composed of activities, which are further composed of tasks producing outcomes that fulfill expected process outputs."

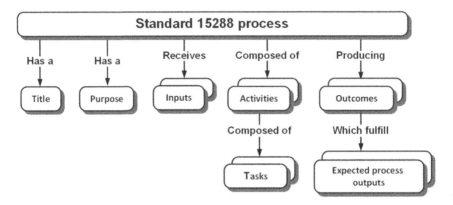

Figure 5.9 Elements of a process: presented by way of a concept map.

5.4 Systems Engineering Deficiencies

5.4.1 Systems Engineering versus Other Engineering Endeavors

The engineering field has contributed immensely to changing the face of the Earth. The innovations and inventions made by men in this area over the years have been extraordinary. Systems engineering is an interdisciplinary field focusing on designing and managing complex projects. Systems engineering (SE) can be traced to the Bell Telephone Laboratories in the 1940s (Schlager, 1956). Since that time, systems engineering has evolved and matured considerably. However, many engineering project failures, disasters, and mishaps occur regularly. If the systems engineering discipline had been robust and thriving, significant disasters and mishaps would not have occurred, at least in the late twentieth and early twenty-first centuries.

One must admit that systems engineering differs from all other traditional engineering disciplines, such as electrical, mechanical, and chemical, based on well-known physical laws and mathematical equations (Figure 5.10).

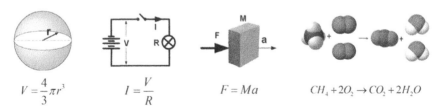

$$V = \frac{4}{3}\pi r^3 \qquad I = \frac{V}{R} \qquad F = Ma \qquad CH_4 + 2O_2 \rightarrow CO_2 + 2H_2O$$

Figure 5.10 Engineering disciplines are based on physical laws and mathematical equations.

In contrast, systems engineering is based on following certain sets of procedures. However, we systems engineers are human. Each person understands, interprets, and applies SE procedures differently. As a result, two systems engineers will interpret requirements and systems' design quite differently. For example, Engel and Reich (2015) describe two approaches to designing interfaces. One systems engineer may design a simple, nonadaptable, inexpensive interface (Figure 5.11a), while another may design a flexible but expensive interface (Figure 5.11b). However, both adhere to the same set of SE procedures.

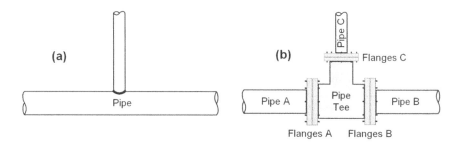

Figure 5.11 Different interface design.

The results indicate that, at this junction, systems engineering practice is, in many ways, disappointing. This realization may be gleaned from many statistical studies of system failures. For example, the US Government Accountability Office (GAO) issued a report in 2008 called "Defense Acquisitions: Assessments of Selected Weapon Programs." The report found that engineering projects exhibit "an average schedule delay of 21 months and average budget overrun of 26 percent" (GAO-08-467SP, 2008).

Another study, conducted by McKinsey and the University of Oxford in 2012,[16] covered more than 5,400 large information technology (IT) projects (with price tags exceeding $15 million per project). The research compared budgets and schedules, as well as predicted performance benefits against actual results. The findings, consistent across industries, indicated that "on average, projects run 45 percent over budget and 7 percent over time while delivering 56 percent less value than expected." In addition, these projects exhibited cost overruns of $66 billion (Bloch et al., 2012).

---

16 See more: Delivering large-scale IT projects on time, on budget, and on value. McKinsey

5.4.2 Systems' Pathologies

Medicine pathology[17] describes the study of natural diseases and their causes and effects. This concept was adapted into *system pathology* or *system engineering pathology*, which studies systems failures and their causes and effects.

For example, the International Council on Systems Engineering (INCOSE) created the Systems Processes and Pathologies project. The group examined known system failures, among other activities, to identify a generalized approach to system dysfunctions. The project's researchers have identified 55 key systems processes that led to pathological outcomes. Table 5.3 depicts 10 widespread systems pathologies (Troncale, 2019).

Table 5.3 Ten widespread systems pathologies.

Pathology	Description
Pathology of channel capacity	Ineffectiveness in transmitting different messages; channel needs to be modified to transmit; needs to account for noise (i.e., disturbance) in transmission; information not received on time
Pathology of autonomy	Subsystems are unable to take actions or make decisions independently; A higher system overconstrains them
Pathology of a balance of tension	Lacking a governing structure that must relieve tension among different subsystems, finding the right balance between the independence of subsystems and integration of the whole, self-organization and structured design, and maintaining a balance between system ability and change
Pathology of dialecticism	Recommendations may be made without the ability to reflect on errors and deploy efforts to correct detected errors, but the system cannot implement the recommendations
Pathology of subsidiarity	Preferring to defer to a higher authority on local issues; elevating subsystem (i.e., local) issues to a higher system level; subsystems should seek system-level solutions only when they have exceeded their capacity to deal with issues
Pathology of buffering	Lacking a surplus of resources; operating a system without sufficient slack; being unaware that unused resources become wasted and take up space
Pathology of morphogenesis	Failing to create new and potentially radically different structures that support existing structures frequently allows new changes without allowing old ones to take hold
Pathology of a system boundary	Having a fuzzy defined line of demarcation that delineates a system and its context; lacks minimum description distinguishing the system

---

17 See Pathology, https://en.wikipedia.org/wiki/Pathology. Accessed: Dec. 2022.

Table 5.3 (Continued)

Pathology	Description
Pathology of circular causality	Using a traditional (linear) causality model of thinking without recognizing the intricate interrelationships in a complex system, assuming it is not possible to have a wide range of conditions leading to the same result, focusing on the cause rather than processes and patterns, assuming superficial cause–effect relationships rather than mutual or multiple causalities
Pathology of well-being	Placing preference on financial profitability above all other measures, lacking balance in material, technical, physical, social, nutritional, cognitive, spiritual, and environmental aspects

A further intent of the INCOSE group is to study how natural systems have evolved to overcome these pathologies. For example, Davidz et al. (2018) suggested using systems engineering pathology as a systematic way to characterize dysfunctional systems engineering processes. Along this line, Katina (2015) proposed a model of systems and function-based pathologies (Figure 5.12).

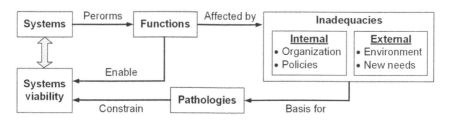

Figure 5.12 Model of systems and function-based pathologies.[18]

5.4.3 Famous Systems Failures

The owners of failed systems and systems projects tend to conceal these systems' failures, so the public is unaware of their distressing prevalence. Sometimes, however, the debacle is impossible to hide. Here are a few short accounts of some of the more significant fiascos over the past century.

The reader is challenged to examine the following intellectual hypothesis: Assuming the engineers involved in the systems described below had been practicing modern systems engineering, would this have eliminated these disasters or mitigated their severity?

---

18 Derived from Katina (2015).

5.4.3.1 The *Titanic* Disaster (1912)

The RMS (Royal Mail Steamer) *Titanic* was a British passenger ship on its maiden voyage from the United Kingdom to New York City. The *Titanic* was the largest and most revered passenger ship ever built. It was about 270 meters in length and displaced over 52,000 tons.

On the night of April 14, 1912, despite repeated warnings from other ships in the area, the *Titanic*, traveling at full speed, struck an iceberg and sank in less than three hours. More than 1,500 people, some two-thirds of the *Titanic*'s passengers and crew, perished, mainly because there were not enough lifeboats to rescue everyone on board (Figure 5.13).

Figure 5.13 Sinking of the *Titanic* (Engraving by Willy Stower, 1864–1931).

Invariably, multiple factors cause most systems disasters and mishaps. The *Titanic* disaster is a prime example of multiple systemic causes beyond engineering mistakes. Figure 5.14 depicts a cause-and-effect (fishbone) diagram of the causes of the *Titanic* disaster. As can be seen, one causation category (flawed ship design) is directly related to engineering. However, three other causation categories (misguided assumptions, disaster management failures, and bad luck) are unrelated to engineering.

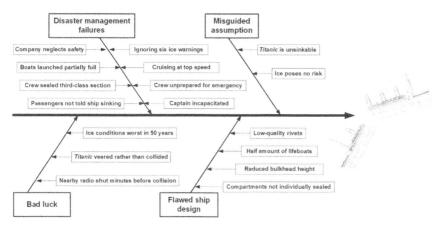

Figure 5.14 Cause-and-effect analysis of the *Titanic* disaster.

5.4.3.2 The Tacoma Narrows Bridge Collapse (1940)

The Tacoma Narrows Bridge spanned the section of the Puget Sound between Tacoma and the Kitsap Peninsula in the US state of Washington. In the 1940s, the Tacoma Narrows Bridge was the third longest suspension bridge in the world. Its ambitious design included a lighter, thinner, and more flexible structure with deep piers driven into the waters below. Though the bridge tended to move vertically in strong winds, this critical problem was not rectified.

So, just four months after it opened to traffic, 65-kilometer-per-hour winds created an undulation that ran the entire bridge length. The built-up torsional vibration caused the bridge to twist in opposite directions, which snapped key suspending cables and culminated in the bridge's collapse. Luckily, there were no human fatalities (Figure 5.15).

Figure 5.15 The Tacoma Narrows Bridge collapsing.

As seen before, most engineering disasters, failures, and mishaps have a systemic origin. However, the Tacoma Narrows Bridge failure is a unique failure caused strictly by an engineering problem associated with a lack of knowledge regarding forced-resonance behavior at the bridge's natural frequency.

5.4.3.3 The Banqiao Reservoir Dam Disaster (1975)

The Banqiao Dam, located on the river Ru near Zhumadian City, Henan province, China, was designed to control regional flooding and generate hydroelectric power. Its construction was completed in 1952.

On August 8, 1975, the dam suffered critical failures and collapsed, releasing 15.7 billion cubic meters of water. The dam collapse created a deadly flood that inundated 12,000 square kilometers, leading to an immediate death toll of 26,000 people. In addition, an estimated 150,000 died due to residual epidemics and famine resulting from the disaster. Ten million people were displaced from their towns and villages.[19] This event is considered the worst engineering disaster ever (Figure 5.16).

Figure 5.16 The aftermath of the Banqiao Dam collapse.

The Banqiao Dam catastrophe resulted from several engineering errors as well as poor management. First, the Banqiao dam had been designed for a calculated 1-in-a-1000-year rainfall event of 300 millimeters per day. However, during Typhoon Nina, some 1060 millimeters of rain fell in just one day. Second, the original engineering design of the dam called for 12 sluice gates to allow the controlled release of water. Management of the project approved only 5 such gates to reduce cost, and even these gates were rendered ineffective due to sediment blockage during the accident. In

---

19 See more: 1975 Banqiao Dam Failure, https://en.wikipedia.org/wiki/1975_Banqiao_Dam_failure. Accessed: Jan. 2023.

addition, the dam suffered numerous structural faults and cracks, which appeared immediately after its completion and were not corrected properly.

5.4.3.4 The Bhopal Industrial Disaster (1984)

The horrific Bhopal industrial disaster occurred at the Union Carbide India pesticide plant in Bhopal, India, on December 3, 1984. Over 40 tons of methyl isocyanate (CH_3NCO), a highly toxic gas used in pesticide production, became contaminated with water. This exothermic chemical reaction increased the temperature and pressure inside its container vessel. As a result, safety relief valves, designed to prevent an explosion of the container vessel, automatically released a massive quantity of this toxic gas into the atmosphere. As a result, some 40 metric tons of heavier-than-air toxic gas floated along with a southeasterly wind into the nearby city of Bhopal. This catastrophe, considered the world's worst industrial disaster, caused 11,000 deaths and more than 550,000 injuries, including about 40,000 "temporary partial" and nearly 4000 "severely and permanently disabling" injuries. Figure 5.17 depicts the Union Carbide pesticide factory in Bhopal.

Figure 5.17   Union Carbide pesticide factory in Bhopal, India (1985).

The Union Carbide pesticide factory remains ruined and abandoned. However, nearly 40 years after the debacle, some 350 metric tons of toxic waste are stored above ground. In addition, many thousands of tons of toxic waste are buried at the local sites untreated. Rainwater continues to run through this buried waste as well as the remains of several abandoned solar evaporation ponds, polluting the groundwater in the Madhya Pradesh region. The land around Bhopal remains blighted and toxic to humans and animals alike.

5.4.3.5 The Space Shuttle *Challenger* Disaster (1986)

The American space shuttle *Challenger* disaster occurred on January 28, 1986. On this calm morning, the *Challenger* spaceflight STS-51L embarked upon its tenth flight, but the vehicle exploded and disintegrated just 73 seconds into the flight.

The crew cabin detached from the wreckage in a single piece and crashed into the ocean at approximately 330 kilometers per hour. All aboard were killed either during the vehicle's disintegration or by the impact's immense force.

The accident occurred due to a joint seal (O-ring) failure at the right solid rocket booster, designed to ensure adequate thermal insulation from the external fuel tank. As a result, hot gas and flames escaped the booster and ignited the external fuel tank, leading to the explosion of the external fuel tank and the disintegration of the *Challenger* space shuttle.

The limited temperature operation of the O-rings had been well known at NASA for nine years but had been ignored. According to Thiokol, the solid rocket booster manufacturer, the O-rings could ensure sufficient sealing capacity only above 12 °C. However, NASA officials disregarded severe warnings from engineers at Thiokol and within NASA. Instead, they proceeded even though the air temperature at the time of the space shuttle *Challenger* launch was 2 °C (Figure 5.18).

Figure 5.18 Ice on the launch tower shortly before the *Challenger* launch.

In the aftermath of the disaster, NASA ordered Thiokol to redesign the solid rocket boosters, incorporating three O-rings instead of the original two. In addition, NASA created an independent decision-making and oversight group where management could consider engineering opinions carefully. Finally, NASA added several checkpoints in the space shuttle administration, including a new NASA safety office and a shuttle safety advisory panel.

5.4.3.6   The Chernobyl Nuclear Power Plant Disaster (1986)

The Chernobyl disaster started on April 26, 1986, at the Chornobyl Nuclear Power Plant near Pripyat in Ukraine, the Soviet Union. The disaster began during a maintenance shutdown, which was utilized to conduct a loss of power test. The test was intended to determine if the turbine would still provide energy to the system to run the cooling water pumps. Testing was conducted during the weekend, at night, when only a skeleton crew of operators remained at the Chernobyl power plant. The operators, by the way, were skilled at running the plant daily, but no one had any nuclear physics background. Also, as it happened, running this test necessitated turning off all the reactor's safety measures.

In contrast to the operators' expectations, the reactor quickly became critical. It exploded, destroying the Unit 4 reactor and causing an open-air graphite fire that sent a massive plume of highly radioactive fallout into the atmosphere (Figure 5.19).

Figure 5.19   The nuclear reactor disaster at Chernobyl, Soviet Union.

Firefighters from the nearby town of Pripyat rushed to the scene, trying heroically to extinguish the conflagration but, having no training whatsoever in dealing with nuclear fire and having no appropriate protective gear, made a bad situation substantially worse, succumbing very quickly to radiation sickness. Most of them died soon after. The contamination spread over most of Europe and the western Soviet Union, requiring the evacuation and resettlement of 350,400 people. Some 30,000 to nearly 1 million individuals living in the broader geographical area are expected to experience premature deaths from cancer and other related diseases. A 2,600-square-kilometer area surrounding the town of Pripyat was defined as an exclusion zone that will not be habitable by humans for the next 20,000 years.

From 1986 to 1989, the military, having been assigned to decontaminate, bury, and clean the Chernobyl immediate area, used some 340,000 reservists and young military recruits from all regions of the Soviet Union for a six-month voluntary stint at Chernobyl. Unfortunately, the vast majority did not have any protective gear and knew very little of the dangerous assignment they were engaged in.

As could be expected in the Soviet Union, the initial accident investigation, released in 1986, blamed the management and operators of the plant for the disaster. Still, a subsequent report, released in 1992, identified extensive engineering and design faults within the facility, including the preliminary design of the control rods and lack of operator training. All in all, it was recognized that virtually all nuclear reactors in the Soviet Union, based on graphite as a nuclear moderator, were fundamentally dangerous and should be phased out (Plokhy, 2018).

5.4.3.7 The Hubble Space Telescope Failure (1990)

The Hubble space telescope, a marvel of engineering and scientific instrument, was launched into low Earth orbit[20] in 1990. After several refurbishing and instrument replacements, the Hubble has remained in operation ever since. Hubble's space location avoids the Earth's atmospheric distortion and encounters substantially lower background light. Over the years, Hubble has captured an extensive array of high-resolution images that have offered insight into immensely remote galaxies of the Universe. Figure 5.20 depicts the Hubble space telescope's 2.4-meter primary mirror, fabricated at Perkin-Elmer's large optics fabrication facility.

Immediately after the Hubble launch, operators found that all incoming images were blurred and out of focus. The problem was traced to a tiny aberration (1/50 the thickness of a human hair) in Hubble's primary mirror, which Perkin-Elmer manufactured.

---

20 A low Earth orbit is a rotation around the Earth with a period of 128 minutes or fewer and an eccentricity of less than 0.25. Eccentricity determines the amount the orbit may deviate from a perfect circle.

Figure 5.20 Hubble space telescope primary mirror.

Replacing the primary mirror was impractical, so during a shuttle mission in 1993, astronauts installed a set of corrective optics on Hubble that countered the flaw's effects. All in all, between 1993 and 2009, astronauts visited Hubble five times, first to repair the optical system (at a cost of more than $2 billion) and then to replace limited-life items such as batteries and gyroscopes and install new scientific instruments.

5.4.3.8 New Orleans Levee Failures (2005)

The New Orleans levee catastrophe occurred after Hurricane Katrina, which made landfall on August 29, 2005. Consequently, the storm surge caused the breaching of more than 50 hurricane protection levees along the seafront and the Mississippi River. These failures enabled more than 80 million cubic meters of water to spill into the inner city of New Orleans and flood more than 100,000 homes and businesses (Figure 5.21). At the height of the debacle, an estimated 80% of New Orleans was flooded, which ushered in a death toll of more than 1,800 persons.

Four major investigations concluded that the primary cause of the flooding was inadequate design and construction by the US Army Corps of Engineers (ACE). The primary mechanisms of the failure of the levees and floodwalls were identified as (1) improper design of the canal floodwalls, (2) overtopping of not sufficiently high levees and floodwalls by the storm surge, (3) the existence of sand in 10% of

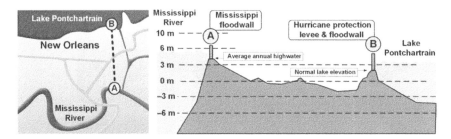

Figure 5.21 New Orleans topology (dotted line describes the A–B cross-section).

places instead of thick Louisiana clay, and (4) overtopping of levees and floodwalls due to negligent maintenance.

In the years after Hurricane Katrina, ACE replaced more than 560 kilometers of levees, floodwalls, and surge barriers, and all are much more robust than before. In addition, ACE built large pump stations in several of New Orleans' key locations.

5.4.3.9 The Fukushima Daiichi Nuclear Disaster (2011)

The Fukushima Daiichi nuclear disaster was initiated on March 11, 2011, by a magnitude 9.1 underwater earthquake with an epicenter about 70 kilometers east of the Oshika Peninsula, some 450 kilometers northeast of Tokyo, Japan. The earthquake triggered a 15-meter-high tsunami that reached the nuclear power plant 50 minutes later, sweeping over the seawall, flooding the four reactors' lower parts, and disabling the emergency diesel generators (Figure 5.22).

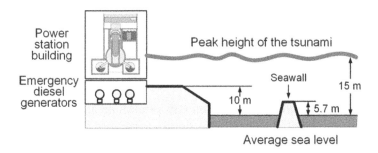

Figure 5.22 Topology of the tsunami and the Fukushima Daiichi nuclear facility.

Japan's Fukushima Daiichi nuclear power plant was one of the world's largest nuclear power stations. It had of six boiling water reactors (BWRs) constructed and run by the Tokyo Electric Power Company (TEPCO), producing a combined power of 4.7 gigawatts. Remarkably, the emergency diesel generators and batteries, which were critical to the survival of the Fukushima Daiichi power plant in an emergency, were located in the basements of the reactor buildings.

Note that providing electricity to a nuclear station—from outside sources like the national electric grid, from the nuclear station itself, or from emergency generators—is vital for the survival of the station. In particular, electricity is needed to power the pumps circulating coolant water through the reactors' cores and monitoring and controlling the reactors.

As it happened, TEPCO's management ignored several critical studies stressing the risks of earthquakes and the system's vulnerability to the loss of grid power. Similarly, TEPCO's management ignored reliable studies regarding the risk from potential tsunamis, which could easily overcome the seawall with waves of more than 10 meters and liable to flood the emergency diesel generators and batteries. Upon detecting the earthquake, all active reactors automatically terminated their everyday operations. As predicted, the earthquake brought down the regional electrical grid, so all the reactors' electricity needs became dependent on emergency diesel generators and a few batteries.

All external power was lost to units 1–4, and all battery power was eventually exhausted. In addition, several steam-driven pumps that provided cooling water to reactors 2 and 3 had ceased operation. As a result, the reactors began to overheat, leading to meltdowns in reactors 1, 2, and 3. This process was followed by three hydrogen explosions occurring in units 1, 2, and 3 (Figure 5.23). Reactors 5 and 6 were not operating when the earthquake struck, and they achieved a successful cold shutdown.

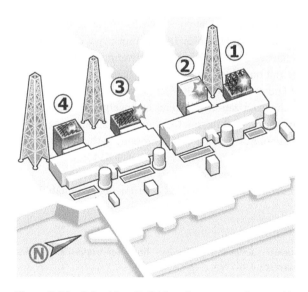

Figure 5.23 Fukushima Daiichi nuclear power plant accident diagram.

Immense amounts of radioactive material were released into the environment during uncontrolled events, venting high-pressure gas into the atmosphere and discharging radioactive coolant water into the sea. Despite sophisticated efforts, seawater continues seeping into the reactors' grounds, mixing with radioactive debris. This contaminated water is stored in large tanks on site and is partially treated to remove radionuclides, except tritium. However, by 2022, space for storage on-site had been exhausted, requiring a controlled spillage of radioactive water into the sea. Following the nuclear accident, some 154,000 residents had to be evacuated from areas up to 20 kilometers from Fukushima Daiichi, the disaster's epicenter.

Several Fukushima nuclear accident investigations were established to identify the disaster's causes and propose policies designed to minimize the damage and prevent the recurrence of similar incidents.[21] The National Diet of Japan found that the causes of the accident had been foreseeable, and the plant operator, TEPCO, had failed to meet basic safety requirements such as risk assessment, preparing for containing collateral damage, and developing evacuation plans. The International Atomic Energy Agency (IAEA) charged the Ministry of Economy, Trade, and Industry with an inherent conflict of interest as the government agency in charge of both regulating and promoting the nuclear power industry. Furthermore, the Japanese nuclear regulatory agency was severely blamed for promoting nuclear industry interests due to the corrupt amakudari[22] system.

5.5 Bibliography

Bloch, M., Blumberg, S., and Laartz, J. (2012, October 1). Delivering large-scale IT projects on time, on budget, and value. McKinsey Digital. https://www.mckinsey.com/business-functions/mckinsey-digital/our-insights/delivering-large-scale-it-projects-on-time-on-budget-and-on-value#. Accessed: Jan. 2023.

Davidz, H.L., Jackson, S., and Thomas, L.D. (July 2018). Systems engineering pathology: Comprehensive characterization of systems engineering dysfunction. INCOSE International Symposium, Washington, DC, July 7–12, 2018.

Engel, A. and Reich, Y. (2015, July). Advancing architecture options theory: Six industrial case studies. *Systems Engineering Journal* 18 (4): 396–414.

GAO-08-467SP. (2008). *Defense Acquisitions: Assessments of Selected Weapon Programs.* Report to Congressional Committees. US Government Accountability Office (GAO).

---

21 See more: Fukushima nuclear accident, Wikipedia. https://en.wikipedia.org/wiki/Fukushima_nuclear_accident. Accessed: Jan. 2023.

22 Amakudari is the institutionalized practice whereby Japanese senior government officials retire to high-paying positions in the private sector (for services rendered).

ISO/IEC/IEEE 15288:2023. (2023). *Systems and Software Engineering: System Life Cycle Processes*. International Organization for Standardization (ISO).

Katina, P.F. (2015, Jan.). Emerging systems theory–based pathologies for the governance of complex systems. *International Journal of System of Systems Engineering* 6 (144): 144–159.

Maier, M.W. and Rechtin, E. (2000). *The Art of Systems Architecting*, third edition. CRC Press.

Owen, P. and Rice, T. (1999). *Decommissioning the Brent Spar*. CRC Press.

Plokhy, S. (2018). *Chornobyl: History of a Tragedy*. Penguin Books.

RAENG. (2010). *Philosophy of Engineering*. Volume 1 of the proceedings of a series of seminars held at The Royal Academy of Engineering, Royal Academy of Engineering (RAENG), London.

Schlager, K.J. (1956, July). Systems engineering: Key to modern development. *IRE Transactions on Engineering Management* 3: 64–66.

Troncale, L.R. (2019). Integrating lists of recurring SE human systems problems. INCOSE International Workshop (IW'19), Torrance, CA, January 26–29, 2019. Joint Systems Science Working Group and Natural Science Working Group (SSWG/NSWG), IW'19 on Recurring SE Dysfunctions and Systems Pathology.

6

Comparative Analysis - Two Domains

Authors: David D'Onofrio[1], Avner Engel

6.1   Introduction

As mentioned, systems science is an interdisciplinary field that studies systems in nature, society, and engineering. Knowledge of systems science provides a common language and intellectual framework for practitioners and researchers in many fields and domains. One of the priorities of systems science is to search for structural and functional similarities as well as integrative concepts that transcend disciplines. A particular focus is on reaching conclusions based on analogies, especially using organismic and functionalist ideas, and describing phenomena in different disciplines.

More specifically, when two systems (A and B) are to be compared, they are considered functionally equivalent if one or more functions that are intrinsic to system A can also be identified in system B. If this functionality can exist in both systems, they are deemed functionally equivalent, even if they are physically different.

This chapter, adapted with permission from D'Onofrio and An (2010), provides a comparison and shows the functional equivalence between aspects of a computer hard drive (CHD) and a DNA hard drive (DHD). First, this comparison is made by identifying four essential properties of information for a centralized storage and processing system: (1) orthogonal uniqueness, (2) low-level formatting, (3) high-level formatting, and (4) translation of stored information to a usable form. Then the complementary aspects of a computer hard drive and DNA complex are categorized using this classification, demonstrating a functional equivalence between the components of the two systems and, thus, the systems themselves.

---

1 Adapted with permission from D'Onofrio and An (2010).

Systems Science for Engineers and Scholars, First Edition. Edited by Avner Engel.
© 2024 John Wiley & Sons, Ltd. Published 2024 by John Wiley & Sons, Ltd.

6.2   A Case for Comparison

A biological cell can be viewed as a dynamic information-processing system that responds to and interacts with a varied and changing environment. Cellular actions rely on operations between the genetic information encoded in the cell's DNA and its intracellular information-processing infrastructure (RNA and proteins). The structure and function of this information-processing complex are of great interest in the study of both normal cellular functions and pathological conditions. To better examine these complex behaviors, it may be beneficial to identify the essential aspects of centralized information processing and seek analogous systems through which comparative analysis can be performed.

Focusing on the interactions between cellular data and data processing can lead to a description of a cell as a biomolecular computer. Alternatively, digital computers are highly engineered information-processing systems, and lessons drawn from computer science may provide a framework for comparing an abstract description of a cell's informational and computational elements and the architecture of a computer system. Since the cell is an order of magnitude more complex than the most sophisticated computer system, caution must be exercised when making such analogies. However, establishing a mapping between the properties and functions of a biological cell and a digital computer may allow lessons learned from the design and engineering of computer systems to be transferred into the biomedical arena. These lessons, in turn, can lead to a greater understanding of the dynamic processes and control mechanisms involved in gene regulation and cellular metabolism.

A central common feature of cellular and silicon systems is a dedicated and distinct centralized information storage and processing complex. In a digital computer, this complex is divided into hardware and software. The hardware of a computer consists of the central processing unit (CPU); the disk of the hard drive, including the servo mechanisms attached to the hard drive; random access memory (RAM); read-only memory (ROM); controllers; and I/O peripherals. The software is a set of instructions that tells the hardware to implement computations and process information. The software consists of the organization of the data; the rules for accessing, storing, and processing it (its format); its operating system; and its users' programs.

Using these definitions, we consider the hardware of the cellular information-processing complex to be represented by its physical, genetic material; its gene expression machinery; and the physical components of the cell (proteins, enzymes, etc.). The cell's general architecture and spatial organization as well as its effect on the manifestation of biochemical laws, can be compared to a computer's instruction set architecture (ISA). The cell's software aspect is represented in its genome sequence's informational content (i.e., the specific pattern of nucleic acids).

The aspects of the DNA sequence that code the structure and function of the molecular machinery of DNA replication, RNA transcription, and protein assembly through translation are analogous to a computer's software instructions concerning its basic input/output system (BIOS) and its operating system. A cell's centralized information-processing complex, composed of its DNA and associated molecular machinery, is analogous to a digital computer hard drive (CHD) and operating system. This descriptive framework is established via comparative analysis between the CHD's architecture and function and eukaryotic[2] DNA's structure and function, defined as the DNA hard drive (DHD).

6.3 Structure and Function of a Computer Hard Drive (CHD)

A computer hard drive (CHD) is the central storage unit containing information about the data, programs, and operating systems that govern digital computers. Modern hard drives can store over 16 terabytes (16 trillion bytes) of coded information, and this is increasing as technology develops. Hard drives store information in magnetized dipole regions of their disk containing magnetic flux lines. The magnetic flux is written to and read from a component known as the servo head. The servo head consists of write and read devices colocated within the control mechanism. It moves radially across the hard disk until it reaches a preset position, where it reads or writes information to the disk. One or more disks may be stacked on each other, forming information cylinders. Figure 6.1 shows a computer hard drive with multiple disks and read/write heads. However, the cylinder will be ignored for this discussion, and the description will be simplified to a single disk.

Figure 6.1 Computer hard drive.

---

2 Eukaryote – Any cell or organism that possesses a clearly defined nucleus. A nucleus is composed of protoplasm encased in a double membrane, directing the cell growth, metabolism, and reproduction.

6.3.1 Property 1: Orthogonal Uniqueness of Magnetic Information

Data stored in any centralized system must exhibit integrity that enables it to be stored and retrieved without ambiguity. Typically, magnetizing regions on a CHD disk consist of north–south (logical 0) or south–north (logical 1) dipoles. Figure 6.2 depicts a typical magnetic disk surface. It shows a pattern of bits: 0 1 1 1 0. By definition, whether represented as magnetic flux, optical bits, or other logical entities, CHD data is considered orthogonal if each data element is unique, is independent, and has no cross-talk characteristics.

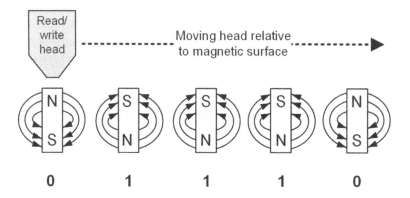

Figure 6.2 Magnetic disk surface structure.

6.3.2 Property 2: Low-Level Formatting of the Computer Hard Drive (CHD)

Organization of the data structures on the CHD is critical for the proper and reliable execution of computer programs. A low-level formatting perspective describes how the CHD is organized so that specific data occupies specific physical space on the hard drive disk.

Information stored on a hard disk is recorded in tracks that are visualized as a thin concentric circle placed on a disk. It would not be efficient for one track to serve as the smallest information storage unit. Programs may not need all the space provided by one complete track. Sectors subdivide tracks into smaller, more manageable units utilizing more functional storage.

A sector subdivides tracks by introducing radially oriented discontinuities in them. This "pie slice" approach of dividing tracks into multiple sectors results in uneven sector lengths. This issue is addressed by creating zones of composite sectors to allow a more even distribution of storage space across the disk. Zoned bit recording organizes the sectors into zones based on their distance from the disk center. Each zone is assigned several sectors per track. Movement from the inner tracks occurs through sectors of arc length with increasing circumference; each zone shows an increase in the number of sectors per track but a corresponding decrease in arc length.

This technique allows for more efficient use of the tracks on the perimeter of the disk and allows the disk to have greater storage capacity. With this configuration, the space made available to hold data has been organized in two-dimensional space to maximize the number of bits per storage unit. In addition, further classifications of functioning and nonfunctioning sectors are identified and cataloged. This information is used by both the CHD controller and operating system so that data is not written to or read from these nonfunctioning sectors.

Each sector has embedded information regarding location, identification, and data attributes within its regions as part of the low-level formatting process. For example, the CHD information that identifies every cylinder and track is called the track index. The track index tells the servo drive electronics where each track starts. In addition, information is provided in a region preceding every sector that guides the servo head to place itself precisely onto the requested track.

6.3.3 Property 3: High-Level Formatting of the Computer Hard Drive (CHD)

The computer's operating system uses higher-level data formatting to locate specifically targeted data packets for storage and retrieval from the CHD. Different operating systems use various ways to control and organize data for storage on media such as hard drives. Operating systems must manage information storage efficiently, which is accomplished through developing partitions and other logical structures on the CHD.

Partitioning the CHD disk is the act of defining areas on the disk that are operationally distinct, each containing the operating system(s) and files that the computer will use. Partitioning divides the hard disk into pieces called logical volumes. Given the number of files and directories that need to be organized for efficient storage and retrieval, these data objects are grouped according to a type of subject or classification paradigm. Files that share some standard functionality or need to share a common space for organizational reasons are grouped into regions called volumes. An operating system uses these logical structures to organize data stored on a medium using a particular file system. A single extended partition can contain one or many volumes of various sizes. Volumes can manifest themselves in drives such as the C: drive and D: drive (commonly used on PCs).

These volumes are part of an organizational method used by a system called file allocation table (FAT). They are part of the high-level formatting operation implemented through software in the disk operating system (DOS). Each partition or volume is put through the high-level formatting process by creating the FAT. Functional sectors, zones, and "bad" sectors where data cannot be written are identified, cataloged, and stored in the FAT. Once this mapping has been implemented, further layers of the organization fit the files and directories contained in the partitions and volumes to assigned sectors on the hard drive. Finally, sectors are grouped into larger blocks called clusters, which occur during the FAT creation. A cluster is now the smallest defined unit of disk space for data storage. For example, if a cluster is determined to contain four sectors equivalent to 2048 bytes (a byte contains 8 bits of data) and a file contains 2000 bytes, then the file is allocated one cluster (Figure 6.3).

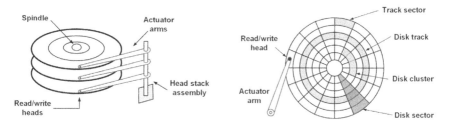

Figure 6.3   Computer disk physical structure and data format.

6.3.4   Property 4: Translation and Access of the Magnetic Information via the Hard Drive Controller

A hard drive controller is necessary to interpret application program interface (API) commands to locate and retrieve data on the disk by steering the servo head to those locations. A servo control system allows the servo head to find the proper location specified by the FAT table. Once there, the servo head reads the data one bit at a time, which is converted to an electrical signal, decoded in hardware, filtered, and loaded into a buffer. Finally, the data is transferred to the system bus via basic input/output system (BIOS) operations. The hard drive controller responds to the previously described low-level formatted information regarding the track index and the grey code. This mechanism allows the servo drive to be positioned accurately onto the right track, allowing the servo head to precisely read or write information from/to the disk.

In the CHD, each sector has its beginning section reserved for management and control information. In addition, each sector contains a portion of space reserved for information-identifying attributes of each sector called the header region. The header contains identification information that the CHD controller uses to identify each sector number and location relative to its track and provides synchronization controls. Hence, the servo head knows where the data begins and ends. It also provides error-checking code to ensure data integrity and indicate if the sector is defective or remapped. In modern drives, the header information is removed from the drive and stored in memory in a format map. This map informs the CHD controller of the sectors relative to the servo information.

6.4 Functional Correlations between the CHD and the DHD

Having described four properties of the CHD essential for its function as a system for information storage and processing, we will now describe those aspects of the DHD that also fulfill these four properties. The emphasis of this section is on describing the structure and machinery concerning the role of DNA in terms of the four functional properties of a centralized information-processing complex while noting specific instances where the implementation of the DHD diverges from the CHD.

6.4.1 Correlation 1: Orthogonality of the DNA Genetic Information

Biological systems also rely upon the property of orthogonality of information to minimize the chance of improper interpretation of the genetic language. Control regions such as the promoters, insulator and enhancer sequences, and codons contained in each gene must be represented in a nontrivial and unambiguous manner. DNA nucleotides have specific attributes that contribute to the integrity of the DNA programmatic language. The field of molecular semiotics suggests that a cellular language exists for the instruction set for cellular processes and that this language manifests in the DNA sequence. The information within DNA consists of a quadruple genetic code consisting of quad bits (Qbits) of the nucleotides adenine (A), cytosine (C), thymine (T), and guanine (G)—which represent a base four system. In the context of the DNA molecule, these nucleotides interact with various structural and functional molecules to form the "language" of genetic information. For example, there is a functional equivalence between the orthogonality of the magnetic representation of data on the CHD and the orthogonal representation of information in the form of Qbits on the DHD (Figure 6.4).

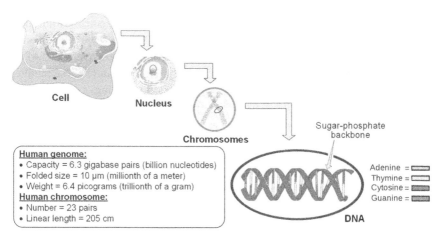

Figure 6.4 DNA within a eukaryotic cell.

Generating various types of RNA from the DNA code converts the coded information into a polyfunctional format throughout the cell. The boundary conditions of the DNA and RNA code arise from integral biochemical properties of the nucleic acids that constrain their possible combinations.[3] The multiple roles of the RNA suggest that RNA may serve as an information interpretation layer similar to the transfer of the magnetic flux encoding of the CHD into electrical voltage logic levels, which are then used everywhere in the computer logic circuitry.

6.4.2 Correlation 2: Low-Level Formatting of the DNA in Eukaryotic Cells

Formatting of the data storage medium represents imposed organizational properties on the medium that facilitate the effective use of the stored information. As human DNA contains about 3 billion nucleotides constituting genes, regulatory

---

3 The interpretation of mRNA in the ribosome represents the "classic" role of RNA as a means of producing proteins. However, other functional RNA such as microRNA (miRNA), large intergenic noncoding RNA (lincRNA), and small interfering RNA (siRNA) serve as critical control elements in cellular information processing.

sequences, and other noncoding regions all residing in a one-dimensional chain organized in three-dimensional space, formatting the DNA data structure is far more complex than that seen in the CHD.

DNA is spatially organized within the nucleus. DNA strands are compacted into chromatin and organized into discrete chromosome territories (CTs). Examination of the subnuclear structure has shown that genes collectively organize within their designated CTs. These regions are anchored to the subnuclear structure by a sequence of matrix attachment regions (MARs) and scaffold attachment regions (SARs). Segments of repetitive DNA are associated with the localization of these binding regions. However, closer examination identifies intervening compartments distributed throughout the nucleus in the space between the CTs. It has been suggested that these compartments create interchromosome domain-containing nuclear bodies that are needed for transcription splicing. These peri-DNA structures demonstrate a level of spatial organization aimed at allocating transcribable domains of active and nonactive genes inside the nucleus (Figure 6.5).

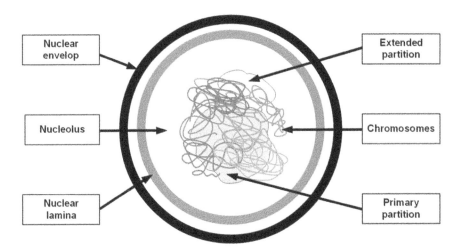

Figure 6.5 Cell nuclear architecture.[4]

The primary function of low-level formatting is to organize the storage space in the DNA/subnuclear hard drive coherently via its subnuclear structure. This organization allows the nuclear machinery to operate upon the euchromatin CTs for copying, splicing, and other regulatory functions. However, a higher-level structural organization is present, and it facilitates the ability of the cellular

---

4 See more: Nuclear organization, Wikipedia. Accessed: Jan. 2023.

machinery to accomplish these tasks and is manifested in the higher-order chromatin domains. The DNA hard drive paradigm can now be assembled using two principles. The first principle involves physical structure (low-level format) and software abstraction (organizational management). The second principle involves the division of the genome into logical pieces called partitions and further organization of the data into volumes and clusters using high-level formatting. Table 6.1 compares the CHD and DHD relative to the low-level formatting process.

Table 6.1 Low-Level Formatting Comparison.

Computer Hard Drive	DNA Hard Drive
Track	The entire DNA strand is one large super track defined by the sugar–phosphate backbone. This super strand exhibits connectivity to the nuclear attachment substrate (NAS) consisting of lamin networks (nuclear lamin regulates replication, transcription, and epigenetic modifications of chromatin).
Sector	The track length encompasses the gene/genes, promoter/ basil transcription complex (BTC) consensus sequences and other outer sites bounded by insulators attached to the nuclear lamina.
Servo information	Promoter regions which are parts of the biological control regions.
Synchronization header	Basil transcription complex consensus sequences enable the sync RNA initiation start site.

6.4.3 Correlation 3: High-Level Formatting of the DNA: Posting a Biological File Allocation Table

Multiple chromosomes in eukaryotic cells can represent multiple "drives" of the DHD. These drives are further divided into primary and extended partitions of euchromatin and heterochromatin (representing control/suppression roles for noncoding DNA). However, the isolation of regions resulting from the "partitioning" of the DHD is not as rigid as in the CHD. In addition, regulatory pathways and metabolic modules may require information that crosses chromosomes, as information for a process initiated on one chromosome can be accessed and acquired from another. Therefore, the functional/logical organization of the DHD calls for further refinement beyond the organization of the CHD.

In a CHD, volumes are logical structures representing the top level (i.e., most inclusive) of file organization. In the DHD analogy, data volumes can be characterized by the content of heterochromatin and euchromatin regions imposed in part by MAR/SAR attachment points and the histone code. There is considerable evidence that nuclear architecture is closely related to genome function and gene expression. The consequences of this spatial organization are evident during cellular differentiation when an alteration in the subnuclear structure enables some types of gene expression while silencing others.

The cluster size is defined by the placement of insulator consensus sequences in the genome that are consequently placed on the DHD by attaching the insulator attachment points to the proper nodal connections on the nuclear lamina. Therefore, the model's genome can be considered a polyfunctional assemblage of nucleotides organized into layers of insulator consensus sequences, regulatory regions, and codons.

Figure 6.6 depicts the organized cluster mapping of DNA to the nucleus. Figure 6.6a shows the DNA strand decomposed into its information structure. The top layer contains the strategic placement of insulators. The middle layer contains the regulatory control regions performing the gene copy process. The bottom layer contains the genes organized into a form that allows coexpression. Figure 6.6b shows the mapping of the insulators to the nuclear lamin substrate to form insulator clusters. These clusters are placed so they structurally partition the genes into organized clusters. The regulatory control regions become specific to the rosette pattern formed from the insulator clusters. This arrangement results in a rosette pattern of genes and their control regions. Figure 6.6c shows the placement of the rosette patterns and the nuclear lamin substrate within the nucleus, which creates the DNA hard drive (the red lines indicate the lamin).

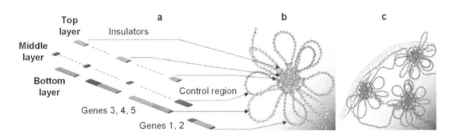

Figure 6.6 Organized cluster mapping of DNA to the nucleus (image: D'Onofrio and an, 2010).

Figure 6.7 depicts a flow chart comparison of high-level formatting models of the DNA hard drive and the computer hard drive. The left-hand side of the figure shows the path for high-level formatting of the DNA molecule. The right-hand side of the figure consists of the computer hard drive, which illustrates high-level formatting processes.

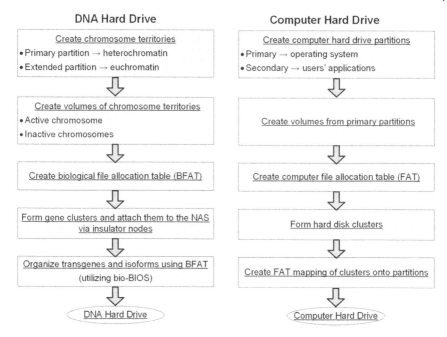

Figure 6.7 Flow chart comparison of high-level formatting of DNA and CHD.

Table 6.2 summarizes the comparison between the high-level formatting of the CHD and that of the DHD.

Table 6.2 High-Level Formatting Comparison.

Computer Hard Drive	DNA Hard Drive
Partitions	The physical compartmentalization of chromosomes and chromosome territories extends to heterochromatin and euchromatin regions. These are imposed partly by the MAR/SAR attachment points, histone code, repetitive DNA, and other noncoding RNA.
Volumes	Logical space is allocated to chromosome territories, including heterochromatin and euchromatin regions.
Clusters	The clustering of insulator nodes defines gene sectors.
File access table (FAT)	Implementing the biological equivalent FAT (BFAT) is manifested by the strategic placement of insulators and enhancer consensus sequences superimposed on the genome. This result insulates clustering with inter-/intracellular communication with the epigenetic system.
	In agreement with the architectural layering of insulator consensus sequences distributed within the genome, BFAT may also be realized within the wetware circuitry of transduction signaling pathways representative of a form of cell firmware.

6.4.4   Correlation 4: Translation and Access of Biological Information via the DNA Transcription Machinery

One of the limitations of the abstract description of a digital computer as a Von Neumann machine is that this representation suggests a linear process: One sequence of DNA leads to one mRNA, which leads to one protein. Clearly, in terms of the cell, this is not the case. The cell manages multiple processes concurrently rather than as a single-threaded sequence. However, despite its multi-threaded computing capacity, a cell retains a single set of chromosomes in a centralized position, both spatially and organizationally. Therefore, to draw our analogy out more completely, the cell is viewed as a complete computational machine in terms that are akin to a multicore computer cluster, where there is a centralized memory and instruction set. Yet, computational tasks are distributed among distinct processing elements. However, to finalize the determination of equivalence between the CHD and the DHD, we will restrict the analogy to a single thread of biological information processing.

For a cell to utilize the information in its chromosome, the intranuclear information encoded in DNA must be converted into a form for use throughout the cell. As alluded to above, the various types of RNA serve as intermediaries in the translation, access, and control of the information encoded in the DNA. The bending of the DNA is a three-dimensional structural change that has no counterpart in the CHD. Because the promoter regions are coupled to their corresponding gene and gene cluster, the protein-centric view of a gene is being reconsidered to include the regulatory and transcriptional regions and other nontranscriptional sequence regions in its definition. It is therefore proposed that the gene, along with its promoter/basal transcription complex, is consistent with the physical layout of the sectors with headers in the CHD and is functionally equivalent to the sectors in the DHD. In both cases, it is up to the controller to identify the requested regions and check and confirm that they are enabled for copying. The controller function comparisons are summarized in Table 6.3.

Table 6.3 Comparison of CHD Controller Functions and DHD Controller Functions.

Computer Hard Drive	DNA Hard Drive
Track index	Unknown (possibly enhancers)
Read head (servo head)	RNA polymerase II (eukaryote)
Synchronization of servo head to read data (located in the header)	Synchronization of RNA polymerase II to initiation start site by proper alignment to the promoter site by transcription factors; this synchronization allows the conformational alignment of RNA polymerase II to the transcription start site (part of the biological header complex)

Table 6.3 (Continued)

Computer Hard Drive	DNA Hard Drive
Identification of active sectors (header)	Implementation of the histone code; in addition, regulatory elements and other possible noncoding RNA influence RNA polymerase II (part of biological header)
Read/write data acquisition through rotation of the disk platter relative to the servo head	Chromatin remolding complex unwinding DNA double helix in conjunction with RNA polymerase II (read head) moving stepwise along the DNA strand
Data buffer and sector editing	Spliceosomes and wetware circuitry of the DHD controller achieve sub-sector editing and multiplexing of both exons and sectors implementation. This machinery reconstructs the requesting genomic information and its derivatives, resulting in a mature mRNA residing in the buffer region of the nucleus
Bios	Bio-BIOS consists of transduction (transfer of genetic material) circuitry resulting in pathways responsible for translating cellular requests into the RNA regulatory language of the DHD

6.5 Conclusions

The comparison of functional and structural characteristics of the DNA complex and the computer hard drive leads to a new descriptive paradigm that identifies DNA as a dynamic storage system of biological information. This system is embodied in an autonomous operating system that inductively follows organizational structures, data hierarchy, and executable operations that are well understood in computer science. Characterizing the "DNA hard drive" in this fashion can lead to insights arising from discrepancies in the descriptive framework, particularly concerning positing the role of epigenetic processes in an information-processing context. Further expansions from this comparison include the view of cells as parallel computing machines and a new approach to characterizing cellular control systems.

Both the DNA complex and the computer hard drive contain components that fulfill the essential properties of a centralized information storage and processing system. The functional equivalence of these components provides insight into the design process of engineered systems and the evolved solutions addressing similar system requirements. However, there are points where the comparison breaks down, mainly when there are externally imposed information-organizing structures on the computer hard drive.

An example is the file allocation table (FAT) imposition during high-level formatting of the computer hard drive and the subsequent loading of an operating system (OS). Biological systems do not have an external source for a map of their stored information or an operational instruction set; instead, they must contain an organizational template conserved within their intranuclear architecture that "manipulates" the laws of chemistry and physics into a highly robust instruction set. It is proposed that the epigenetic structure of the intranuclear environment and the noncoding RNA may play the roles of a biological file allocation table (BFAT) and biological operating system (Bio-OS) in eukaryotic cells.

6.6 Acknowledgments

This chapter is based on D'Onofrio and An's (2010) paper. The author of this book is deeply indebted to Professor D'Onofrio for his permission to embed text and graphics from said paper in this chapter.

6.7 Bibliography

Capelson, M. And Corces V.G. (2004). Boundary elements and nuclear organization. *Biology of the Cell* 96 (8): 617–629.

D'Onofrio, D.J. and An G. (2010). A comparative approach for the investigation of biological information processing: An examination of the structure and function of computer hard drives and DNA. *Theoretical Biology and Medical Modelling* 7 (1): 1–29.

Part II

Holistic Systems Design

7

Holistic Systems Context

7.1 Introduction

Systems context is, by definition, the environment of a system of interest (SoI). Fundamentally, part or all of the system context may influence the SoI or be affected by the SoI. Unfortunately, most systems engineers view systems context very narrowly, considering only a few elements of direct contact with the SoI as relevant.

According to advocates of the narrow view, this limited approach is justified because systems engineers do not have control beyond the boundaries of their system. A more holistic view of systems context recognizes that the broad environment of SoIs has myriad and settled influences over SoIs. Many minor and spectacular engineering failures can be traced to systems whose designers ignored such consequences. In addition to the above, this chapter includes the following elements:

- Rethinking the context of the systems
- Components of systems context

7.2 Rethinking the Context of the System

Systems are part of the universe being studied, whereas the context of the system is the remainder of the universe that lies outside the boundaries of the system. According to the International Council on Systems Engineering (INCOSE), the system under study has been designated the system of interest (SoI), and the relevant remainder of the universe is designated the system context. Since the SoI and the system context have reciprocal relations, the current systems engineering worldview implies that its context must also be explored and understood. All open systems interact with their context by exchanging material, energy, or information. Unfortunately, systems engineers have traditionally tended to somewhat belittle the context of their SoIs, except regarding the most immediate interactions.[1]

However, as we have seen in previous chapters, many systems engineering undertakings fail due to errors often associated with their context rather than the engineered systems themselves. For example, the space shuttle *Challenger* failure in 1986 occurred due to NASA management's decision, against engineering advice, to launch the shuttle when the ambient temperature was much below the permitted level. The 2010 *Deepwater Horizon* oil spill fiasco was blamed on rig operators and contractors for multiple cost-cutting actions and inadequate safety systems. In contrast, the 2011 Fukushima Daiichi nuclear power disaster was related to a significant engineering blunder. However, warnings from geologists regarding loss of grid power due to large-scale earthquakes and risks from mega-tsunamis that could easily overcome the seawall protecting the nuclear power station were ignored by the management of the TEPCO utility company.

Under extreme conditions, complex systems, like the ones described above exhibit emergent behaviors that are difficult to understand or predict. However, the prevalence of failures of such systems can often be attributed to their context. Therefore, systems engineers should be motivated to expand their worldview and pay more attention to the context than they currently do. As discussed before, systems engineers have no control over the various elements that make up the context. However, exploring them and identifying their potential harmful effects on the SoI is essential. Doing so allows engineers to design reasonable defense mechanisms in preparation for a wide range of undesirable contextual impacts (SEBoK, 2023; Stevens, 2005).

7.3   Components of Systems Context

Figure 7.1 depicts a model of an engineered system of interest (SoI) and its context. The SoI should be analyzed through the perspectives of 10 fundamental principles of systems science, which include (1) universal context, (2) boundary, (3) hierarchy, (4) interactions, (5) change, (6) input/output, (7) complexity, (8) control, (9) evolution, and (10) emergence.

In addition, the context of the SoI should be examined through 12 individual context perspectives, which include (1) natural systems, (2) social systems, (3) research systems, (4) formation systems, (5) sustainment systems, (6) business systems, (7) commercial systems, (8) financial systems, (9) political systems, (10) legal systems, (11) cultural systems, and (12) biosphere systems.

The following is a short description of the typical context of a given SoI. A detailed description of typical systems' context is provided in Chapters 9 and 10.

---

1 See more: Environment (Systems), https://en.wikipedia.org/wiki/Environment_(systems). Accessed: Jan. 2023.

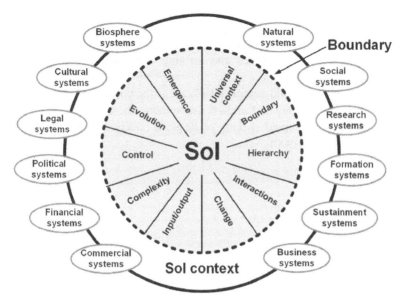

Figure 7.1 System of interest (SoI) and system context.[2]

7.3.1 Natural Systems

Natural systems exist in nature, and, by definition, they are independent of humanity. They comprise the physical and biological materials and their interrelated processes and interactions. All SoIs are affected, in one way or another, by natural systems. Figure 7.2 depicts an example of a natural system, the Bernese Oberland, Switzerland.

Figure 7.2 Natural systems

2 Figure inspired by SEBoK (2023).

7.3.2 Social Systems

Social systems are "the patterned series of interrelationships existing between individuals, groups, and institutions and forming a coherent whole."[3] Most components of social systems affect SoIs in one way or another. Figure 7.3 depicts a caricature of a social pyramid. Simple people are at the bottom; capitalists and rich people above them; army and soldiers above them; the clergy above them; and finally, at the top, Leopold II, king of Belgium (election poster from the Belgian Labor Party, circa 1900).

PYRAMIDE A RENVERSER

La Royauté. — Je règne sur vous.

Le Cléricalisme. — Je prie pour vous.

Le Militarisme. — Je tire sur vous.

Le Capitalisme. — Je mange pour vous.

La Peuple. — Je travaille pour vous.

Figure 7.3 Social systems

7.3.3 Research Systems

Research systems are systemic investigative processes establishing facts and natural principles. They include facilities and appropriate human resources as well as funding resources. By and large, research systems affect SoIs during their various life cycles. Figure 7.4 depicts a technology readiness level (TRL),[4] estimating the maturity of technologies.

---

3 See more: https://en.wikipedia.org/wiki/Social_system#cite_note-:0-1. Accessed: Jan. 2023.

4 See more: Technology readiness level (TRL). https://en.wikipedia.org/wiki/Technology_readiness_level. Accessed Jan. 2023.

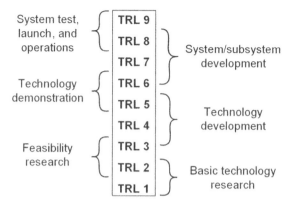

Figure 7.4 Research systems

7.3.4 Formation Systems

"Formation systems create growth, progress, positive change, or the addition of physical, economic, contextual, social, and demographic components."[5] Formation systems include facilities, appropriate human resources, and funding resources to modernize SoIs. They affect SoIs during all phases of the systems' life cycles. Figure 7.5 depicts a generic formation system model comprising definition, design, implementation, integration, qualification, production, and deployment.

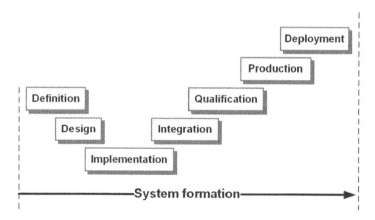

Figure 7.5 Formation systems

---

5 SID Israel. (2021, February). What is development? The Israeli branch of the Society for International Development (SID). https://www.sid-israel.org/en/Development-Issues/What-is-Development. Accessed: Jan. 2023.

7.3.5 Sustainment Systems

Sustainment systems are mechanisms for "keeping an existing system operational and maintaining its ability to manufacture and field updated versions of the systems that satisfy the original and evolving requirements."[6] According to SEBoK (Systems Engineering Body of Knowledge), "Sustainment involves the supportability of operational systems from the initial procurement to disposal. Sustainment is a key task for systems engineering that influences product and service performance and support costs for the entire life of the program."[7] Figure 7.6 depicts the key components of sustainment systems. The figure is based on the SEBoK definition of system sustainment and the US Joint Chiefs of Staff doctrine focus paper: "Sustainment - Insights and Best Practices Focus Paper."[8]

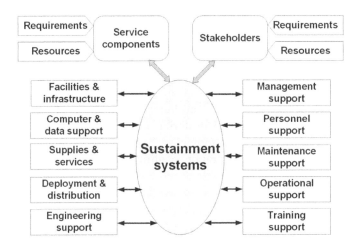

Figure 7.6 Sustainment systems

7.3.6 Business Systems

Business systems are enterprising entities engaged in commercial, industrial, or professional activities. Business systems constitute a combination of policies, personnel, equipment, and computer facilities designed to coordinate the governing of relevant organizations. Business systems affect SoIs in multiple ways.

---

6 Sandborn and Myers. (2008). Designing engineering systems for sustainability. https://www.semanticscholar.org/paper/Designing-Engineering-Systems-for-Sustainability-Sandborn-Myers/b99d488bf843f76c7ec1869d8230270fb1a02e73. Accessed: Jan. 2023.

7 See: https://sebokwiki.org/wiki/Service_Life_Management#:~:text=Sustainment%20involves%20the%20supportability%20of,entire%20life%20of%20the%20program. Accessed: Jan. 2023.

8 See: https://www.jcs.mil/Portals/36/Documents/Doctrine/fp/sustainment_fp.pdf?ver=2018-05-17-102011-017. Accessed: Jan. 2023.

Figure 7. 7 depicts the components of business systems: intelligence, planning, engineering, purchasing, sales, accounting, human resources (HR), and finance.

Figure 7.7 Business systems

7.3.7 Commercial Systems

Commercial systems are objects conceived, designed, produced, and marketed solely for economic profit. Commercial systems affect the SoIs in multiple ways. Figure 7.8 depicts the production line of the Cromemco C-10 computer (circa 1983).

Figure 7.8 Commercial systems

7.3.8 Financial Systems

Financial systems are mechanisms of interacting institutions and markets aiming to maintain investments and payments within commercial activities. They include banks, credit card companies, insurance companies, accountancy companies, stock brokerages, investment funds, and individual managers. Financial systems affect SoIs in multiple ways. Figure 7.9 depicts a caricature of J.P. Morgan as a bull blowing bubbles of inflated values for which people are reaching (Wall Street bubbles - Always the same - Keppler 1901. Source: Puck (magazine), Vol. XL, No. 1264, centerfold).

Figure 7.9 Financial systems

7.3.9 Political Systems

Political systems are mechanisms for making official governing decisions. They affect SoIs by combining factors like the prevailing political systems at the federal, state, and local political levels, as well as the government's overall policies. In general, stable and functioning political systems are essential to the stability and success of SoIs. Naturally, political systems affect SoIs in numerous ways. Figure 7.10 depicts a caricature of William Pitt wearing a regimental uniform and hat while dining with Napoleon. Each carves the world, which is depicted as a large plum pudding (drawing: James Gillray, 1805).

Figure 7.10 Political systems

7.3.10 Legal Systems

Legal systems are "procedures and processes for interpreting and enforcing the law."[9] They affect SoIs through the endurance of the legal framework. Also, well-defined and adhered-to national and international laws are essential to the stability and success of SoIs. Figure 7.11 depicts an engraving of the code of Hammurabi scrawled on a stela created in 1750 BC. This relief shows Hammurabi standing before a seated Shamash, the Babylonian sun god, receiving a legal text containing 282 of the most advanced ancient civil laws.

Figure 7.11 Legal systems

7.3.11 Cultural Systems

Cultural systems are societal attributes of species. Among humans, they are typically comprised of knowledge, beliefs and religion, customs and habits, laws, language, music, and arts. Cultural systems are the interaction of different elements within a culture.[10] They affect SoIs in numerous ways. Figure 7.12 depicts a model of a sociocultural system. The model embodies three concepts: (1) society, which is the collection of interdependent organisms of the same species; (2) culture, which is the learned behaviors and material products that are shared

---

9 See https://www.coursehero.com/file/70657994/A-legal-system-is-a-procedure-or-process-for-interpreting-and-enforcing-the-law-1docx/. Accessed: Jan. 2023.
10 See https://en.wikipedia.org/wiki/Cultural_system. Accessed: Jan. 2023.

by a given society; and (3) systems, which are a collection of parts interacting with each other to function as a whole.

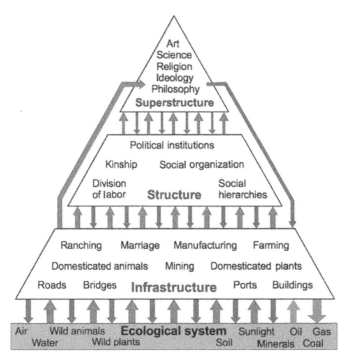

Figure 7.12 Cultural systems

7.3.12 Biosphere Systems

The biosphere consists of living organisms and nonliving components on Earth. It consists of parts of the following: (1) the lithosphere, which is the thin crust between the Earth's mantle and the atmosphere; (2) the atmosphere, which is composed of a mixture of nitrogen, oxygen, and traces of carbon dioxide, argon, water vapor, and other components; and (3) the hydrosphere, which is the accumulation of water in its common states (solid, liquid, and gas) as well as the elements dissolved in it. The biosphere systems affect SoIs in numerous ways. Figure 7.13 depicts the Earth system comprising the atmosphere, lithosphere, and hydrosphere.

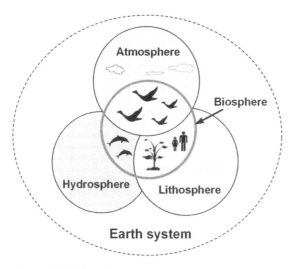

Figure 7.13 Biosphere systems

7.4 Bibliography

Sandborn, P. and Myers, J. (2008). Designing engineering systems for sustainability. In K.B. Misra (Ed.), *Handbook of Performability Engineering*. Springer, London. https://doi.org/10.1007/978-1-84800-131-2_7. Accessed: Jan. 2023.

SEBoK, Guide to the Systems Engineering Body of Knowledge. (May 2023). Cloutier J.R. and Hutchison, N. (Eds.), Version 2.8, INCOSE. https://sebokwiki.org/w/images/sebokwiki-farm!w/0/0a/Guide_to_the_Systems_Engineering_Body_of_Knowledge.pdf. Accessed: Oct. 2023.

SID Israel. (2018, March 11). What is development? Society for International Development (SID) Israel. https://www.sid-israel.org/en/Development-Issues/What-is-Development. Accessed: Jan. 2023.

Stevens, R. (2005). Systems engineering in the information age: The challenge of mega-systems. Presentation to the Naval Post Graduate School Systems Engineering Management Course.

8

Example: UAV System of Interest (SoI)

8.1 Introduction

This chapter provides a comprehensive example of an unmanned air vehicle (UAV) system of interest (SoI). This description focuses on the 10 systems science principles: universal context, boundary, hierarchy, interactions, change, input/output, complexity, control, evolution, and emergence. The following two chapters provide a holistic description of the context of this UAV system.

We define three terms related to unmanned air vehicles: drones, UAVs and UAS. However, users disagree on the exact meanings of the first two terms. Therefore, we will explain the specific definitions adopted for this book.

1. Drones, within the context of this book, are reusable flying unmanned vehicles powered by batteries and one or more electric motors. By and large, drones are relatively small aerial vehicles with limited range and payload capacity, often operated by recreational hobbyists and commercial service providers.
2. Unmanned aerial vehicles (UAVs) are classified by the International Civil Aviation Organization (ICAO) as pilotless (reusable) aircraft that are flown without an onboard pilot and are either remotely controlled from another place or programmed and fully autonomous. In the context of this book, UAVs are powered by liquid fuel and one or more internal combustion engines. By and large, UAVs are larger aerial vehicles with autopilot systems, often operated by government agencies as well as the defense sector.
3. UAS (unmanned aircraft systems) are defined by the US Department of Defense (DoD) as a set of unmanned aircraft, together with their ground control station, data links, and other support equipment. The convention adopted in this book is to use the terms *UAV* and *UAV systems* instead of *UAS*.

Systems Science for Engineers and Scholars, First Edition. Edited by Avner Engel.
© 2024 John Wiley & Sons, Ltd. Published 2024 by John Wiley & Sons, Ltd.

8.2   Example: UAV System

A UAV system generally consists of (1) an unmanned aircraft, (2) a remote pilot station, (3) a command-and-control transceiver, and (4) a payload specific to the intended application/operation. This payload may include cameras or other sensors that collect imagery data. For example, multispectral cameras can be used in agriculture operations to determine the relative health of crops and accurately distribute fertilizer or insecticides. In addition, the command-and-control link of most UAVs will support the transmission of collected data for analysis.

The utility of UAVs has significantly disrupted aviation-related industries. As technology develops, this disruption will likely impact the industries even more. The following example utilizes an unmanned aerial system of interest, demonstrating the 10 perspectives of systems science.

8.2.1   Systems Science Principle 1: Universal Context

An artist's view of the UAV system is depicted in Figure 8.1. The system's mission is to collect ground information in various civilian environments and deliver it in real time to multiple users. UAVs are widely used in modern societies. Their missions may include (1) search, rescue, and emergency response; (2) traffic monitoring and control tasks; (3) city policing and crime prevention; (4) energy and electrical grid monitoring; (5) pipeline (water, oil, and gas) inspection; (6) infrastructure and agriculture surveys; (7) border patrol and coast guard patrolling as well as smuggling prevention; (8) forest protection and wildfire management; and (9) environmental monitoring and the like.

The UAV system in this example encompasses the following subsystems: (1) ground control station (GCS), (2) ground communication (GCO), (3) air system (AS), (4) UAV launcher (LNCR), (5) support equipment (SE), (6) training simulator (TS), and (7) remote terminals (RT).

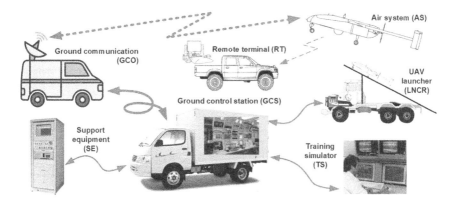

Figure 8.1   An artist's view of a UAV system.

The physical air system used in this example is shown in Figure 8.2.

Figure 8.2 US Navy RQ-2B Pioneer UAV (Image: US DoD).

8.2.2 Systems Science Principle 2: Boundary

As mentioned before, the system's scope and the boundary between the system and its context may be determined arbitrarily by the system engineer. Accordingly, the interior of the SoI includes all the subsystems and components that are (1) needed to fulfill the system's purpose and (2) can be controlled by the system engineers, owners, or managers of the system. The SoI receives inputs from the context of the system or other components within the system, performs the functionality within the system, and then sends outputs to the context of the system or other elements within the system.

As depicted in Figure 8.3, the interior of the UAV system includes the following subsystems: GCS, GCO, SE, TS, AS, LNCR, AS, and RT. The context (environment) of the UAV system includes the following elements: (1) Global Positioning System

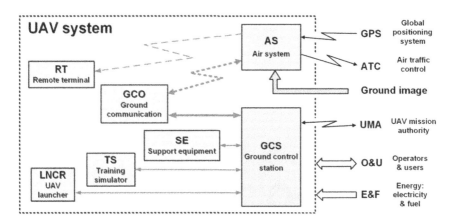

Figure 8.3 UAV system: internal and external components.

(GPS), (2) air traffic control (ATC), (3) ground image, (4) UAV mission authority (UMA), (5) operators and users (O&U), and (6) energy: electricity and fuel (E&F).

8.2.3 Systems Science Principle 3: Hierarchy

Hierarchy is a formal or implied arrangement where people, objects, or processes are organized so that each is placed above, below, or at the same level. Hierarchy is an essential concept in management and systems theories. In addition, hierarchy serves a great purpose in ensuring that every component is appropriately placed vis-à-vis the rest of the system. Finally, a hierarchical structure chart is easy to depict and understand. Figure 8.4 shows the UAV system composed of the ground system (GS) and the air system (AS). The GS is comprises the GCS, GCO, RT, LNCR, SE, and the TS.

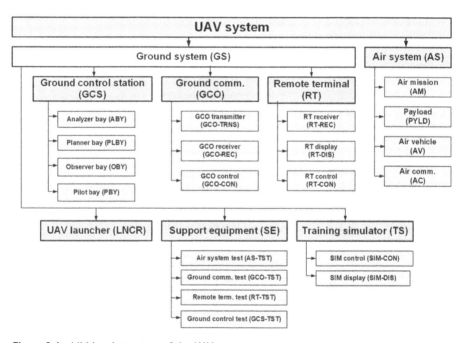

Figure 8.4 Mid-level structure of the UAV system.

8.2.4 Systems Science Principle 4: Interactions

A typical UAV system operational scenario starts when the UAV mission authority (UMA) generates a specific task for the UAV system. This task is transformed by the UAV operators, located at the GCS, into specific commands which are uploaded through the GCO to be executed by the AS. Relevant AS status data as well as daytime video and night infrared images are transmitted from the AS through the GCO to the

GCS. An appropriate subset of this information is then sent to the UAV mission authority. The AS is manually controlled from the GCS or automatically via a UAV mission plan loaded from the GCS and stored onboard the AS. The UAV system may launch the AS manually or automatically from the LNCR or from an airstrip.

Similarly, the AS may be recovered manually or automatically at an airstrip. In addition, the UAV system encompasses support capabilities through the SE and the operator's training simulator (TS). Finally, the AS provides data and ground images to several remote terminals (RT), for the benefit of passive observers located within the transmission range of the AS. Table 8.1 and Table 8.2 depict the UAV system's internal and external interactions.

Table 8.1 UAV Internal Interactions.

From	To	Internal Interaction
GCS	GCO	Control commands to the GCO and AS
GCO	GCS	Video and IR data stream from AS Status data from the GCO and the AS
GCS	SE	Status data from the GCS
SE	GCS	Control commands the GCS
GCS	TS	Control commands to the simulated GCO and AS
TS	GCS	Simulated video and IR data stream from AS Simulated status data from the GCO and the AS
GCS	LNCR	AS launch commands
LNCR	GCS	Status data from the LNCR and AS
GCO	AS	Control commands to the AS
AS	GCO	Video and IR data stream from AS Status data from the AS
AS	RT	Video and IR data stream from AS Status data from the AS

Table 8.2 UAV External Interactions.

From	To	External interaction
GPS	AS	AS position in three-dimensional space
AS	ATC	AS location in three-dimensional space
Ground	AS	Visible and IR images of the ground
UMA	GCS	UAV tasking commands
GCS	UMA	Video and IR data stream from AS Status data from the UAV system

Table 8.2 (Continued)

From	To	External interaction
O&U	UAV	Commands to the UAV system
UAV	O&U	Video and IR data stream from AS
		Status data from the UAV system
E&F	UAV	Electricity and fuel to operate the UAV system

8.2.5 Systems Science Principle 5: Change

As discussed in Chapter 2, the UAV system changes over time, primarily due to the aging and decay of mechanical, electronic, and software components.

1. **Changes in mechanical systems.** Over time, the air system (AS) exhibits the most significant mechanical changes in the UAV system. Mechanical variations are caused by friction between moving parts, corrosion due to chemical reactions, and residue deposition in pipes and other narrow passages. Other mechanical changes often occur due to a creep phenomenon that leads to components' deformation under stress. Finally, some mechanical changes often occur due to fatigue of mechanical parts and failure of components caused by the propagation of cracks that ultimately break the part.

2. **Changes in electronic systems.** The UAV system contains many electrical and electronic subsystems and components. Indeed, many of these components change their electric properties over time, often causing failures at the UAV system level. For example, the following electronic semiconductors are particularly susceptible to aging and decay: integrated electronic systems with analog and mixed-signal (AMS) fabricated using complementary metal oxide semiconductor (CMOS) technology as well as operational amplifiers, ring oscillators, switched capacitors, successive approximation register, and sigma delta analog to digital converters. Similarly, thick-film resistors (TFR) also progressively degrade over time. In addition, under certain circumstances, they tend to increase their resistance by an order of magnitude relative to the original fabrication. Finally, polymer-based insulation materials used in electronic systems, transformers, capacitors, electrical cables, and so on change their dielectric properties over time, causing harmful electrical current leakage.

3. **Changes in software systems.** The UAV system contains many software packages and components. Invariably, this software is modified over time to meet changing stakeholders' needs. Furthermore, modifying software continuously is essential because computers and other hardware components are changing and becoming obsolete. In addition, operating systems and many other software elements are enhanced, and older versions are no longer supported. Maintaining software also causes aging because often, the people

who perform it do not understand the original design concept, thus driving the structure of the programs to degrade. The aging process of the software tends to be exacerbated by the fact that maintainers regularly fail to update the documentation, thereby making future maintenance even more difficult.

8.2.6 Systems Science Principle 6: Input/Output

Figure 8.5 depicts an activity model describing the UAV system's three main processes and their system level, inputs, and outputs. An activity model represents the end-to-end operational process of the system. In other words, such a model shows how specific inputs are transformed into desired outputs. In addition, a control mechanism should include sufficient internal assets and appropriate rules to govern these transformations.

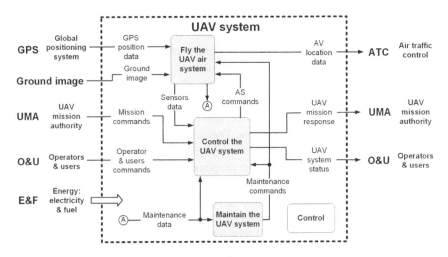

Figure 8.5 UAV system inputs, processes, and outputs.

1. **Fly the UAV air system.** This activity is responsible for bringing the air system (AS) to its destination, acquiring video and IR image data from the ground, and returning the AS to its landing location. The inputs to this activity are GPS position data, ground image, AS commands, and maintenance commands. The outputs from this activity are AV location data, sensor data, and maintenance data.

2. **Control the UAV system.** This activity is responsible for managing the overall UAV system. The inputs to this activity are operators and user commands, mission commands, and sensor data. In addition, inputs to this activity are maintenance commands and maintenance data. The outputs from this activity are AS commands, UAV mission response, and UAV system status.

3. **Maintain the UAV system.** This activity is responsible for the overall maintenance of the UAV system. The input to this activity is maintenance data, and the output is maintenance commands.

8.2.7 Systems Science Principle 7: Complexity

Figure 8.6 depicts a schematic diagram of the UAV system with its data flow. Behind this image lie the fundamental principles of systems science embedded in the UAV system (i.e., universal context, hierarchy, interactions, change, boundary, input/output, control, evolution, and emergence) along with the hardware, software, communication, and so on needed to implement the system.

As discussed in Chapter 3, "Principles of Systems Science (Part II)," there are several complexities, depending on different criteria proposed by systems scientists. Therefore, is the UAV system a complex one? And if yes, to what level?

Reanalyzing Chapter 2 suggests that the UAV system is complex, according to Maier and Rechtin (2000). Still, according to the more stringent definitions advocated by Sussman (2000), Senge (2006), and Gutierrez (2012), it is not. So, the UAV system may be characterized as a complex low-level system.

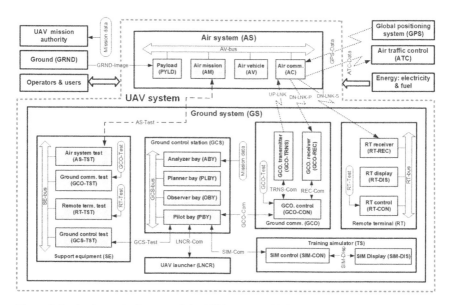

Figure 8.6 A schematic diagram of the UAV system with its data flow.

8.2.8 Systems Science Principle 8: Control

Systems control in living organisms, society, or engineering is echoed through three distinct mechanisms: command, control, and communication (C3 in military jargon). In general, (1) command is the functional exercise of authority based upon a desire to attain an objective, (2) control is the process of verifying and correcting activity such that the original objective will be accomplished, and (3) Communication is the ability to ensure the necessary interface to exercise effective command between relevant actors. Control is impossible unless feedback in some form can take place. So briefly, command and control cannot be accomplished without two-way communication.

In the case of the UAV system, Figure 8.7 depicts the primary external and internal UAV system command, control, and communication flow. The UAV mission authority transmits mission tasking to the UAV system. Operators at the GCS forward these tasking commands to the GCO, which then sends the commands via telemetry to the air system. The air vehicle maneuvers into the desired position and obtains the requested imagery. This information and relevant air system status data are transmitted to the GCO, the GCS, and then to the UAV mission authority. In addition, the air system receives GPS position data and transmits this information to the UAV system's ground portion as well as the air traffic control (ATC). Sometimes, the air system violates its defined air space restrictions. In such cases, the ATC alerts the UAV mission authority, which, in turn, commands the operators at the GCS to take appropriate corrective actions. In addition, the air system uses a secondary channel to transmit ground images and some limited data to one or more remote terminals for passive viewing by selected observers.

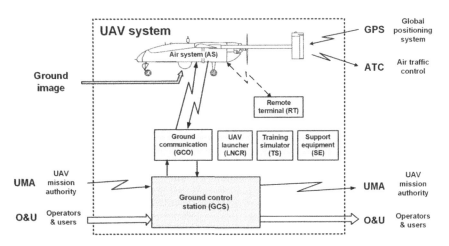

Figure 8.7 UAV command, control, and communication.

The top-level control chart of the UAV system is depicted in Figure 8.8 using Statechart notation.[1] The top-level modes of the system are (1) power off, (2) initiation mode, (3) operation modes, (4) nonoperation modes, and (5) termination mode. The operation modes include (1) automatic takeoff, (2) cruise to target,

---

1 See Harel and Politi (1998); Lavi and Kudish (2001).

(3) perform mission, (4) cruise to home, and (5) automatic landing. The nonoperation modes include (1) maintenance mode and (2) training mode.

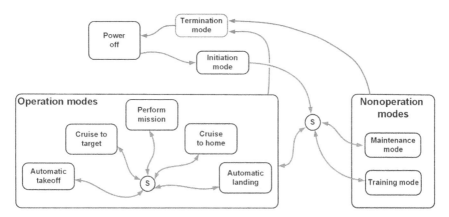

Figure 8.8   UAV system control chart.

8.2.9   Systems Science Principle 9: Evolution

Engineered systems often undergo cycles of adaptation to meet the prevailing stakeholders' needs, which constitute the context of the system. Along this line, an open system has external interactions with its context. Such exchanges may constitute material, energy, or information transfers into or away through the system boundary. Therefore, openness in a system may be defined as the flexibility of the system's design to expand and incorporate components, resources, and functions as well as new ideas, which hitherto were outside the system, into the domain of the system and expand the range of its external system's interactions. For example, in the case of the UAV system, its evolution may involve expanding its payload functionalities as described below.

1. **Expanding existing UAV payload capabilities.** The current UAV payload may be extended by providing the tracking capability of moving objects on the ground. The operator can identify the target and zoom in. At the same time, the onboard processor will hold the moving target in the center of the video screen regardless of the UAV movement or direction. Another UAV payload expansion may include onboard image processing capability. This capability will improve the quality of the image and ensure solid target-tracking performance. In addition, image processing can support data compression, which will significantly reduce the data link bandwidth.

2. **Introducing other UAV payloads.** A new UAV payload may include a phased-array radar. This system uses a grid of antennas that emit radio waves in precisely defined patterns. By controlling this pattern, the radar can scan an entire field of view without moving the device. Phased-array radar is

particularly well suited for UAV operations because it has a reasonably small size, low power requirements, and no moving parts. However, the most significant advantage is that its signals propagate through the atmosphere unaffected by rain, blizzards, or clouds, and they work at any time of day or night.

Another new payload may include a microwave imaging sensor that can penetrate the ground surface and be used for various applications like soil moisture analysis, buried pipeline detection, or mine identification. Yet another payload may include a multispectral imaging camera. In agriculture, for example, remote sensing imaging technology uses green, red, red-edge, and near-infrared frequencies to capture visible and invisible vegetation images. Such information can enhance farming by minimizing pesticides, fertilizers, and water wastage while increasing farms' yield.

3. **Introducing data encryption.** Another evolutionary step may involve encrypting images as well as UAV commands and status data so unauthorized agents cannot eavesdrop on the transmitted information or even seize the air vehicle.

8.2.10 Systems Science Principle 10: Emergence

The concept of emergence has been around since the time of Aristotle. Emergence occurs when a system exhibits properties its parts do not have. These properties emerge when the components of the UAV system interact under specific rules of engagement. Thus, a system's emergent behavior can be ascertained only by understanding its parts and their relationships and governance.

Figure 8.9 depicts the emerging top-level UAV system accomplishments. This artist's view characterizes five phases of acquiring day and night images from afar, which is the fundamental purpose of the UAV system and an objective none of its parts can achieve on their own.

1. During phase 1, the UAV system initiates a manual or automatic takeoff of the air system from an airstrip or from a UAV launcher.
2. During phase 2, the air system cruises to its destination. This cruise is done through manual commands from the ground control station (GCS) or automatically through a mission plan generated at the GCS and uploaded into the air system.
3. During phase 3, the air system performs its mission, which involves flying in a particular pattern over the target and directing its day and night cameras to appropriate locations. This process may be accomplished manually in real time or automatically using a mission plan stored within the air system.
4. During phase 4, the air system cruises back to its home. This cruise is also done by way of manual commands or automatically.

5. Finally, during phase 5, the UAV air system performs a manual or automatic landing at the home airstrip.

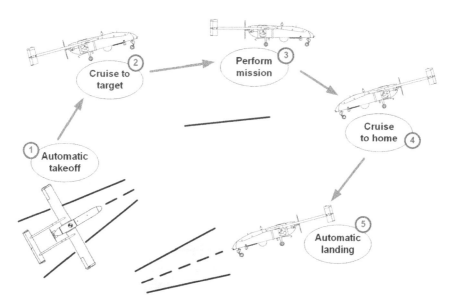

Figure 8.9 Emerging UAV system accomplishment.

8.3 Bibliography

Harel, D. and Politi, M. (1998). *Modeling Reactive Systems with Statecharts: The STATEMATE Approach*. McGraw-Hill.

Lavi, J.Z. and Kudish, J. (2001). *Systems Modeling and Requirements Specification Using ECSAM: An Analysis Method for Embedded and Computer-Based Systems*. Dorset House.

Maier, M.W. and Rechtin, E. (2000). *The Art of Systems Architecting*, second edition. CRC Press.

9

Example: UAV Context (Part I)

9.1 Introduction

As mentioned earlier, most engineers need to appreciate the SoI context's vastness, which affects their systems. For example, some spectacular systems disasters described in Chapter 5 could be attributed to limited engineering attention to the SoI's overall context. The purpose of this and the following chapters is to illuminate the holistic nature of SoI context issues through examples related to the UAV SoI described in the previous chapter.

For clarity, the 12 subtopics of the UAV system context are presented in two chapters. This chapter describes the following UAV system subcontexts: (1) natural system, (2) social system, (3) research system, (4) formation system, (5) sustainment system, (6) business system, and (7) commercial system. The next chapter describes the following UAV system subcontexts: (8) the financial system, (9) the political system, (10) the legal system, (11) the cultural system, and (12) the biosphere system.

As mentioned before, the context (environment) of any given system of interest (SoI) is, by definition, a system of systems that affect the SoI in many ways. Therefore, engineers should thoroughly investigate how their SoI may be affected by its context. Such investigation could lead engineers to design their SoI in a way that will reduce the potential negative impact of these effects. Conversely, engineers are encouraged to take advantage of the positive aspects of these effects.

Systems Science for Engineers and Scholars, First Edition. Edited by Avner Engel.
© 2024 John Wiley & Sons, Ltd. Published 2024 by John Wiley & Sons, Ltd.

9.2 UAV Context: Natural Systems

Definition: Natural systems exist in nature, and, by definition, they are independent of humanity. They comprise the physical and biological materials and their interrelated processes and interactions. All SoIs are affected, in one way or another, by natural systems.

This analysis describes the natural systems context of the UAV SoI. These biological systems, that is, the global environment, are mainly affected by the disposal of UAV systems and other electronic and electrical waste. In turn, the global environment affects the UAV SoI and, more broadly, society at large.

9.2.1 Electrical and Electronic Waste[1]

Electrical and electronic waste is a form of pollution caused by discarding such products. This waste, also called e-waste, is created when users throw away used equipment upon completing its useful life. In 2019, some 54 million metric tons of e-waste were produced worldwide. China, followed closely by the United States, takes the lead in e-waste creation. However, excessive e-waste generation per capita characterizes most Western developed countries.

The US Environmental Protection Agency (EPA) monitors hazardous waste management systems on a cradle-to-grave basis. The EPA provides the legal and social foundation to keep land and people safe in the United States. In addition, many state, national, and international regulations mandate the safe disposal of certain waste materials and systems. These regulations also require the salvaging of specific substances for industrial recycling.

Within the European Union (EU), there are numerous environmental protection regulations related to electrical and electronic systems. For example, European Union directive 2002/95/EC[2] on "restriction of the use of certain hazardous substances in electrical and electronic equipment," as well as directive 2002/96/EC[3] on "waste, electrical and electronic equipment," are designed to confront the fast-increasing waste stream of electrical and electronic equipment and add to EU measures on landfill use and incineration of waste. Increased recycling of electrical components will limit the total quantity of waste moving into final disposal. Producers will have to take back and recycle their electrical and electronic equipment. This approach will also incentivize designing environmentally efficient systems that consider waste management.

---

1 Portions of this and the next section have been adapted with permission from Engel (2010).

2 Directive 2002/95/EC of the European Parliament and of the Council of January 27, 2003, on the restriction of the use of certain hazardous substances in electrical and electronic equipment.

3 Directive 2002/96/EC of the European Parliament and the Council of January 27, 2003, on waste electrical and electronic equipment (WEEE).

However, as of 2018, only about 20% of global e-waste was documented, collected, and recycled under an adequately controlled environment. This recycling included the retrieval of valuable materials as well as precious and rare-earth metals. Nevertheless, 80% of this global e-waste has yet to be collected for recycling. As of now, it is not even documented, and its fate is unknown.

Solid waste landfill disposal is the most common method for disposing of electrical and electronic components. Consequently, thousands of tons of obsolete systems containing vast quantities of toxic materials enter the waste stream annually. These materials cause severe health problems and significant environmental damage near electronic dump sites. The other "disposable method" is to export them, often illegally, to countries with minimal environmental regulations or enforcement of such rules, for example, China, India, and some parts of South America and Africa. There, inevitably, e-waste ends up in crude and toxic recycling garbage dumps and landfills (Figure 9.1).

Figure 9.1 Men burning electrical wires to recover copper at Agbogbloshie, Ghana.

9.2.2 E-Waste and the Environment

All dumped e-waste poses serious environmental and health issues because toxic chemicals from hazardous materials tend to disperse into the atmosphere as well as leach from the hazardous materials and contaminate the aquifer. The enormous number of obsolete electrical and electronic systems that are disposed of yearly generates massive hazardous waste. In general, waste is dangerous if it is toxic to living organisms, ignitable, corrosive, or reactive, or if it appears on a list of about 100 industrial waste streams (Lippitt et al., 2000). Obsolete e-systems like electrical and electronic equipment, automobiles, industrial machinery, aircraft, and ships often contain hazardous waste. This waste may include contaminated sludge, solvents, acids, heavy metals, and other chemical wastes. Improper waste disposal harms human and animal health as well as the environment, representing a significant economic loss. Table 9.1 lists the potential health hazards of materials commonly used in electronic equipment.

Table 9.1 Hazardous Materials in Electrical and Electronic Systems

Material	Characteristic Location in Systems/Nature of the Hazard
Lead	Lead is a metal used for soldering electronic components onto printed circuit boards and in cathode ray tubes (CRT). Lead causes damage to the circulatory, renal, nervous, and reproductive systems in humans.
Cadmium	Cadmium occurs in specific components such as chip resistors, infrared detectors, semiconductor chips, and batteries. Cadmium and its compounds are toxic to humans and animals, accumulating in their bodies, particularly the kidneys.
Mercury	Mercury is often used in electrical and electronic equipment. For example, it is used in thermostats, sensors, relays, switches, medical equipment, lamps, mobile phones, and batteries. However, mercury can damage human organs, especially the brain and kidneys. In addition, fetus development is highly susceptible to mercury exposure.
Chromium	Chromium is used as corrosion protection for untreated and galvanized steel plates and as a decorative or hardener for steel housings. It is easily absorbed into the human body, where it produces toxic effects within the contaminated cells. Chromium can cause DNA damage and is highly toxic in the environment.
PVC	Polyvinyl-chloride (PVC) is mainly found in cabling and computer plastic housings, although many computer moldings are now made with somewhat more benign ABS[4] plastics. As with other chlorine-containing compounds, dioxin can be formed when PVC burns.
BFR	Brominated flame retardant (BFR) is used in plastic housings of electronic equipment and circuit boards. However, the US Environmental Protection Agency (EPA) identifies toxic chemical compounds that use BFR that could harm humans and animals.
Beryllium	Beryllium is commonly found on electronic motherboards. Beryllium is classified as a human carcinogen because exposure to it can cause lung cancer. However, this metal's primary health concern is inhaling beryllium dust, fumes, or mist.
Phosphor	Phosphor is applied as a coat on the interior of the CRT faceplate. Phosphor is toxic, and its coating contains very toxic heavy metals, such as cadmium, zinc, and vanadium, as additives.
Toners	Toner is stored in plastic printer cartridges. Black toner ingredients have been classified as possibly carcinogenic to humans. In addition, some reports indicate that color toners (cyan, yellow, and magenta) contain heavy metals that are hazardous to animals and humans.

4 ABS (acrylonitrile, butadiene, and styrene) is used to prepare a broad spectrum of plastics that combine the properties of resins and elastomers, offering toughness, high-impact strength, and surface hardness.

9.2.3 Combating Global E-Waste Failures

The US Environmental Protection Agency (EPA) and the European Union devised a pollution prevention strategy to combat global e-waste practices.[5] The idea is to reduce, eliminate, or prevent pollution at its source. This approach is fundamentally different and more desirable than recycling, treatment, or disposal. Moreover, this strategy can recover raw materials and yield cost-effective changes in production and operation.

In particular, design for the environment (DfE) is an advanced design approach aiming to reduce the adverse human health and environmental impacts of products, processes, and services. Here, results are considered across the entire product's life cycle. Using the same rationale, the US EPA has proposed a design for disposal (DfD) approach, which considers how to reuse or refurbish products' end of life. This approach will affect the design of systems and the materials used.

Another approach for combating global e-waste assumes manufacturers are responsible for their products "from the cradle to the grave." As such, they should repossess each product at the end of its life. Presumably, this measure will ensure that e-waste will be diminished, collected, recycled, and reused, with the remaining waste being adequately treated.

For example, as of 2005, the European Union mandated all manufacturers to take back all electrical and electronic waste free of charge.[6] In the United States, Congress has debated national takeback and recycling legislation for many years. However, as this book goes to print, no agreement has been reached among stakeholders (i.e., manufacturers, retailers, recyclers, states, nongovernmental organizations [NGOs], etc.). The bottom line is that the United States has no established federal takeback program. However, without relevant national legislation, some companies in the United States, notably Panasonic, Sony, Toshiba, Canon, and Sharp Corporation, created voluntary takeback programs, offering monetary incentives for recyclable electronic equipment. In addition, this is an excellent way to help conserve resources and protect natural materials.

9.2.4 Implications: The System of Interest and Society

The natural systems context of the UAV SoI, that is, the global environment, affects manufacturers and users of UAV systems and the public. To increase their competitive advantage, UAV manufacturers should design their systems to meet environmental considerations, especially concerning the disposal of their products. Similarly, UAV manufacturers are advised to join takeback and the

---

5 See more: Pollution Prevention (P2) at https://www.epa.gov/p2. Last accessed: Jan. 2023.

6 Based on EU Directive on Waste Electrical and Electronic Equipment (WEEE).

circular economy, offering monetary incentives for obsolete UAV systems. In addition, users of obsolete UAV and drone systems should participate in a takeback program or, in their absence, follow environmentally safe disposal practices.

9.3 UAV Context: Social Systems

Definition: Social systems are "the patterned series of interrelationships existing between individuals, groups, and institutions and forming a coherent whole."[7] Most components of social systems affect SoIs in one way or another.

This analysis describes the social systems context of the UAV SoI. Figure 9.2 and the text below depict this social system in a hierarchical form.

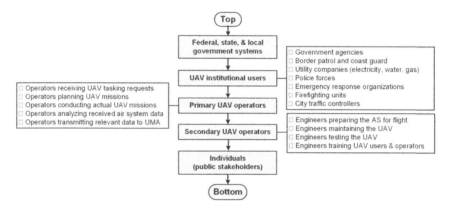

Figure 9.2 UAV context: hierarchical and social system.

1. **Federal, state, and local government systems.** Federal, state, and local governments have hierarchical supremacy over the rest of the UAV system context. These organs define the rules of engagement for the institutions, organizations, and individuals involved and dictate operational standards, activity zone boundaries, and operators' licensing procedures.

2. **UAV institutional users.** The UAV institutional users include (1) government agencies, (2) border patrol and coast guard, (3) utility companies (electricity, water, gas), (4) police forces, (5) emergency response organizations, (6) firefighting units, and (7) city traffic controllers.

3. **Primary UAV operators.** The primary UAV operators include (1) operators receiving UAV taskings requests, (2) operators planning UAV missions,

---

7 See more: https://en.wikipedia.org/wiki/Social_system#cite_note-:0-1. Accessed: Jan. 2023.

(3) operators conducting actual UAV missions, (4) operators analyzing received air system data, and (5) operators transmitting relevant data to UMA.

4. **Secondary UAV Operators.** The secondary UAV operators include (1) engineers preparing the air system for flight, (2) engineers maintaining the UAV system, (3) engineers testing the UAV, and (4) engineers training UAV users and operators.

5. **Individuals (public stakeholders).** These people indirectly benefit from various UAV services. For example, an emergency response team can locate, reach, and help injured individuals faster. Police can identify trouble spots and protect bystanders. Firefighting units can quickly identify fires and extinguish them while watching people in the neighborhood.

Individual components of the federal, state, and local governments; the UAV SoI institutional users; and up to the last UAV operator can, intentionally or unintentionally, bring the UAV SoI down and even cause significant harm to people and property. Therefore, a smooth and successful UAV system operation depends upon the dedicated and harmonious work of a fair number of people who are often distributed in many organizations in different land regions.

9.4   UAV Context: Research Systems

Definition: Research systems are systemic investigative processes establishing facts and natural principles. They include facilities and appropriate human resources as well as funding resources. By and large, research systems affect SoI during its various life cycles.

This analysis describes the research systems context of the UAV SoI. It involves three aspects of advanced UAV systems related to (1) new types of air systems and their operations, (2) new types of payloads, and (3) advanced software that provides new functional capabilities. The technological expansion will likely significantly influence the UAV SoI because it will accelerate its obsolescence.

9.4.1   New Types of Air Systems

This section depicts the following types of UAV air systems: (1) single-rotor UAV helicopters, (2) fixed-wing vertical takeoff and landing (VTOL), (3) multirotor drones, (4) swarm drones' operation, and (5) other types of UAV.

9.4.1.1   Single-Rotor UAV Helicopter

The most crucial advantage of single-rotor UAV helicopters, relative to fixed-wing UAVs, is their ability to hover at the same spot for a long time. In addition, they can carry a relatively heavy payload and have vertical takeoff and landing

(VTOL) properties. They do not need a runway or a catapult to launch them into the air.

However, single-rotor UAVs helicopters are much more complex than fixed-wing UAV, leading to higher operational risks and maintenance costs. Also, flying UAV helicopters is intricate, requiring special training not least because the large rotor blades threaten people and property. Finally, UAV helicopters generate significant vibration, affecting various applications like quality photography. Figure 9.3 depicts a single-rotor Alpha 800 UAV Helicopter manufactured by Alpha Unmanned Systems of Spain.

Figure 9.3 UAV: Single-rotor helicopter.

9.4.1.2 Fixed-Wing VTOL

Fixed-wing VTOL combines the benefits of fixed-wing UAVs with single or multirotor UAVs. Some of these types attach several rotors to the body or wings of fixed-wing UAVs, providing them with VTOL capability. Others rest on their tails on the ground, pointing straight up for takeoff, and then pitch over to fly horizontally. A third variant contains two pivots attached to the end of each of the two wings. This assembly swivels from pointing upward for takeoff to pointing horizontally for forward-motion flights.

The advantage of a fixed-wing VTOL UAV is its VTOL capability, as well as its long-flight endurance. However, the drawback of fixed-wing VTOL UAVs is that their technology is somewhat experimental, and the system exhibits substantial operational risk, especially during the transition from hovering flight mode to forward flight mode.

Figure 9.4 depicts a fixed-wing, vertical takeoff and landing (VTOL) UAV prototype, Greased Lightning, developed by NASA (National Aeronautics and Space Administration) advanced UAV systems research.

Figure 9.4 UAV fixed-wing VTOL (Image: NASA).

9.4.1.3 Multirotor Drones

Multirotor drones are the most common type of UAV used by the public. They are easy to operate, but because of their short flying time (i.e., 20 to 30 minutes) and other limitations, these drones are most often utilized for recreational purposes.

The advantage of multirotor drones is their VTOL capability and general flying stability, which contribute to ease of operations even in a confined space. In addition, multirotor drones are generally safe, easy and inexpensive to manufacture, and readily available to the public. However, the popular and relatively inexpensive multirotor drones exhibit limited flying time, speed, and substantially restricted payload-carrying capacity. These limitations are mainly because multirotor drones require a massive portion of their energy just to overcome gravity and stay in the air. Therefore, they are unsuitable for certain commercial operations like long-distance aerial mapping or surveillance. Figure 9.5 depicts a multirotor XENA-8F coax drone manufactured by OnyxStar.

Figure 9.5 UAV: multirotor drone.

9.4.1.4 Swarm Drone Operation

Swarm robotics offers a promising new technology for coordinating multidrone systems whereby each unmanned aerial vehicle makes its own decisions and acts in concert with information shared by the rest of the swarm. More specifically, a drone swarm can move autonomously, know each other's position, plan the movements of other drones, and avoid collisions between them. In short, a drone swarm can work successfully, exhibiting an emergent behavior that conforms to desired objectives.

Figure 9.6 depicts a swarm of drones demonstrated by the US Air Force (USAF) Research Laboratory Information Directorate in Rome, NY, SWARM project, an evolutionary operational concept of advanced drone system research.

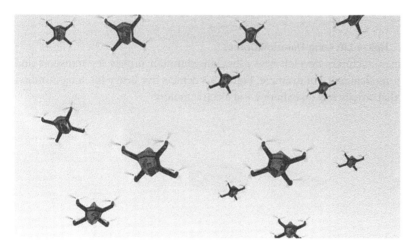

Figure 9.6 UAV swarm drone operation (Image: US DoD).

9.4.1.5 Satellite and Relay Drone Operation

Another example of a UAV swarm application is designed to extend the full range of UAVs capable of flying beyond the limits of the horizon. As depicted in Figure 9.7, long-range UAVs are limited, communication-wise, by the Earth's curvature. For example, a UAV flying at a distance of 200 kilometers must maintain an altitude of at least 3,200 meters to communicate with its ground station. Solutions for this constraint are to utilize a relay UAV or a high-altitude satellite for communication with a distant UAV.

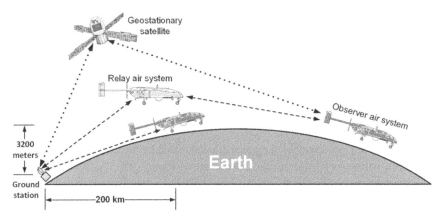

Figure 9.7 Line of sight and Earth's curvature.

9.4.1.6 Heavy-Lift Long-Duration Drones

Some manufacturers develop heavy-lift, long-duration drones for transport and military applications. For example, Figure 9.8 depicts five heavy-lift, long-duration drones that strictly rely on batteries and electric motors.

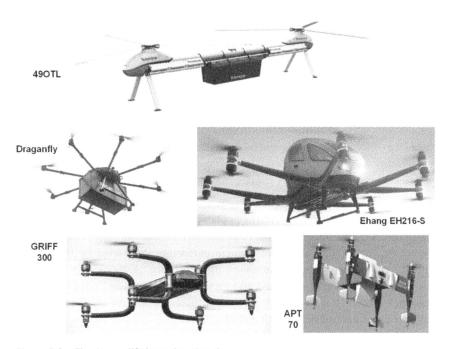

Figure 9.8 Five heavy-lift, long-duration drones.

Table 9.2 presents the unique characteristics of the five drones shown in Figure 9.8.

Table 9.2 Characteristics of the Five Drones Shown in Figure 9.8.

Drone Name	Manufacturer	Max Payload (kg)	Drone Weight (kg)	Range (km)	Flight Duration (minutes)	Max Speed (km/hr)
49OTL	Avidrone Aerospace, Canada	25	26	150	90	100
Draganfly	Draganfly, Canada, US	30	44	30	55	80
APT 70	Bell-APT, US	45	135	56	60	240
EHANG 216L	Ehang H.L Limited, China	220	380	35	20	130
GRIFF 300	Griff Aviation, Norway	225	75	15	45	60

By and large, commercial delivery services could be implemented using a heavy-lift, long-duration, multidrone application. For example, several companies (e.g., Amazon, UPS, etc.) have indicated an interest in using such drones for package delivery. However, this effort has been unsuccessful so far due to many technical, safety, legal, and other issues.

9.4.2 New Payloads and Capabilities

In our context, payloads are any device from which one can obtain information about the context of the UAV. Payloads may be divided into (1) passive instruments, which detect specific signals from the Earth's surface, for example, a sensor that detects reflected sunlight, and (2) active instruments, which emit preliminary irradiation of the relevant objects, for example, radar devices. The UAV SoI consists of two sensors:

1. **Visible-light (VL) sensor.** This imaging sensor covers the visible wavelengths, that is, it provides daytime situational awareness. By and large, it can identify targets and track their movements. Critical features of this sensor are long-range imaging abilities and image stabilization.
2. **Infrared (IRS) sensor.** This sensor produces images based on infrared (IR) radiation emitted from objects. This feature makes it possible to obtain information at night and to find objects by the thermal signature that they generate.

However, the context system consists of more than 10 sensors. This fact poses two challenges to the manufacturers of current UAV systems: (1) Users of UAV systems expect their systems to provide new capabilities by integrating new sensors, and (2) users of UAV systems consider the current system obsolete and opt for replacement by a more capable system. In both cases, the context system significantly influences the current UAV system. The currently available context systems consist of the following sensors:

1. **Near-infrared (NIR) sensor.** This imaging sensor is widely used in diverse remote earth sensing like forestry and agriculture. This sensor and similar ones utilize the characteristics of many chemical and molecular compounds in nature that emit a unique set of spectral emission or absorption lines. These spectral lines identify targets' features when illuminated by a light source.

2. **Ultraviolet (UV) instrument.** This imaging sensor captures images using ultraviolet (UV) light. In the UAV, ultraviolet images may reveal artifacts within archaeological sites and traffic patterns not otherwise apparent under visible light.

3. **Multispectral (MS) sensor.** This imaging sensor captures image data within the wavelength ranges across the electromagnetic spectrum. Usually, frequencies are outside the visible human range. Subsequently, multispectral imaging reveals information that the human eye cannot capture.

4. **Hyperspectral (HS) sensor.** This imaging sensor is similar to a multispectral sensor. Still, this sensor can detect large numbers of frequency channels, often up to 450 different channels, thus identifying various objects of interest, chemical materials, and natural or artificial processes.

5. **Gamma-ray spectrometer (GRS).** This sensor quantifies the energy spectra of gamma-ray sources in, for example, the nuclear industry and geochemical studies. All radioactive sources produce gamma rays that are generated at different energies and intensities. However, gamma rays are the highest-energy form of electromagnetic radiation, exhibiting high photon energy due to their short wavelength.

6. **Magnetometer sensor.** This sensor is an instrument that measures the characteristics of the Earth's magnetic field, that is, the direction, strength, and relative changes in the magnetic field at appropriate locations. Geologists use magnetometers to detect iron ore areas within the earth.

7. **Laser range finder (LRF) sensor.** This sensor uses a laser beam to measure the distance and orientation of an object located in space relative to the LRF sensor. This measurement is done by sending a laser pulse toward the object and measuring the time and orientation of the pulse as it reflects off the target and returns to the sensor.

8. **Laser illumination sensor.** This sensor comprises a concentrated light source directed toward a stationary or moving object in space. A third party may use a reciprocal instrument to locate and identify the illuminated object.

9. **Laser imaging, detection, and ranging (LIDAR) sensor.** This imaging sensor is an advanced variant of the laser range finder (LRF) sensor. However, LIDAR sensors can make digital three-dimensional representations of remote objects and surfaces. Consequently, LIDAR is used in many mapping applications, including surveying, geography, geology, geodesy, seismology, archaeology, forestry, and atmospheric physics.

10. **Synthetic aperture radar (SAR) sensor.** This imaging sensor is a radar system that can create three-dimensional reconstructions of objects. However, the SAR sensor uses no moving parts (as ordinary radar systems do); instead, it controls the timing and polarization of many individual stational micro antennas. Beyond the elimination of the moving antenna, the advantage of the SAR sensor is that both the transmitted and received signal polarizations can be precisely controlled, so analyzing the signal strength from these different polarizations provides valuable information about the structure of the imaged surface.

11. **Collision avoidance system (CAS) sensor.** This imaging sensor is a radar that detects and prevents potential collisions among aerial moving objects, thus supporting safe navigation in clouds, fog, smog, and other challenging weather conditions. Typically, CAS sensors provide output data of distance, speed, and angle information of approximately 50 obstacles up to roughly 100 meters. In addition, CAS exhibits anti-interference abilities, which include external lights, noise, and electromagnetic interference.

9.5 UAV Context: Formation Systems

> **Definition:** "Formation systems create growth, progress, positive change, or the addition of physical, economic, contextual, social, and demographic components."[8] Formation systems include facilities, appropriate human resources, and funding resources to modernize SoIs. They affect SoIs during all phases of the systems' life cycles.

This analysis describes the formation systems context of a UAV SoI. Systems formation typically refers to all phases involved in bringing a system from a concept or an idea to a functioning product available to its users. From a life cycle timeline, the formation stage occurs from the system's definition phase to its deployment phase (left part of Figure 9.9).

---

8 SID Israel. (2021, February). What is development? The Israeli branch of the Society for International Development (SID). https://www.sid-israel.org/en/Development-Issues/What-is-Development. Accessed: Jan. 2023.

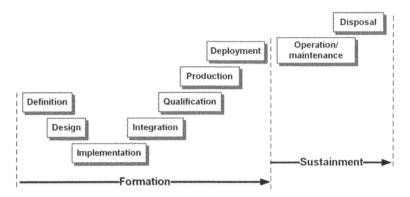

Figure 9.9 SoI: System formation and sustainment stages.

As mentioned earlier, system engineers can define their SoI as being composed of operational and enabling products. However, the UAV SoI example described earlier encompasses only the former. Therefore, the enabling products constitute part of the context of these particular SoI. Consequently, these enabling products, described in the upper portion of Figure 9.10 and the text below, exert considerable influence on the UAV SoI.

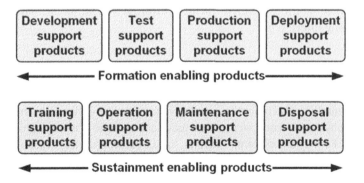

Figure 9.10 SoI formation and sustainment enabling products.

9.5.1 Enabling Products in Support of SoI Formation

Enabling context products supporting the UAV SoI formation comprise laboratory equipment, mechanical devices, computers, workstations, electronic hardware, firmware and software support tools, simulators, and system prototypes. In addition, these enabling products include a collection of established systems methodologies, processes, and procedures, as well as relevant professional books (SEBoK, 2023).

Various system formation documents are also at the heart of the SoI context. For example, typical management enabling documents may include a work breakdown structure (WBS), project schedule, system engineering management plan (SEMP), system integration plan (SIP), and the like. Similarly, typical technical enabling documents may include system requirements specification (SRS), system/subsystem design document (SSDD), and various technical reviews like system requirements review (SRR), system/subsystem design review (SSDR), etc.

9.5.2 Enabling Products in Support of SoI Testing

The enabling products supporting the SoI testing include infrastructure similar to that discussed above, as well as special test tools, test facilities, and test laboratories (e.g., test-measuring tools; environmental test facilities; and ground, flight, and operational test facilities). In addition, typical test facilities may also include a system integration laboratory (SIL), as depicted in Figure 9.11.

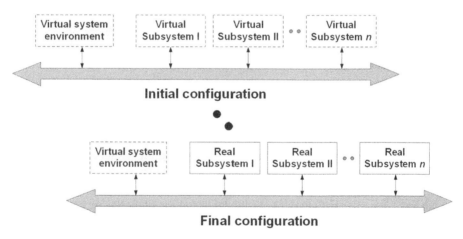

Figure 9.11 Virtual and real system integration laboratory (SIL).[9]

Furthermore, specific enabling system documents in support of SoI testing include an overall verification validation and test management (i.e., VVT management plan [VVT-MP]), traceability matrix (e.g., requirement verification matrix [RVM]), and system test plan/description/results (e.g., STP/STD/STR). Finally, system testing methodologies and procedures, as well as relevant books and articles on verification and validation, also constitute elements within the context of the UAV SoI.

---

9 Adapted from Engel (2010).

9.5.3 Enabling Products in Support of SoI Production

A manufacturing plant and a factory are industrial sites with buildings and machinery, where workers operate machines and other people provide various support functions to manufacture goods. A factory, including all its components, is a vital enabling element supporting SoI production (Figure 9.12).

Figure 9.12 A typical manufacturing plant model with its enabling components.

9.5.4 Enabling Products in Support of SoI Deployment

In general, systems deployment processes involve relocating systems from their formation environment, establishing them in a customer's or user's site, and making them operational for the people using them. Deployment of commercially available drone SoI follows regular business transactions. However, deploying commercially available drone SoI amounts to ordering a small drone package from an appropriate store and then using it.

However, the deployment of large or complex UAV SoI is an entirely different matter. First, often both the customer and the producer of the SoI are involved in the deployment process, where the customer gradually takes over responsibility as deployment proceeds. However, in "turnkey" contracts, the system's producer assumes sole responsibility for system deployment. Second, the deployment process can vary from simply updating a software package on an existing system to constructing new facilities with complete infrastructure and deploying newly produced systems. Third, a freshly developed SoI deployment must often be synchronized with an operating live environment to minimize disruption to ongoing operations.

9.5.5 Context Consequences on the UAV SoI

The formation systems context of the UAV SoI changes and evolves. These changes are reflected in the UAV SoI. For example, the SEMP document develops during SoI formation, affecting various SoI components. Similarly, other enabling products associated with SoI testing, production, and deployment change throughout its formation and often affect the SoI itself. Therefore, it is incumbent upon the engineering formation team to invest time and effort to assemble a set of enabling products as robust as reasonably possible. Thus, changes in the formation context of the SoI will be minimized, leading to the optimal formation of the SoI.

9.6 UAV Context: Sustainment Systems

Definition: Sustainment systems are mechanisms for "keeping an existing system operational and maintaining the ability to manufacture and field updated versions of the systems that satisfy the original and evolving requirements."[10] According to SEBoK (Systems Engineering Body of Knowledge), "Sustainment involves the supportability of operational systems from the initial procurement to disposal. Sustainment is a key task for systems engineering that influences product and service performance and support costs for the entire life of the program"[11].

The analysis of the sustainment system context of a UAV SoI is presented here in two contexts (1) a narrow context, considering the immediate, daily sustainment process of the UAV SoI, and (2) a broad context of the UAV SoI, that is, the broad interrelations between the UAV SoI and its surroundings.

9.6.1 The Narrow Context of the UAV SoI

This analysis describes the sustainment system context of a UAV SoI. UAV system sustainment typically refers to the operations, maintenance, and disposal of the UAV SoI at the end of its life (right part of Figure 9.9). The enabling products associated with the narrow context of the UAV SoI are described in the lower detail of Figure 9.10 and the text below. They are affected by the UAV SoI and, in turn, affect the UAV SoI considerably.

The training support products may include specialized tools, simulators, operation manuals, system schematics, etc. In addition, the operation support products may consist of various manuals (e.g., operation manuals, hardware and software manuals). Finally, the maintenance support products may include relevant system schematics, system diagnostic manuals, troubleshooting manuals, test documentation, etc.

Under the narrow context of the UAV SoI, disposal support products contain statutory requirements related to hazard and safety considerations. The optimal

---

10 Sandborn and Myers (2008). Designing engineering systems for sustainability. https://www. semanticscholar.org/paper/Designing-Engineering-Systems-for-Sustainability-Sandborn-Myers/ b99d488bf843f76c7ec1869d8230270fb1a02e73. Accessed: Jan. 2023.

11 See: https://sebokwiki.org/wiki/Service_Life_Management#:~:text=Sustainment%20involves% 20the%20supportability%20of,entire%20life%20of%20the%20program. Accessed: Jan. 2023.

disposal context of small drones could be achieved through takeback and recycling programs. However, disposal of large UAV SoI includes a formal disposal plan and appropriate disposal facilities. These elements should have been initially addressed during the system definition, design, and production phases, so critical environmental and material recovery should be considered at the beginning of the process.

9.6.2 The Broad Context of the UAV SoI

This analysis describes the broad sustainment system context of the UAV SoI. Accordingly, this context system includes the following elements: (1) electricity and (2) fuel, (3) UAV mission authority (UMA), (4) Ground Positioning System (GPS), (5) air traffic control (ATC), (6) UAV operators, (7) UAV users, and (8) ground image (Figure 9.13).

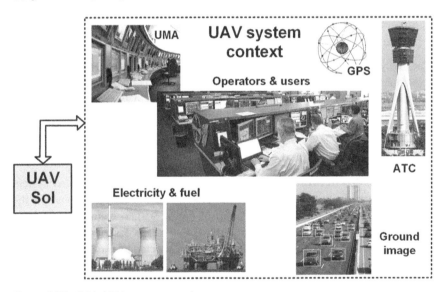

Figure 9.13 Wide UAV context: sustainment system.

1. **Electricity.** The UAV system requires electricity to perform its mission. Failures in the power generation or the electrical distribution grid will cause an immediate cessation of all UAV SoI operations. Also, if such termination occurs when the air system (AS) is flying, it may cause the loss of the AS itself.
2. **Fuel.** The UAV requires energy to feed the air system (AS) engine. Therefore, failures in oil extraction and refinery facilities, oil distribution, or the supply chain will cause the cessation of all UAV SoI operations.
3. **UAV mission authority (UMA).** The UAV system requires tasking commands to perform its mission. In addition, the UAV SoI generates relevant images and other data, which must be transmitted to the UAV mission

authority (UMA). If the UAV SoI does not receive tasking information, it is practically disabled because it cannot act without the specific instructions of the UMA. Similarly, if relevant data cannot be transmitted from the UAV SoI to the UMA, the UAV SoI is practically disabled. This limitation is because users can utilize the data only through UMA channels.

4. **Global positioning system (GPS).** The UAV system must obtain exact information regarding its position, elevation, orientation, speed, acceleration, and other critical AS spatial data. Therefore, the availability of GPS signals is vital to the smooth and safe operation of the UAV SoI. Loss of GPS data for any reason (e.g., a jamming process created erroneously or intentionally) endangers the AS and ground objects and thus disables all UAV SoI operations.

5. **Air traffic control (ATC).** An essential safety feature adhered to by all UAV systems sharing flying space is transmitting the AS location and other spatial and dynamic information to the nearest or the most relevant air traffic control (ATC). Operators at the ATC direct the UAV SoI operators if any spatial restriction is about to be violated so that the AS is commanded to exit such restricted spaces. So again, for safety reasons, no UAV SoI operations should be permitted if the ATC does not receive transmissions from the AS, which results in disabling all UAV operations.

6. **UAV SoI operators.** Human operators constitute a crucial element in operationalizing the UAV SoI. First, some operators are directly involved in performing the mission of the UAV system. These include operators who receive UAV tasking from the UMA; plan the specifics of the UAV SoI mission; conduct the actual AS takeoff, flight, and landing of the air system; as well as others involved in analyzing the data received from the AS and transmitting relevant results to the UMA. Second, many human operators are involved in multilevel maintenance, testing, preparations, training, and so on, which are needed to effect the smooth operation of the UAV SoI.

   The effectiveness of the UAV SoI is critically dependent on the expertise and dedication of these UAV operators. Operating an air system that had not been thoroughly checked before flights may end with the loss of the AS and, possibly, harm and damage to third parties. Leaving bugs in one of the many software packages in the system may lead to similar results. Setting incorrect parameter values or flying the AS into an obstacle can easily lead to accidents and mishaps.

7. **UAV users.** Typically, civilian UAV systems are used by specially trained units belonging to involved organizations like the police force, emergency response teams, city traffic controllers, utility companies, regional and national firefighters, border patrol and coast guard, and various government agencies. Often, these units obtain limited control of the UAV system so they can fly the AS in a predefined pattern and operate its day video and night infrared sensor at will. In most countries, these invasive operations are regulated, and unauthorized operations (e.g., contravening privacy laws or utilizing the system for other

purposes or private gains) are strictly prohibited. Indirect users are the multitude of ordinary individuals and stakeholders that, by and large, derive benefits from these civilian UAV systems. For example, these benefits may be obtained through better police protection, quicker emergency response, etc.

8. **Ground image.** The UAV SoI is designed for missions collecting ground information in various civilian environments. Consequently, the AS subsystem contains a payload of day video cameras and night infrared images. End users of the system receive this streaming data and manipulate it according to their needs. For example, Figure 9.13 depicts the use of real-time UAV SoI data for traffic monitoring by the police. However, day images may not be available when heavy fog or low clouds are present. Similarly, infrared images of cold (not emitting infrared signature) traffic obstacles cannot be detected at night.

9.7   UAV Context: Business Systems

Definition: Business systems are enterprising entities engaged in commercial, industrial, or professional activities. Business systems constitute a combination of policies, personnel, equipment, and computer facilities designed to coordinate the governing of relevant organizations. Business systems affect SoI in multiple ways.

This analysis describes the business systems contexts of the UAV SoI. From a business standpoint, the UAV system rose to prominence in the 1980s based on military technology. Advances in microelectronics and software led the vigorous drone markets for hobbyists and photography enthusiasts. However, with new software; advanced battery technology; and vast improvements in light, small-size sensors, commercial drones appear to be gaining distinct commercial viability across numerous industries. In addition, new UAV regulations enacted by the Federal Aviation Agency (FAA) and other national bodies organized and resolved many issues related to operating UAVs and drones in public space. The combined effects of these facts led governments to encourage industrial corporations to invest heavily in the UAV and drone business.

9.7.1   Economic Impact

According to McKinsey,[12] by 2026, commercial drones, both corporate and consumer applications, will contribute $30 billion to $50 billion to the annual US gross domestic product (GDP). In particular, drone-enabled productivity improvements

---

12 Cohn et al. (2017, December 5). Commercial drones are here: The future of unmanned aerial systems. McKinsey. https://www.mckinsey.com/industries/travel-logistics-and-infrastructure/our-insights/commercial-drones-are-here-the-future-of-unmanned-aerial-systems.   Accessed: Jan. 2023.

will be created by UAV manufacturers and associated services, enabling efficient operations in many sectors of the economy.

Along this line, a Barclays analysis suggests that the global commercial drone market will grow by a factor of 10, from $4 billion to $40 billion between 2019 and 2024. Consequently, it is estimated that using UAVs/drones will save some $100 billion.[13]

Thus, the projected number of commercial UAVs/drones produced will exceed 2.5 million, and the worldwide industry revenue will exceed $12 billion by 2025 (Figure 9.14). Another study by the Association for Unmanned Vehicle Systems International (AUVSI) anticipates that within the United States alone, UAV/drone-related business could generate more than 100,000 new jobs as well as an economic gain of $82.1 billion by 2025 (Jenkins and Vasigh, 2013).

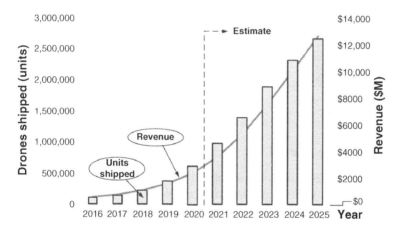

Figure 9.14 Commercial drone shipments and revenue: world market, 2016–2025.[14]

9.7.1 Applications

UAVs and drones have numerous civilian, commercial, military, and aerospace applications. Table 9.3 presents some of them. In addition, Figure 9.15 shows a set of commercial applications and the estimated market size of UAVs and drones by 2024.

---

13 McGee, P. (2019, November 27). How the commercial drone market became big business. *Financial Times*.

14 Adapted from Haller, L. (2020, May 26). Industry news: Drone market recap 2019. https://www.unmannedairspace.info/latest-news-and-information/commercial-drone-shipments-will-rise-from:-500000-in-2019-to-150000-in-2020-new-study/. Accessed: Jan. 2023.

Table 9.3 Examples of UAV and Drone Applications.

1. Defense	7. Environmental conservation	13. Telecommunications
2. Transport (cargo)		14. Mapping and GIS
3. Emergency response	8. Healthcare	15. Photography and TV
4. Urban planning	9. Agriculture	16. Toys
5. Construction	10. Weather forecasting	
6. Surveillance and inspection	11. Waste management	
	12. Mining	

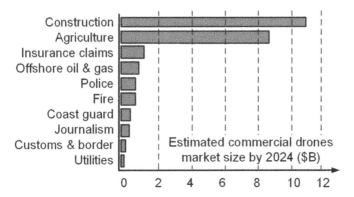

Figure 9.15 Commercial applications and market size of UAVs and drones by 2025.[15]

9.7.3 Effects on the UAV SoI

The UAV/drone business is open to many applications, is growing exponentially, and is clearly a disruptive technology. This characteristic deeply affects the UAV SoI. Therefore, adapting this system to support new applications in different fields as well as the ability to use different technologies should be readily available in the current commercially expanding environment. From a business standpoint, the UAV SoI is affected by the UAV context, which projects the following UAV/drone features:

1. **Versatility.** UAVs/drones can fly into difficult-to-reach or hazardous areas relatively cheaply.
2. **Cost-effectiveness.** UAVs/drones can perform specific tasks at a fraction of the cost and time of conventional means.
3. **Deployability and controllability.** Operators should get appropriate training to deploy and control their UAV/drones.
4. **Applications.** UAVs/drones and appropriate sensors can be utilized in many applications.

---

15 Adapted from McGee, P. (2019, November 27). How the commercial drone market became big business, *Financial Times*. https://www.ft.com/content/cbd0d81a-0d40-11ea-bb52-34c8d9dc6d84. Last access: Jan. 2023.

9.8 UAV Context: Commercial Systems

Definition: Commercial systems are objects conceived, designed, produced, and marketed solely for economic profit. Commercial systems affect SoIs in multiple ways.

This analysis describes the commercial systems context of the UAV SoI. Over the past decade, UAV prices have dropped considerably, making their operations more accessible. As a result, the use of UAVs has extended from the military, government agencies, and niche hobbyists to many industries and services. Utilizing UAVs offers many possible applications and benefits because they can perform dangerous, time-consuming, or complex tasks while protecting human operators. For example, CBInsights (2020) as well as Heutger and Kuckelhaus (2014), and others describe many such applications, some of which are outlined below.

9.8.1 Emergency Response

UAVs outfitted with visible and thermal imaging cameras provide emergency response teams with an ideal vantage point to conduct search-and-rescue missions; locate victims; and, sometimes, deliver aid. In addition, UAVs offer an excellent platform to survey disaster zones and assess local damage. For example, after the earthquake and tsunami devastated Fukushima, Japan, the entire nuclear power plant became heavily contaminated with radioactive substances. As part of the emergency response, several Honeywell T-Hawk Micro UAVs[16] (Figure 9.16) were utilized to collect insights from

Figure 9.16 The Honeywell T-Hawk Micro UAV.

---

16 A VTOL, powered by a two-stroke gasoline engine. The Micro UAV weighs 8.4 kilograms with an endurance of 40 minutes, an operating radius of 11 kilometers, and forward speeds of up to 130 kilometers/hour.

the heart of a destroyed plant. Consequently, on June 24, 2011, one T-Hawk Micro UAV crashed on the roof of Fukushima's number 2 reactor building.

9.8.2 Fighting Crimes

As mentioned before, UAVs are also used by law enforcement for crime prevention and surveillance. Similarly, security companies use UAVs to provide comprehensive aerial surveillance systems for industrial, commercial, and residential properties. For example, some UAVs are programmed to fly autonomously, scanning for suspicious activities near selected locations.

9.8.3 Environmental Protection

Nowadays, UAVs play a vital role in environmental protection. For example, several conservation game reserves in South Africa use UAVs to scan large areas in real time to protect endangered rhinos from poachers. In addition, these UAVs are combined with geospatial imagery to study, monitor, and track the movement of animals within their global ecosystems. Other environmental groups launch UAVs from their ships in the Antarctic Ocean to challenge Japanese whaling ships and protect whales.

9.8.4 Land Surveying

UAVs equipped with GPS and three-dimensional multispectral instruments are used for land surveying in support of many industries and fields (e.g., forestry management, mining, oil and gas, urban planning, construction, flood and pollution monitoring, and archaeology). Topographic reference data provides highly accurate (i.e., 1- to 2-centimeter resolution) digital maps at a fraction of the time and expense of ground-based surveys.

9.8.5 Precision Agriculture

As mentioned above, UAVs can support precision agriculture by creating various surveys. Such surveys provide valuable agricultural data, including soil hydration, soil composition variations, and pest and fungal infestations. This data may be gathered through automated and repetitive weekly or monthly processes, reducing farmers' labor and overall cost and improving the efficiency and productivity of agricultural efforts.

Another area where UAVs are gaining traction is the physical cultivation of crops. This capability may include crop irrigation, fertilization, and pest control (Figure 9.17). Combining the strategies of precision agriculture and UAV crops, cultivation yields a substantial reduction in water consumption and lowers the use of fertilizers, herbicides, and pesticides while maximizing crop yields.

Figure 9.17 Agricultural UAV capable of carrying 25 kilograms of water, pesticides, and so on.

9.8.6 Urban Planning

Urban planning encompasses the design and regulation of spaces used within urban environments. More specifically, it concerns advancing open land and revitalizing existing city areas. Increasingly, geographic information systems (GIS) are utilized to map the current urban system and project the consequences of changes. Along this line, UAVs gather dynamic topographic data regarding mass population movements, traffic patterns, and congestion within population-dense areas. Using real-time UAV data with artificial intelligence (AI) technology allows urban planners to control city-wide traffic patterns and affect urban planning for optimal design. For example, combining UAV data, GIS, and AI helps city planners determine how to assign certain city areas to specific zones (e.g., commercial, residential, park, and recreational spaces). In addition, with many municipalities operating on limited budgets, UAVs can provide a relatively low-cost way to capture valuable urban data.

9.8.7 Construction Planning and Management

Construction planning is the way engineers define how to conduct a specific construction project. This type of planning may include creating the structure, purchasing or ordering construction materials and support infrastructures, and planning how to deploy workers and subcontractors to complete various tasks. In addition, construction management entails tracing project progress during execution, assessing project health, identifying problems, and implementing timely corrective actions in response to anticipated schedule delays or other project obstacles.

While ground surveying is still essential to construction planning and monitoring, using UAVs has become increasingly important. Instrumented UAVs are used extensively throughout the construction life cycle to measure topography and soil type as well as monitor the status of buildings and other structures as they evolve. For example, UAVs can perform a close-up inspection of the exterior of a building and produce a high-resolution video of the roof, gutters, chimneys, and building envelope. Such operations invariably reduce operational costs while minimizing hazards to workers and bystanders, particularly on multistory structures.

9.8.8 Infrastructure Development and Inspection

Infrastructure inspection using UAVs equipped with appropriate sensors and cameras has been adopted in many countries. First, this technology offers significant economic and time savings relative to manned helicopters. Second, the vast size and scale of various infrastructures combined with geographically challenging environments present a tedious and, by and large, quite risky situation for the individuals involved. Third, UAVs can follow a planned flight path and fly closer to the infrastructure, yielding increased repeatability and higher data accuracy. Finally, UAVs are generally less vulnerable to extreme weather conditions and more accessible to deploy than manned helicopters.

1. **Transportation infrastructure.** The US interstate highway system, created in the 1950s, has surpassed its design life. Furthermore, more than 55,000 bridges in the United States are now considered structurally deficient. This infrastructure must be inspected frequently and efficiently. For example, a survey conducted in 2018 by the American Association of State Highway and Transportation Officials (AASHTO) indicates that around 80% of US state transportation departments utilized UAVs. Uses included monitoring the progress of highway construction projects; surveying new sites; and inspecting roads, railroad tracks, bridges, and more. Another study indicated that the time required to collect data on busy existing railroad tracks near London was reduced from several months to about two days, with UAV-generated photographs providing 1-to-2-millimeter accuracy levels.

   In addition, UAVs equipped with chemical detectors are used over highways and congested roads to detect greenhouse gas (GHG) emissions and pinpoint specific vehicles that violate emission regulations and standards. By and large, trucks account for 24% of transportation-related GHG emissions.

   In addition, the Federal Aviation Administration (FAA) in the United States and similar organizations in many other countries apply a rigorous UAV-based inspection regime to the airline industry. For example, aircraft must be thoroughly checked after every 125 hours of flight time. In addition, the aircraft's exterior must be inspected before every flight. Typically, this is done manually by walking around the aircraft, which is a minimal inspection. Recently, Airbus conducted experimental exterior aircraft inspections using UAVs outfitted with cameras and other sensors. This procedure allows operators to collect images, create detailed three-dimensional models of the aircraft, and then use AI software to seek surface abnormalities relative to an intact aircraft model.

2. **Energy infrastructure.** In most of the United States, 1 million kilometers of high-voltage transmission lines, 8 million kilometers of distribution lines, and thousands of electric power generation facilities have reached their design life expectancy. As such, they tend to fail frequently, and the only way to inspect this massive system quickly and at a reasonable cost is to use autonomous UAVs. For example, high-resolution images collected from the air can reveal corrosion on transmission line conductors. In addition, thermal sensors attached to UAV hovering near pipelines can detect electricity leakages.

In the same vein, more than 270,000 wind turbines are operating globally, and they are rotating thanks to approximately 800,000 turbine blades battered by the elements that need regular inspections for wear and tear (Figure 9.18). UAVs provide close-up images of this equipment so inspectors can remain safely on the ground. Regarding utility-scale solar facilities, many of the 6,000-plus renewable energy plants in the United States use UAVs to inspect solar arrays. These systems use a thermal sensor that detects specific panels that have gone offline or are underperforming.

Figure 9.18 Offshore electricity wind farm near Copenhagen, Denmark.

The United States has over 4 million kilometers of oil and gas (O&G) pipelines. So naturally, this O&G infrastructure is susceptible to periodic failures. Two UAVs equipped with appropriate sensors are used to survey this vast system as they seek to detect underground pipeline leaks. For example, UAVs carrying LIDAR (light identification detection and ranging) can pinpoint underground pipeline leaks by examining high-resolution vegetation maps showing plant kill-off zones, a sign of leaks. Similarly, UAVs carrying infrared cameras can create thermal imagery of pipeline routes; hotspots may point to potential defects in pipeline insulation or leaks that are invisible to the human eye.

In addition, UAVs are equipped with infrared devices to survey O&G sites and identify ozone and other types of air pollution that may exceed allowable limits.

3. **Water systems.** The US drinking water supply infrastructure includes dams, reservoirs, well fields, pumping stations, aqueducts, canals and canal locks, water treatment plants, water towers, and approximately 3 million kilometers of distribution lines. Of the 160,000 public water systems in the United States, 34% are community systems and 66% are noncommunity systems. From a public safety standpoint, dams present the most dominant risks to downstream communities due to the tremendous destructive energy accumulated in the water held by the dams and levees. In addition, more than 90,000 state, federal, and privately owned dams in the United States are approaching the end of their useful lives.

UAVs equipped with infrared sensors are commonly used to inspect various structures within the water infrastructure system to detect water leaks. In addition, UAVs equipped with ground-penetrating radar are used experimentally to detect undesired water leakage.

9.8.9 Mining Operations

Mining is a capital-intensive venture that demands ongoing status assessment. Within the mining industry, UAVs replace many manual operations, improving efficiency and safety while drastically reducing the time and human resources required. UAVs provide critical information in the following areas:

1. **Effective stockpile management.** UAVs equipped with photogrammetry or LiDAR, utilizing high-quality digital three-dimensional models on the ground, provide accurate and detailed measurements and profiling of ore grades throughout the life of mines.

2. **Terrain mapping and change detection.** UAVs routinely survey and map industrial environments and collect ongoing aerial data for precise measurements while saving time, money, and human resources. This data generates orthophotos and digital elevation models to supplement formal survey reports.

3. **Infrastructure and equipment inspection.** Automatic and autonomous UAV are programmed to monitor and inspect difficult-to-access areas near mines, providing a safe and cost-efficient way of gaining insight into operation-critical processes. Similarly, UAVs can augment manual design, analysis, optimization, and construction of haul roads near mines. In particular, ongoing UAV inspections of haul roads are beneficial as these roads undergo constant wear and tear from heavy machinery and harsh weather conditions.

4. **Security and surveillance.** Mining and, in general, industrial operations face constant safety and security threats, which require real-time, precise,

and reliable situational awareness. Autonomous preprogrammed UAVs can augment security officers in support of such needs. Either routinely or in an emergency, UAVs can quickly reach critical locations (e.g., gates, fences, necessary infrastructures) and provide real-time aerial videos and photos delivered directly to personnel on the ground.

9.8.10 Aerial Photography and Gaming

In addition to the above uses, aerial photography is widely used in many applications. Here are some examples:

1. UAVs have been beneficial in capturing pictures of real estate and high-value properties. For example, several companies in the United States offer on-demand UAV photography of residential and commercial real estate, primarily for marketing purposes. Similarly, insurance companies have started augmenting manual property inspections with UAVs, using high-resolution cameras to assess damage in hard-to-reach structures.
2. Television outlets and other news media use UAVs routinely following FAA regulations, allowing journalists to use drones in newsgathering. For example, UAV obtained aerial video depicting the aftermath of Hurricane Irma in 2017, several California wildfires of recent years, and many other significant events.
3. Small service providers, as well as well-established film industry giants, routinely use UAVs to capture dramatic aerial perspective scenes for films and photographs, replacing helicopters at a fraction of the cost. Similarly, many sporting events are televised using UAV-mounted cameras. Likewise, some companies concentrate on producing live entertainment with UAVs or drones, including live synchronized drone performances for audiences, advertising banners, and the like.
4. In-flight technology and portable photography advances have reduced the cost of UAVs and drones, making them attractive as consumer goods for amateur and professional photographers as well as recreational tools for those who enjoy the great outdoors. In addition, some companies organize various UAV gaming like drone races and high-tech battles via augmented reality and sophisticated obstacle courses.

9.8.11 Delivery of Goods

Experiments with UAVs delivering goods from local retailers are ongoing in several countries. Similar attempts to deliver food from restaurants and takeaway outlets are being experimented in some more developed countries. Amazon is well known for its innovations in this regard. UAV deliveries are economical within cities where people live within a 15-kilometer radius, and UAVs can avoid heavy traffic and other impediments. However, safety, collision avoidance, delivery security, insurance, and other operational barriers must be overcome before such services are commercialized.

9.8.12 Current UAV Challenges

1. **Battery-based drones versus gasoline-based UAVs.** The Achilles heel of battery-powered drones is the limited electrical capacity of their batteries. Most consumer drones use rechargeable lithium-ion batteries with energy density by mass of 0.4 to 0.9 millijoule/kilogram and charge/discharge efficiency in the range of 80% to 90%. By and large, these types of drones can fly for about 30 minutes. Then they must land to recharge their batteries or have them replaced with fully charged ones. In contrast, heavier and larger UAVs use gasoline, a clear petroleum-derived flammable liquid used primarily for internal combustion engines (e.g., automobiles). Gasoline energy density by mass is 46.4 millijoule/kilogram, with an overall efficiency of about 30%.[17]

   The low energy-to-weight ratio limits drones' ability to achieve long flight durations and ranges as well as to carry relatively heavy payloads. By designing UAVs with larger fuel tanks, flight duration, capacity, and weight bearing may easily be extended. Another aspect being considered is that while the fuel weight of gasoline-based UAVs diminishes as the fuel is consumed, the weight of battery-based drones is constant whether they are fully charged or empty. Also, batteries exhibit limited operations in low temperatures (i.e., typical operations at high altitudes and in the more northern and southern regions of the globe). In addition, batteries age relatively quickly, delivering about half their rated capacity after just a few years of operation. In contrast, combustion engines deliver full power at various temperatures and have performed well for many years.

   In summary, as of this writing, battery-based drones are unsuitable for many of the practical applications discussed in the previous sections. The flip side of this issue is that gasoline-powered UAVs produce substantial noise, especially during horizontal takeoffs. This limitation is a severe hindrance in urban areas but a relatively minor issue in rural and open country areas.

2. **Autonomous, reliable, and safe flights.** A second critical challenge for fully embracing UAV technology is the requirement for reliable and secure autonomous flights. This reliability and safety requirement means drones and UAVs must have the ability to (1) know their exact three-dimensional position, trajectory, and velocity using GPS and other means in case GPS signals are degraded or eliminated; (2) transmit their three-dimensional data to other airborne elements within their vicinity as well as with air traffic control centers in areas near airports; and (3) implement a self-detect-and-avoid functionality, routing and control the UAV to fly reliably toward its target.

---

17 See more: Energy Density, https://en.wikipedia.org/wiki/Energy_density. Last accessed: Jan. 2023.

9.9   Bibliography

CBInsights. (2020, January 9). 38 ways drones will impact society: From fighting war to forecasting weather, UAVs change everything. Research *Briefs*. https://www.cbinsights.com/research/drone-impact-society-uav/. Accessed: Jan. 2023.

Cohn, P., Green, A., Langstaff, M., and Roller, M. (2017, December 5). *Commercial Drones Are Here: The Future of Unmanned Aerial Systems.* McKinsey.

Engel, A. (2010). *Verification, Validation and Testing of Engineered Systems* (Wiley Series in Systems Engineering and Management). Wiley.

Federal Aviation Administration (FAA). (2020, October 6). Fact sheet: Small unmanned aircraft systems (UAV) regulations (Part 107). https://www.faa.gov/news/fact_sheets/news_story.cfm?newsId=22615. Accessed: Jan. 2023.

Haller, L. (2020, May 26). Industry news: Drone market recap 2019. https://www.unmannedairspace.info/latest-news-and-information/commercial-drone-shipments-will-rise-from:-500000-in-2019-to-150000-in-2020-new-study/. Accessed: Jan. 2023.

Heutger, M., & Kückelhaus, M. (2014). Unmanned aerial vehicles in logistics a DHL perspective on implications and use cases for the logistics industry. *DHL Customer Solutions & Innovation, Troisdorf, Germany.*

SEBoK, Guide to the Systems Engineering Body of Knowledge. (May 2023). Cloutier J.R. and Hutchison, N. (Eds.), Version 2.8, INCOSE. https://sebokwiki.org/w/images/sebokwiki-farm!w/0/0a/Guide_to_the_Systems_Engineering_Body_of_Knowledge.pdf. Accessed: Oct. 2023.

Jenkins, D. and Vasigh, B. (2013, March). The economic impact of unmanned aircraft systems integration in the United States. https://higherlogicdownload.s3.amazonaws.com/AUVSI/958c920a-7f9b-4ad2-9807-f9a4e95d1ef1/UploadedImages/New_Economic%20Report%202013%20Full.pdf. Accessed: Jan. 2023.

Lippitt, J., Webb, P., and Martin, W. (2000). *Hazardous Waste Handbook*, third edition, Butterworth-Heinemann.

McGee, P. (2019, November 27). How the commercial drone market became big business. *Financial Times.*

Sandborn, P. and Myers, J. (2008). Designing engineering systems for sustainability. *Semantic Scholar.* https://www.semanticscholar.org/paper/Designing-Engineering-Systems-for-Sustainability-Sandborn-Myers/b99d488bf843f76c7ec1869d8230270fb1a02e73. Accessed: Jan. 2023.

SID Israel. (2018, March 11). What is Development? The Israeli branch of the Society for International Development (SID). https://www.sid-israel.org/en/Development-Issues/What-is-Development. Accessed: Jan. 2023.

10

Example: UAV Context (Part II)

10.1 Introduction

As mentioned earlier, most engineers need to appreciate the SoI context's vastness, which affects their systems. For example, some spectacular systems disasters described in Chapter 5 could be attributed to limited engineering attention to the overall context of the SoI. Therefore, the purpose of Chapter 9 as well as this chapter is to illuminate the holistic nature of SoI context issues by an example related to the UAV SoI described in a previous chapter.

For clarity, the 12 subtopics of the UAV system context are presented in two chapters. The previous chapter describes the following UAV system subcontexts: (1) natural systems, (2) social systems, (3) research systems, (4) formation systems, (5) sustainment systems, (6) business systems, and (7) commercial systems. This chapter describes the following UAV system subcontexts: (8) financial systems, (9) political systems, (10) legal systems, (11) cultural systems, and (12) biosphere systems.

As mentioned before, the context (environment) of any given system of interest (SoI) is, by definition, a system of systems that affect the SoI in many ways. Therefore, engineers should thoroughly investigate these systems' contexts to ascertain how they may affect their SoI. Such investigation could lead engineers to design their SoI in a way that will reduce the negative impact of these effects. Conversely, engineers are encouraged to take advantage of the positive aspects of these effects.

Systems Science for Engineers and Scholars, First Edition. Edited by Avner Engel.
© 2024 John Wiley & Sons, Ltd. Published 2024 by John Wiley & Sons, Ltd.

10.2 UAV Context: Financial Systems

Definition: Financial systems are mechanisms of interacting institutions and markets aiming to maintain investments and payments within commercial activities. They include banks, credit card companies, insurance companies, accountancy companies, stock brokerages, investment funds, and individual managers. Financial systems affect SoIs in multiple ways.

This analysis describes the financial systems context of the UAV SoI. As mentioned before, rapid technological innovation has offered consumers cutting-edge UAVs and drones at affordable prices. In addition, UAVs can perform tedious and sometimes hazardous tasks, such as inspecting high-voltage power transmission lines, with higher precision and cost-effectiveness than conventional methods. As a result, the market for drones in agriculture, infrastructure, and various industries exceeds $127 billion. At the same time, integrating UAVs into the economy is expected to create more than 100,000 jobs.

Despite the clear economic advantage of UAV and drone usage, many people are concerned about intrusive data collection issues practiced by corporations and governments. In addition, drone delivery services must overcome security and safety risks, traffic management issues, and liabilities regarding damaged or stolen property incurred during the delivery of goods. Furthermore, an unmanned aerial vehicle cannot access apartment units within cities without a man in the loop. Another concern relates to safety issues. As the number of UAVs in the sky increases, the likelihood of bird collision increases. This risk may lead to injury and death of birds as well as damage to UAVs, their cargo, and people and property on the ground.

10.2.1 UAV Systems and Banks

Commercial banks are essential in financial systems and the UAV/drone industry. Banks allocate funds to industry borrowers and provide specialized financial services to their customers. More specifically, (1) banks provide funding mechanisms for UAV/drone companies to spend on the development, manufacturing, and sales of their products, and (2) banks provide fast and safe mechanisms for UAV/drone companies to perform financial transactions with suppliers, customers, and workers.

10.2.2 Global UAV Stock Market

As the FAA and other worldwide government bodies open the air space for commercial UAV activities, the relevant global stock markets are expanding swiftly. This expansion is mainly because such actions tend to lower the entry barriers for new UAV startups and innovators. In particular, the small-cap stock sector is affected by relatively small drones and UAVs, which are offered at around $2,000 per unit and equipped with infrared cameras and other sensors. Moreover, these UAVs and drones provide enhanced productivity; cost-effective operation; and commercial services like building inspections, land surveying, transport, logistics, and precision agriculture.

The UAV industry analysis projects the market to grow at a 16.6% compound annual growth rate based on value during the forecast period from 2016 to 2027 (Figure 10.1). As of 2019, the North American sector dominates the international UAV market with a share of 51%. However, the Asia Pacific (APAC) countries, particularly China, Japan, South Korea, Australia, and Singapore, have rapidly become the second-largest UAV market.

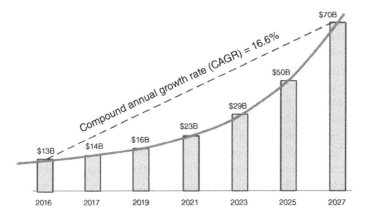

Figure 10.1 Global UAV and drone stock market forecast.[1]

Experts predict that by 2030, agriculture will claim most of the commercial market for drones and UAVs because most farms will use them to assess water and insect problems as well as monitor localized crop yields, saving farmers time and money.

As of 2020, the most dominant UAV/drone corporations in the stock market are (1) DJI of China, (2) General Atomics of the United States, (3) Aurora Flight of the United States, (4) AeroVironment Inc. of the United States, (5) BAE Systems PLC of the UK, (6) Denel Dynamics of South Africa, (7) Draganfly of Canada, (8) Elbit Systems Ltd. of Israel, (9) General Dynamics Corporation of the United States, (10) Lockheed Martin Corporation of the United States, and (11) Northrop Grumman of the United States.

---

1 Source: Drones market: Global major key players research. Forecast to 2023, June 2018. https://www.webpackaging.com/en/portals/marketresearchfuture/assets/11964671/drones-market-global-major-key-players-research-forecast-to-2023. Last accessed: Jan. 2023.

10.2.2.1 Segmentation of the UAV Stock Market

From the stock market point of view, UAV and drones are segmented along with several orthogonal criteria, including segmentation by (1) UAV type, (2) UAV class, (3) UAV range, (4) UAV end user, (5) UAV component, and (6) UAV region.

1. **Segmentation by UAV type.** Segmentation by UAV type includes commercial UAVs (fixed-wing, VTOL, etc.) and military UAVs (small tactical, medium-altitude long endurance, high-altitude long endurance, and combat air systems).
2. **Segmentation by UAV class.** Segmentation by UAV class includes small, tactical, strategic, and special-purpose UAVs. The relatively small UAV sector is expected to grow at a high annual growth rate due to strong demand by the commercial sector for applications like precision agriculture, logistics and transportation, search and rescue operations, firefighting, law enforcement, photography, and disaster management.
3. **Segmentation by UAV range.** Segmentation by UAV range includes an extended as well as beyond visual line of sight. These segments are expected to grow at the highest annual growth rate due to the increased use of these UAVs in commercial and consumer applications.
4. **Segmentation by UAV application.** Segmentation by UAV application includes the following: (1) the commercial segment;[2] (2) the government and defense segment;[3] and (3) the consumer segment, which includes primarily drones and UAVs hobbyists. As of 2020, the UAV commercial segment was projected to grow at the highest annual rate due to the increased adoption of UAV for many commercial applications.
5. **Segmentation by UAV component.** Segmentation by UAV component includes (1) propulsion, (2) power, (3) navigation, (4) control, (5) communication, (6) camera, and (7) sensors.
6. **Segmentation by UAV propulsion and power.** The propulsion systems may include a single propeller, multiple propellers, a jet, etc. The power source may include a battery, gasoline, etc.
7. **Segmentation by UAV navigation.** The navigation systems may consist of an inertial navigation system, global positioning system, geographic information system, and so on.
8. **Segmentation by UAV control and communication.** The UAV control may include manual or autopilot capability. The communication systems have different types of transmission for UAV commands, status, and payload data streams.

---

2 Including inspection and monitoring, surveying and mapping, logistics and transport, oil and gas, construction, healthcare, precision agriculture, retail and food, energy and power, media and entertainment, education, and so on.

3 Including law enforcement, homeland security, and military operations.

9. **Segmentation by UAV payloads and sensors.** The systems may include a multispectral camera, thermal camera, LIDAR (Light Identification Detection and Ranging) camera, high-resolution camera, and so on. The sensor systems may consist of a motion sensor, light sensor, proximity sensor, sense and avoid sensor, temperature sensor, etc.

10. **Segmentation by UAV global region.** Segmentation by UAV global region includes North America, Europe, Asia Pacific, and the rest of the world. The North American area has the largest market share, followed by the European region; however, the Asia Pacific region is slated to demonstrate the highest growth rate during the next decade.

10.2.3 Insurance and UAV Systems

The potential for expensive liability claims increases as the UAV industry becomes more regulated. The most common UAV/drone insurance types are (1) liability insurance and (2) hull insurance.

1. **UAV/drone liability insurance.** UAV/drone liability insurance protects against liability claims against UAV manufacturers, businesses, and operators for property damage, bodily injuries, and other financial damage. Therefore, organizations and individuals tend to obtain insurance policies to manage relevant risks effectively. For example, general UAV liability insurance protects a company from expenses associated with accidental property damage or bodily injuries caused to third parties while operating its UAVs/drones. Along this line, aviation product liability is a subcategory of general liability insurance covering liability and costs related to the risk of a defective aviation product, such as UAVs and drones.

2. **UAV/drone hull insurance.** UAV/drone hull insurance covers accidental damage that UAVs or drones may suffer while operating commercially. For example, when the payload consists of costly equipment like a multispectral or LIDAR camera, obtaining added payload and UAV/drone-specific insurance is often desired.

10.2.4 Implications to the UAV SoI

UAV and drone SoI are affected by financial systems. To begin with, banks are a vital component in the operations of any company and corporation. Unstable, inefficient, or unsafe banks can quickly ruin a UAV/drone company, thus rendering some UAV SoI unattractive and even obsolete.

The stock market also affects UAV/drone companies and, therefore, any UAV SoI. For example, UAV/drone companies may choose to go public to raise money to fund the company through inexpensive capital. Such companies tend to project robust financial health and profitability for shareholders. Another reason UAV/drone companies issue stock is to compensate employees and acquire and retain employees. Another way UAV/drone companies may obtain funding is to issue bonds. Bonds function as loans between investors and given corporations. Here, investors agree to provide corporations with certain amounts of money for a specific period. In exchange, corporations provide investors with periodic interest payments.

All in all, companies may raise capital by taking a loan from a bank or issuing either stocks or bonds. Generally, bond financing is often advantageous over bank loans, as it may be structured differently with different maturities. Also, bond financing is often less expensive than equity and does not require giving up any company control. So, a UAV/drone company with good financial standing can maintain and upgrade its UAV SoI and continue offering new and advanced features to its portfolio of UAV systems.

10.3 UAV Context: Political Systems

Definition: Political systems are mechanisms for making official governing decisions. They affect the SoIs by combining factors like the prevailing political systems at the federal, state, and local levels as well as the government's overall policies. In general, stable and functioning political systems are essential to the stability and success of SoIs. Naturally, political systems affect SoIs in numerous ways.

This analysis describes the political systems context of the UAV SoI.

10.3.1 Politics of Recreational Drones

By and large, personal use of drones involves photography, videography, or simple recreation. However, over a relatively short time, recreational drones have increased in physical size and technical capability. This increase enables drones to traverse longer distances, achieve higher altitudes, and accomplish more advanced functionalities. In addition, these capabilities are available to relatively unskilled and unsophisticated operators who can, inadvertently or maliciously, create dangerous situations. These situations may include losing control of a rather large drone, threatening sensitive systems like nuclear power plants or military installations, disrupting and even ceasing normal operations at airports, risking injury to members of the public, and threatening personal privacy.

Politically, public regulators must address many problems related to recreational drone use. These regulations may include economic or transportation disruptions, injury risk to members of the public, or threats to personal privacy. Regulators must consider the political conflict between issues of public freedom and challenges posed by the unrestricted use of drones. These challenges may be divided into three categories. First is where drones should be allowed and not allowed to fly. These limits include the need to identify appropriate airspace and assign them to different uses and classes of drones. The second challenge relates to who should be allowed to use drones. These restrictions include the assignment of responsibility for damages to people and property.

The third and most difficult challenge is detecting, delaying, and neutralizing suspected drones. By and large, drone detection may be achieved through various types of radar reflectance and acoustic emissions, electromagnetic emissions, and induced magnetic fields. Delay may be achieved by detecting a suspicious drone or UAV as far as possible from a vulnerable target. Another delay strategy is to install closely spaced obstacles within the facility to deny adversary drones from landing. Yet another delay strategy is to cover vital structures with mesh netting. All these delay approaches provide more time for the facility to mobilize against the threat. Finally, neutralization is initiated after a drone has been detected and positively identified as a threat. One nondestructive neutralization approach is to exploit a cyber-attack to gain control of the drone and capture it. Another nondestructive neutralization approach is to use a protective drone with a net to capture an attacking drone. Other destructive neutralization approaches include antidrone laser systems, radar-controlled firearms, and miniature surface-to-air missiles.

10.3.2 Politics of Civil Government UAV

The vast majority of the civil government UAVs are relatively small, under 25 kilograms. These UAVs are utilized in many applications, including environmental and wildlife monitoring, firefighting, disaster recovery, search and rescue, meteorology studies, natural resources management, surveying, agriculture, traffic monitoring, and transportation.

A paper released by the US Department of Justice (DoJ) in 2016 analyzed the political ramifications of law enforcement agencies using UAVs (NCJ 250283). Accordingly, current UAV public safety uses include responding to hazardous materials incidents, explosive ordnance disposal incidents, crime scenes, individuals under surveillance, execution of search warrants, active-shooter incidents, disasters and recovery efforts, search and rescue missions, assistance requests from local and state fire authorities, and training support. Other potential law enforcement uses of these platforms are:

- Forensic photography/crime scene mapping
- Damage assessment
- Public safety communications enhancement

- Emergency response/disaster management/postdisaster assessment
- Operational planning
- Border patrol
- Aerial photography and security patrolling of critical infrastructures
- Three-dimensional mapping of major transportation accidents
- Aerial surveillance
- Public safety/life preservation missions
- Alarm response (roof checks, inaccessible fenced-in areas)
- Crowd monitoring

However, from a political standpoint, the general public in the United States raises significant privacy and civil liberty concerns over the use of UAVs, especially concerning performing the following law enforcement assignments:

- Monitor traffic for issuing traffic citations
- Pursue suspects beyond the "visual line of sight"
- Conduct surveillance over large groups of people
- Drop objects, such as tear gas
- Exercise force via weaponized UAV
- Act as weapon target (laser) designator

As the capabilities of UAVs evolve and their costs decrease, the political chasm between privacy advocates and representatives of the law enforcement community increases. The first group objects to the excessive use of UAV technology and would like more robust controls. Conversely, the second group opposes the imposition of excessive controls that inhibit their ability to respond quickly to life-threatening situations or conduct public safety missions. All parties concur that the challenge of using UAVs should include formulating policies that will accommodate the needs of public safety and law enforcement. In addition, these policies should also ensure privacy and civil liberty protections based on existing laws and regulations.

The Federal Aviation Administration (FAA) issued a 2020 small unmanned aircraft systems regulation that elevated the political controversy.[4] The regulation deals with the following issues: (1) operating requirements, (2) registration, (3) pilot certification, (4) drone certification, (5) other requirements, and (6) airspace authorizations.

---

4 Federal Aviation Administration (FAA). (2020, October 6). Fact sheet: Small unmanned aircraft systems (UAV) regulations (Part 107). https://www.faa.gov/news/fact_sheets/news_story.cfm?newsId=22615. Last accessed: Jan. 2023.

10.3.3 Politics of the Military's UAVs

The US armed forces have large, strategic, medium, and high-altitude long-endurance UAVs that operate over long distances through satellite links (Figure 10.2). In addition, the US armed forces have several medium and small tactical surveillance UAVs.

The Predator is a 2.5-ton military UAV used primarily for offensive operations by the US Air Force and the Central Intelligence Agency (CIA). The Predator can fly at a ceiling of 7.6 kilometers for up to 740 kilometers to a given destination, stay overhead for 14 hours, and then return to its base. It carries cameras, other sensors, and two Hellfire missiles.

The Global Hawk is a 14-ton military UAV operated by the US Air Force as a high-altitude, long-endurance platform that provides a broad ground overview and systematic surveillance. This UAV can cruise at an altitude of more than 18 kilometers and fly continuously for more than 32 hours under a complete operational configuration. It carries 910-kilogram payloads, including high-resolution synthetic aperture radar and long-range electro-optical/infrared sensors. Consequently, the Global Hawk can have long loiter times over target areas, surveying some 100,000 square kilometers of terrain daily. In addition, the Global Hawk is fitted with a self-protection suite consisting of a laser warning receiver, a radar warning receiver, a jamming system, and a towed deception decoy to protect against adversaries' attacks.

Figure 10.2 US strategic UAV: (L) Predator and (R) Global Hawk (Images: US DoD).

The rise of UAV technology has effectively lowered the cost of military engagements and allowed the United States to undertake significant military action across the globe. For example, the Predator UAV system was used extensively in Afghanistan, Pakistan, Bosnia, Serbia, Iraq, Yemen, Libya, Syria, and Somalia. The current political controversy over UAVs is multifaceted, as discussed below.

1. **Global use of lethal UAVs.** UAVs offer three clear benefits for the party deploying them: (1) safety of military personnel who are not exposed to retaliatory actions; (2) persistence because UAVs can stay in the theater of operations for a relatively long time and thus offer their service on a nearly continuous basis; and (3) opportunities for improved intelligence gathering, analysis, and lethality.

   However, using UAVs raises a fundamental problem, as they lower the threshold for using military force. That is because they decrease the risk for the deploying side. As a result, that party is more inclined to use them in situations that could have been resolved through other, more benign means. Overall, the controversies over the global use of lethal UAVs focus on (1) the effectiveness of UAVs in targeted killings; (2) the legality of these actions in the context of state sovereignty; and (3) the ethics of UAVs operations in contexts of inevitable collateral damage.

2. **The government and the UAV manufacturers.** In developed democratic countries, the government maintains a monopoly on defense but relies heavily on private defense-related industries. These political public–private linkages influence defense policy and defense funding. Ideally, decisions by governments would be made to promote the general interests of their citizens. However, this is often not the case because UAV-related legislation is enacted under intense pressure from various interest groups, the military, and lobbyists from UAV manufacturers.

   The case of the United States is a good example. In the military UAV arena, five significant players (the Big Players) dominate the US Congress: Lockheed Martin, Northrop, Boeing, General Dynamics, and General Atomics. In addition, lobbyists, acting on behalf of the Big Four and the US armed forces, utilize various means to reap multiple benefits for their members, often circumventing the broader interests of the public. As a result, Congress is under intense political pressure to relax many rules limiting the use of UAVs in domestic US airspace. Similarly, pressure is exerted on various government agencies to repeal current guidelines prohibiting UAV sales abroad.

10.3.4 Implications for the UAV System of Interest

The lesson learned from analyzing the political environment of current UAV systems may be the following. First, recreational UAVs should be designed to meet regulatory obligations. These obligations may include adherence to defined UAV classifications and built-in unique identification of individual UAVs. In addition, certain classes of UAVs should be designed to carry active transponders so that they can be detected by relevant authorities. Finally, different governments should create proper regulations similar to statutes issued by the US Department of Justice (DoJ) and the US Federal Aviation Authorities (FAA). In particular, regulations should mandate the use of collision avoidance equipment on certain classes of UAVs to enhance operational safety.

10.4 UAV Context: Legal Systems

Definition: Legal systems are "procedures and processes for interpreting and enforcing the law."[5] They affect the SoIs through the endurance of the legal framework. Also, well-defined and adhered-to national and international laws are essential to the stability and success of SoIs.

This analysis describes the legal systems context of the UAV SoI. Figure 10.3 defines the six legal components that affect UAV systems of interest.

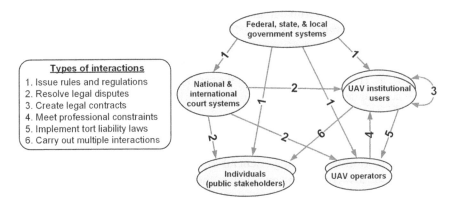

Figure 10.3 UAV context: legal interactions among SoI context.

Engineers and technical individuals dealing with complex concepts, designs, and products should be familiar with relevant legal issues that affect their work and careers. Engineering law is a segment of the legal body that is applicable to professional engineering practice. Some of its elements that are appropriate to the context of the UAV system are described below.

1. **Professional ethics.** The universal basis of professional behavior is avoiding unethical conduct such as offering bribes or engaging in fraudulent[6] practices.

---

5 See https://www.coursehero.com/file/70657994/A-legal-system-is-a-procedure-or-process-for-interpreting-and-enforcing-the-law-1docx/. Accessed: Jan. 2023.

6 Fraud is the "Wrongful or criminal deception intended to result in financial or personal gain" (Oxford Languages Dictionary).

2. **Product liability.** Product liability deals with the law through which manufacturers and others who make products for public use are held responsible for injuries those products cause. By law, engineers involved in designing and manufacturing the product are responsible for assisting the general public in obtaining information about risks associated with these products.

3. **Environmental regulations.** Managers and engineers involved in designing and manufacturing products are legally obligated to uphold environmental regulations within the United States and other countries.

4. **Workplace laws.** Engineers and managers must implement various workplace laws regulating health and safety issues. Similarly, engineers and managers are bound by laws related to hiring, preventing discrimination in the workplace, managing medical leave, and protecting workers' rights.

5. **Disability laws.** Disability laws are primarily applicable to US federal agencies and their suppliers. Under these laws, engineers and managers are prohibited from discriminating against people with a disability who are seeking employment. They are further required to ensure that all information and communications technology the federal government develops, procures, maintains, and uses is accessible to people with disabilities.

6. **Technical standards.** Standards are not legally binding in engineering projects; however, their use becomes binding when stipulated in legislation or a contract. Nevertheless, engineers and managers are encouraged to use technical standards because in case of product liability disputes, courts can examine the use of standards to determine whether a product is defective.

7. **Contract laws.** Contract law is a segment of the legal body that is applicable to agreements between people, businesses, and groups. Contracts are, by definition, legally binding agreements that govern the parties' rights and duties of an accord. They typically involve the exchange of goods, services, money, or the promise of any of those.

8. **Bidding process.** Bidding is a legal form of competitive solicitation used to acquire goods and services. First, an organization issues a request for proposal (RFP) detailing the required products or services. Then bidders submit bids proposals containing both technical and price proposals. These proposals are evaluated, and a contract is awarded to the bidder whose proposal is selected.

9. **Intellectual property laws.** Intellectual property laws constitute a segment of the legal body that is applicable to individuals' or organizations' property, including intangible creations of the human intellect. There are many types of intellectual property, including copyrights, patents, trademarks, and trade secrets.

From the standpoint of the UAV SoI, adherence to this body of law by all involved parties is paramount. Any violation of one or more of these laws can have damaging and destructive effects on the operational capability and effectiveness of the UAV system.

10.5 UAV Context: Cultural Systems

Definition: Cultural systems are societal attributes of species. Among humans, they are typically comprised of knowledge, beliefs and religion, customs and habits, laws, language, music, and arts. Cultural systems are the interaction of different elements within a culture.[7] They affect SoIs in numerous ways.

This analysis describes the cultural systems context of the UAV SoI. These cultural systems have typical organization and affect the UAV SoI in many ways.

10.5.1 Cultural Layers

According to Erez and Gati's (2004) model of cultural layers, culture is comprised of five hierarchical layers consecutively nested inside each other (Figure 10.4). These layers are described below.

Figure 10.4 Model of cultural layers.[8]

1. **Global culture.** Different cultures have always influenced one another through trade, travel, wars, conquests, etc. However, as the internet, electronic communications, and the entertainment and news mass media expand rapidly, cultural diffusion increases dramatically. The result is that cultural elements like ideas, language, technology, financial markets, media conglomerates, and international law become components that transcend the boundaries of nation-states and reflect a standardized cultural expression around the world.

---

7 See https://en.wikipedia.org/wiki/Cultural_system. Accessed: Jan. 2023.

8 Adapted from: Erez and Gati (2004).

2. **National culture.** Differences among nations stem from diversity in national history, values, and practices of behaviors. Geert Hofstede and his research fellows conducted the most authoritative study on national and organizational cultural dimensions (Hofstede, 2001; Hofstede et al., 2010). The Hofstede model of national culture is comprised of six dimensions that distinguish countries from each other. They are:

- **Power distance dimension.** Power distance describes the degree to which the weak members of a society accept power unequally in society. In high power distance societies, people acknowledge the existing hierarchical order in which everybody has a fixed place in society. In contrast, within power-distance societies, people seek to equalize power distribution, demanding justification for power inequalities.

- **Individualism versus collectivism dimension.** Individualism versus collectivism describes the degree of individuals' integration into primary groups. Individualism reflects peoples' preference for a loosely knit social framework in which they are expected to care only for themselves and their immediate families. In contrast, collectivism reflects peoples' choice for a tightly knit social framework in which they are expected to exhibit loyalty and care for community members.

- **Masculinity versus femininity dimension.** Masculinity versus femininity describes the degree of difference in practical and emotional roles between men and women. Masculinity represents a preference for achievement, assertiveness, and material rewards for success. Femininity represents prioritizing cooperation, caring for the weak, and seeking quality of life. Masculine society tends to be more competitive, while feminine society tends to be more consensus oriented.

- **Uncertainty avoidance dimension.** Uncertainty avoidance characterizes the degree to which people feel distressed due to uncertainty and ambiguity. Societies exhibiting strong uncertainty avoidance are intolerant to eccentric behavior, ideas, and belief codes. They generally maintain rigid principles of belief and behavior. Communities showing weak uncertainty avoidance allow a more lenient attitude toward peculiar behavior and controversial ideas.

- **Long- versus short-term orientation dimension.** This national difference expresses the degree of societal focus on the future versus the present and past. For example, societies with a short-term orientation prefer maintaining time-honored traditions and norms. On the other hand, societies focusing on long-term directions take a more pragmatic approach to life and business.

- **Indulgence versus restraint dimension.** Indulgence versus restraint orientation describes how society condones or forbids human desires related to enjoying life. For example, a tolerant society allows relatively free gratification of natural human drives connected to enjoying life and having fun. In contrast, a restrained society tends to suppress human gratifications by regulating strict social norms.

3. **Organizational Culture.**[9] Different researchers have proposed contrasting definitions and descriptions of organizational cultures. By and large, organizational culture is the set of expectations, values, and practices that guide the actions of individuals within an organization; that is, the collection of traits that make an organization what it is. A good culture embodies positive attitudes that lead to improved performance, while an inferior culture brings out qualities that hinder an organization. Wong (2020) and other researchers further describe the general qualities of good organizational cultures:

   - **Alignment.** A culture where the organization's objectives and its members' motivations are pulling in the same direction. Exceptional organizations work to build continuous alignment with their vision, purpose, and goals.
   - **Appreciation.** A culture where recognition of achievements and appreciation of individuals is frequently provided in the forms of public kudos, notes of thanks, promotions, and the like.
   - **Trust.** A culture where individuals within the organization can express themselves freely and rely on others for support when they try something new.
   - **Performance.** A culture where talented individuals motivate each other to excel, leading the organization to productivity and success.
   - **Resilience.** A culture where, within a highly dynamic environment, individuals constantly watch for and respond to change.
   - **Teamwork.** A culture where individuals collaborate with, communicate with, support, and respect each other.
   - **Integrity.** A culture where individuals can trust, make decisions and rely on each other, interpret results, and form partnerships where everyone practices honesty and transparency.
   - **Innovation.** A culture where individuals apply creative thinking to available technologies, resources, and markets as well as other relevant aspects of the organization.
   - **Psychological safety.** A culture that ensures a safe environment where everyone feels comfortable contributing. In particular, it supports individuals when they take risks and provide honest feedback.

---

9 Adapted from Wong (2020).

4. **Group culture.** By and large, group culture is different from organizational culture. A group is an assemblage of individuals who connect based on attributes commonly shared by most members. Typically, such a group creates a specific culture that tends to evolve based on beliefs, standard practices, and behaviors prevailing within the group. Group culture often creates cohesion, trust, and a sense of safety among the members, leading to further collaboration. In general, group culture is made up of the following elements:

   - **Common expectations.** Common expectations impact group culture in a significant way. In particular, they motivate group members to accomplish common desired goals, strengthening a sense of cohesion and purpose within the group.
   - **Common language.** Language is a primary means to communicate as well as understand ideas and actions. As such, it is a critical element in shaping a group culture. In addition, language is a necessary component in developing individuals' thinking and group affinity.
   - **Common context.** Group context (environment) presents physical space for the group and a specific social, business, financial, political, legal, and cultural framework for any group. This group culture "body language" shares values and key messages.
   - **Common routines.** Routines are shared practices involving participation, discussions, learning, or thinking to simplify interactions and minimize confusion. In short, habits serve as scaffolding for groups and individuals to learn and think.

5. **Individual culture.** Individual culture characterizes group members' and organizations' preferences for things and values through personal experiences, including the influence of one's family, peers, school, media, etc. In other words, individual culture is based on who one is and one's social upbringing.

10.5.2 Nature of a Cultural System

In social sciences, culture is the sum of human lifeways, behavior, beliefs, feelings, and thoughts. The following section describes a cultural system in terms of (1) definition of culture, (2) functions of culture, (3) components of culture, (4) characteristics of culture, and (5) aspects of culture.

1. **Definition of culture.** Many scholars have defined human culture. A consolidated description would be: "Culture is defined as the shared patterns of behaviors and interactions, cognitive constructs, and affective understanding learned through socialization."[10]

---

10 Source: Culture: Definition, Functions, Characteristics, Elements of Culture, iEduNote. https://www.iedunote.com/culture. Last accessed: Jan. 2023.

2. **Functions of culture.** Culture provides specific functionality for individuals and groups within human society.
   - **Enabling communication.** Culture provides an infrastructure for maintaining human contact using verbal and nonverbal language.
   - **Transfer of knowledge.** Culture helps transmit customs, rituals, and learning from generation to generation. In particular, the natural socialization process transfers specific cultural expertise to individuals as they grow up and mature.
   - **Define daily situations.** Culture helps define everyday situations by giving individuals additional background knowledge about them and teaching how to behave and act within a given situation.
   - **Define norms.** Culture defines the standards expected of individuals. Culture defines a behavioral boundary demanded from individuals within a given society.
   - **Create identities.** Culture influences how people think of themselves and others regarding values, ethnicity, gender, age, and so on. As such, culture promotes the feeling of social connectedness with family, friends, and people in the wider community who share beliefs, identities, and commitments.
   - **Establish stratification.** Culture differentiates among individuals and social groups based on various criteria like social class (e.g., economic standing), social rank (e.g., political positions), gender, age, and the like.
3. **Components of culture.** By and large, culture has the following essential components: (1) Cognitive components are people's knowledge about the universe, its creation and existence, and its behavior; (2) material components are all the tangible things humans use and appreciate; and (3) Normative components are society's values, beliefs, rules, and norms that guide and regulate individuals' behavior.
4. **Characteristics of culture.** All cultures share five essential elements. Culture is learned, shared, based on symbols, holistic, and dynamic.
   - **Culture is learned.** One learns culture unconsciously from families, peers, institutions, and the media. This process, ingrained in all human societies and known as enculturation, differs from basic biological needs like sleep, food, and sex.
   - **Culture is shared.** One shares behavioral actions and attitudes within a given culture with other group members. Thus, all members of the group act in socially appropriate ways. Nevertheless, an individual's behavior within a given culture is acceptable within varying degrees of tolerance from the norm (also a factor of the culture itself).
   - **Culture is based on symbols.** A symbol is an arbitrary element that stands for something else. For example, wedding rings stand for marriage, and in a traffic light, red means stop and green means go. In particular, language is the essential symbolic component of culture.

- **Culture is holistic.** All aspects of a given culture are interconnected and related to one another. Therefore, understanding a culture involves learning as many parts of the culture as possible.
- **Culture is dynamic.** As time passes, cultures encounter other cultures. Inevitably these cultures exchange ideas and symbols. In the process, each culture changes and adapts to its environment.

5. **Aspects of culture.** Based on the above explanation, one can identify three elements of any given culture: (1) Culture is a pattern of behavior—it refers to the behavior exhibited by most people in a particular culture; (2) culture is learned—one learns it through experiences and interactions with other individuals within the given society; and (3) culture is transmitted from generation to generation—thus, cultural elements endure the entire life span of an individual and, naturally, are transmitted from one generation to the next.

10.5.3 Implications for the UAV SoI

According to Anhée and Dignum (2018), Culture influences individual decisions and collective behavior. However, the exact mechanism of how personal choices affect collective behavior is not so apparent. Therefore, the authors suggest a model that depicts the relationships between culture, individual decisions, and collective behavior (Figure 10.5).

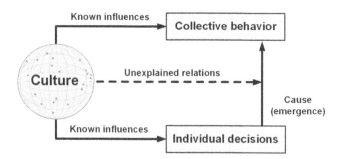

Figure 10.5 Influence of culture on individual decisions and collective behavior.[11]

Cultures reflect fundamental inequalities and individuals' divergences, leading to contrasting patterns of collective behavior. Thus, people worldwide are affiliated with different cultures,[12] which influence UAV systems. Let us illustrate some general examples that, by nature, are very broad and somewhat porous.

---

11 Adapted from Anhée and Dignum, 2018.

12 See more: The University of Hawaii (Pressbooks). Divergent Cultural Characteristics.

1. **Individualistic versus collectivist cultures.** People in individualistic cultures (e.g., the United States, Europe, etc.) value personal freedom and independence. In contrast, people in collectivist cultures, including many in Asia and South America, appreciate the needs of the nation, community, or family. Along this line, the first set of people will probably seek UAV systems that are versatile, reliable, and easy to operate for business and pleasure. In contrast, the second set of people will probably seek UAV systems that are inexpensive and specifically adaptive for use by governments, law enforcement bodies, the military, and the like.

2. **Explicit-rule versus implicit-rule cultures.** In explicit-rule cultures like Germany and Switzerland, the rules are clear, and the people, by and large, are aware of them. In contrast, in implicit-rule cultures like many African countries, the rules are often ambiguous and only partially communicated to the public. Along this line, using relevant languages, the first set of people will probably seek UAV systems that are well documented in their operations, safety, maintenance, and so on. In addition, manufacturers of these UAV systems will be expected to provide sufficient infrastructure for spare parts and operational training tailored to the country's specifics. In contrast, the second set of people will probably seek UAV SoI that, by and large, contain the primary system and little else.

3. **Uncertainty-accepting versus uncertainty-rejecting cultures.** In uncertainty-accepting cultures, such as the United States and Britain, people tolerate life's ambiguities and function efficiently within reasonable levels of instability. In contrast, in uncertainty-rejecting cultures such as the Arab world, people will often attempt to reduce the element of surprise. Along this line, the first set of people will probably seek to purchase and operate the most advanced UAV systems, including the latest and most advanced bells and whistles (gadgets). In contrast, the second set of people will probably seek well-proven and famous UAV systems.

4. **Monochronic versus polychronic cultures.** In monochronic time-oriented cultures, as in North America and north and central Europe, people consider time to be a tangible commodity. Consequently, schedules are carefully planned and are often oriented toward "doing one thing at a time." Along this line, interruptions are to be avoided as much as possible. In contrast, in polychronic time-oriented cultures such as those prevalent in the Mediterranean, South America, Africa, and Asia, time is considered more fluid, the schedule may involve many things simultaneously, and multitasking is valued. Along this line, the first set of people will probably seek an entirely dependable UAV systems that is available for operations whenever needed without surprises. In contrast, the second set of people will probably seek UAV systems designed with sufficient backup capabilities, extra spare parts, and skilled operators who can improvise operational solutions.

5. **Short-term versus long-term cultures.** People in short-term cultures, often located in the United States and other Western countries, revere quick results, seeking to reach success soonest and concentrating on the financial bottom line. In contrast, people in long-term cultures, often located in Asian countries, are influenced by the teachings of Confucius; often value a long-term orientation; and tend to focus on long-term planning, postponing success to a later date. In addition, these people emphasize persistence, personal adaptability, saving, and being thrifty. Along this line, the first set of people will probably seek to buy or trade in older UAV systems with the latest and most sophisticated version of UAV SoI and any relevant gadget available. In contrast, the second set of people will probably seek to keep and maintain existing UAV systems or possibly purchase a used or older version of UAV systems.

6. **Masculine versus feminine cultures.** In general, masculine culture stresses different expectations for men and women. For example, men in countries like Japan, Italy, and Venezuela are expected to be competitive, assertive, and focused on material success. In contrast, women are expected to focus on people, nurturing, and seeking quality family life. Feminine culture that is prevalent in countries like Sweden, Norway, and the Netherlands emphasizes similarities between gender roles, and women and men are expected to be nurturing and focus on people and quality of life. Along this line, people in masculine cultures will probably seek high-performance UAV systems equipped with sophisticated payloads and advanced flight management systems. In contrast, feminine cultures will probably seek UAV systems that can support environmental protection and other quality-of-life missions.

7. **Direct versus indirect communication cultures.** In direct communication cultures, which are common in the United States and most Western countries, parties express their true intentions, needs, and desires freely and explicitly. By and large, the communicating parties take each other's words at face value. They expect short, direct verbal interactions and value honesty and frankness. In contrast, in indirect communication cultures, which often prevail in Japan, China, India, Latin America, Saudi Arabia, and so on, the parties' true intentions are hidden. In particular, indirect speakers tend to avoid statements that might cause tension or result in an uncomfortable situation. In addition, indirect communicators believe that being polite, showing respect, and avoiding humiliation of other people is more important than giving an accurate response. Along this line, individuals from one communication culture attempting to interact with individuals from other communication cultures to achieve a business goal related to UAV systems must respect, understand, and internalize the cultural gap and the language barriers that must be overcome.

8. **Materialism versus human relationships cultures.** Anyone will agree that a certain income and level of material goods are necessary to sustain life.

Still, in worldly cultures that are prevalent in countries like Romania, the United States, New Zealand, Ukraine, and Germany, people often value and place exceeding importance on money and consumption along with acquiring wealth and material possessions. In contrast, in cultures that value human relationships rather than material objects, which prevail in some East Asian countries, people tend to put more value on personal relationships. Such relationships are based on attitudes toward other people as well as ideas and ideals inherited from parents, ancestors, and schools as the primary life drivers. Along this line, the first set of people will probably seek to purchase and use UAV SoI that could be used commercially, that is, by and large the more upscale systems and sensors. In contrast, the second set of people will probably seek to purchase and use UAV systems oriented to hobbyists and photography enthusiasts, which naturally belong to the more economical UAV systems.

9. **Low-power-distance versus high-power-distance cultures.** In low-power-distance cultures, people relate to one another as equals regardless of their formal roles. So, for example, a student will interact with parents, teachers, and other adults in the same way as they deal with their peers and other students. In contrast, the way people relate to one another in high-power-distance cultures reflects their dominant or subordinate formal roles. So, for example, an employee will interact with a manager with appropriate formality, respect, and reverence. Along this line, the first set of people will probably discuss issues related to UAV systems in an accessible, democratic manner, arriving at the best economical and technical solution. In contrast, the second set of people will probably accept a decision regarding, for example, the purchase and use of UAV systems made by senior individuals within the relevant hierarchical group.

10.6 UAV Context: Biosphere Systems

Definition: The biosphere consists of living organisms and nonliving components on Earth. It consists of parts of the following: (1) the lithosphere, which is the thin crust between the Earth's mantle and the atmosphere; (2) the atmosphere, which is composed of a mixture of nitrogen, oxygen, and traces of carbon dioxide, argon, water vapor, and other components; and (3) the hydrosphere, which is the accumulation of water in all its common states (solid, liquid, and gas) as well as the elements dissolved in it. The biosphere systems affect SoIs in numerous ways.

The following analysis describes the biosphere systems context of the UAV SoI.

10.6.1   UAV SoI and the Biosphere

The biosphere involves all living organisms on Earth and their interactions with one another as well as their environment. UAVs can be affected by the biosphere in several ways. The most notable biosphere impact on UAVs involves collision with living organisms like birds, animals, and tree branches. The inevitable results are damage to the UAV, leading to their crash as well as injury or death to the involved birds and other animals. Other impacts may be caused as ants, bees, or other insects penetrating the sensors or other electronic parts of the UAV, causing the UAV to malfunction or crash. Overall, UAVs can be affected by the biosphere in various ways. Therefore, UAV systems designers, builders, and operators must consider these factors.

10.6.2   UAV SoI and the Lithosphere

The lithosphere is the outer solid layer of the Earth, which is comprised of the crust and upper mantle. UAVs can be affected by the lithosphere in several ways. Again, the direct impacts of the lithosphere on UAVs are collisions. For example, UAVs may crash into the terrain they fly over, such as mountains and tall structures such as buildings, bridges, or towers. These conditions can make navigating and performing their intended tasks more challenging for UAVs. In addition, sometimes, UAVs may be employed to assess damage from all types of natural or human-made disasters. Therefore, UAV systems designers, builders, and operators must consider these factors as they design their systems.

10.6.3   UAV SoI and the Atmosphere

The atmosphere is the Earth's protective layer of gases that surround the planet. UAVs are affected by the atmosphere in several ways. Air temperature may affect UAVs, impacting their performance and ability to fly. For example, UAVs that fly in hot temperatures may experience reduced lift and increased drag, which affects their flight stability and control. Conversely, UAVs that fly in frigid temperatures may be affected by ice or frost forming on their surfaces, which can also impact their performance.

Similarly, UAVs may be affected by changes in air pressure, which can impact their performance and ability to fly. For example, UAVs that fly at high altitudes may experience reduced lift due to the lower air pressure, which can affect their flight stability and control. Wind also affects UAVs, impacting their performance and ability to fly. For example, even moderate wind can affect the speed and range of a UAV. Also, strong gusts can cause UAVs to lose stability and control and, in extreme cases, can knock UAVs off course or cause them to crash. Finally, UAVs are affected by precipitation such as rain, snow, or hail, which impacts their performance and ability to fly. Again, UAV systems designers, builders, and operators must consider these factors, interact with users, and design and build their systems to surmount these conditions.

10.6.4 UAV SoI and the Hydrosphere

The hydrosphere is the Earth's water cycle and all of the Earth's bodies of water, including oceans, rivers, lakes, and groundwater. UAV can be affected by the hydrosphere in several ways. First, UAV SoI stored and operated from ships are particularly vulnerable to salt water and fungus growth, which can quickly diminish or hinder their ability to perform their mission. In particular, salt vapor may condense on electronic circuitry, causing corrosion and shorts of electrical connections.

Also, UAVs may be affected by low flying over large bodies of water. For example, UAVs used for military, marine research, or search and rescue operations may need to navigate over choppy or rough seas, impacting their stability and performance. Therefore, UAV systems designers and builders should apply appropriate protection to electronic boards and other sensitive UAV equipment when the system is slated to be stored on and operated from ships. Similarly, navigation and stability systems must be designed for the unique condition of the given UAV SoI operational theater.

10.7 Bibliography

Anhée, L. and Dignum F. (2018). Explaining the emerging influence of culture, from individual influences to collective phenomena. *Journal of Artificial Societies and Social Simulation* 21 (4): 11. http://jasss.soc.surrey.ac.uk/21/4/11.html. Accessed: Jan. 2023.

The University of Hawaii (Pressbooks). Divergent cultural characteristics. https://pressbooks-dev.oer.hawaii.edu/cmchang/chapter/18-4-divergent-cultural-characteristics/. Accessed: Jan. 2023.

Erez, M. and Gati, E. (2004). A dynamic, multi-level model of culture: From the micro level of the individual to the macro level of a global culture. *Applied Psychology: An International Review* 53 (4): 583–598.

Federal Aviation Administration (FAA). (2020, October 6). Fact sheet: Small unmanned aircraft systems (UAV) regulations (Part 107). https://www.faa.gov/news/fact_sheets/news_story.cfm?newsId=22615. Accessed: Jan. 2023.

Hofstede, G. (2001). *Culture's Consequences: Comparing Values, Behaviors, Institutions, and Organizations Across Nations.* Sage.

Hofstede, G., Hofstede, G.J., and Minkov, M. (2010). *Cultures and Organizations: Software of the Mind.* McGraw-Hill Education.

iEduNote. Culture: Definition, functions, characteristics, elements of culture. https://www.iedunote.com/culture. Accessed: Jan. 2023.

NCJ 250283. (2016 December). Considerations and Recommendations for Implementing an Unmanned Aircraft Systems (UAV) Program, US Department of Justice Office of Justice Programs, National Institute of Justice. https://www.ncjrs.gov/pdffiles1/nij/250283.pdf. Accessed: Jan. 2023.

WebPackaging. (2018, June). Drones market: Global major key players research. Forecast to 2023. https://www.webpackaging.com/en/portals/marketresearchfuture/assets/11964671/drones-market-global-major-key-players-research-forecast-to-2023. Accessed: Jan. 2023.

Wong, K. (2020). Organizational culture: Definition, importance, and development. https://www.achievers.com/blog/organizational-culture-definition/#:~:text=Organizational%20culture%20is%20the%20collection,your%20company%20what%20it%20is. Accessed: Jan. 2023.

Part III

Global Environment and Energy: Crisis and Action Plan

11

Global Environment Crisis

11.1 Introduction

As of this writing, humanity faces many global predicaments. The author of this book considers the two most challenging systemic global issues to be the global environmental crisis and its twin, the global energy crisis. Notable environmental research published over a decade ago (Rockstrom et al., 2009) calculated a safe operating space for humanity. It identified 10 areas of global concern, 3 of which were particularly alarming: loss of biodiversity, the nitrogen cycle, and the climate crisis. An updated research, "Earth beyond six of nine planetary boundaries" (Richardson et al., 2023), was released, indicating a significant deterioration of the current earth's environmental conditions[1] (Figure 11.1 and Table 11.1).

Biermann and Kim (2020) reviewed the original planetary boundaries framework. They observed that the 2009 research generated widespread academic debate among social scientists, economists, lawyers, and others, exploring these boundaries and proposing different policy recommendations worldwide. As part of this debate, the planetary boundaries framework aroused three main categories of criticism:

1. **Critique from Earth system science.** Earth system scientists expressed skepticism over the planetary boundaries framework as being too long-term oriented, with some of the global limits being too general and some boundary definitions being inadequate.
2. **Critique from a development perspective.** The planetary boundaries approach has met broad criticisms from scholars and commentators from the Global South (mainly Africa, Asia, and Latin America). In particular, the criticism has centered around the framework boundaries being defined from a planetary perspective, with no concern for local global inequalities and social justice.

---

1 See more: Planetary boundaries - Wikipedia.

Systems Science for Engineers and Scholars, First Edition. Edited by Avner Engel.
© 2024 John Wiley & Sons, Ltd. Published 2024 by John Wiley & Sons, Ltd.

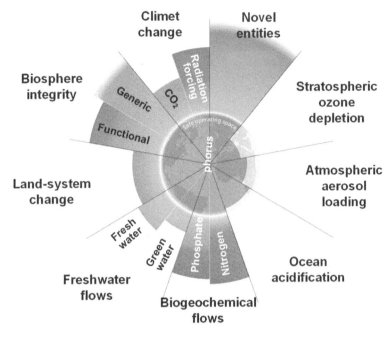

Figure 11.1 Planetary Boundaries (as defined in 2023).

Table 11.1 Planetary Boundaries (as defined in 2023)

Earth-system process	Control variable	Boundary value in 2023	Current value
1. Climate change	Atmospheric carbon dioxide concentration (Parts per million [ppm] by volume)	350	417
	Anthropogenic radiative forcing, top of the atmosphere (Watts per meter squared [W/m²])	1.0	2.91
2. Biosphere integrity	Genetic diversity, Extinction rate (Extinctions per million species-years [E/MSY])	<10	<100
	Human appropriation of net primary production (Percent of preindustrial Holocene)	<10	30
3. Biogeochemical flows	Phosphate (P) flows from freshwater into the ocean and from fertilizers to erodible soils [Tg/year]	11	22
	Nitrogen (N) industrial and intentional fixation [Tg/year]	62	190

Table 11.1 (Continued)

Earth-system process	Control variable	Boundary value in 2023	Current value
4. Ocean acidification	Global mean of calcium carbonate in surface seawater (saturation level)	2.75	2.8
5. Land-system change	Part of the forests rested intact (%)	75	60
6. Freshwater change	Bluewater: human-induced disturbance of flow (Percent of preindustrial Holocene)	10.2	18.2
	Green water: human-induced disturbance of water available to plants (Percent of preindustrial Holocene)	11.1	15.8
7. Stratospheric ozone depletion	Stratospheric ozone concentration (Dobson units [DU[2]])	276	284
8. Atmospheric aerosol loading	Interhemispheric difference (Aerosol optical depth [AOD])	0.1	0.076
9. Novel entities	Synthetic chemicals released to the environment (%)	0	Transgressed

3. **Critique from social science, humanities, and technology perspectives.** Another issue of criticism has been the relevance of the planetary boundaries framework to actual governance. The issue is whether such planetary threshold values are externally determined boundaries or politically decided targets. For example, the definition of the maximum discharge level of pollutants into bodies of water can be framed as an environmental target. In that case, it will be up to policymakers to balance the level of environmental pollution based on prevailing local regulations and societal norms. However, permitted discharge levels can also be framed as a "natural" boundary condition. In that case, the value identification would be in the realm of the experts.

In response, especially to critiques from the social sciences and humanities, the economist Kate Raworth (2018) developed and then expanded a doughnut-shaped visual framework (Figure 11.2) that combines the concept of planetary

---

2 Dobson unit (DU) is a unit of measurement of the amount of a trace gas in a vertical column through the Earth's atmosphere.

environmental boundaries with the reciprocal concept of social boundaries. The outer area of the doughnut represents the planetary boundaries of life. The inner area of the doughnut represents the fraction of people who lack access to life's essentials (i.e., the level of social foundations that are not yet met).

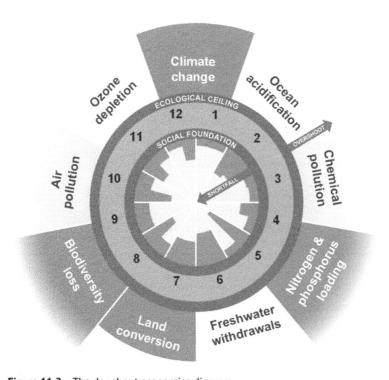

Figure 11.2 The doughnut economics diagram.

The ecological ceilings are adapted, with some modifications, from the planetary boundaries put forward by Rockstrom et al., 2009 study. They are (1) climate change, (2) ocean acidification, (3) chemical pollution, (4) nitrogen and phosphorus loading, (5) freshwater withdrawals, (6) land conversion, (7) biodiversity loss, (8) air pollution, and (9) ozone depletion.

The social foundations are inspired by the 12 social aspirations of the UN Sustainable Development Goals.[3] These are (1) food security, (2) health,

_____
3 See Sustainable Development Goals, Sustainable Development Goals, Wikipedia. Accessed: Jan. 2023.

(3) education, (4) income and work, (5) peace and justice, (6) political voice, (7) social equity, (8) gender equality, (9) housing, (10) networks, (11) energy, and (12) water.

This chapter describes and systemically analyzes the human race's environmental issues so readers can appreciate this vital challenge to humankind. The chapter presents the following:

- Climate change, including the global temperature increase, as well as its causes and impacts on the Earth's lithosphere, hydrosphere, and atmosphere systems (Figure 11.3).
- Biodiversity loss, including the linkage between environmental change and biodiversity loss. In addition, the International Union for Conservation of Nature (IUCN) Red List of endangered species, statistical data, examples, and factors affecting biodiversity. Finally, this chapter portrays the impacts of biodiversity loss on humans.

Chapter 12 proposes a no-nonsense, systemic environmental action plan for humankind based on the global environment's impending adversity.

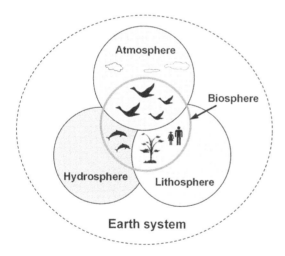

Figure 11.3 Earth system.

11.2 Climate Change

11.2.1 Global Temperature Increase

Several independent researchers have shown that the Earth's climate system is warming. In the 2011 to 2020 decade, the Earth's climate was warmed by an average of 1.09 °C compared with the preindustrial baseline (1850–1900). Surface temperatures are increasing by about 0.2 °C per decade, with 2020 reaching a temperature of 1.2 °C above the preindustrial era. The 2014 Intergovernmental Panel on Climate Change (IPCC) reported that recent global climate change had affected people and nature on every continent and in the oceans (IPCC, 2014). Global shifts in temperature, precipitation, ocean levels, and the frequency of extreme weather events have impacted plant, animal, and human populations. The resulting extinction, migrations, and behavioral shifts fundamentally change our world, leading to catastrophic effects on ecosystems.

For example, global climate change has altered the abundance of food and habitat as well as the latitude and altitude of many species' ranges, transformed interspecies interactions, and changed the locations and timing of migratory species' behaviors. In addition, human-induced nonclimate causes, such as the introduction of invasive species and habitat destruction, contribute to the rapid annual extinction of species worldwide. Still, human-caused climate change plays a significant role, and its influence is expected to grow with time.

Climate change is created by the emission of greenhouse gases, chiefly carbon dioxide (CO_2) and methane (CH_4). Most of these emissions are created by burning fossil fuels for energy production. Certain agricultural practices, industrial processes, and forest loss are additional sources. Many of these impacts are already recognized at the current 1.2 °C level of warming (Figure 11.4 and Figure 11.5). However, additional warming will increase these impacts and may trigger the melting of the Greenland ice sheet.

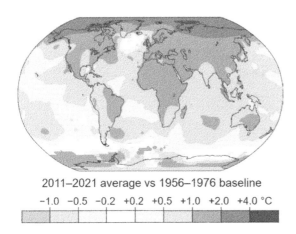

2011–2021 average vs 1956–1976 baseline

−1.0 −0.5 −0.2 +0.2 +0.5 +1.0 +2.0 +4.0 °C

Figure 11.4 Average temperatures from 2011 to 2021 compared to 1956–1976 (Image: NASA).

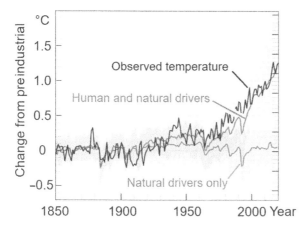

Figure 11.5 Change in average air temperature since the Industrial Revolution.

11.2.2 Causes of Climate Change

An essential approach to determining the human contribution to climate change is to ascertain the individual nature of the causes and then compare these findings with observed patterns of climate change. Analysis shows that climate change occurs in response to several drivers. Among these drivers, the most important ones are (1) greenhouse gases, (2) nitrogen pollution, (3) land surface changes, and (4) climate change feedback.

11.2.2.1 Greenhouse Gases

The four greenhouse gases of interest to this discussion are carbon dioxides, methane, nitrous oxides, and water vapor. In the past 250 years, atmospheric carbon dioxide and methane concentrations have increased, along with human-created emissions such as hydrofluorocarbons, perfluorocarbons, and sulfur hexafluoride. These pollutants are emitted into the atmosphere by burning fossil fuels, deforestation, and harmful agricultural practices—thus amplifying the effects of climate change.

Greenhouse gases are transparent to sunlight that passes through the atmosphere and heats the Earth's surface. The Earth radiates it as heat at an infrared frequency. Much of this heat is absorbed by greenhouse gases. This process decreases the heat escaping into space and traps it near the Earth's surface. Human activity, mainly burning fossil fuels (i.e., coal, oil, and natural gas), has increased the amount of CO_2 and methane, resulting in a radiative imbalance that increased by about 48% and 160%, respectively. For example, the CO_2 levels in the atmosphere are higher now than at any time during the past 2 million years. Likewise, methane concentration is far higher than at any time during the previous 800,000 years.

Figure 11.6 depicts CO_2 emissions per capita versus GDP per capita (as of 2018). For example, with about 1.4 billion inhabitants, China produces 10.2 billion tons of CO_2 annually. In contrast, with approximately 330 million inhabitants, the United States produces 5.2 billion tons of CO_2 annually, which is more than two times China's per capita amount.

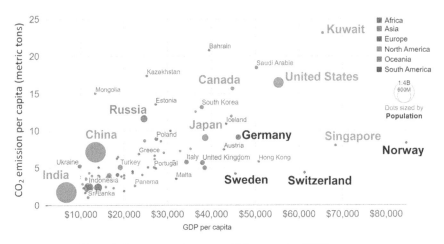

Figure 11.6 CO_2 emissions per capita versus GDP per capita, 2018.

11.2.2.2 Nitrogen Pollution

Two different ongoing human activities create nitrogen pollution. The first is capturing pure nitrogen from the air and converting it into a large amount of synthetic fertilizer like ammonia and nitrous oxide, which help crops grow. In many modern farming systems worldwide, synthetic fertilizers are used instead of nitrogen-fixing crops and manures. As a result, the use of global fertilizer is high, and it continues to grow. This practice responds to attempts to increase food production to feed a growing global population (Figure 11.7).

Manufacturing and using synthetic nitrogen fertilizers contribute to climate change in two ways. First, nitrogen fertilizers can oxidize and evaporate into the air as nitrous oxide when used in excess. Nitrous oxide is a durable greenhouse gas that contributes to global warming. It stays in the atmosphere for many years and is significantly more potent than carbon dioxide (CO_2). In addition, fossil fuels underpin the production of synthetic nitrogen fertilizers.

The other distinct artificial pollution activity stems from the high volume of animal manure and slurry dumped into the environment. This is often created within intensive livestock production farming. This high volume generates vast quantities of the greenhouse gas methane. This gas is around 80 times worse than CO_2 at trapping the Earth's heat, and it persists for a decade or two until it becomes

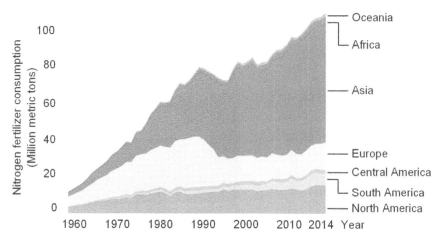

Figure 11.7   Yearly global synthetic nitrogen-based fertilizer consumption.

oxidized and its global warming potential is reduced. In addition, the impact of manure and slurry on waterways is quite significant. This impact occurs through accidental spillages, flooding, and corrupt practices of people and organizations deliberately dumping excess waste into rivers, making the water toxic to fish and other aquatic life forms and unusable for human consumption.

11.2.2.3   Land Surface Changes

The Earth's land surface is a significant carbon sink for CO_2, particularly its forests. Land-surface carbon fixation in the soil and through photosynthesis remove about 30% of annual global CO_2 emissions. The ocean is also a significant carbon sink as CO_2 dissolves in the surface water and sinks into the ocean's interior. All in all, environmental change includes deforestation, intensive monocropping, and urbanization. Deforestation is the purposeful clearing of forested land, often to make space for agriculture and animal grazing as well as to obtain wood for fuel, manufacturing, and construction. Monocropping is growing a single crop (e.g., maize, soybeans, wheat) year after year on the same land. Finally, urbanization is the societal population shift from rural to urban areas. Under this process, towns and cities are formed and become more prominent (Figure 11.8 and Figure 11.9).

This process creates agricultural land-producing products such as beef, corn, palm oil, and logging to produce wood products. As a result, forested land decreased significantly (Figure 11.10), dramatically exacerbating global warming. Furthermore, deforestation prevents trees from absorbing CO_2 in the future. In addition, deforestation is implemented by burning trees, which releases additional CO_2 into the environment.

Figure 11.8 Burning rainforest in Brazil (Image: NASA).

Figure 11.9 Tree clearcutting in southern Finland.

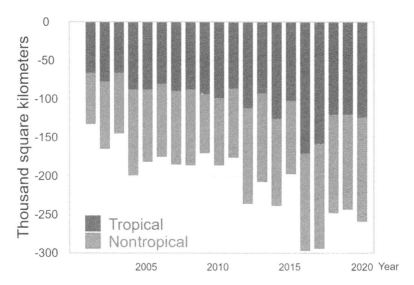

Figure 11.10 Global tree cover annual loss.

11.2.2.4 Climate Change Feedback

Negative and positive heat feedback modify the Earth's response to climate change. Negative feedback reduces the effects of climate change through radiative cooling. As a result, climate change tends to slow down as the Earth radiates more heat to space in response to rising temperatures. Conversely, positive feedback increases the effects of climate change. The main positive feedbacks are water vapor feedback and ice albedo[4] feedback. Water vapor, being a greenhouse gas, holds more moisture and thus further heats the atmosphere. Similarly, as the snow cover and ice in Arctic regions decline, their overall heat reflectivity decreases, contributing to the amplification of Arctic temperature changes.

11.2.3 Climate change impact on the Lithosphere

The Lithosphere is the solid outer skin of the earth. It comprises a brittle crust and the top of the earth's upper mantle (Figure 11.11). Also, it is the most rigid and cold part of the earth, distinguished by its chemistry and mineralogy. From a mechanical standpoint and over thousands of years, the Lithosphere behaves elastically.

---

4 Albedo is the measure of the diffuse reflection of solar radiation out of the total solar radiation.

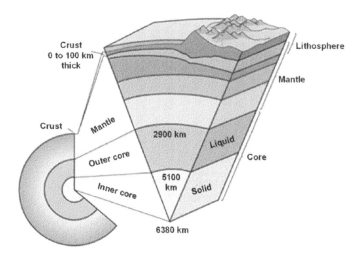

Figure 11.11   Cross-section showing the internal structure of the Earth (Image: derived from USGS).

The environmental effects of climate change dominate the entire globe. For example, since the mid-twentieth century, droughts and heat waves have arisen simultaneously with increasing frequency. Similarly, excessively wet and excessively dry events have dramatically increased worldwide. In addition, the intensity of hurricanes and typhoons is steadily increasing, and tropical cyclones' geographic range is extending poleward.

The impact of climate change on humans can be seen on all continents and ocean regions (Figure 11.12). Extreme weather leads to crop failures and undernutrition. For example, climate change caused a significant reduction in global yields of maize, wheat, and soybeans between 1980 and 2020. Further

Figure 11.12   Worldwide extreme and frequent wildfires and floods.

future warming is expected to negatively affect crop production in low-latitude countries. Similarly, already dry regions and those that are dependent on glacier water have a higher risk of water shortage. In addition, various infectious diseases, such as dengue fever and malaria, are more easily transmitted in warmer climates.

Economic damages due to climate change usher in disastrous consequences for hundreds of millions of people. Moreover, climate change has already increased global economic inequality, which is projected to continue. For example, the most severe impacts occur in sub-Saharan Africa and Southeast Asia, where most local inhabitants depend on natural and agricultural resources. In conclusion, worst-case climate change models project that by the end of this century, almost a quarter of humanity will live in regions where extreme temperatures and rising sea levels will drive unprecedented environmental migration.

11.2.4   Climate Change Impact on the Atmosphere

The atmosphere is comprised of a gaseous layer that is primarily carbon, nitrogen, oxygen, and hydrogen. The atmosphere receives energy from the Sun and vapor from the Earth's surface. The atmosphere then redistributes the heat and moisture across the Earth's surface.

11.2.4.1   Impact on the Atmosphere's Chemical Content

Scientific measurements show shifts in the chemical content of the earth's atmosphere, which will adversely affect the future of human societies. The origin of some of these changes is natural, for example, variations in the intensity of solar radiation, which affect the energy balance and chemistry of the atmosphere. Similarly, volcanic eruptions inject a variety of chemical compounds into the atmosphere. However, such events tend to be periodical and, historically, do not threaten the equilibrium of the global Earth system.

In contrast, human activities change the long-term chemical composition of the atmosphere in a potentially irreversible way by injecting billions of tons of greenhouse gases every year into the atmosphere. For example, burning fossil fuels increases the worldwide concentration of carbon dioxide in the atmosphere. Similarly, human activities like combustion and the use of nitrogen fertilizers increase the engagement of nitrous oxides in the atmosphere. Raising many animals for the meat industry also increases the atmospheric methane concentration.

The results of all of this, depicted in Figure 11.13, are an ever-faster increase in the concentration of greenhouse gases in the atmosphere. This increase is the primary cause of the Earth's warming, amounting to about 1 °C over the past century.

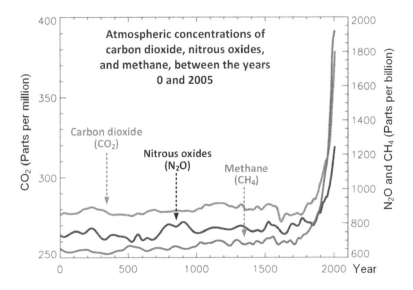

Figure 11.13 Concentration of greenhouse gases over the past 2000 years.[5]

11.2.4.2 Impact on the Nitrogen Cycle

The air in the Earth's atmosphere is comprised of nearly 80% pure nitrogen. However, in an inorganic form (N_2), this abundance of atmospheric nitrogen cannot be used directly by plants or animals because the latter use only various nitrogen compounds rather than its pure form. The nitrogen cycle (Figure 11.14) is a biochemical process in which nitrogen is converted into several compounds, transitioning from the atmosphere to the soil to organisms and back into the atmosphere. It involves several techniques, such as nitrogen fixation, nitrification, denitrification, decay, and putrefaction. Organic nitrogen in various chemical compounds is available to plants via symbiotic soil bacteria, which can convert the inert nitrogen into usable forms such as nitrites and nitrates.

Similarly, the marine nitrogen cycle occurs in aquatic ecosystems, where marine bacteria carry it out. Nitrogen is also created by human activities such as fuel combustion and nitrogen fertilizers. These processes increase the levels of nitrogen-containing compounds in the atmosphere. In addition, nitrogen fertilizers are washed away in lakes and rivers, resulting in eutrophication.[6]

---

5 Adapted from Forster, P.V. et al. (2007). Changes in atmospheric composition. In *Climate Change*. https://www.e-education.psu.edu/meteo300/print/book/export/html/606. Accessed: Jan. 2023.

6 Eutrophication is an excessive richness of nutrients in bodies of water, which causes dense growth of plant life and extinction of marine life from lack of oxygen.

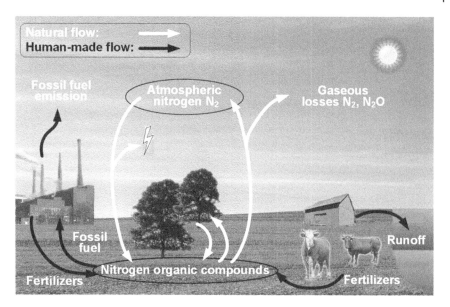

Natural flow: ⟶
Human-made flow: ⟶

Fossil fuel emission

Atmospheric nitrogen N_2

Gaseous losses N_2, N_2O

Fossil fuel

Runoff

Fertilizers

Nitrogen organic compounds

Fertilizers

Figure 11.14 The natural and human-made nitrogen cycle.

11.2.5 Impact of Climate Change on the Hydrosphere

The hydrosphere consists of water in the Earth's oceans, ice sheets, and glaciers; its lakes, rivers, and moisture found in the soil; and within rocks and areas of permafrost, as well as its atmospheric humidity.

11.2.5.1 Impact on the Oceans

Over the past century, the quantity of heat stored in the ocean has increased dramatically. This ocean heat has led to an increase in sea surface temperature at an accelerating rate. Half of this sea-level rise emanates from the natural expansion of the warming water. The other half stems from land-based snow and ice melting into the ocean.

Over the twenty-first century, the sea level is expected to rise by approximately 1.2 meters. However, continued high emissions of greenhouse gases coupled with increased ocean warmth threaten to melt the Antarctic glacier, leading to the possibility of a 2-meter sea level rise by 2100 (Figure 11.15).

Along this line, rising ocean temperatures feed hurricanes and typhoons, which blow harder, drop more rain, and cause increased levels of damage. Also, this high-water temperature shifts global ocean currents that melt Antarctica's ice, which slowly contributes to sea-level rise. A related problem is frequent coastal flooding, affecting much low-lying land worldwide. In addition, the world's oceans have become more acidic due to higher atmospheric CO_2 concentrations in the water.

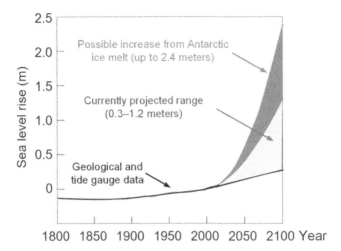

Figure 11.15 Historical sea level projections up to 2100.

11.2.5.2 Impact on the Ice Caps, Glaciers, and Permanent Snow

The latest measurements suggest that Arctic sea ice has decreased over time. This decrease is because the length of its melt season has grown, and the ice has become thinner. In contrast, Antarctic sea ice seems to have increased slightly. Nevertheless, the decline of the former substantially outweighs any growth of the latter.

Similarly, glaciers worldwide have diminished since the 1960s, and the rate at which they melt has accelerated over recent decades. Naturally, this glacier ice loss contributes to rising sea levels. Along the same line, between 1972 and 2015, North America's average snow-covered area decreased by about 8500 square kilometers per year. Furthermore, the average snow depth throughout the United States declined by about 25% between 1955 and 2016.

11.2.5.3 Impact on Groundwater, Ground Ice, and Permafrost

Over recent decades, atmospheric warming has contributed to a significant decrease in the distribution and thickness of permafrost in many northern regions of the world, and this degradation is expected to accelerate during the next century. Permafrost acts as an impenetrable barrier, confining the flow of groundwater and methane. However, as permafrost thaws, groundwater storage, and connectivity increase, impacting wetlands and surface water bodies that rely on groundwater exchange.

In addition, the permafrost in the Arctic region acts as a store of the greenhouse gas methane. So, with the declining volume of permafrost, methane from this repository created by rotting biomass is released into the atmosphere, thus increasing global warming and the greenhouse effect.

11.3   Biodiversity Loss

11.3.1   Environmental Change and Biodiversity

The biosphere is the domain of life on Earth. More specifically, it is the total of all Earth places where organisms live, including portions of the lithosphere, hydrosphere, and atmosphere. Under ecological equilibrium, all organisms live in balance with one another and the environment, so these organisms evolve and change while maintaining their stable biodiversity.

Biodiversity may be defined as the spectrum of life on Earth in various forms, including species diversity, genetic variations, and the interaction among these lifeforms. Biodiversity loss consists of the worldwide extinction of different species and the local reduction or loss of species in various habitats. As mentioned above, the current global biodiversity loss, driven by human activities, has, so far, proven irreversible. The global diversity loss rate is the fastest in human history and is expected to accelerate in the coming years. These rapidly rising extinction trends impact numerous species, including mammals, birds, reptiles, amphibians, fish, and humans.

11.3.2   Biodiversity Loss: IUCN Classification

The International Union for Conservation of Nature (IUCN) Red List[7] classifies species into nine groups depending upon criteria such as (1) rate of decline, (2) population size, (3) area of geographic distribution, and (4) degree of population and distribution fragmentation.[8] These IUCN Red List categories are:

1. **Extinct (EX).** A species is extinct when there is no reasonable doubt that the last individual has died. This condition happens when exhaustive surveys in known and/or expected habitat, at appropriate times (diurnal, seasonal, annual), throughout its historic range have failed to record an individual. Surveys should be over a time frame appropriate to the species' life cycles and life forms.
2. **Extinct in the wild (EW).** A species is extinct in the wild when it is known to survive only in cultivation, in captivity, or as a naturalized population well outside its past range. A species is presumed to be extinct in the wild when exhaustive surveys in known and/or expected habitat, at appropriate times, throughout its historic range have failed to record an individual.

———

7 The International Union for Conservation of Nature (IUCN). Red list of threatened species. https://www.iucnredlist.org/.

8 Guidelines for using the IUCN red list categories and criteria, version 15.1. (2022, July). https://www.iucnredlist.org/resources/redlistguidelines. Accessed. Jan. 2022.

3. **Critically endangered (CR).** A species is critically endangered when the best available evidence indicates that it is facing an extremely high risk of extinction in the wild.

4. **Endangered (EN).** A species is endangered when the best available evidence indicates it faces a very high risk of extinction in the wild.

5. **Vulnerable (VU).** A species is vulnerable when the best available evidence indicates that it faces a high risk of extinction in the wild.

6. **Near threatened (NT).** A species is near threatened when it does not qualify for the critically endangered, endangered, or vulnerable categories now but is close to qualifying for or is likely to qualify for a threatened category soon.

7. **Least concern (LC).** A species is of least concern when it does not qualify for the critically endangered, endangered, vulnerable, or near threatened categories. Widespread and abundant species are included in this category.

8. **Data deficient (DD).** A species is considered to be data deficient when there is inadequate information to directly or indirectly assess its risk of extinction based on its distribution as well as the population status.

9. **Not evaluated (NE).** A species is considered to be not evaluated when it has not yet been evaluated against any criteria.

11.3.3 Biodiversity Loss: Statistical View

An endangered species is threatened with extinction in the near future. This status applies to both global and local areas. The survival of endangered species is at risk due to habitat loss, poaching, and invasive species. The IUCN Red List identifies the conservation status of many species, and various other agencies assess the status of species within specific areas. As of 2022, the IUCN Red List had assigned more than 42,100 species to a threatened category (EX, CR, EN, or VU), which is almost 30% of all assessed species (Figure 11.16).

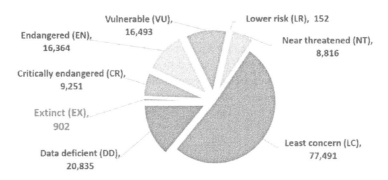

Figure 11.16 Species assigned to IUCN Red List categories, 2022.

The set of nearly 30% of the assessed species indicated in Figure 11.16 is shown in Figure 11.17, organized along 14 groups of species (i.e., cephalopods; bony fishes[9]; gastropods; birds; insects; reptiles; mammals; crustaceans; conifers; reef-forming corals; sharks, rays, and chimeras; dicots; amphibians; and cycads).

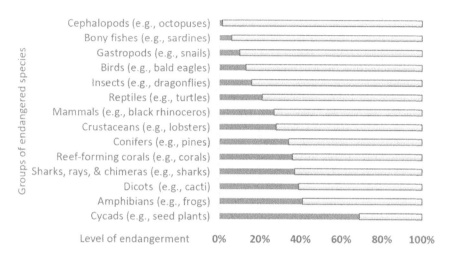

Figure 11.17   ICUN Red List endangered species groups, 2022.

11.3.4   Examples of Endangered Species

The following text provides examples of species from each species group identified in Figure 11.17.

1. Example from the cephalopods group

The cephalopods group comprises intelligent ocean-dwelling species, including octopuses, squids, cuttlefishes, and shelled-chambered nautiluses.

Example image: The giant Australian cuttlefish sepia apama is listed in the IUCN Red List as near threatened.

9 The term fishes is used as a plural when there are more than one species, especially in scientific settings.

2. Example from the bony fishes group

Bony fishes are a diverse superclass of vertebrates[10] with skeletons primarily composed of bony tissue. They include anchovies, herrings, sardines, angelfishes, billfishes, blennies, bonefishes, butterflyfishes, cornet fishes, croakers and drums, dragonfishes, and light fishes.

Example image: The proterorhinus tataricus is listed in the IUCN Red List as critically endangered.

3. Example from the gastropods group

Gastropods are a large group of mollusks, including abalones and cone snails. They have muscular feet, eyes, tentacles, and specialized rasp-like feeding organs.

Example image: The achatinella fuscobasis is listed in the IUCN Red List as critically endangered.

4. Example from the birds group

Birds are a group of warm-blooded vertebrates characterized by feathers, toothless beaked jaws, and a strong yet lightweight skeleton. Birds lay hard-shelled eggs and have a high metabolic heart rate.

Example image: The kakapo strigops habroptila fuscobasis is listed in the IUCN Red List as critically endangered.

---

10 Vertebrates: large group of animals that includes mammals, birds, reptiles, amphibians, and fishes. They are distinguished by the presence of a backbone or spinal column.

5. Example from the insects group

Insects are the largest group of animals, and they are diverse. They have a three-part body (i.e., head, thorax, and abdomen), three pairs of jointed limbs, compound eyes, and one pair of antennae.

Example image: The Lord Howe Island stick-insect dryococelus australis is listed in the IUCN Red List as critically endangered.

6. Example from the reptiles group

Turtles, crocodilians, lizards, and snakes are reptiles. The origin of the reptiles lies about 300 million years ago, in the steaming swamps of the late Carboniferous period.

Example image: The calumma tarzan is listed in the IUCN Red List as critically endangered.

7. Example from the mammals group

Mammals are vertebrate animals. They are characterized by a neocortex region of the brain, as well as a body covered by fur or hair and milk-producing mammary glands for feeding their young.

Example image: The eastern lowland gorilla is listed in the IUCN Red List as critically endangered.

8. Example from the crustaceans group

Crustaceans are diverse invertebrate animals, including crabs, lobsters, shrimps, krill, copepods, and less dynamic sessile creatures like barnacles. All crustaceans have hard but flexible shells.

Example image: The tadpole shrimp triops gadensis is listed in the IUCN Red List as endangered.

9. Example from the conifers group

Conifers are a group of cone-bearing seed plants. Conifers are ecologically important because they are the dominant plants over large land areas, most notably in mountains and cool climate areas of the Earth.

Example image: The wollemia nobilis is listed in the IUCN Red List as critically endangered.

10. Example from the reef-forming corals group

Corals are marine invertebrates that form large colonies of many identical individual polyps. They build reefs that inhabit tropical oceans and secrete calcium carbonate to form hard skeletons. Coral colonies constitute many genetically identical polyps that are typically a few centimeters in height and a few

millimeters in diameter. Over many generations, a colony creates a typical structure for each species. Corals contribute to the physical structure of the coral reefs that evolve in tropical waters, such as the Great Barrier Reef east of Australia.

Example image: The staghorn coral acropora cervicornis is listed in the IUCN Red List as critically endangered.

11. Example from the sharks, rays, and chimeras group

Sharks are a group of fish distinguished by a cartilaginous skeleton and pectoral fins not fused to the head. Sharks range in size from the small deep-sea species that are less than 20 centimeters long to the whale shark, reaching approximately 12 meters. They are found in all seas and are common in depths up to 2 kilometers.

Rays are also cartilaginous fish. They are the largest group of cartilaginous fish, with more than 600 subspecies. Rays are also distinguished by their flattened bodies and pectoral fins fused to the head and located on their ventral surfaces.

Chimeras are also cartilaginous fish that are primarily confined to deep waters. Chimaeras' ancestors lived nearly 400 million years ago.

Example image: The green sawfish pristis zijsron is listed in the IUCN Red List as critically endangered.

12. Example from the dicots group

The dicots group consists of birches, cacti, magnolias, maples, oaks, the protea family, southern beeches, teas, and similar plants.

Example image: The golden barrel echinocactus grusonii is listed in the IUCN Red List as endangered.

13. Example from the amphibians group

Amphibians are four-limb vertebrates that depend on external sources of body heat (i.e., they are ectothermic). They live in various habitats, with most species living within aquatic ecosystems. By and large, amphibians start as larvae living in the water.

Example image: Rabb's fringe-limbed treefrog ecnomiohyla rabborum is listed in the IUCN Red List as critically endangered.

14. Example from the cycads group

Cycads are seed plants with stout and woody trunks and a crown of large, strong, stiff evergreen leaves. These leaves are often organized in a multidivided arrangement, growing from both sides of a standard stem. The species is characterized by individual plants that are either male or female. Cycads vary in size, from trunks that are only a few centimeters to several meters tall. Cycads have naked seeds exposed to the air to be directly fertilized by pollination.

Example image: The palmita zamia inermis is listed in the IUCN Red List as critically endangered.

11.3.5 Factors Affecting Biodiversity Loss

11.3.5.1 Climate Change

Plants and animals are accustomed to living in environments within a well-defined temperature spectrum, but those ranges are moving. A study of more than 1700 animal and plant species demonstrated that in every decade since 1950, species have shifted on average 6.1 kilometers toward the poles to compensate for increasing global temperatures. A more recent study suggested that, on average, 23 groups of species moved nearly 17 kilometers toward the poles per decade. Similarly, marine species have moved to colder waters over the past century.

However, individual species' ability to respond depends on mobility, size, longevity, and life cycle. For example, most plants cannot keep up with changing global temperatures in the twenty-first century, whereas most animals can adapt (through migration) to the current slow rates of climate change. Nevertheless, even species that can outrun climate change are often confined to their natural indigenous ecosystem. For example, although primates are highly mobile, most are limited to forest habitats that are being rapidly destroyed by humans.

Furthermore, a warmer upper layer in lakes reduces oxygen flow into deeper water. This process creates large areas of water that are depleted of oxygen and thus cannot support life. Persistent "dead zones" produce toxic algal blooms, massive fish kills, and foul-smelling drinking water. In addition, increasing amounts of rain rather than snow and more severe and frequent flooding, which are linked to global warming, stress native aquatic plants and animals. For example, ongoing measurements in rivers and streams show that, for various reasons, the survival rates of fish species have been diminishing over time.

Plant and animal species native to polar latitudes gradually go extinct as their environments warm beyond their tolerance ability. For example, in Antarctica, penguin populations are declining, while polar bear populations in the Arctic have been decimated due to shorter hunting seasons and receding sea ice.[11]

Relatively rapid changes in the climate also affect normal evolutionary processes because only a tiny portion of a species' population possesses the genetic makeup to survive in warmer climates. This limitation creates a narrow population bottleneck, limiting genetic diversity due to increasing inbreeding.

In addition, global climate change influences species' geographic ranges. For example, a study of bird species in the Sierra Nevada Mountains showed that rising temperatures pushed some species to higher, cooler elevations. However, increasing rain upslope forced others to move downslope. Clearly, some species react more to changes in temperature, while others react more to changes in precipitation. Changing global temperatures also shift the cycle of life in nature.

---

11 As the fall freeze-up of ice over the shallow waters is delayed, polar bears face a shorter period to hunt in areas where seals tend to concentrate.

Thus, seasonal events in animal and plant life cycles occur earlier and earlier with each passing decade. For example, this timing disruption leads flowers to bloom when pollinators are in hibernation, mammals to awake from winter hibernation with less food available, and butterflies and birds' early migration disrupt the timing of interspecies interactions.

11.3.5.2 Land-Use Intensification

There is no doubt that land-use change is having a profound impact on biodiversity. Agricultural intensification, urbanization, deforestation, and other significant land-use changes are affecting the abundance and diversity of many species.

A recent global biodiversity assessment concluded that land-use change has had the most significant relative negative impact on terrestrial and freshwater biodiversity (Intergovernmental Science-Policy Platform on Biodiversity and Ecosystem Services [IPBES], 2019). The impact of land-use change on biodiversity is evident at the local level. For example, a study of the impact of forest clearance and conversion to other land uses in Cameroon found a reduction of 75% in bird species diversity.

In addition, extensive human global intervention in free-flowing rivers utilizing dams, levees, hydropower, and habitat degradation has reduced the number of earth's longest free-flowing rivers by two-thirds (Figure 11.18).

Figure 11.18 The Gordon River dam, Southwest National Park, Tasmania, Australia.

11.3.5.3 Global Habitat Loss

Habitat destruction is critical in species extinctions, especially in tropical forest destruction. This process stems directly from the systematic linkage between habitat size and the number of species. In particular, physically larger species living in forests and oceans are sensitive to reduced habitat size. So, all forms of agricultural practices—like clearing and draining the land, eradicating weeds and pests, and supporting just a limited set of domesticated plant and animal species—affect the habitats and their species. In addition, some countries' property rights practices and lax laws/regulatory enforcement are associated with deforestation and habitat loss.

11.3.5.4 Global Pollution

Pollutants created by industrial and agricultural activities are sulfur dioxide and nitrogen oxides. They are emitted into the atmosphere by burning fossil fuels and biomass, deforestation, and various agricultural practices. Sulfur dioxide and nitrogen oxide introduced into the atmosphere react with cloud droplets, raindrops, or snowflakes, creating sulfuric and nitric acids. During precipitation, this process creates acid rain, destroying forests and agricultural assets at a significant distance (hundreds of kilometers) from the emission source (Figure 11.19).

Figure 11.19 Effects of acid rain in the woods of Jizera Mountains, Czech Republic.

11.3.5.5 Overexploitation and Unsustainable Use

Overexploitation occurs when renewable resources are harvested to the point of destruction of the resource. Exploitation often occurs with water aquifers, grazing meadows, forests, wild medicinal plants, fish, and other wildlife. All of this occurs in the context of human economic activity that involves exploiting organisms and biological resources in more significant numbers than their populations can withstand.

For example, current human demands and consumption have resulted in overfishing, which has led to a loss in marine biodiversity, with reduced fish species richness and depletion of large fish at the top of the marine food chain. A UN Food and Agriculture Organization (FAO, 2020) report classified 34% of the fish stocks of the world's marine fisheries as overfished. By 2020, global fish populations were reduced by 38% compared to 1970. It is chiefly fishery methods such as longline fishing and bottom trawling that have caused habitat destruction and regional species richness to decline.

11.3.5.6 Invasive Species

Biodiversity loss includes migrant species that displace native species. This process alters species richness and changes ecosystems' functions and services. Biological invasions contributing to biodiversity loss have increased immensely worldwide due to economic globalization and global warming. Ecosystems susceptible to biological invasions include coastal areas and freshwater ecosystems. Invasive species are introduced to the new habitat, intentionally or unintentionally, by human activities and global warming, which induce more significant migration and distribution of species dependent on warm climates.

For example, recent warming has driven many species poleward, seeking colder temperatures. For example, the Florida Fish and Wildlife Conservation Commission (FWC) listed eight "Reptiles of Concern."[12] This list includes three snakes distinguished by their large size and aggressive nature: (1) the Burmese python (*Python molurus bivittatus*), which is typically found in Southeast Asia; (2) the African rock python (*Python sebae*), which is typically found in central and south Africa, and (3) the yellow anaconda (*Eunectes notaeus*), which is typically found in tropical South America (Figure 11.20).

Figure 11.20 Invasive species migrating north: snakes as an example.

---

12 Florida Fish and Wildlife Conservation Commission (FWC). Reptiles of concern. https:// myfwc.com/license/captive-wildlife/reptiles-of-concern/. Accessed: Jan. 2023.

In addition, climate change affects wildlife behavior, including foraging, migration, and reproduction. Drivers of phenology such as mating, breeding, hibernation, and post-hibernation benefit some species and harm others. For example, some climate parameters, such as photoperiod (the daily duration each organism receives illumination), are constant, while the timing of spring weather changes because of greenhouse gases. In summary, climate change endangers native terrestrial wildlife and alters the function and structure of their ecosystem.

11.3.5.7 Impacts of Biodiversity Loss on Humans

The impacts of biodiversity loss on people include impacts on economic and societal systems as well as on human health. First, humans rely on various plants, animals, and other organisms for food and other needs, and their availability is vital to all cultures. In 2019, the UN's FAO produced a report on the state of the world's biodiversity for food and agriculture, which warned, "Many key components of biodiversity for food and agriculture at genetic, species and ecosystem levels are in decline" (FAO, 2019). The report also indicated that "loss and degradation of forest and aquatic ecosystems and, in many production systems, transition to intensive production of a reduced number of species, breeds, and varieties, remain major drivers of loss of Biodiversity for Food and Agriculture (BFA) and ecosystem services."[13]

In addition, biodiversity losses reduce the utilization of medicinal plants, which is especially significant to some 70% to 80% of individuals worldwide who rely solely on plant-based medicine. Furthermore, the biological diversity of microorganisms, flora, and fauna provides extensive benefits for natural, health, and pharmacological sciences. These developments also hinder medical and pharmacological discoveries, which rely on discovering active biological ingredients and applying them to modern medicine. Finally, patterns of infectious diseases are sensitive to decreased biodiversity and thus to ecosystem changes. Significant processes affecting infectious disease reservoirs and transmission include deforestation, land-use changes, water management, large-scale irrigation projects, and uncontrolled urbanization.

11.4 Bibliography

Biermann, F. and Kim, R.E. (2020). The boundaries of the planetary boundary framework: A critical appraisal of approaches to define a "safe operating space" for humanity. *Annual Review of Environment and Resources* 45 (1): 497–521.

---

13 See: Biodiversity loss. Biodiversity loss - Wikipedia. Accessed Jan. 2023.

Brondizio, E.S., Settele, J., Díaz, S., and Ngo, H.T. (Eds.). (2019). Global Assessment Report on Biodiversity and Ecosystem Services of the Intergovernmental Science-Policy Platform on Biodiversity and Ecosystem Services (IPBES).

Food and Agriculture Organization of the United Nations (FAO). (2019). The state of world biodiversity for food and agriculture. https://www.fao.org/3/CA3129EN/CA3129EN.pdf. Accessed: Jan. 2023.

Food and Agriculture Organization of the United Nations (FAO). (2020). The state of world fisheries and aquaculture: sustainability in action. https://www.fao.org/3/ca9229en/ca9229en.pdf. Accessed: Jan. 2023.

Forster, P.V. et al. (2007). Changes in atmospheric composition. In *Climate Change*. https://www.e-education.psu.edu/meteo300/print/book/export/html/606. Accessed: Jan. 2023.

Intergovernmental Panel on Climate Change (IPCC). (2014). Fifth assessment report: Impacts, adaptation, and vulnerability. http://www.ipcc.ch/report/ar5/wg2/. Accessed: Jan. 2023.

Raworth, K. (2018). *Doughnut Economics: Seven Ways to Think Like a 21st-Century Economist,* illustrated edition. Chelsea Green Publishing.

Richardson K. et al. (2023 Sep.). Earth beyond six of nine planetary boundaries. *Science Advances*, 15; 9 (37). Earth beyond six of nine planetary boundaries - PMC (nih.gov). Accessed Nov., 2023.

Rockstrom, J., Steffen, W., Noone, K., et al. (2009). A safe operating space for humanity. *Nature* 461: 472–475. https://doi.org/10.1038/461472a. Accessed: Jan. 2023.

Schwartz, M. (2014, June 30). Ecosystem shift: How global climate change is reshaping the biosphere. Blog, Special edition on climate change, Harvard University. http://sitn.hms.harvard.edu/flash/2014/ecosystem-shift-how-global-climate-change-is-reshaping-the-biosphere/. Accessed: Jan. 2023.

12

Systemic Environment Action Plan

12.1 Introduction

The author of this book believes that humankind faces its most challenging undertaking involving the Earth's environment and the production of renewable and clean energy. Only concerted efforts by governments, scientists, engineers, and the world public can address these issues effectively. Currently, little is being done about the environmental problem. However, this benign attitude will change drastically as life on this planet becomes more and more unbearable for more and more people. Then federal, state, and local governments; environmental scientists; engineers; and the public will unite to propose and carry out measures to combat global environmental threats to the human species.

The following is this author's opinion regarding what can be done about the environmental problem and what is practical.[1] This opinion may not coincide with official, governmental, and some pundits' declarations and official boasting, so the reader should make up his own mind regarding the following proposed systemic action plan. This chapter contains the following parts:

- Sustaining the earth's environment, which includes sustaining an eco-friendly lithosphere, atmosphere, hydrosphere, and biosphere
- Sustaining human society, including providing food for humankind, implementing a circular economy, reducing materials consumption, legislating ecological taxation, curbing human population, and supporting political action

12.2 Sustaining the Earth's Environment

This section describes practical means to sustain the Earth's system. It includes sustaining the lithosphere, atmosphere, hydrosphere, and biosphere.

---

1 Credit for some of the ideas presented in this chapter is due to Miller and Spoolman. (2018). *Environmental Science*. Cengage Learning.

Systems Science for Engineers and Scholars, First Edition. Edited by Avner Engel.
© 2024 John Wiley & Sons, Ltd. Published 2024 by John Wiley & Sons, Ltd.

12.2.1 Sustaining an Eco-Friendly Lithosphere

The lithosphere is the solid outer skin of the Earth. Sustaining an eco-friendly lithosphere involves the following practical actions.

12.2.1.1 Protecting, Restoring, and Expanding Critical Ecosystems

Governments should protect, restore, and expand critical ecosystems within national parks, national marine conservation areas, and other places to combat climate change. Typically, mangroves and other, forests, wetlands, rivers, and oceans absorb large quantities of carbon, which slows warming. In addition, wetlands absorb excess water from floods, while mangroves serve as an excellent barrier against tropical storms, two extreme weather phenomena that are exacerbated by climate change.

12.2.1.2 Dealing with Hazardous Waste

A sustainable approach to hazardous waste management is producing less, recycling and reusing, converting the remaining products to less hazardous substances, and safely putting the remainder into perpetual storage (Figure 12.1). For example, coal ash ponds (called surface impoundments) created in a coal-fired power plant are depicted in Figure 12.2.

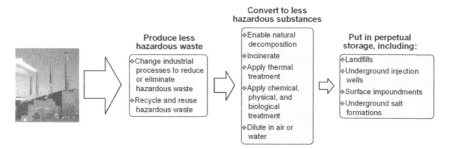

Figure 12.1 Sustainable hazardous waste management.

Figure 12.2 Coal-fired power plant with ash impoundments at image background.

12.2.2 Sustaining an Eco-Friendly Atmosphere

The atmosphere is the whole mass of gases surrounding the Earth. Sustaining an eco-friendly atmosphere involves the following practical actions.

12.2.2.1 Carrying out Environmental Actions

First, governments should make it easier to live without automobiles. City planners should redesign city streets, providing safe and convenient walkways and bike trails. In addition, the reckless destruction of forests, especially in the Amazon basin, cannot be tolerated by the global community anymore. Therefore, countries and states should evolve aggressive global treaties on deforestation. The treaties should prohibit cutting down tropical forests. In particular, rogue nations should have to accept that the deforestation treaties supersede national laws and regulations. In addition, the treaties should include a transborder international enforcement body with powers to inspect tree-cutting activities on the ground, including forceful prevention of illegal logging action (Figure 12.3).

Figure 12.3 Criminal gangs are responsible for illegally clear-cutting timber in Brazil.

12.2.2.2 Carrying Out Technological Actions

Another critical action relates to the systemic sequestration of greenhouse gases from heavy industry, especially coal-fired power plants. Practical greenhouse gas mitigation is an array of systems and techniques that mitigate the air pollution created by such industries (Figure 12.4).

First, the focus should be on removing particulates that cause air pollution, illness, and premature deaths. Next, sulfur dioxide (SO_2) and nitrogen oxides (NO_x), gases that cause acid rain, should be removed. A much more complex and expensive undertaking is the carbon sequestration process, that is, indefinitely capturing, transporting, and storing carbon dioxide (CO_2) in a deep underground geological formation.

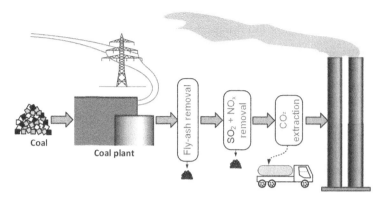

Figure 12.4   Coal pollution mitigation.

Figure 12.5 depicts how the carbon capture and storage (CCS) process is realized. Carbon dioxide from industrial sources is extracted, liquefied, transported by ship or pipeline, and stored in reservoirs like geological cavities or exhausted oil and gas wells at depths of a few kilometers. Although the coal energy return on investment (EROI) value is relatively high, coal pollution mitigation and primarily carbon sequestration are energy-intensive processes that reduce the net coal EROI value significantly.

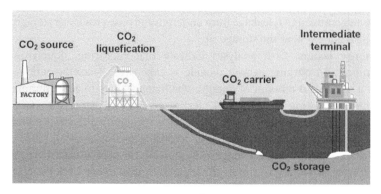

Figure 12.5 CO_2 sequestration system.[2]

This strategy is studied by the US National Energy Technology Laboratory (NETL), which reports that the United States and Canada have enough storage capacity for more than 900 years of CO_2 at current production rates.

---

2 Adapted from Metz et al. 2005.

Experts believe that large-scale industrial carbon dioxide sequestration must be examined while considering the following concerns:

1. **Untested/unproven technology.** Large-scale industrial carbon dioxide sequestration is an untested and unproven technology. Opponents of CO_2 sequestration believe that further testing and analysis must be done before such new technology is used. For example, CO_2 in deep ocean storage may not stay on the bottom of the ocean; instead, it could leak upward into the atmosphere. Another concern related to deep ocean storage is that the carbon dioxide added to the ocean will turn it acidic and endanger aquatic life.

2. **Safety concerns.** Accidents during the transport of carbon dioxide must be considered. Accidents may result from leakage in pipelines or transport ships carrying liquid CO_2 as well as from onshore or offshore CO_2 storage facilities. According to the Intergovernmental Panel on Climate Change (IPCC), leaking CO_2 from components of the transportation chain at concentration levels of about 10% in the air could pose an immediate threat to human life (Metz et al. 2005).

   Leakage from underground storage facilities where carbon dioxide is stored in huge volumes is also possible. This risk is severe because carbon dioxide gas is denser than air and would remain near the Earth's surface for a relatively long time. A sudden leak of CO_2 could endanger people and animals in the surrounding area. Similarly, gradual leaks from CO_2 injection wells can contaminate the soil and groundwater surrounding the storage site. Finally, natural calamities such as powerful seismic events or human-induced incidents may cause a CO_2 leakage from underground or sea reservoir storage, disrupting the areas near the storage site.

3. **Cost/energy issues.** Cost analyses indicate that capturing, liquefying, transporting, and burying carbon dioxide is expensive. Also, the process requires a significant amount of energy, which contributes to air pollution. So, equipping existing industry and electric generation plants with CCS technology will necessarily increase the cost of generating electricity and creating various products. For example, according to Davies et al. (2013), paying for CCS technology is estimated to increase the cost of electricity by 50% to 80%. So, without government financial incentive to use CCS, the cost of equipment to separate CO_2, build and operate infrastructure to transport it, and store it may be prohibitively high.

In summary, as of 2022, carbon capture and storage have a limited role in mitigating climate change. Currently, CCS captures only about one-thousandth of global CO_2 emissions; most projects involve natural gas processing. Moreover, the technology has a success rate of only between 50% and 70% of captured carbon.

---

3 Adapted from Carbon capture and storage. Wikipedia. https://en.wikipedia.org/wiki/Carbon_capture_and_storage. Last accessed: Jan. 2023.

Nevertheless, at this writing, more than 200 carbon capture and storage projects are operational or under development worldwide[3] (Figure 12.6). For example, Denmark has assumed a pioneering role among European countries with Project Greensand, the first storage of CO_2 in a depleted oil well in the Danish North Sea.

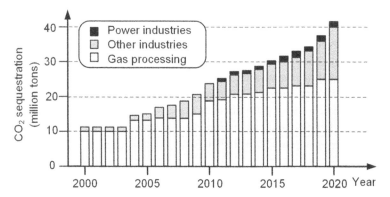

Figure 12.6 Historical data on CO_2 sequestration.

12.2.2.3 Carrying Out Economic Actions
Countries and states should incentivize using low-sulfur coal, remove sulfur from coal, and convert coal into liquid or gaseous fuel. Similarly, governments should subsidize various public transportation—trains, buses, and subways—that is clean, safe, and frequently run throughout metropolitan areas and among cities. These incentives should be made by putting an economical price on each unit of these greenhouse gases emitted by fossil fuel use and, in parallel, reciprocating by reducing taxes on income, wages, and profits. In parallel with the above, governments should phase out all subsidies and tax breaks for environmentally harmful fossil fuels and phase in government subsidies and tax breaks for energy efficiency technologies, carbon-free renewable energy sources, and more sustainable agriculture.

12.2.2.4 Carrying Out Legal Actions
Governments and states should undertake the following actions. First, strictly regulate carbon dioxide (CO_2) and methane (CH_4) as the primary source of climate-changing pollutants. This regulation should be applied to all polluters: power stations, big industries, and transport vehicles. In particular, power plants and industries using low-grade coal should be gradually replaced with less polluting systems. Second, states should set stringent emission standards, require emission control devices, inspect automobile exhaust systems yearly, and get older polluting cars off the road. In addition, states should incentivize people to use mass transit and purchase low-polluting, energy-efficient vehicles.

Similarly, states should set stricter emissions standards for organic compounds (e.g., formaldehyde) used in carpets, furnitures, and building materials. In addition, organizations and households should use fewer polluting substitutes for cleaning agents, paints, and other products. Finally, buildings should be designed for adequate air circulation, and air should be changed frequently within buildings.

12.2.2.5 Carrying Out Educational Actions

Schools and universities should be involved in environmental education so that most people worldwide will be familiar with environmental issues, engage in problem-solving, and take action to improve the environment. The components of environmental education are awareness, understanding, and sensitivity to the environment and its challenges. Education should also instill an attitude of concern for the environment; help develop skills to identify and help resolve environmental challenges; and, most importantly, encourage participation in activities that resolve environmental challenges.

12.2.3 Sustaining an Eco-Friendly Hydrosphere

The hydrosphere constitutes all the Earth's water in all its forms, including ice, liquid, and vapor. Sustaining an eco-friendly hydrosphere involves the following practical actions.

12.2.3.1 Water Use and Scarcity

Over the past 125 years, annual global water consumption increased by a factor of five (Figure 12.7). The main reasons for this increase are the growth of the world population, improving living standards, changing consumption patterns, and expanding irrigated agriculture. In addition, climate change, deforestation, increased water pollution, and wasteful use of water contribute to increased global water consumption.

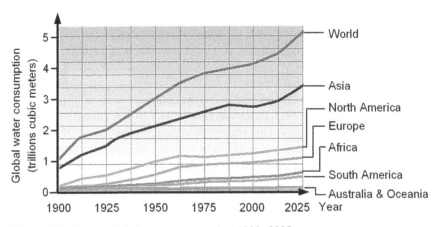

Figure 12.7 Annual global water consumption, 1900–2025.

Despite this increased consumption, according to the UN Sustainable Development Goals Report of 2022, some 2 billion people worldwide currently do not have access to safe drinking water (Jensen, 2022). Also, according to the IPCC, roughly half of the world's population is experiencing severe water scarcity for at least part of the year (Lee and Romero, 2023). Along with this line, the World Meteorological Organization (WMO) estimates that these numbers will increase, exacerbated by climate change and population growth.

Surface water, such as lakes and rivers, provides water to many world population segments. Where these sources are scarce or inaccessible, people extract and use groundwater. Groundwater is the source of drinking and agriculture water for much of the Earth's population. Groundwater depletion may be defined as long-term water-level declines caused by sustained groundwater pumping, often coupled with long-term droughts. These processes are the reason for groundwater depletion in many parts of the world, reducing water in streams and lakes, drying up wells, and causing a deterioration of water quality.

12.2.3.2 Increasing Water Supplies

One solution to the projected groundwater shortages is diverting surface water to recharge aquifers. Another solution is providing more water by reducing unnecessary water waste. These solutions may be achieved by subsidizing water conservation and taxing and raising water prices to discourage waste. Yet another strategy is for states and municipalities to discourage farmers from growing water-intensive crops in dry areas.

A different solution is building dams and reservoirs in appropriate geographic locations. Dams and reservoirs capture and store runoff water and release it as needed to control floods; generate electricity; and supply water for irrigation, towns, and cities. Reservoirs also provide recreational activities such as swimming, fishing, and boating.

On the downside, dams and reservoirs flood areas of the most productive land, displace millions of people from their homes, and damage rivers' critical ecological services. For example, a 2007 World Wildlife Fund (WWF) study estimated that about one-fifth of the world's freshwater fish and plant species are either extinct or endangered, primarily because dams and water withdrawals have sharply decreased water flow.

Finally, seawater desalination is a process that creates fresh water by removing salts and mineral components from seawater. Desalination processes use either thermal methods (in the case of distillation) or membrane-based methods (e.g., reverse osmosis). Alix et al. (2022) estimated that in 2018, there were more 18,000 desalination plants operating in more than 150 countries. These plants produced 87 million cubic meters of fresh water daily, supplying more than 300 million people. The average energy intensity for seawater desalination in

2018 was about 3 kWh/m^3 (kilowatt-hour for one cubic meter of fresh water). This energy amounted to a worldwide consumption of about 260 gWh (gigawatt-hour) per day.

12.2.3.3 Using Water More Sustainably

Humankind can use water more sustainably by reducing water waste for the public and reducing irrigation in agriculture and industrial processes.

1. **Reducing water waste for the public at large.** Reducing water waste is always quicker and easier than providing new water supplies. It is also cheaper unless supply systems are subsidized, which makes water prices artificially low. The fact of the matter is that (1) about two-thirds of the water used throughout the world is unnecessarily wasted through evaporation, leaks, and other losses, and (2) it is economically and technically feasible to reduce such water losses in order to meet most of the world's water needs for the foreseeable future.

   The leading cause of water waste is its low cost to users. Such underpricing is primarily the result of government subsidies that provide irrigation water used by farmers at below market price. Higher water prices encourage water conservation but make it difficult for low-income farmers and city dwellers to buy enough water to meet their needs. The remedy for this dilemma is to provide each household with a set amount of low-priced water to meet basic needs. Users who exceed this amount pay higher prices as their water use increases.

2. **Reducing water waste in irrigation.** About 60% of the irrigation water worldwide does not reach the targeted crops. Most irrigation systems obtain water from groundwater wells or a surface water source. The water then flows by gravity through unlined ditches in crop fields so the crops can absorb it. This irrigation method delivers far more water than is needed for crop growth and typically loses 40% of the water through evaporation, seepage, and runoff.

   More efficient and environmentally sound irrigation methods significantly reduce farm water waste by delivering water more precisely to crops. For example, drip irrigation is the most efficient way to precisely deliver small amounts of water to crops (Figure 12.8). In addition, irrigation water waste may be reduced by following these measures: (1) using treated urban wastewater for irrigation, (2) limiting irrigation to nighttime to reduce evaporation, (3) regularly monitoring soil moisture and adding water only when necessary, and (4) avoiding growing water-intensive[4] crops in dry areas.

3. **Reducing water waste in industry.** Producers of chemicals, paper, oil, coal, primary metals, and processed food consume almost 90% of the water

---

4 The most popular water-intensive crops include rice, soybeans, wheat, sugarcane, cotton, alfalfa, and pasture.

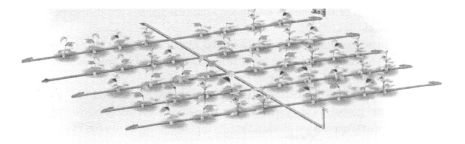

Figure 12.8 Drip irrigation delivers 90% of the water to crops.

industry uses. Their wastes include garbage; scrap metals; chemicals; dirt; gravel; concrete; trash; cleaning fluids; pesticides; and metals like mercury, lead, nitrate, oils, and petrochemicals. More often than not, industrial waste is discarded via wastewater. Unfortunately, this untreated wastewater contaminates the groundwater, thus polluting and harming the environment, humans, animals, and flora.

Some industries recapture, purify, and recycle water to reduce water use and treatment costs. For example, more than 95% of the water used to make steel is recycled in the United States. Even so, most industrial processes could substantially reduce their water waste. For example, manufacturers should be incentivized to redesign their water usage systems if states and municipalities raise the price of water and reciprocally reduce corporate taxes.

From a technical point of view, the industry's most desired method for reducing water pollution is to reduce or eliminate the dangerous materials used in the production process. However, in most cases, this approach is not feasible. The next best thing is to use small-scale water treatment plants. Water treatment processes can eliminate most of the dangerous components from the water using one or more of the following methods: (1) reverse osmosis; (2) ultrafiltration, nano, and microfiltration; (3) absorption desalination; (4) membrane distillation; and (5) forward osmosis. After treatment, the wastewater can be reused or released into the environment.

12.2.4   Sustaining an Eco-Friendly Biosphere

The biosphere includes all the Earth's plants and animals as well as all its land, water, and air where these organisms live. But, according to the United Nations Environment Program (UNEP), humanity is experiencing an alarming biosphere decline that can be attributed to human activity. This decline includes the following:

- Humans use the equivalent of 1.6 times what the Earth can produce to maintain their current way of life. Our ecosystems cannot keep up with these demands.

- One million of the world's estimated 8 million species are threatened with extinction.
- Human actions have significantly altered 75% of the Earth's land surface.
- Human activities, including overfishing and pollution of seas and estuaries, impact nearly 70% of the ocean area.
- Nearly 90% of marine fish stocks are overexploited or depleted.
- Humans' global food system is the primary driver for biodiversity loss. Agricultural expansion alone accounts for 70% of the terrestrial biodiversity loss.

Yet, some people doubt the importance of biodiversity to them personally. The short answer is that nature loss has far-reaching consequences for the human species. Degraded ecosystems exacerbate climate change, undermine food security, and put people and communities at risk. So, the following is a set of practical eco-friendly biodiversity actions related to protecting, managing, and sustaining wild species, forests, grasslands, and terrestrial and aquatic biodiversity. The problem, though, is the global community's inability to enforce treaties and agreements on various rogue states that violate them (e.g., deforestation of the Amazon basin in Brazil and Colombia, as well as illegal animal poaching in Africa and Asia).

12.2.4.1 Protecting Wild Species

Humankind can reduce wild species extinction (Figure 12.9) and help protect overall biodiversity by establishing national environmental laws and creating a variety of protected wildlife sanctuaries. International treaties can also help in protecting wild species. One of the most far-reaching is the 1975 Convention on International Trade in Endangered Species. One hundred seventy-four countries have now signed this treaty. It lists 900 species and bans hunting, capturing, and selling them as live specimens or wildlife products.

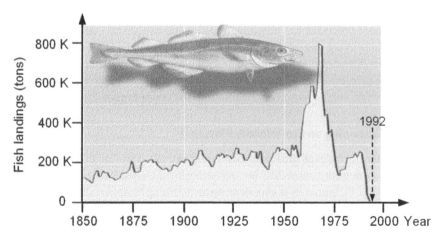

Figure 12.9 Collapse of Atlantic cod landings off the east coast of Newfoundland.

12.2.4.2 Managing and Sustaining Forests

Humankind can manage and sustain forests by emphasizing their economic value. In addition, removing all government subsidies to the logging industry is vital. Similarly, governments should ban road building into uncut forest areas and clear-cutting on steep slopes. Furthermore, humankind should protect old-growth forests and prohibit logging in these forests. In addition, governments should support tree planting, primarily on deforested and degraded land, and enforce strict rules allowing forest harvesting to be no faster than replenishing. Finally, consumers should sustain forests by demanding certification of timber and products grown under sustainable forest management.

12.2.4.3 Managing and Sustaining Grasslands

People use grasslands to provide forage and grazing of vegetation for cattle, sheep, and goats. From an ecological standpoint, grasslands provide essential environmental benefits, including soil formation, erosion control, nutrient cycling, maintenance of biodiversity, and storage of atmospheric carbon dioxide in biomass. However, overgrazing arises when too many animals graze for too long, exceeding the growth capacity of a given area. In addition, such land abuse exposes the soil to water and wind erosion and compresses it, which diminishes its ability to hold water.

Grasslands' well-being can be sustained by limiting the number and dispersion of grazing livestock and restoring degraded grasslands. The most widely used method for sustainable management of grasslands is to limit the number of cattle and the duration of their grazing in each area so that the area's carrying capacity is not exceeded.

12.2.4.4 Sustaining Terrestrial Biodiversity

The Earth's species are not evenly distributed on the planet. For example, a few countries with extensive tropical forests contain most of the Earth's species. Along this line, biodiversity scientists believe that protecting threatened habitats and ecosystems is the best way to prevent extinction. This undertaking involves mapping the world's terrestrial and aquatic ecosystems and creating an inventory of each species and the ecosystem benefits they deliver, protecting the most endangered ecosystems and species, protecting ecosystems' plant and wildlife biodiversity, and restoring as many degraded ecosystems as possible. So, given the political will, humankind can help sustain terrestrial biodiversity by identifying and protecting severely threatened areas, rehabilitating damaged ecosystems, and sharing much of the land people dominate with other species.

12.2.4.5 Sustaining Aquatic Biodiversity

Human activities are destroying or degrading large portions of the world's coastal wetlands, mangroves, coral reefs, and ocean bottom, disrupting many of the world's freshwater ecosystems. For example, trawlers drag huge nets weighted down with heavy chains over ocean bottoms to harvest tens of tons of fish at one scoop. Each year, thousands of such vessels scrape and disturb large seabed areas. This ongoing process causes the depletion of marine life and the loss and degradation of many sea-bottom habitats. However, given the political will, humankind can help to sustain aquatic biodiversity by establishing protected sanctuaries; managing coastal development; and, most importantly, preventing overfishing and prohibiting environmentally damaging fishing methods.

12.3 Sustaining Human Society

This section describes practical means to sustain global human society. It includes providing food for humankind, supporting and implementing a circular economy, legislating ecological taxation, curbing the human population, and supporting political action.

12.3.1 Providing Food for Humankind

The following section describes practical means to provide food for humankind.

12.3.1.1 Producing Food More Sustainably
More sustainable food production involves reducing soil erosion and shifting to more sustainable agriculture.

1. **Reducing soil erosion.** Using land to produce food requires fertile topsoil. Unfortunately, such fertile topsoil takes hundreds of years to evolve. Thus, reducing soil erosion is the most critical component of sustainable agriculture. Soil conservation involves using diverse ways to reduce soil erosion as well as restore soil fertility, primarily by keeping the soil covered with vegetation. For example, terracing enables growing food on steep slopes without depleting the topsoil. It is done by converting steeply sloped land into nearly level terraces across its contours (Figure 12.10).

   Another method to reduce soil erosion is to eliminate conventional plowing and tilling of the soil. This conservation tillage farming uses special tillers and planting machines that drill and place seeds directly into the undisturbed soil. The only soil disturbance is a narrow slit in the ground. No-till and minimum-tillage farming also increase crop yields and lower water, pesticide, and tractor fuel use.

Figure 12.10 Terraces near the village of Pisac on the Urubamba River, Peru.

2. **Shifting to more sustainable agriculture.** Modern agriculture produces large amounts of food at reasonable prices. But the current form of agriculture is unsustainable because (1) it relies more on fossil fuels than on naturally available resources; (2) it reduces agrobiodiversity[5]; and (3) it does not emphasize conservation and recycling of nutrients in topsoil, the irreplaceable base of all food production on land.

The market prices of food should reflect these harmful environmental costs so that consumers will select less expensive food grown in a more sustainable agricultural environment. This food will be grown in a perennial, high-yield polyculture environment and undergo regular crop rotation, organic fertilization, biological pest control, and efficient irrigation and soil conservation.

12.3.1.2 Improving Food Security

Pests are species that interfere with human welfare by competing with us for food, spreading disease, or invading ecosystems. Worldwide, only about 100 species of plants, fungi, microbes, and insects cause most of the damage to the crops people grow. In natural ecosystems, natural enemies (predators, parasites, and disease organisms) control the populations of most potential pest species. However, when

---

5 Agrobiodiversity refers to the variety and variability of living organisms that contribute to humans' food consumption and are associated with cultivating crops and rearing animals.

people clear forests, destroy grasslands, plant monoculture crops, and douse fields with chemicals that kill pests, they upset many natural population ecosystems that support biodiversity and sustainability. Then people must use chemical pesticides to protect monoculture crops from insects and other pests that nature once primarily controlled.

Humankind can reduce pesticide use without decreasing crop yields by using various cultivation techniques, biological pest controls, and small amounts of selected chemical pesticides. Conventional chemical pesticides have advantages and disadvantages. Their main advantages are that they save human lives[6] and increase food supplies.[7] On the other hand, however, chemical pesticides promote genetic resistance, kill natural pests and enemies, pollute the environment, harm wildlife and people, and are expensive for farmers and consumers.

12.3.1.1 Reducing Wasted Food

Controlling the amount and distribution of food production more effectively should eliminate or drastically reduce wasted food, which, for example, accounts for up to 40% of the food created in the United States. In addition, such policies should increase food recycling through composting or producing biogas and biofertilizers in sealed, oxygen-free tanks.

12.3.1.2 Curbing the Meat and Dairy Industry

According to a UN report published in 2021[8], almost 90% of the financial support for agriculture is "harmful," and much of it goes to the meat and dairy industry, which is considered the most environmentally damaging type of farming. Currently, $540 billion is paid to farmers worldwide every year, and these subsidies are expected to grow to $1.8 trillion by 2030.

Governments should regulate and curb the effects of meat and dairy farming. The best mechanism to do so is through taxation on methane production through a vigorous global "antimeat" campaign. In particular, this action should address the factory-farm model of livestock production. After fossil fuels, the food industry, particularly the meat and dairy sector, is an influential contributor to greenhouse gases and climate change. For example, the worldwide livestock sector discharges more greenhouse gas emissions than all cars, trains, planes, and ships combined.

---

6 For example, DDT (dichlorodiphenyltrichloroethane, which is currently banned due to health reasons) and other insecticides prevented the premature deaths of millions of people from insect-transmitted diseases such as malaria, bubonic plague, and typhus.

7 According to the UN Food and Agriculture Organization (FAO), more than 50% of the world's human food supply is lost to pests. Without pesticides, these losses would be worse and food prices would rise.

8 A Multi-Billion-Dollar Opportunity Repurposing Agricultural Support to Transform Food Systems, Food and Agriculture Organization of the United Nations, Rome, 2021.

Another consideration relates to the global livestock industry, a significant factor in water utilization and contamination. Today, 80% of all agricultural production goes to feeding animals. This animal feeding process is realized by expanding land for raising crops to feed livestock, much of it by deforestation in the Amazon and other regions.

12.3.2 Implementing a Circular Economy

The current linear economic concept is based on extracted natural resources that are turned into products destined to become waste. The price people pay for such products includes direct costs related to the given product. For example, if one buys a car, the price includes the direct costs of raw materials, labor, shipping, etc. Similarly, when using a car, one pays the direct costs of fuel, maintenance, repairs, and insurance.

A circular economy (CE) is vital to societal preservation in these challenging times. A circular economy is an economic and social model of producing and consuming goods and services. It involves sharing, leasing, reusing, repairing, refurbishing, and recycling existing products. CE aims to combat global challenges such as climate change, biodiversity loss, waste, and pollution by emphasizing three principles of the model: (1) eliminating waste and pollution, (2) circulating products and materials, and (3) regenerating nature (Figure 12.11).

Circular economy concepts have been studied in academia, business, and government in the past few decades. It gained popularity because it helps minimize harmful emissions, reduce raw material consumption, open new market prospects, and improve resource efficiency. A circular economy keeps products, materials, equipment, and infrastructure in use for longer, thus improving resources' productivity. Finally, at the end of their life, products are recycled, and viable parts

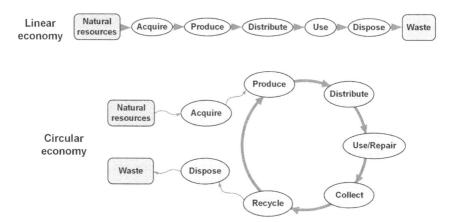

Figure 12.11   Linear and circular economies.

and base materials are inserted back into the production process and reused multiple times. Materials that cannot be reused are disposed of in a controlled manner, minimizing pollution effects. In other words, a circular economy may be defined as an industrial economy that is both regenerative and restorative by value and design.

According to CE philosophy, prices of products and services include their benefits to the environment as well as their harmful environmental impacts. Therefore, under the concept of full-cost pricing, the cost of a car should also include environmental costs related to extracting and processing raw materials; the cost of manufacturers using nonrenewable energy and mineral resources; as well as costs related to the creation of hazardous wastes, releasing greenhouse gases into the atmosphere, and polluting the water.

Adopting full-cost pricing would also enable consumers to make more informed choices. Jobs and profits would be eliminated in environmentally harmful businesses as consumers would more often choose green products. However, more jobs and profits would be created in environmentally beneficial businesses. This economic doctrine will reduce resource waste, pollution, and environmental degradation and improve human health by encouraging producers to invent more resource-efficient and less polluting production methods. Such shifts in job markets, profits, and types of businesses are a normal part of market-based capitalism.

12.3.2.1 Shifting to a Circular Economy

Governments should adopt a combination of taxes and subsidies to incentivize people, institutions, and industries to shift toward a circular economy. This shift means changing from a traditional linear economy (make, use, discard) to an alternative economy whereby resources are used as needed and then regenerated to be used again or recovered by recycling their components and materials.

For example, a car manufacturer "loans" its cars to customers. Later, these customers can trade their old vehicles for new ones. Then the car manufacturer may refurbish and upgrade the old cars, sell them again, or disassemble them and recycle their parts and materials in its manufacturing plants.

12.3.2.2 Reducing Materials Consumption

The following are ideas regarding what can be done to reduce material consumption.

1. **Conserving resources.** Conserving resources should be encouraged. For example, some ways of conserving nonrenewable resources are working from home in relevant industries; using public transport instead of individual vehicles; carpooling, where several people with a common origin and destination go together in one vehicle; and turning off lights and air conditioners when they are not needed.

   Similarly, substituting traditional materials with new materials could reduce resource waste, for example, replacing copper and aluminum wires with fiber-optic glass cables that transmit information, using light and high-strength composite materials, and using glass fibers instead of metals in the automobile and aerospace industries. All of the above cost less to produce, do not need painting (which reduces pollution and costs), and can be molded into different shapes, thus increasing the systems' EROI.

2. **Recycling resources.** Most materials—metal, glass, paper, plastic, and so on—can be recycled and used again. States and local municipalities should establish regulations and the means for collecting and recycling such materials and bringing them back to society as new products. For example, recycling paper helps conserve forests, and recycling aluminum cans reduces excavation and production efforts and energy. Furthermore, recycling plastic saves energy because producing plastics consumes a good deal of manufacturing fuel. In addition, recycling plastic will reduce the amount of plastics in oceans, on beaches, and at garbage dumps. In short, recycling helps to conserve resources and energy and to reduce solid pollution.

3. **Repair and use.** Producing consumer goods generates a lot of carbon pollution. For example, the electronics industry use parts that harm the environment when dumped untreated into landfills. Mining rare-earth metals produces harmful emissions that kill plants and animals around nearby waterways and can have serious health consequences for people. Often people and organizations dispose of faulty products because they find that repairing them is not viable and purchasing new ones is more accessible and less annoying. Unfortunately, dumping old consumer goods, especially electronic equipment, leads to further ecological damage. For example, most of a smartphone's carbon pollution comes from its manufacture and disposal, not its use. Similar situations occur with other consumer goods. For example, people and organizations sell automobiles after a few years as soon as minor operational problems emerge. Later, 99% of good motor vehicles are scrapped due to repair costs, lack of spare parts, or a notion that they have reached the end of their life.

   Extending the life of consumer goods will dramatically reduce the volume of new goods that need to be manufactured. Therefore, reversing the current trend will be beneficial to society. First, repairing helps conserve resources. Second, it creates an economy based on recycling, reusing, and repairing rather than replacing. Third, it reduces global societal waste and various types of pollution. Fourth, when the repair infrastructure is established, the cost of repairing consumer goods will be a small fraction relative to replacing these goods.

12.3.2.3 Transitioning to a Sustainable Low-Waste Society

For decades, industrialized countries shipped hazardous wastes to developing countries. In 1989, the United Nations Environment Program (UNEP) developed an international treaty called the Basel Convention. The treaty banned such practices and was ratified by 122 countries. The provisions of the Convention concentrate on the following principal aims: (1) reduction of hazardous waste generation and promotion of environmentally sound management of hazardous wastes, (2) restriction of transboundary movements of hazardous wastes, and (3) implementation of a regulatory system applying to permissible transboundary movements.

Over the past 30 years, the Basel Convention has been essential in attempting to achieve environmental sustainability through waste minimization, recycling, and reuse. In addition, state-of-the-art recycling following agreed-upon standards has created numerous business and job opportunities. Conservation of precious resources through extraction and reuse rather than primary mining has provided better protection of the air, soil, water, and thus human health. It was realized that this potential might also lessen incentives for unlawful recycling operations by providing legal, safe, and economically rewarding alternatives. Unfortunately, the treaty does not eliminate the profitable illegal global waste trade. Smugglers evade the laws by using various tactics, including bribes, false permits, and mislabeling of hazardous wastes as materials to be recycled.

Shifting to a low-waste society requires individuals and organizations to reuse and recycle waste at local, national, and global levels following these principles: (1) Polluters and producers should pay for the waste they produce; (2) different categories of hazardous waste and recyclable waste should not be mixed; and (3) municipalities should provide means for reusing, recycling, or composting all solid wastes produced in the community.

12.3.3 Legislating Ecological Taxation

Ecological taxation should be levied on the activities of people and organizations that produce carbon dioxide (CO_2), methane (CH_4), and other greenhouse gases. This tax is intended to promote environmentally friendly activities via economic incentives. Ecological taxation is the process of adjusting market prices to include the direct environmental impact on measurable parameters such as, for example, pollution created in power plants and exhaust gases emanating from automobiles.

An ecological tax aims to implement a "true cost accounting" using fiscal policy. As a result, polluters, paying their ecological taxes, will tend to increase their products' prices. This scheme will reduce the attractiveness of their products in the public eye, and relatively fewer polluting products will be sold and used. Similarly, users of polluting products (e.g., automobiles) and services (e.g., electricity, heating), paying their ecological taxes, will be incentivized to change their habits and reduce their use of such devices and services. The following are four examples of ecological taxes that should be considered:

1. Impose a carbon tax on individuals and organizations that use fossil fuels
2. Impose an import tax on goods containing significant nonecological energy inputs

3. Impose resource exploitation taxes on the extraction of mineral, energy, and forestry products
4. Impose waste disposal taxes depending on the type of waste and the nature of the disposal

In complementing ecological taxation, states and municipalities should use a balanced taxation scheme to subsidize all industries that reduce greenhouse gases in the biosphere; that is, they should maintain a revenue-neutral status by proportionately reducing other taxes. This action will compensate the general population and organizations as well as control the cost of living. The following are three examples of taxes that should be reduced in proportion to ecological taxes:

1. Income and sales taxes
2. Corporate taxes
3. Property taxes

12.3.4 Curbing the Human Population

Population projections show how the human population might change (Figure 12.12). This data forecasts the population's impact on the future ill-being of this planet and humanity. For example, by 2100, the UN projects the world's population will grow to 10 billion people, while the population in sub-Saharan Africa alone will reach 3.8 billion.

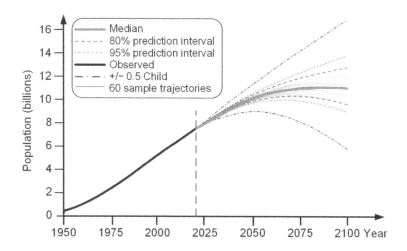

Figure 12.12 World population prospects, 2022 and beyond (Image: UN DESA).[9]

---

9 DESA = United Nations Department of Economic and Social Affairs.

Overpopulation is a major cause of many world problems. First, an increase in the world's population will strain global resources. More people means an increased demand for food, water, housing, energy, healthcare, transportation, and so on. From an ecological standpoint, the population increase will cause more deforestation, decreased biodiversity, and spikes in pollution and emissions—all of which will exacerbate climate change. So, unless people take action to minimize further population growth, the additional stress on the planet's resources will lead to ecological disruption and collapse so severe that it will threaten the viability of our current notion of life on Earth. Finally, scarcity brought about by environmental disruption and overpopulation will trigger mass migration from South America and Central Africa northward. This migration of many millions of individuals will probably trigger increased political unrest, violence, and wars. The best way to slow human population growth is by encouraging quality education, promoting family planning, empowering women, and applying economic and legal measures.

12.3.4.1 Providing Quality Education

One of the most effective ways to achieve sustainable population growth is to provide quality education to all children. Many children, especially girls, in developing countries are not attending school due to poverty and gender inequality. In addition, there is a direct correlation between women's duration of education and the number of children they have. For example, studies show that African women with no formal education have, on average, 5.4 children, whereas women who have completed high school have 2.7 children. Reciprocally, when family sizes are smaller, women are more incentivized to gain education and work, as well as to improve their economic opportunities. Educating people about family planning and injecting topics related to population growth and family planning into politics and economics courses in high school and college are beneficial.

12.3.4.2 Promoting Family Planning

Governments should support family planning through clinical services that help couples choose when to have children and how many. In addition, such clinical services should provide information on birth control and healthcare for pregnant women and infants.

Along this line, governments should remove barriers to contraception. The fact is that more than 200 million women worldwide who wish to avoid pregnancy are not using modern contraceptives due to lack of access, concerns about side effects, and social pressure not to use them.

In summary, family planning has become a significant factor in reducing the worldwide number of births. It has also reduced the number of abortions performed each year and the number of deaths of mothers and fetuses during pregnancy.

12.3.4.3   Empowering Women and Girls

Several studies show that women tend to have fewer children if they have formal education, can control their own lives, hold a paying job outside the home, and live in societies that do not suppress their rights. Therefore, governments should provide incentives (financial or otherwise) for women and girls to choose what happens to their bodies and lives. Empowerment provides freedom to pursue education, career, economic independence, and access to reproductive healthcare. Therefore, governments should outlaw child marriages and gender-based abuses. In summary, promoting the rights of girls and women is a powerful solution to human population growth.

12.3.4.4   Legislating Economic Measures

Governments' actions regarding policies and laws, as well as their spending and tax programs, influence family planning and population growth.

- **Government policy and laws.** As mentioned above, a government's policy and laws greatly influence its citizens. For example, the promotion of later marriage and more extended breastfeeding can reduce the birth rate and, at the same time, raise a family's welfare. Similarly, laws about education affect fertility by altering decisions about children's education.
- **Government spending.** As mentioned above, government spending on programs like education, primary healthcare, family planning, fertility control, and old-age security influences family decisions on fertility. For example, in developed countries, parents are incentivized to raise large families to ensure their own financial support and protection in old age.
- **Government tax programs.** Similarly, government tax programs like family allowances, subsidies on children's services, and support fees for larger families offer specific incentives and disincentives to limit a family's fertility. The effects of taxes and subsidies can differ depending on the situation. For example, tuition and book charges might discourage parents from sending children to school and indirectly contribute to higher fertility. However, once education is considered valuable, people will be encouraged to have fewer children to give them a better education.

12.3.5   Supporting Political Action

12.3.5.1   Invigorating International Environmental Treaties

Many international environmental treaties and agreements have been signed in the past century. Some are bilateral, that is, between two countries, and others are multilateral, that is, among several countries. Typically, these agreements belong to different environmental categories: (1) conservation and protection of resources;

(2) interaction with mammals, agriculture, and marine life; (3) pollution of the air, land, oceans, and freshwater systems; (4) maintenance of ecosystems; and (5) regulation of freshwater resources in lakes and rivers. The discussion below concentrates on two key environmental treaties, the 1997 Kyoto Protocol and the 2015 Paris Agreement. Finally, the text explains the barriers to their implementation and the likelihood of their success.

1. **The Kyoto Protocol.** The Kyoto Protocol was an international accord that committed the parties to reducing greenhouse gas emissions. It was adopted in Kyoto, Japan, in 1997, and by 2020, there were 192 parties to the Protocol. The Kyoto Protocol's objective was to reduce greenhouse gas concentrations in the atmosphere and thus mitigate the dangerous human-made pollution interference with the climate system. The Protocol applied to the following seven greenhouse gases: (1) carbon dioxide (CO_2), (2) methane (CH_4), (3) nitrous oxide (N_2O), (4) hydrofluorocarbons (HFCs), (5) perfluorocarbons (PFCs), (6) sulfur hexafluoride (SF_6), and (7) nitrogen trifluoride (NF_3).

2. **The Paris Agreement.** The Paris Agreement is a legally binding international treaty on climate change. Nearly 200 parties adopted it in Paris in 2015. The Paris Agreement aims to curb global warming below 2 °C relative to preindustrial levels. Governments should reach a climate-neutral world by mid-century to achieve this temperature goal. This agreement constitutes a milestone in climate change action because, for the first time, a binding agreement unites all nations into a common cause to combat climate change and its effects.

3. **Understand the barriers to implementation.** The differences and conflicts within the world's existing political systems pose barriers to implementing significant environmental protocols. First, state sovereignty means no country can be forced to participate or fully implement agreements. Second, the north–south conflict can block cooperation and cause conflicts. Third, the Global South countries argue that the north has had opportunities to develop and thus has harmed the environment during their industrial development, so now it is their turn.

Most importantly, countries often lack the motivation to change their environmental policies due to conflict with other local interests, especially economic prosperity. If adherence to environmental protocols will cause economic difficulties or harm to a country, it may not implement the protocols. Due to these barriers, environmental protocols often do not produce anywhere near the desired effects or, at best, tend to gravitate toward the least common denominator.

What is needed most is for environmental treaties to include the means to monitor and enforce adherence to all parts of the treaty. However, this scheme is impossible under the world's existing political systems. Therefore, this author assesses that the Kyoto Protocol and the Paris Agreement are unlikely to achieve their objectives.

12.3.5.2 Sustaining Environmental Policies

The role played by a government is primarily determined by its policies, the set of laws and regulations it enforces, and the programs it funds. Therefore, environmental policies should be guided by principles designed to minimize environmental harm. Consider, for example, the following eight principles:

1. **The humility principle.** People's understanding of nature and how human actions affect nature is limited.
2. **The reversibility principle.** People should try to make decisions that can be reversed later if a decision turns out to be wrong.
3. **The net energy principle.** People should not be encourage to use energy alternatives with low net energy yields that cannot compete energy-wise with other forms of energy sources.
4. **The precautionary principle.** People should take precautionary measures to prevent or reduce potential environmental harm due to their activities.
5. **The prevention principle.** People should make decisions that prevent environmental problems from occurring or becoming worse.
6. **The polluter-pays principle.** People should demand that environmental regulations include economic tools such as ecological taxes to ensure they bear the costs of the pollutants and wastes they produce.
7. **The public participation principle.** People should have access to environmental data and information and the right to participate in developing, criticizing, and modifying environmental policies.
8. **The environmental justice principle.** People should establish environmental policies so that no one individual and no group shall bear an improper burden created by pollution, environmental degradation, or the execution of environmental laws.

12.3.5.3 Becoming Environmentally Literate

There is widespread evidence and agreement that we are a species in the process of degrading our life support system and that, during this century, this behavior will threaten human civilization as well as the survival of up to half of the world's species. Part of the problem stems from ignorance about how the Earth works, how our actions affect its life-sustaining systems, and how people can change their behavior toward the Earth. Correcting this begins by internalizing three crucial ideas:

1. Natural capital matters because it supports the Earth's life and our economies.
2. Humans' ecological footprints are immense and are expanding rapidly. They already exceed the Earth's ecological capacity.
3. Ecological and climate change tipping points are irreversible and should never be crossed. Nevertheless, humans have crossed several of these points, and neither money nor technology will save us from harmful consequences that could last for thousands of years.

Learning how to live more sustainably requires a foundation of environmental education to produce environmentally literate people. Here are some key goals for each person seeking environmental literacy:

1. Understand how the earth works and sustains itself as much as possible, and use such knowledge to guide your life, community, and society
2. Understand the relationships between the economy and the Earth's natural support systems and the role of economics in making the transition to a more sustainable society
3. Use critical thinking skills to become a seeker of environmental wisdom instead of overfilled vessels of environmental information and misinformation
4. Understand and evaluate our environmental worldviews and continue this as a lifelong process

12.4   Bibliography

Agardy, F.J. and Nemerow, N.L. (2010). *Environmental Solutions: Environmental Problems and the All-Inclusive Global, Scientific, Political, Legal, Economic, Medical, and Engineering Bases to Solve Them*. Academic Press.

Agardy, F.J., Sullivan, P.J., Nemerow, N.L., and Salvato J.A. (2009). *Environmental Engineering: Environmental Health and Safety for Municipal Infrastructure, Land Use and Planning, and Industry*. Wiley.

Alix, A., Bellet, L., Trommsdorff, C. and Audureau, I. (Eds.). (2022, June). *Reducing the Greenhouse Gas Emissions of Water and Sanitation Services: Overview of Emissions and Their Potential Reduction Illustrated by Utility Know-How*. IWA Publishing.

Davies, L.L., Uchitel, K., and Ruple, J. (2013). Understanding barriers to commercial-scale carbon capture and sequestration in the United States: An empirical assessment. *Energy Policy* 59: 745–761.

Hickel, J. (2020). *Less Is More: How Degrowth Will Save the World*. Cornerstone Digital.

JensenL. ed. (2022). The Sustainable Development Goals Report 2022. United Nation. https://unstats.un.org/sdgs/report/2022/The-Sustainable-Development-Goals-Report-2022.pdf. Accessed: Oct. 2023.

Lee, H. and Romero, J. eds. (2023). IPCC, Summary for Policymakers. In: Climate Change 2023: Synthesis Report. Contribution of Working Groups I, II and III to the Sixth Assessment Report of the Intergovernmental Panel on Climate Change. https://www.ipcc.ch/report/ar6/syr/downloads/report/IPCC_AR6_SYR_SPM.pdf. Accessed: Oct. 2023.

Metz B. et al. eds. (2005). Special Report on Carbon Dioxide. *Capture and Storage.* https://www.ipcc.ch/site/assets/uploads/2018/03/srccs_wholereport-1.pdf. Accessed: Jan. 2023.

Miller, G.T. and Spoolman, S. (2018). *Environmental Science.* Cengage Learning.

Myers, N. and Spoolman, S. (2013). *Environmental Issues and Solutions: A Modular Approach.* Cengage Learning.

13

Global Energy Crisis

13.1 Introduction

As of this writing, humanity faces many global predicaments. The author of this book considers the two most challenging, systemic global issues to be the global environmental crisis and its twin, the global energy crisis. This chapter describes and systemically analyzes the second issue so readers can appreciate this vital challenge to humankind. The next chapter proposes a no-nonsense, systemic energy action plan for humankind based on this impending global energy adversity.

The chapter describes the following:
- Current global energy status and crisis, causes of the global energy crisis, and effects of the global energy crisis
- Energy return on investment (EROI), including EROI concept and controversy
- Renewable energy, including general observations, solar energy, wind energy, hydroelectric energy, geothermal energy, ocean energy, biomass energy, and exclusive global renewable energy
- Fossil fuels energy, including general observations, crude oil, natural gas, and coal
- Conventional fission reaction energy

13.2 Current Global Energy Status

This section describes the current global energy status, as well as the causes and effects of the global energy crisis.

13.2.1   Global Energy Status

Figure 13.1 depicts the past 20 years of global consumption of energy. As can be seen, by and large, global energy consumption has tended to increase over the previous two decades. As of 2020, some 83% of worldwide energy consumption was based on fossil resources, namely crude oil, natural gas, and coal. Just over 4% of global energy was derived from nuclear reactors using uranium. The rest of global energy is derived from the world's renewable energy supply. Biofuel and waste generate 68% of it, mostly in industrialized countries; hydropower generates 18%; and biomass, geothermal, hydropower, solar, tidal wave, and wind generate 14%.[1]

Table 13.1 shows total global energy consumption for 2020.

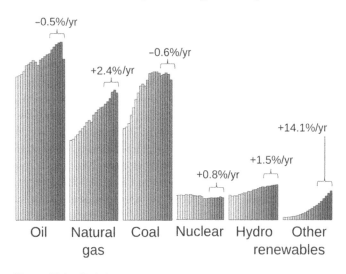

Figure 13.1   Global energy consumption, 2000–2020.

Table 13.1   Global Energy Consumption, 2020.

Energy Type	Percent of Global Consumption
Crude oil	31.2%
Natural gas	24.7%
Coal	27.2%
Nuclear	4.3%
Hydro	6.9%
Other renewables	5.7%

---

1 World energy supply and consumption. Wikipedia. https://en.wikipedia.org/wiki/World_energy_supply_and_consumption. Accessed: Jan. 2023.

13.2.2 Global Energy Crisis

The world faces three energy problems: (1) Most global energy produces greenhouse gas emissions; (2) billions of people lack access to sufficient energy; and (3) the availability of global fossil fuel is steadily diminishing, and the world lacks large-scale low-carbon energy alternatives.

1. **Fossil fuel produces greenhouse gas emissions.** Environmental risk is considered the most important global energy crisis, especially climate change. This climate change emanates from greenhouse gas emissions produced by the increasing world population. Of course, the problem is more significant for affluent societies but isn't limited to them.

2. **Billions of people lack access to sufficient energy.** About 2 to 3 billion people worldwide lack access to modern forms of energy. As a result, people in developing countries produce very low greenhouse gas emissions due to their lack of access to advanced energy and technology. Therefore, one may define the energy dilemma of the poorer half of the world as energy poverty. When people experience energy poverty, they rely on solid fuel sources, mainly firewood, dung, and crop waste. However, this action comes at a high cost to the health of these people living in energy poverty. For example, indoor air pollution is a significant risk for early death. In addition, utilizing wood as an energy source inevitably leads to deforestation. This deforestation occurs across vast portions of Africa, where wood provides more than half the total energy.

3. **The availability of global fossil fuels is diminishing.** Another international component of the energy crisis stems from recognizing the foreseeable end of the oil, gas, and coal fossil cycle. The resources needed to power industrial societies are diminishing, threatening social stability and security worldwide.

13.2.3 Causes of the Global Energy Crisis

In general, there are four causes of the global energy crisis: (1) overpopulation, (2) overconsumption, (3) poor infrastructure, and (4) wasted energy.

1. **Overpopulation.** One cause of the global energy crisis has been an accelerated increase in the global population and its demands for fuel and other products. All these products are made and transported using energy resources. Moreover, energy demands are amplified by demographics, as the world population is expected to reach nearly 10 billion people by 2050. As a result of the growing global population, global energy demand is expected to increase by more than 50% by 2030.

2. **Overconsumption.** The energy crisis results from many strains on our natural resources. In particular, there is stress on fossil fuels (i.e., oil, gas, and

coal) due to overconsumption. For example, oil will run out in 40 to 60 years at the current consumption rate. On the other hand, natural gas could be mined for another 70 years, and coal will be available for around two centuries.

3. **Poor infrastructure.** The aging infrastructure of power-generating equipment and power transportation affects energy shortage as energy-producing firms continue to use outdated equipment that restricts energy production and limits the efficiency of their processes.

4. **Wasted energy.** In the world's developed countries, people and governments must realize the importance of conserving energy. Global energy could be saved through concerted governmental guidance to individuals that stresses saving energy at home and in the workplace. In addition, governments and municipalities could reduce their energy consumption in myriad ways.

13.2.4 Effects of the Global Energy Crisis

1. **Environmental effects.** Most global energy is produced by burning nonrenewable fossil fuels. They release greenhouse gases, creating a blanket on the Earth's surface that traps heat. Consequently, the energy crisis facilitates the Earth's warming, promoting global warming.

2. **Increased price of fuel resources.** One should recognize that the abundance and availability of fossil fuels are limited. Therefore, increasing fuel resource usage leads to the gradual depletion of these resources. This depletion, in turn, leads to a gradual increase in their price. This process is expected to continue, with an increasing influence on the global economy.

3. **Political disturbances.** As prices of energy rise and availability declines, it is reasonable to expect that the global energy crisis will create political disturbances across the globe.

13.3 Energy Return on Investment (EROI)

This section describes the energy return on investment (EROI), including discussion of the EROI concept and related controversy.

13.3.1 EROI Concept

Energy return on investment (EROI) is the mathematical relationship between the energy delivered and the energy source. For instance, the ratio would describe how much energy is delivered to users relative to the energy required to find, extract, deliver, and refine crude oil. EROI is crucial in determining an energy source's overall value. When the EROI is high, producing energy from that source is relatively easy and energy-effective. However, when the EROI is small, obtaining energy from that source is difficult and energy-expensive. In the extreme, when this ratio is 1.0, there is no return on energy invested. In its simplest form, EROI is computed as:

$$\text{EROI} = \frac{\text{Energy output}}{\text{Energy input}} = \frac{\text{Energy delivered}}{\text{Energy invested}}$$

If the EROI is less than or equal to 1, the system is considered an "energy sink." Therefore, this system should no longer be used as an energy source. From an economic standpoint, an EROI score of 7 represents a break-even point. Therefore, a system with an EROI of less than this value is considered unviable and not profitable as an energy source. The EROI function measures input and output energies used in the energy production domain. These inputs and outputs are described below.

- **Inputs.** (1) On-site energy consumption. This includes labor, health, safety, and transportation costs. (2) The energy embedded in materials used. This includes the materials consumed during construction, operational stages, and decommissioning. (3) Energy used in labor. Transportation and energy used for a laborer's entire workday are included in the input calculation.
- **Outputs.** (1) Heat, motion, and electricity. Any energy production's desired outcome is heat, motion, or electricity. (2) Environmental factors. Energy-producing plants and technologies can be directly affected by the environment. For example, an earthquake can dislodge a wind turbine or destroy a power plant.

The critical energy sources are described below:

1. **Photovoltaic energy.** Photovoltaic energy is one type of solar energy that is clean and renewable. Solar radiation is captured using solar panels that produce electricity. However, in EROI, photovoltaic energy ranges are shallow.
2. **Biomass energy.** Biomass energy is extracted from plant-based material. It is utilized as fuel to produce heat or electricity. Examples of biomass are wood and wood residues; various energy crops; agricultural residues; and waste from industry, farms, and households.
3. **Wind energy.** Wind energy is obtained by using wind turbines to generate electricity. Wind power is a partially sustainable (depending on location and wind pattern) renewable energy source with a limited environmental impact.
4. **Solar thermal energy.** Solar thermal energy is a form captured by mirrors and other technical means. The system converts it to thermal energy, used directly by industry or converted into electricity.
5. **Gas energy.** Gas energy is obtained from a naturally occurring mixture of hydrocarbon gasses consisting primarily of methane.
6. **Coal energy.** Coal energy is obtained from coal, a combustible black sedimentary rock. Coal is mostly carbon formed when living organisms decay

and are converted into coal by the heat and pressure within the Earth's crust over millions of years.

7. **Hydroelectric energy.** Hydroelectric energy is electricity generated from hydropower (water power). Hydropower supplies more energy than all other renewable sources combined and more than nuclear power.

8. **Nuclear energy.** Nuclear energy is derived from controlled nuclear reactions. This process produces heat, which is then converted into electricity. Nowadays, most of the electricity obtained from nuclear power plants is produced by uranium and plutonium atomic fission.

Energy experts say the EROI score must be above 7 for a system to be considered economically viable. Figure 13.2 shows that, as of 2020, investing in photovoltaic, biomass, and wind energies is typically not economically viable.

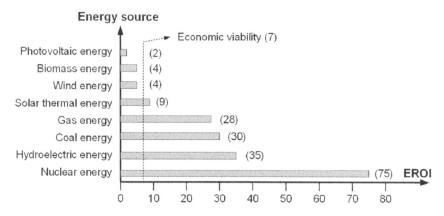

Figure 13.2   EROI for energy sources (derived from CFI, 2020).

13.3.2 EROI Controversy

There are dramatic differences in how EROI is calculated and, in particular, how specific steps of the input process are measured. In addition, this measurement is complex because the inputs are diverse, and there is uncertainty about how far back these inputs should be taken in the analysis.

For example, consider a wind turbine. The energy inputs include the energy required to (1) mine and process the materials needed for turbine construction and its connection to the grid, (2) erect the turbine and construct its infrastructure, (3) operate and maintain the turbine and its infrastructure over its lifetime, and (4) decommission and remove the turbine then remediate the site after its useful life is over. This final energy cost may seem trivial for a wind turbine, but this is not the case for a large nuclear reactor and its spent fuel.

Researchers publish EROI values for similar systems, depending primarily on the system boundary (Figure 13.3 and Figure 13.4). That is, the EROI of an energy resource may be calculated at the point of extraction from the geo-biosphere or where it is used (e.g., refined petrol at the pump or electricity at customers' locations). So, if the input and output parameters are not determined strictly, EROI will be one-sided and misleading.

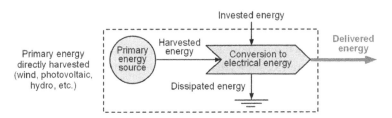

Figure 13.3 Primary energy directly harvested (Raugei et al., 2016).

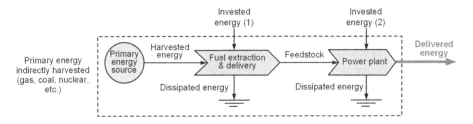

Figure 13.4 Primary energy indirectly harvested (Raugei et al., 2016).

A further reason EROI estimates are challenging is the need to consider all input energy costs. All energy production methods, whether fossil, nuclear, or renewable energy, generate externalities[2] that should be considered in the EROI computation. Consider, for example, energy costs related to suppressing air pollution and thermal pollution emissions in fossil fuel power stations.

Another EROI computation issue is the intermittent nature of renewable energy production, mainly wind and solar systems. By and large, conversion and storage are often needed. Energy can be stored in batteries, compressed air, or pumped hydro schemes, but this storage comes at a heavy energy cost. In addition, conversion and storage equipment, as well as increased input energy costs and the inevitable energy losses, reduce output energy. Both of these factors reduce the EROI of renewable energy systems.

---

2 Externalities occur when some of the costs or benefits of a transaction fall on someone other than the producer or the consumer.

13.4   Renewable Energy

13.4.1   General Observations

On the surface, renewable energy, primarily Sun and wind sources, are ideal because they provide energy with minimal ecological impact. Using a mix of renewable energy sources can reduce pollution, greenhouse gas emissions, and biodiversity losses. Available technologies provide energy from solar and wind farms to be stored and released whenever power is needed. Also, pairing renewable generators and battery storage technologies at residential homes in small off-grid communities in remote locations can provide reliable and relatively cheap electricity.

But on deeper examination, prospects for renewable energy sources are limited, mainly because alternative energy sources such as photovoltaics and wind turbines are not nearly as cheap energetically or economically as crude oil, natural gas, and coal are. Moreover, by nature, renewable energies are defused and uneven sources. Therefore, people must build large systems to harvest these resources. This undertaking is expensive, especially when backup costs for a continued flow of electricity are considered. Thus, the global transition to renewable energies would require massive investments in finance and energy (which probably will come from fossil fuels). Also, most importantly, when their total EROI is computed, their energetic value to society is limited. Therefore, despite many claims to the contrary and the current hype, this book's author considers these solutions a temporary stopgap at best.

Renewable energy (RE) constitutes electricity or heat from solar, wind, hydroelectric, geothermal, ocean, and biomass energy. The main advantages of RE are inexhaustibility and minimal impact on the environment. However, the main disadvantages of RE are its low energy density and the requirements to place these systems in specifically defined locations on the Earth.

13.4.2   Solar Energy

Solar energy generation involves using solar thermal energy or solar photovoltaic energy systems to harvest energy from sunlight.

13.4.2.1   Types of Solar Energy Systems

Solar energy is harvested using two different systems and methodologies.

1. **Solar thermal energy.** Systems based on mirrors spread over extensive areas concentrate sunlight onto a target in which liquid is heated, driving a turbine connected to electrical generators. Under this approach, sunlight energy is converted to heat energy, which is then converted to mechanical energy, which is finally converted to electrical power (Figure 13.5).

Figure 13.5   Ashalim solar power station in Israel.

2. **Solar photovoltaic energy.** Systems based on photovoltaic cells spread over large areas convert sunlight energy into electricity directly. Photovoltaic (PV) systems generate electricity directly from solar energy radiation. PV power plants are based on semiconductor materials (Figure 13.6). Their significant advantage is that they do not release CO_2 and greenhouse gases, nor do they emit particles that cause respiratory complications in humans and animals during their operation.

Figure 13.6   Photovoltaic Park at Perovo, Crimea.

13.4.2.2   Efficiency and Environmental Considerations

1. **General.** The great benefit of solar energy is that its production creates a minimal amount of pollution. However, sunlight is an intermittent energy source. Therefore, it must be operated with an energy storage facility or

external power sources to continuously provide a reliable electricity supply. In addition, solar energy production requires ample sunlight and space as well as a high upfront investment. Finally, and most importantly, due to its low energy return on investment (EROI), most researchers believe it will not achieve significant results as a replacement for traditional nonrenewable energy sources.

2. **Manufacturing/installation.** Mining, manufacturing, and transporting PV systems require substantial energy. In addition, producing solar-grade silicon semiconductor processing involves hazardous chemicals. Often, these chemicals are disposed of into the environment, but this action depends on the manufacturer and country of origin.

    Finally, building a utility-scale solar power facility requires a large area of land. Often covering many square kilometers of ground, these facilities usually require clearing and grading of land, which causes soil compaction, erosion, and alteration of drainage channels.

3. **Operation/maintenance.** After PV systems are manufactured and installed, they produce emission-free energy for more than 25 years. However, the environmental impacts associated with solar power fluctuate depending on the scale of the system and the specific photovoltaic technology used. For example, solar panels require periodic maintenance that involves washing their porous surfaces, which leads to pollution in the water table in the area of operation. Furthermore, larger PV plants create habitat loss and negatively impact local flora and fauna.

4. **Decommissioning.** Over time, solar panels break or lose their original physical characteristics. Therefore, they eventually must be replaced or recycled. In addition, solar panels are mostly made of glass that contains small amounts of heavy metals (cadmium, lead, etc.) that are considered hazardous. Because of their toxic content, solar modules must be disposed of following standard e-waste procedures. However, the cost of solar panel recycling is high, resulting in many solar panels ending up in landfills.

13.4.3 Wind Energy

The wind is, essentially, the movement of air due to pressure differences within the atmosphere. More specifically, pressure differences cause air masses to move from a high pressure location to a low-pressure location. Wind energy is harvested by capturing wind flow. Here, the wind kinetic energy exerts pressure on the turbine blades, which rotate the turbine's rotor. The turbine rotor is attached to an electrical generator, which, in turn, converts the kinetic energy into electrical energy. Modern wind turbines are enormous machines with energy production that is dependent on air mass and wind speed (Figure 13.7).

Figure 13.7 Wind farm in southern California.

13.4.3.1 Efficiency and Environmental Considerations

1. **General.** The great advantage of systems based on wind energy is that they do not produce CO_2 or release harmful products. However, wind energy production is intermittent, like sunlight-based energy systems. In an average year, wind energy is produced for only a limited number of hours per month. This characteristic necessitates energy storage facilities or operations with other power sources to provide a continuous electricity supply.

   In addition, power systems based on wind energy are primarily made from aluminum (e.g., the tower, turbine blades, and turbine-generator housing). First, much of the bauxite (aluminum ore) is mined in remote places like Australia, China, and Guinea. Then some of the aluminum ore is smelted either in its country of origin (e.g., Australia) or is shipped overseas, often to India, China, Russia. Then pure aluminum ingots are transported to various places (e.g., China, European Union, the United States), where the wind turbines are built and installed onshore or offshore.

   Furthermore, most individual wind turbines are placed in remote onshore or offshore wind farms far from the urban centers where electricity is needed. They are connected to local or national electric grids by long transmission lines with typical losses, which naturally reduces their overall EROI. Considering all of the above, research shows that the EROI of wind energy is relatively low. As a result, most researchers believe that wind energy cannot be expected to replace or even significantly affect the use of traditional nonrenewable energy sources.

2. **Manufacturing/installation.** The area occupied by one wind energy unit is about 30 square meters, and the land between different wind energy towers may be used for farming and agriculture. However, producing the metals and other materials used to make wind turbines impacts the environment because the removal of raw materials and the manufacturing and installation of these systems use, by and large, fossil fuels.

3. **Operation/maintenance.** Wind turbines often cause substantial ecological harm to bird populations. Birds are frequently injured and sometimes killed when they fly through the blades of wind turbines. The US Energy Information Administration (EIA) indicates that wind turbines have caused thousands of bat and bird deaths. In addition, wind turbines produce significant noise pollution; therefore, these plants are regularly built outside populated areas. However, animals get used to them and return to their habitat. Wind power plants affect the electric grid stability in many ways, creating electric voltage and frequency variations due to changes in wind speed. Additionally, wind farms produce electromagnetic disturbances that affect communication and cause transmission interference.

4. **Decommissioning.** Decommissioning wind turbines includes removing all physical material and equipment related to the system, including their concrete bases. Although most materials used to make wind turbines can be reused or recycled, turbine blades cannot be recycled as most are currently constructed. Wind turbine rotor blades are up to 100 meters long and are made of a mix of resin, fiberglass, and carbon fibers that emit dust and toxic gases. Rotor blades are difficult and expensive to decommission and must be partitioned on-site before getting trucked away on specialized equipment to a landfill.

13.4.4 Hydroelectric Energy

Hydroelectric energy is also considered renewable energy that exploits the kinetic energy of moving water to generate electricity. The water flow activates turbines connected to a generator, producing electricity. Hydroelectric power does not create pollution and is considered an environmentally friendly energy option. However, hydroelectric power generation requires specific geographical and hydrological conditions that can be found in only a few places on Earth. In addition, hydroelectric power generation disrupts waterways and disturbs the animals in them. This disturbance includes changing water levels and currents, as well as obstruction of migration paths for many aquatic species. Therefore, future expectations are for limited use of this technology, so it will minimally affect global energy needs.

13.4.5   Geothermal Energy

Geothermal energy is heat captured from beneath the Earth's crust and used to produce steam for heating urban areas and operating turbines that produce electricity. Geothermal energy is naturally replenished and therefore is not expected to be depleted in the foreseeable future. However, as with hydroelectric energy, geothermal energy production is viable in only a few locations on Earth. Another primary concern regarding geothermal energy production is its vulnerability to volcanic eruptions and earthquakes. Again, future expectations are for minimal use of this technology, so it will minimally affect global energy needs.

13.4.6   Ocean Energy

Oceans' natural energy can be harvested to produce two types of energy: thermal and kinetic. Ocean thermal energy generators produce energy by harnessing the temperature differences between ocean surface waters and deep ocean waters. Ocean kinetic energy generators use the tides' ebbs and flows to generate energy.

Unlike other forms of renewable energy, ocean energy is predictable, and estimating the expected energy production is easy. In addition, this type of renewable energy is abundant, and production facilities may be located near populated centers by oceans. Most tidal energy generators use turbines placed in tidal streams and extract energy from seawater flow. Because water is much denser than air, tidal energy may be generated using turbines that are smaller than wind turbines. Tidal energy production is still in the experimental stage. So far, the amount of power produced has been small, and very few commercial-sized tidal power plants are operating worldwide. In addition, relatively large machinery must be built to harvest ocean energy. Assembling such structures may disrupt the ocean floor and its sea life habitats. Currently, the prospects of using large-scale global ocean energy production systems look dim.

13.4.7   Biomass Energy

Biomass energy is mainly produced from burning organic matter from recently living plants and organisms. To a lesser extent, biomass energy is produced by harnessing methane gas produced by decomposing organic materials. Unfortunately, using biomass in energy production creates carbon dioxide that pollutes the atmosphere.

13.4.8   Exclusive Global Renewable Energy[3]

Moriarty and Honnery (2020) examined the feasibility of RE fueling all the current and future global energy needs by 2050. RE encompasses all direct and indirect

---

3 This section is derived from Moriarty and Honnery's (2020) paper.

solar energy sources (direct solar, wind, wave, ocean thermal, and hydro energy) and two nonsolar sources (geothermal and tidal energy.

Admitting that there is no agreement among energy researchers as to whether RE can provide for all global energy needs, the authors conclude that by 2050, hydro, geothermal, and biomass energy constraints will limit RE's scope to mostly wind and solar energy. The overall conclusion of this analysis is that for high levels of energy use, 100% RE is unlikely to be obtained by 2050. Below are key takeaway points.

1. **Constraints on hydro, geothermal, and biomass energy.** The leading form of RE today is biomass, mainly wood consumed in low-income countries. However, other biomass usages like food, forage, fiber, and forestry restrict its future growth. Also, the output from other energy sources, like bioenergy and geothermal, is negligible and only grows slowly. In short, sustainable biomass potential for all energy uses, including electricity production, is limited. For example, the global potential for geothermal electricity is minimal and could never supply more than a small fraction of global needs. The potential for tidal electricity is likewise small. The conclusion is that for an RE future, we must rely heavily on intermittent RE sources, chiefly wind and solar.

2. **Future global energy needs under 100% RE scenario.** In 2018, global consumption of primary energy was 580 exajoules.[4] Fossil fuel use accounted for 84.3% of this total and still rose in absolute terms. However, in 2019, solar and wind contributed only 8.0% of global electricity. Moreover, conservative global long-range primary energy projections for 2050 increase global energy needs by 25%, reaching 730 exajoules.

3. **Declining quality of inputs.** Wind farm EROI will gradually decrease because the availability of prime locations with high wind speed will slowly diminish. In addition, solar geographical resources will be constrained due to their remoteness from load centers and lack of infrastructure and fresh water in desert areas. As a result, an increasingly important component of input energy will be needed to mine and process parts for PV and wind turbine manufacture. Furthermore, in the expanded economy assumed for 2050, materials demand in the nonenergy sectors of the economy will also grow. Studies show that proven reserves of several metals, particularly cadmium, cobalt, lithium, and nickel, are insufficient to build RE systems at the predicted level of future global energy demand. Similarly, the energy costs of mining and processing of refined material are expected to rise as progressively lower-grade ores must be used.

---

4 Exajoules is 10^{18} joules.

4. Need for energy conversion and storage. In electrical wind/solar energy systems, conversion and storage of some or all of the intermittent electricity output are needed. These needs emerge because (1) output energy varies over time due to the availability of wind and sunlight, and (2) output does not usually match variations in instantaneous demand load.

In conclusion, given the enormous uncertainties, it is impossible to arrive at a precise figure for the technical potential of wind and the technical potential of solar power. However, it is likely that, given the assumption of continued business-as-usual economic growth, the world in 2050 could not obtain anywhere near the 600+ exajoules of primary intermittent electric energy that it would need. Heavy fossil fuel use will need to continue (perhaps with some form of CO_2 removal), or energy use will need to be significantly reduced.

13.5 Fossil Fuel Energy

13.5.1 General Observations

Global use of fossil fuels is deeply ingrained in modern societies. A realistic expectation is that eliminating these energy sources is impossible because no leader will sanction policies that drastically reduce living standards for people who are expected to keep them in their leadership positions. The best we can hope for is some reduction in greenhouse emissions through other means.

Today, 80% of total global energy each year comes from fossil fuels (i.e., crude oil, natural gas, and coal). Additionally, coal has been the fastest-growing primary global fuel, surpassing all other electricity-generating fuels. And, assuming current consumption levels, coal is expected to become the world's largest energy source. Along this line, it is estimated that the global reserves of coal are the largest and, at the current utilization rate, will last until 2200. On the other hand, relatively inexpensive crude oil and natural gas are limited and are expected to last until about 2070.[5] All these three dominant nonrenewable energy sources produce greenhouse gases. In relative terms, coal is the worst environmental offender, and natural gas is considered the cleanest-burning fossil fuel.

13.5.2 Crude Oil

Crude oil is a natural fossil occurring as a liquid mixture of the main hydrocarbons in geological formations. Crude oil is produced when large quantities of dead organisms are buried in the Earth's crust and subjected to prolonged heat and

---

5 See: When Will Fossil Fuels Run Out? (January 18, 2021). https://group.met.com/en/mind-the-fyoutre/mindthefyoutre/when-will-fossil-fuels-run-out. Accessed: Jan. 2023.

pressure for millions of years. Crude oil's EROI is significantly higher than that of renewable energy sources. However, its value has declined globally over the past decade or two. In addition, energy-intensive carbon capture and sequestration (CCS) requires reducing fossil fuel emissions to levels equivalent to wind or photovoltaic electricity production, which would considerably reduce the final crude oil EROI value. Based on historical world energy consumption data and global governments' reluctance to deal seriously with global warming issues, it is reasonable to expect that the trends shown in Figure 13.8 will continue for the foreseeable future.

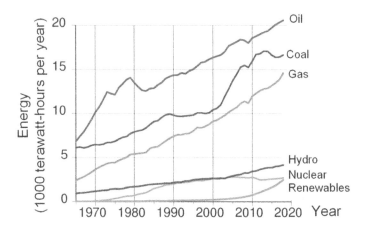

Figure 13.8 Global energy consumption per year.

13.5.3 Natural Gas

Natural gas consists primarily of methane. It is a nonrenewable fossil fuel formed when layers of organic matter (principally marine microorganisms) break down under anaerobic conditions and are subjected to extreme pressure and immense heat for millions of years. Natural gas may be found in underground geologic cavities, and its extraction and consumption contribute to climate change. Methane and carbon dioxide are released when natural gas is burned. As a result, natural gas produces more greenhouse gas emissions during production and transport than other primary fossil fuels. However, when burned for heat or electricity, natural gas produces 25% to 30% less carbon dioxide than crude oil and 40% to 45% less than coal.

13.5.4 Coal

Coal is a combustible sedimentary rock. It is mainly comprised of hydrogen, sulfur, oxygen, and nitrogen–carbon traces. Coal is formed when dead plants decay and are transformed by pressure and heat over millions of years. During the late Carboniferous and Permian times, vast coal deposits originated in former wetlands that covered much of the Earth's tropical land. Coal, primarily used as fuel, provided one-quarter of the global energy in 2020. Over a third of it is used to generate electricity; the rest is used to make iron and support other industrial processes. However, using coal causes significant environmental damage by creating carbon dioxide and sulfur dioxide.

13.6 Conventional Fission Reaction Energy

Nuclear power plants produce heat by way of a fission reaction. This heat generates steam that drives turbines connected to a generator producing electricity (Figure 13.9). As of 2022, the International Atomic Energy Agency reported 439 nuclear power reactors operating in 32 countries worldwide.

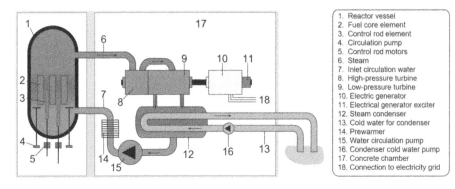

1. Reactor vessel
2. Fuel core element
3. Control rod element
4. Circulation pump
5. Control rod motors
6. Steam
7. Inlet circulation water
8. High-pressure turbine
9. Low-pressure turbine
10. Electric generator
11. Electrical generator exciter
12. Steam condenser
13. Cold water for condenser
14. Prewarmer
15. Water circulation pump
16. Condenser cold water pump
17. Concrete chamber
18. Connection to electricity grid

Figure 13.9   Boiling water reactor (BWR).

Conventional nuclear reactors operate based on fission reactions. Uranium-235 nuclei absorb neutrons. The kinetic energy of the neutrons splits the uranium into fission products (i.e., krypton and barium). The loss of mass associated with this physical interaction produces heat. In addition, the process releases several free neutrons, which continue the chain reaction (Figure 13.10).

Nuclear power plants create a minimal CO_2 footprint (comparable to that of renewable energy). This footprint is much lower than that of fossil fuels. However, nuclear reactors require continuous temperature monitoring to prevent a core meltdown. Such meltdowns have occurred on several occasions through accidents, releasing large doses of radiation and making the surrounding area uninhabitable. In addition, nuclear plants must be protected against theft of nuclear material and attacks by saboteurs or enemy military forces.

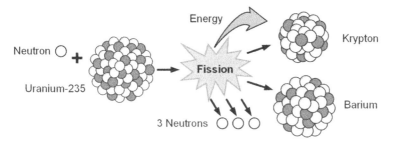

Figure 13.10 Fission nuclear reaction.

Generally, nuclear power plants are considered safe. However, the nuclear industry has suffered many nuclear and radiation accidents and incidents that have released radiation into the environment and have cost millions and even billions of dollars to fix. The most severe and well-known disasters[6] include (1) the 1979 partial core meltdown of one reactor power plant at Three Mile Island in the United States; (2) the 1986 total core meltdown of one reactor at Chernobyl, a nuclear power plant in the former USSR; and (3) the 2011 total core meltdown of three reactors and damage to a fourth reactor at Fukushima Daiichi, a nuclear power plant in Japan. Finally, there are significant concerns about long-lived radioactive wastes, vulnerability to sabotage, and the potential for spreading nuclear weapons technology and material.

In conclusion, electricity generation in nuclear power plants currently constitutes a minor and declining share of global electricity production. However, there is a relatively ample fuel supply (uranium) and low air and water environmental impacts. However, building, maintaining, and decommissioning nuclear power plants is costly, and their net energy yield is relatively low during day-to-day operations. So, despite their well-known shortcoming, a conventional (fission) nuclear energy source seems to be the best energy solution for the immediate future. Therefore, more nuclear energy plants should be built, and nonrenewable and old coal-burning plants should be decommissioned worldwide.

13.7 Bibliography

Banik A. (Ed.). (2022). *Transition in Energy Sector: Scope, Challenges and Future Opportunities (Energy and Environment)*. Central West Publishing.

---

6 Nuclear and radiation accidents and incidents. https://en.wikipedia.org/wiki/Nuclear_and_radiation_accidents_and_incidents. Accessed: Jan. 2023.

CFI. (2020, August 24). Energy return on investment (EROI). Corporate Finance Institute (CFI). https://corporatefinanceinstitute.com/resources/knowledge/other/energy-return-on-investment-eroi/. Accessed: Jan. 2023.

Moriarty, P. and Honnery, D. (2020). Feasibility of a 100% global renewable energy system. *Energies* 13 (21): 5543. https://www.mdpi.com/1996-1073/13/21/5543. Accessed: Jan. 2023.

Raugei, M., Frischknecht, R., Olson, C., Sinha, P., and Heath, G. (2016). Methodological guidelines on net energy analysis of photovoltaic electricity, IEA-PVPS Task 12, Report T12- 07. https://iea-pvps.org/wp-content/uploads/2020/01/Task12_-_Methodological_Guidelines_on_Net_Energy_Analysis_of_Photovoltaic_Electricity.pdf. Accessed: Jan. 2023.

14

Systemic Energy Action Plan

14.1   The Global Energy Dilemma

In a most profound sense, humanity's quality of life depends on the availability of reasonably priced energy compatible with the environment. Four key climate change indicators—greenhouse gas concentrations, sea level rise, ocean heat, and ocean acidification—are clear signs that human activities cause global-scale shifts on land, in the ocean, and in the atmosphere, with dramatic and long-lasting ramifications. So, to have a chance of keeping climate change below 2 °C, nations must achieve net zero emissions worldwide in less than 30 years. At the same time, continued use of traditional energy sources would lead to temperatures of 50 °C, increasing sea levels of up to 1 meter, and violent weather phenomena in many parts of the world. These phenomena will naturally lead to a mass migration of millions upon millions of people, mainly from central Africa and South America to the north, mainly to the United States and Canada, as well as to Europe.

Thus, society seems to be caught in a dilemma unlike anything experienced in the past. All of this was possible because there was abundant cheap, high-quality energy, primarily crude oil, gas, and coal. However, the author believes the future will likely be very different. For a while, considerable energy will remain in the ground; however, over the long haul, it is unlikely to be cheaply exploitable because of its decreasing energy return on investment (EROI).

The following is this author's opinion regarding what can be done about the future energy problem. This opinion may not coincide with official, governmental, and some pundits' declarations and official boasting, so the readers should make up their own minds regarding the information in the following sections. This chapter provides a systemic action plan for the energy predicament. It contains the following parts:

- The global energy dilemma
- Renewable energy and action plan, including general observations, characteristics of renewable energy, and a renewable energy action plan

Systems Science for Engineers and Scholars, First Edition. Edited by Avner Engel.
© 2024 John Wiley & Sons, Ltd. Published 2024 by John Wiley & Sons, Ltd.

- Fossil fuel energy and action plan, including general observations, characteristics of fossil fuel energy, and a fossil fuel energy action plan
- Cars, trucks, and electric vehicles, including myths about electric vehicles and cars and trucks action plan
- Fission reaction energy and action plan, including conventional fission reaction energy and action plan
- Short-term future energy and action plan, including small modular reactors (SMR), SMR characteristics, global status, and a short-term future energy action plan
- Long-term future energy and action plan, including fusion nuclear energy, international and national nuclear fusion research, other state-funded fusion research, commercial fusion research, and a long-term future energy action plan

14.2 Renewable Energy Action Plan

The following action plan is proposed concerning renewable energy.

1. **Solar energy**. The advantage of this energy source is that it has a minimal ecological impact on the environment. On the other hand, by nature, its production is intermittent and thus it must be connected to the national electric grid. An optimal action plan is to use it extensively on rooftops and sides of buildings and to use inexpensive conventional batteries to store a relatively small amount of electricity locally at home. However, despite the current hype, erecting large solar panel farms may be a short-term stopgap. Fundamentally, this approach is ineffective and not advisable for the long term.

    This view is derived from the following reasons: (1) The energy return on investment (EROI) is too low. (2) The intermittent nature of solar energy raises the need to either store large amounts of energy using expensive and inefficient means or rely on external fossil fuel energy sources. (3) Ideal locations for harvesting solar energy are desert areas within a belt centered on the Earth's equator. However, most population centers are far away from these optimal places, and the energy losses associated with such energy transportation are prohibitive. (4) These systems' up-front investment and upkeep costs, especially in countries with abundant daylight conditions, are high and unrealistic.

2. **Wind energy.** The benefits and deficiencies of wind energy are similar to those of the abovementioned solar energy situation. However, wind energy is inappropriate for rooftops or sides of buildings. Another restricting factor in utilizing wind energy is the limited availability of geographical locations

where relatively strong and steady wind occurs. So, despite the current hype, erecting large wind farms may be a short-term stopgap. Fundamentally, this approach is ineffective and not advisable for the long term.

3. **Hydroelectric energy.** The advantage of this power source is that it does not create pollution. However, hydroelectric energy requires particular geographical and hydrological conditions. Therefore, from a worldwide energy perspective, hydroelectric energy is quite negligible.

4. **Geothermal energy.** The advantages, limitations, and conclusions regarding this energy source are similar to hydroelectric energy discussed above.

5. **Ocean energy.** This energy source is in its infancy. More data should be gathered before making a solid conclusion.

6. **Biomass energy.** In contrast with the previously mentioned energy sources, this energy source negatively impacts the environment. Although burning wood for cooking and other usages is widespread in less-developed regions, the fact of the matter is that biomass energy is not precisely "renewable" because, by and large, the rate of usage far exceeds the rate of regeneration, leaving large portions of the Earth bare of trees and other plants. Ideally (although not practically), the action plan regarding this energy source is to decrease it as much as possible.

14.3 Fossil Fuel Energy Action Plan

The following action plan is proposed concerning fossil fuel energy.

1. **Crude oil.** This energy source contributes, of course, to environmental pollution and the creation of greenhouse gases. Oil utilization is at the heart of the modern economy and is expected to dwindle by the mid-twenty-first century. Oil EROI is significantly higher than that for all renewable energies. So, from an action plan standpoint, this energy source is here to stay for the foreseeable future, and no other energy source can remove it from its prominent position.

2. **Natural gas.** This energy source is quite similar to crude oil, as discussed above. However, natural gas is considered the cleanest-burning fossil fuel. So, from an action plan viewpoint, no other energy source can replace it for the foreseeable future, probably up to the end of the twenty-first century.

3. **Coal.** This energy source is similar to crude oil and natural gas, as discussed above. Coal is mainly used for generating electricity and powering heavy industry. Unfortunately, in relative terms, coal is considered the worst environmental offender relative to crude oil and natural gas. So, from an action plan viewpoint, governments should incentivize the industry to phase

out coal-burning plants, replacing them with oil or, better yet, natural gas–burning facilities.

14.4 Cars and Trucks Action Plan

14.4.1 Myths about Electric Vehicles

One myth about electric vehicles is that they deliver higher energy efficiency than fossil fuel–based vehicles. For example, a typical passenger car using a diesel engine has an overall energy efficiency of about 30%, while similar vehicles using gasoline engines have an energy efficiency of about 20%. However, as depicted in Figure 14.1, the system-wide efficiency of electric vehicles (EVs) is approximately 30%. Nevertheless, governments should encourage the use of EVs because the source of pollution is, by and large, outside metropolitan areas. Similarly, the hype that electric cars do not produce greenhouse gases and thus do not impact the environment is also a myth. The fact is that greenhouse gases are created at the electrical plant rather than the vehicle itself.

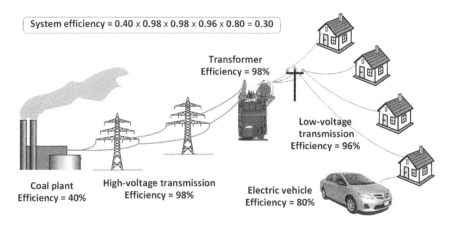

System efficiency = 0.40 × 0.98 × 0.98 × 0.96 × 0.80 = 0.30

Transformer
Efficiency = 98%

Low-voltage
transmission
Efficiency = 96%

Coal plant
Efficiency = 40%

High-voltage transmission
Efficiency = 98%

Electric vehicle
Efficiency = 80%

Figure 14.1   System-wide electric vehicle energy efficiency.

14.4.2 Car and Truck Action Plan

Despite the current hype fueled by various commercial interests and ignorant or corrupt governments, electric vehicles have no energetic advantage relative to conventional vehicles. So, a recommended action plan is to develop vehicles that run on natural gas rather than oil in their different forms (e.g., gasoline, diesel, etc.). As mentioned above, natural gas is considered the cleanest-burning fossil fuel.

14.5 Fission Reaction Energy Action Plan

On the pro side, conventional nuclear power plants create a minimal CO_2 footprint. Also, there is a relatively ample fuel (uranium) supply. And most importantly, the EROI associated with nuclear energy is far higher than that for any fuel source available today. On the con side, the fission reaction produces radioactive waste that is difficult to store and maintain. In addition, one of the byproducts of nuclear reactions is plutonium, which is used to build nuclear weapons and has a half-life of more than 20,000 years.

From a safety point of view, nuclear reactors require extreme day-to-day vigilance. Several significant accidents have occurred in different parts of the world, releasing radioactive materials into the environment and costing many billions of dollars to clean up. Also, building, maintaining, and decommissioning nuclear power plants is costly and hazardous.

An action plan dilemma regarding nuclear power is whether to maintain the current worldwide energy production balance (fossil energy at 83% and nuclear energy at 4.3%). So, for the immediate future, an action plan recommended for governments and the conventional (fission) nuclear energy industry is to substantially increase the number of nuclear power plants in countries and regions that can ensure their safety. These new power plants should replace existing coal-burning power plants worldwide.

14.6 Small Modular Reactor (SMR) Action Plan

14.6.1 Small Modular Reactors (SMRs)

Economic factors of scale are significant in the nuclear industry. However, the 1986 Chernobyl and the 2011 Fukushima nuclear disasters caused a significant setback for the nuclear industry, with the worldwide suspension of development and the closure of reactor plants. In response, a new strategy was introduced to build smaller reactors quickly to maximize return on investment (ROI). Despite the limited output power, the economics of these systems seem to be sustained due to the introduction of modular construction and a shorter expected building timescale.

Small modular reactors (SMRs) are a class of nuclear fission reactors that can be built modularly in one or more locations and then moved, commissioned, and operated at another location. Various components of the nuclear industry have proposed multiple SMRs designs. Some are simplified versions of current reactors, and others involve entirely new technologies. However, all proposed SMRs use nuclear fission with designs that include thermal-neutron and fast-neutron nuclear reactors (Figure 14.2).

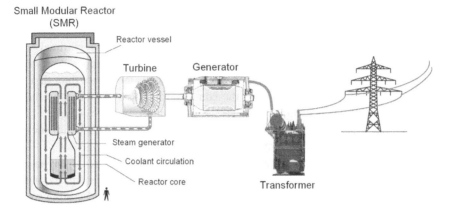

Figure 14.2 Light water small modular reactor (SMR) system.

By and large, SMRs have a power capacity of 300 mW[1] (electric) or less than 1000 mW (thermal) per unit. This power capacity is about one-third that of traditional nuclear power reactors. That is, SMRs are (1) small relative to conventional nuclear power reactors and (2) modular, which enables portions of SMRs to be built and assembled at authorized factories and then transported to designated locations for final installation.

14.6.2 SMR Characteristics and Global Status

14.6.2.1 SMR Safety
As mentioned above, most SMRs system designs are based on a passive core cooling architectures. As a result, no human intervention is required to shut down the reactor system in an emergency. These increased safety margins significantly lower the potential for radioactivity to be released into the environment in case of an accident.

Another safety aspect relates to the limited amount of nuclear fuel maintained within each SMR unit. First, lower radioactive inventory per reactor means substantially less environmental damage in case of an accident. Second, safety is enhanced because SMRs require occasional refueling, typically every three to seven years of operations, as contrasted with conventional plants, which require refueling every one to two years.

On the other hand, more small reactors pose a higher security risk, requiring more nuclear fuel transportation. Overall, SMRs are based on new designs and technology, the safety of which has yet to be proven. In summary, small reactors will not be safe without public regulation. This stipulation means that the security of systems that generate electricity, regardless of the type of fuel used, must be watched by accountable and responsible government agencies.

---

1 mW – megawatt. One million watts.

Then one should remember the matter of waste disposal, which is relevant to all nuclear power plants. Although these plants don't produce greenhouse gases, they do create toxic waste that will stay with us for thousands of years. So, safe storage is an issue with small nuclear reactors, as well as with big ones. So, where will we store the waste from all these wonderful small nuclear reactors?

14.6.2.2 SMR Advantages

Many SMR benefits are linked to the nature of their small modular design.

1. **SMR production and installation.** In contrast with existing reactors, SMRs designs are generally more straightforward. In addition, portions of SMRs can be manufactured, transported, and installed on site (Figure 14.3). This advantage makes them more affordable than large power reactors, which are often custom-designed for a particular location. Furthermore, given their smaller footprint, SMRs can be sited in places that are unsuitable for larger nuclear power plants and offer a reduction in construction time. However, the modular building will be cost-effective only with high quantities of the same types of SMRs. Therefore, a high market share is needed to obtain sufficient orders.

Figure 14.3 Artist concept: transporting SMR unit (Image: NuScale Power).

2. **SMR flexibility.** Small nuclear reactors offer notable technological and management advancements due to their flexibility and modularity. This flexibility and modularity of SMR systems enable units to be incrementally added when the load on the grid increases. They also allow units to be offline for refueling and maintenance while other reactors stay online. Additionally, the standardization and modularity of SMRs designs support rapid production at a decreasing cost following the completion of early reactors.

3. **SMR cooling.** SMRs core cooling uses natural convection circulation to remove decay heat after reactor shutdown. This cooling process, in turn, eliminates the need for pressure injection systems, so emergency external grid power, as well as battery sources and the diesel generator, are not required for core cooling. In summary, passive cooling systems are more straightforward and require less testing. Finally, SMRs do not require an emergency feedwater system to enhance safety.

4. **SMR base load capability.** Many power plants, such as large oil, coal, and nuclear plants, can't change their power output rapidly. These plants are called baseload power plants, meaning they must provide a minimum energy level to the electrical grid over a given unit of time (e.g., one week). In contrast, SMR systems are designed to adjust their output based on demand. Thus, in rural areas lacking sufficient electrical transmission lines or grid capacity, SMR can operate off the grid, providing low-carbon electric power for industry and the local population.

14.6.2.3 SMR Disadvantages

SMRs exhibit several types of disadvantages, which are related primarily to their economics. Here are some of them[2]:

1. **As long as coal and natural gas are cheap, SMRs do not make economic sense.** Small nuclear reactors will never make sense financially—except in a few locations—as long as natural gas is inexpensive and readily available, as it is new and will likely remain. Probably the only way to make nuclear reactors competitive would be to impose a steep carbon tax that increases the price of coal and natural gas.

2. **SMRs are not as cheap to build and maintain.** Bringing an acceptable small nuclear reactor design from the drawing board to approval by a nuclear regulatory authority and building and operating them will cost hundreds of millions of dollars. Along this line, serious efforts to develop SMR in the United States, the United Kingdom, Russia, and China receive vast amounts of government money.

3. **Small atomic reactors are less economical to run than big atomic reactors.** Reactors producing 300 mW of electricity will not generate as much revenue as currently built reactors that create 1000 to 1600 mW of electricity, especially when small atomic reactors' research and development costs are comparable to those of big ones.

4. **As long as nobody manufactures SMR modules, economies of scale cannot be realized.** SMR module manufacturing will occur when a relatively large number of SMRs are achieved. This economic advantage will happen only when small reactors' costs decrease significantly.

---

2 Adapted with permission from Climenhaga (2020).

14.6.2.4 SMR Global Status

The International Atomic Energy Agency currently identifies about 50 SMR concepts of modular reactor designs. Still, there have been only a handful of attempts to build them, all with massive government funding.

1. **Russia.** The only small nuclear reactor plant operating worldwide is the Akademik Lomonosov atomic power plant (Figure 14.4). This system is a barge docked at the Pevek harbor. It supplies electricity to the region and heat to the town. Pevek is an Arctic port town located in the northeastern portion of Russia. The power plant, commissioned in 2020, has two modified nuclear reactors (icebreaker type), each producing 150 mW thermal energy and 35 mW electric energy.

   The concept of prefabricated SMR modules, manufactured and then shipped and installed on-site, and all the other nice SMR trimmings, is absent in the case of the Akademik Lomonosov power plant. Also, from an original cost estimate of US$140 million in 2006, its cost increased to US$740 million when the vessel was launched.

Figure 14.4 The Akademik Lomonosov atomic power plant.

2. **China.** The ACP100 is the world's first onshore SMR and is undergoing construction at China's Linglong-One nuclear power facility. In April 2022, China National Nuclear Corporation (CNNC) completed hoisting the lower section of the containment shell into place. The overall height of the steel containment's lower cylinder is about 15 meters, and the structural weight is 450 tons (Figure 14.5).

   The multipurpose 385 mW (thermal) and 125 mW (electrical) SMR is a pressurized water reactor for electricity generation and other functions. The Linglong-One development started in 2010, construction began in 2021, and stable operation is expected to commence by the end of 2026. Then the system will produce electricity for 526,000 households.

By examining the ACP100 reactor data and viewing Figure 14.5, it is pretty clear that, despite its name, this is not an SMR, as discussed above. Standard modules are too heavy to be manufactured elsewhere and brought to the site for assembly. In addition, construction seems to follow a development process used by extensive nuclear facilities.

Figure 14.5 Linglong-One reactor pit 2022 (Image: CNNC).

3. **United States.** NuScale Power, founded in 2000, is an American company headquartered in Oregon. The company designs nuclear plans made of one or more SMR, where each reactor vessel is 2.7 meters in diameter by 20 meters in height. A single SMR unit runs on low-enriched uranium fuel assemblies, uses a passive cooling method, and is expected to produce about 60 mW of electricity. NuScale Power and its SMR design were approved for certification in 2022. They are contracted with the Utah Associated Municipal Power Systems to deliver 12 small modular reactors by 2030 at a cost of $6.1 billion.

4. **United Kingdom.** Rolls-Royce SMR, located in the United Kingdom, is developing and will eventually build SMR. In 2022, the company disclosed that it was examining eight possible sites in the UK to build three factories

that will manufacture modules of their SMR. In addition, Rolls-Royce plans to build a nuclear power station using its first-produced SMR in 2029. The company estimates that the 470-mW (electric) units will cost around £1.8 billion once they are in total production, compared with £22 billion for a full-sized nuclear power station. The UK government supported Rolls Royce's SMR development with $275 million.

14.6.3 SMR Action Plan

True SMR. SMRs of the type proposed by NuScale Power are characterized by (1) their power capacity of about 300 mW, roughly one-third of traditional nuclear power reactors; (2) their small physical size relative to conventional nuclear power reactors; and (3) their modularity, which enables portions of the reactor system to be built and assembled at different locations and then transported to designated locations for final installation. Also, SMR designs promise to be substantially safer than conventional nuclear reactors and, generally, more flexible to operate. On the other hand, small nuclear reactors are less economical to run than big atomic reactors, so, generally speaking, as long as fossil fuels are cheap, SMR do not make economic sense. The recommended action plan for true SMR is to encourage the nuclear industry to experiment and build SMR in the immediate future.

Fictional SMR. The author believes Russia's nuclear floating power station, the Akademik Lomonosov, does not merit the name SMR. Indeed, it produces power and its physical size is small, but it is not modular in the sense described above. Nevertheless, the experiment of building a moveable nuclear power plant on a ship to provide electricity to individual coastal cities seems interesting. Similarly, naming China's ACP100 as an SMR is even more inappropriate, judging from its size and complete absence of modularity.

14.7 Fusion Nuclear Energy Action Plan

14.7.1 Fusion Nuclear Energy

In many respects, a planned nuclear power plant will be similar to other thermal power stations, except that its heat source will use a fusion nuclear reactor. According to current plans, this will be achieved by a Tokamak, an experimental machine producing energy through nuclear fusion reactions (Figure 14.6).

Nuclear fusion is an atomic reaction where two light atoms are combined to form a single heavier atom and a neutron. The overall difference in mass between

Figure 14.6   A Tokamak model presented by ITER in 2013 (Image: IAEA).

the reactants and products leads to the release of energy. Such an atomic reaction is the process that powers the stars.

The planned fusion reactions within the Tokamak combine nuclei of deuterium (a stable isotope of hydrogen) with tritium (a radioactive isotope of hydrogen), creating helium and freeing a neutron, and in the process, releasing a large amount of energy (Figure 14.7).

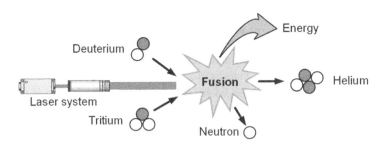

Figure 14.7   Fusion nuclear reaction.

Fusion power is the only promising solution to humankind's renewable energy dilemma. Fusion power is a form of power creation that generates electricity using heat from nuclear fusion reactors. As mentioned, light atoms combine to form a heavier nucleus, releasing considerable energy. Fusion processes occur continuously in the Sun and the stars, where hydrogen is converted to helium on a grand scale, producing a colossal amount of light and heat for billions of years. Similarly, fusion processes also occur in thermonuclear explosions. Nuclear fusion offers many advantages over current fission technology, including safe operation, reduced radioactivity, elimination of most high-level nuclear waste, and ample fuel supplies (i.e., primarily deuterium, which exists abundantly in the Earth's oceans).

However, the problem is that fusion can occur only at more than 100 million °C and extreme pressure within a confined vessel. These conditions present extreme scientific, engineering, and management challenges. So, despite declarations to the contrary, the more realistic fusion researchers agree that, in the best of cases, commercial fusion energy will be achieved toward the end of the twenty-first century. Such a timeframe means fusion technology is a long-term solution to low-carbon energy needs. In other words, fusion will not get here in time to make a real contribution to slowing or reversing climate change. Therefore, government funding for research and development along with generous tax breaks are needed to help develop this energy solution.

14.7.2 International and National Nuclear Fusion Research

The following describes international and national nuclear fusion research.

1. **The International Thermonuclear Experimental Reactor (ITER).**[3] A consortium of 35 nations is building the world's most extensive Tokamak system. This magnetic fusion device has been built to prove the feasibility of the fusion process as a large-scale and carbon-free energy source. ITER officials expect their Tokamak to be the first fusion device to produce net energy, maintaining fusion for relatively long periods. The ITER project was officially initiated in 1988. Then in 2007, site construction in southern France began. After that, in 2013, the Tokamak complex construction started. The plan calls for achieving the first plasma in 2025 and the start of deuterium–tritium operations in 2035.

2. **The National Ignition Facility (NIF).**[4] NIF is a US government–based facility at the Lawrence Livermore National Laboratory in Livermore, California. NIF is involved in inertial confinement fusion (ICF) research, and its mission is to achieve fusion that results in high energy gain. It studies

---

3 The International Thermonuclear Experimental Reactor (ITER). https://en.wikipedia.org/wiki/ITER. Accessed: Jan. 2023.
4 National Ignition Facility (NIF). https://en.wikipedia.org/wiki/National_Ignition_Facility. Accessed: Jan. 2023.

the behavior of matter under the conditions found within thermonuclear explosions. NIF works on the most potent ICF device built to date. Its basic concept is to use a highly energetic laser system to squeeze a small amount of deuterium–tritium fuel pellets to reach the pressure and temperature necessary for fusion.

A top-level history of the NIF started in 1995 when a decision regarding the facility took place. Accordingly, in 1997, the US House Armed Services Committee approved the NIF project, which was designed to produce, in a laboratory setting, matter with temperatures and densities comparable to those found in nuclear explosions.

Actual work on the NIF started with a single laser beamline demonstrator in 1994 and was completed in 1997. By 2003, the NIF had achieved the "first light" on a bundle of four laser beams, producing a 10.4-kilojoule pulse in a single beamline. By 2007, 96 laser lines have been completed and commissioned, creating total energy of more than 2.5 megajoules. In 2012, NIF produced a 1.85-mJ pulse with an increased power of 500 tW[5].

In 2016, NIF successfully executed its first gas pipe experiment to study the absorption of a large quantity of laser light within 1-centimeter-long targets relevant to high-gain magnetized liner inertial fusion. Finally, in 2021, the NIF experiment yielded the world's first burning plasma, where the yield was approximately 70% of the laser input energy.

3. **The JT-60SA experimental fusion reactor.**[6] This research facility is located in the city of Naka, Ibaraki Prefecture, Japan. It is managed by Japan's national institutes for quantum science and technology (QST) in cooperation with the European ITER project. The JT-60SA research reactor aims to complement the ITER objectives and accelerate the development of fusion power. The work includes the construction of the JT-60SA fusion device and research into well-suited materials for use in future fusion reactors.

Construction of the JT-60SA (Figure 14.8) has been ongoing since 2013, with a significant delay due to a 2011 earthquake that saw a planned 2016 debut pushed back several years. In December 2023, the JT-60SA fusion reactor was inaugurated (EU, 2023) in Naka, Japan, 130 km northeast of Tokyo. It became the world's biggest and most advanced tokamak-type fusion reactor. Upon activation, the plasma current achieved a one million ampere. The discharge time was 10 seconds, creating around 140 cubic meters of plasma—the most significant quantity of superheated matter humanity has yet created.

As mentioned, the generation of fusion energy does not produce carbon dioxide. In addition, the fusion reaction is intrinsically safe: It stops when the fuel supply or power source is shut down and generates no high-level,

---

5 tW – terawatt is one trillion watts.

6 The JT-60SA Construction. https://www.qst.go.jp/site/jt60-english/6599.html. Accessed: Jan. 2023.

Figure 14.8 The JT-60SA experimental fusion reactor (Courtesy: QST).

long-lived radioactive waste. Therefore, fusion qualifies as the next-generation energy source that simultaneously addresses energy supply and environmental challenges.

14.7.3 Other State-Funded Fusion Research

The following describes other state-funded fusion research.

1. **The Experimental Advanced Superconducting Tokamak (EAST).**[7] This research facility is located in Hefei, China. It is an experimental superconducting Tokamak magnetic fusion energy reactor. It has operated since 2006, and, according to official reports, the project's budget is approximately US$40 million, approximately one-twentieth the cost of comparable reactors built in other countries.

   The EAST project was proposed in 1996 and approved in 1998. In 2006, the first plasma was achieved. In 2007, the reactor generated plasma lasting nearly five seconds and 500,000 amperes of electric current. In 2011, EAST became the first Tokamak to successfully sustain high-confinement mode

---

7 Experimental Advanced Superconducting Tokamak (EAST). https://en.wikipedia.org/wiki/Experimental_Advanced_Superconducting_Tokamak. Accessed: Jan. 2023.

plasma for over 30 seconds at approximately 50 million °C. Then, in 2021, EAST produced a 120 million °C electron temperature for 101 seconds, and later, EAST achieved a long-pulse high-parameter plasma operation of 1056 seconds.

2. **The Joint European Torus (JET).**[8] This research facility is an operational magnetically confined plasma physics experiment located at Culham Centre for Fusion Energy in Oxfordshire, UK. Based on a Tokamak design, the fusion research facility is a joint European project with the primary purpose of opening the way to future nuclear fusion grid energy. JET began operating in 1983; achieved the first plasma in JET; and between 1991 and 1993, conducted experiments using tritium and deuterium. In 1997, JET produced 16 mW of fusion power while injecting 24 mW of thermal power to heat the fuel, reaching an input/output efficiency (Q) of 0.67. In 2021, JET used deuterium–tritium fuel, producing 59 megajoules during a five-second pulse with $Q = 0.33$.

14.7.4 Commercial Fusion Research

According to the Global Fusion Industry in a 2021 report, there are now 35 fusion firms worldwide. The four most promising commercial firms are described below.

1. **Commonwealth Fusion Systems (CFS).**[9] This American company was founded in 2018 to design and build a fusion power plant based on the affordable, robust, compact (ARC) Tokamak concept. The company, based in Cambridge, Massachusetts, is associated with the Massachusetts Institute of Technology (MIT). CFS successfully demonstrated a 20-T high-temperature superconductor magnet, and simulations suggest that this magnet could be powerful enough to let the firm's Tokamak reactor achieve net energy from fusion. As a result, CFS plans to construct the world's first fusion power plant, provide power onto the grid, and demonstrate the technical and economic competitiveness of fusion power. This process will pave the way for fusion systems to provide carbon-free, safe, limitless power for the world. Actual systems development is expected to begin in 2025.

2. **General Fusion (GF).**[10] This Canadian company was founded in 2002 and is based in Vancouver, British Columbia. It is developing a fusion power system based on magnetized target fusion (MTF). The device under development

---

8 Joint European Torus (JET). https://en.wikipedia.org/wiki/Joint_European_Torus. Accessed: Jan. 2023.

9 Commonwealth Fusion Systems (CFS). https://en.wikipedia.org/wiki/Commonwealth_Fusion_Systems. Accessed: Jan. 2023.

10 General Fusion (GF). https://en.wikipedia.org/wiki/General_Fusion. Accessed: Jan. 2023.

injects plasma mass, a compact toroid cylinder of spinning liquid metal. The material is mechanically compressed to fusion-relevant densities and pressures by a dozen to hundreds of steam-driven pistons.

In 2013, GF constructed a prototype compression system with 14 full-size pistons placed around a 1-meter-diameter spherical compression chamber. In 2017, GF demonstrated a plasma injector that utilized 15 tons of liquid lead reservoir to pump lead at 100 kg/s into a 1-meter spherical compression chamber. The company plans to demonstrate an experimental fusion device, 70% of the size of a commercial power plant in Oxfordshire, at Culham, the center of the UK's nuclear R&D.

3. **TAE Technologies (TAE).**[11] TAE is an American company based in California. Founded in 1998, TAE is developing an aneutronic fusion power system relying on an advanced beam-driven field-reversed configuration (FRC), which uniquely combines features from accelerator physics and other fusion concepts and is optimized for hydrogen-boron fuel.

In 2013, TAE received a powerful plasma injector that produces a 5 to 20 mW neutral beam. This device was produced by the Budker Institute of Nuclear Physics in Novosibirsk, Russia. This device injects energy into a reactor to generate fusion plasma. In 2015, TAE demonstrated the ability to heat plasma to 10 million °C for five milliseconds. In 2017, TAE achieved plasma within their reactor, operating at temperatures between 50 million and 70 million °C. After that, in 2021, TAE announced that their reactor was regularly producing a stable plasma at temperatures greater than 50 million °C.

4. **Tokamak Energy (TE).**[12] TE is a British firm based in Oxfordshire, United Kingdom. The company has been involved in fusion power research since its inception in 2009. The company has built several versions of spherical Tokamaks to reach commercial fusion power generation. In 2018, the most recent Tokamak developed reached 15 million °C. Then, in 2022, the spherical Tokamak created a plasma temperature of 100 million °C.

14.7.5 Long-Term Future Energy Action Plan

Fusion power is the only promising solution to humankind's renewable energy dilemma. Realistically speaking, the author believes that real, practical benefits from fusion power plants could be achieved toward the end of the twenty-first century. However, conquering this technology is necessary for the human population's survival with a reasonable quality of life.

---

11 TAE Technologies (TAE). https://en.wikipedia.org/wiki/TAE_Technologies. Accessed: Jan. 2023.

12 Tokamak Energy (TE). Tokamak Energy Wikipedia. Accessed: Jan. 2023.

However, to achieve this goal, the first action plan is for governments and the public to realize that current renewable energy schemes are delusional. Looking at the big picture reveals that solar and wind farms are, by far, not going to solve human energy needs. The author believes a critical action plan involving substantial acceleration of nuclear fusion research and a significant increase in government funding and subsidies to national and international nuclear fusion research like the ITER, NIF, EAST, and JET are needed. In addition, the author believes that a meaningful action plan is needed to increase commercial fusion research funding, significantly subsidizing research undertaken in the most advanced and promising facilities, for example, CFS, GF, TAE, and TE.

14.8 Bibliography

Climenhaga, D.J. (2020, December 8). Economics behind Jason Kenney's small nuclear reactor dream don't add up. rabble.ca. https://rabble.ca/politics/canadian-politics/economics-small-nuclear-reactors-touted-jason-kenney-game/. Accessed: Jan. 2023.

Dyatlov, S.A., Didenko, N.I., Ivanova, E.A., Soshneva, E.B., & Kulik, S.V. (2020). Prospects for alternative energy sources in the global energy sector. In IOP (Institute of Physics. Learned society for physics in the UK and Ireland) conference series: *Earth and Environmental Science* 434 (1): 012014. IOP Publishing. https://iopscience.iop.org/article/10.1088/1755-1315/434/1/012014/pdf. Accessed: Jan. 2023.

EU. (2023 December 1). News announcement: EU and Japan celebrate start of operations of the JT-60SA fusion reactor and reaffirm close cooperation on fusion energy. European Union (EU), Directorate-General for Energy. https://energy.ec.europa.eu/news/eu-and-japan-celebrate-start-operations-jt-60sa-fusion-reactor-and-reaffirm-close-cooperation-fusion-2023-12-01_en. Accessed: Dec. 2023.

Ongena, J. and Oost, G.V. (2004). Energy for future centuries: Will fusion be an inexhaustible, safe, and clean energy source? *Fusion Science and Technology* 45. 2T: 3–14.

Part 4

More Systems Science for Engineers and Scholars

15

Engineering and Systemic Psychology[1]

15.1 Introduction

This chapter aims to link key psychological aspects with systems engineering. In particular, it describes schema theory and cognitive biases because they sometimes lead to failed design, building, and systems operations. The chapter describes a systemic link between psychology and engineering and ways to achieve cognitive debiasing. It includes the following elements:

- **Schema theory.** Including the concepts of role schema, object schema, self-schema, and event schema.
- **Cognitive biases.** Including the concept of cognitive biases and selected cognitive biases.
- **Systems failures.** Including the Bay of Pigs fiasco (1961), the disastrous 747 collision at Tenerife (1977), the space shuttle *Columbia* disaster (2003), the *Deepwater Horizon* BP oil spill (2010), and the collapse of the Morandi Bridge in Genoa (2018).
- **Cognitive debiasing.** Including Abraham Lincoln's legacy, cognitive biases, strategic decisions, categories of cognitive biases, strategic decision processes, and cognitive biases versus strategic decision processes.

15.2 Schema Theory

A schema is a mental, psychological framework that helps organize and interpret information. Schemas can be helpful because they allow people to take shortcuts in processing the vast amount of information in their environment. On the other

---

1 Parts adapted with permission from Engel (2018).

Systems Science for Engineers and Scholars, First Edition. Edited by Avner Engel.
© 2024 John Wiley & Sons, Ltd. Published 2024 by John Wiley & Sons, Ltd.

hand, schemas often cause us to exclude pertinent information, focusing only on things that confirm our worldviews, beliefs, and ideas (Figure 15.1).

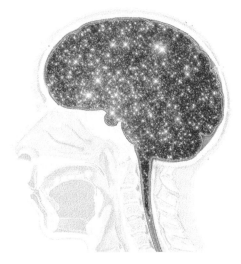

Figure 15.1 Schema: the cognitive framework that organizes and interprets information.

As a fundamental concept, schemas were first used by Frederic Bartlett (1886–1969) as part of his learning theory. Later, Jean Piaget (1896–1980) introduced the term *schema* as part of his theory of cognitive development in children and adults. According to Piaget, a schema is a type of knowledge and the process of attaining it. He believed that people constantly create and adapt their schema as new information is presented.

For example, a child may develop a schema for a cat. The schema defines a cat as a small animal with four legs and a tail. When the child encounters a dog for the first time, he may initially call it a cat because it fits in with his schema of a cat. However, once the child is told that there are different animals called a cat and a dog, he will modify his schema for a cat and create a new one for a dog.

Schemas make it easier for people to act within the world around them. New information may be classified and categorized by comparing existing schemas with new experiences. Furthermore, due to the existing schemas, people do not usually have to spend much time interpreting further information, as they can assimilate it quickly and automatically. By and large, when learning new information that does not fit existing schemas, people often tend to distort or alter the latest data to adjust it with what they already know. Traditionally, four basic types of schemas have helped people comprehend and interpret the world around them.

1. **Role schema.** Role schema defines models and expected behavior from individuals with specific societal roles. These societal roles include (1) achieved roles that encompass both occupation and professions, such as teachers or engineers, and (2) ascribed roles, including social categories such as age, gender, and race.
2. **Object schema.** Object schema defines the meaning of inanimate objects. It explains how various objects function and what one can expect from them. For example, object schema describes how to open a door, use scissors, turn on a TV, start a car, and so on.
3. **Self-schema.** Self-schema defines knowledge people accumulate about themselves through interactions with the natural world and human beings around them. Self-schema is based on past individual experiences, self-memories, and expectations.
4. **Event schema.** Event schema refers to cognitive scripts describing daily activities, behavior, and event sequences. It provides a foundation for anticipating the future, setting goals, and making plans. For example, the event schema for the appropriate behavior sequence associated with eating at a coffee shop is to enter the shop, wait to be seated, examine the menu, select the desired dish, eat, pay the bill, and then leave.

By and large, the processes through which schemas are altered occur when a person learns new information and/or undergoes new experiences. This process typically occurs during childhood but becomes infrequent as people age. Adults' schemas often persist even when they are presented with evidence contradicting their outlook. Even then, many younger persons and older adults may slowly change their schemas only after being inundated with evidence pointing to the real world's facts.

In addition to the above, motor schemas are memory representations of movement and sensory consequences. According to Schmidt (1975), the production of movement patterns involves a set of specified motor commands that are retrieved from memory and then adapted to a particular situation. Thus, the motor system must learn the initial situational conditions, generate appropriate motor commands, and use motor commands' sensory consequences to control the movement's outcome.

Riding a bicycle is considered a combination of perceptual-motor and cognitive tasks. Usually, children learn how to pedal and steer their bicycles using training wheels. Then they learn how to balance without training wheels. Later, they learn how to jump makeshift ramps with the neighborhood kids and no longer need to put much brainpower toward pedaling, steering, or balancing. So, the two functional levels of tasks, control and maneuvering of the bicycle, require cognitive abilities that become automatized through extensive experience. However, the strategic task of riding a bike toward a specific destination is not usually automated and generally requires rider attention.

15.3 Cognitive Biases

This section describes the concept of cognitive biases and provides a selected list of cognitive biases.

15.3.1 Concept of Cognitive Biases

In 1972, Amos Tversky and Daniel Kahneman[2] identified the phenomena of cognitive biases. They conducted experiments and empirical studies proving that traditional economic assumptions of rationality theory are often invalid. Framing bias, for example, arises when a problem is presented with two equal solutions that are expressed in different ways. People tend to choose one answer or another depending on how they are stated. For instance, 600 participants in an experiment were asked to choose between two treatments for individuals affected by a deadly disease. The first treatment was expected to save 200 lives, whereas the second treatment was predicted to result in 400 deaths. The "positive" treatment (A) was chosen by 72% of the participants, whereas only 22% of them chose the "negative" treatment (B).

Generally speaking, each person acquires a unique set of cognitive biases during their lifetime. This set leads individuals to create their subjective reality from their perceptions of themselves and their environment. As a result, an individual's reality dictates that person's behavior. Thus, cognitive biases cause many people's irrationality (e.g., perceptual distortion, inaccurate judgment, and illogical interpretation). Therefore, systems engineers who are responsible for large and complex systems should do their utmost to recognize and mitigate their cognitive biases. Furthermore, they should discover their tendencies to think along repeatable patterns, which may lead to systematic deviations from rationality and good judgment.

15.3.2 Selected Cognitive Biases

Since the innovative work of Tversky and Kahneman, many cognitive biases have been identified. Understanding of human biases has been expanded regarding their experimental context and conclusions about the broader implications of each mental bias effect. Interested readers may refer to Pohl (2022) for a comprehensive

---

2 Kahneman is an Israeli American psychologist who was awarded the 2002 Nobel Prize in Economic Sciences for his groundbreaking work with Amos Tversky.

3 See more: List of cognitive biases. https://en.wikipedia.org/wiki/List_of_cognitive_biases. Accessed: Jan 2023.

analysis of cognitive illusions. In addition, a more accessible (though somewhat less reliable) list of cognitive biases is available on Wikipedia.[3] Cognitive biases can be divided into three groups, and the more important of these are described below.

15.3.2.1 Decision-Making, Belief, and Behavioral Biases

These cognitive biases affect individuals' decision-making processes, belief systems, and behavior within widespread domains like engineering, business, and economics.

- **Anchoring.** The tendency to rely too heavily on an "anchor" (i.e., one piece of information) when making decisions.
- **Availability heuristics.** The tendency to exaggerate the probability of events with greater "availability" (e.g., recent, unusual, or emotional events).
- **Bandwagon effect.** The tendency to accept things because many other people believe the same.
- **Bias blind spot.** The tendency to perceive oneself as less biased than others or attribute more cognitive biases to others than to oneself.
- **Confirmation bias.** The tendency to interpret, focus on, or remember information in a way that confirms one's original preconceptions.
- **Courtesy bias.** The tendency to give socially expected opinions more than one's genuine opinion to avoid offending anyone.
- **Curse of knowledge.** The tendency of better-informed people to overlook the comprehension problems of lesser-informed people.
- **Endowment effect.** The tendency to demand much more to relinquish an object or an idea than one would be willing to pay to acquire or adopt it.
- **Expectation bias.** The tendency to believe in the validity of data that agrees with one's expectations and to disbelieve and ignore data that conflicts with those expectations.
- **Focusing effect.** The tendency to assign too much importance to one dominant aspect of an event or knowledge.
- **Framing effect.** The tendency to conceive different conclusions from the same data, depending on how it is presented.
- **Mere exposure effect.** The tendency to express an excessive liking for things merely because of familiarity.
- **Neglect of probability.** The tendency to completely disregard probability when making decisions under uncertainty.
- **Normalcy bias.** The tendency to refuse to plan for a disaster that has never happened before.
- **Not invented here.** The tendency to reject or avoid using products or knowledge developed outside an individual's group.
- **Ostrich effect.** The tendency to ignore an apparent negative situation.
- **Pessimism bias.** The tendency to overestimate the negative likelihood that things will happen.

- **Planning fallacy.** The tendency to underestimate the time or effort needed to complete a task or a project.
- **Pro-innovation bias.** The tendency to exhibit excessive optimism regarding the prospect of an invention or its usefulness while often failing to perceive its limitations and weaknesses.
- **Zero-sum bias.** The tendency to perceive situations solely in terms of one person's gains must be at the expense of another.
- **Loss aversion.** The tendency to feel the psychological pain of losing something as much more powerful than the pleasure of gaining it.
- **Sunk cost.** The tendency to follow continued endeavors one has already invested time, effort, or money into, even if the expected costs outweigh their benefits.

15.3.2.2 Attributional Biases
These cognitive biases refer to the systematic errors made by individuals who evaluate themselves or try to find reasons for other people's behavior.

- **Authority bias.** The tendency to attribute greater weight and be more influenced by the opinions of authorities, regardless of their content.
- **Egocentric bias (attributional variant).** The tendency of individuals to claim more responsibility for themselves than they deserve for the success of a joint action.
- **Illusory superiority.** The tendency of individuals to overestimate their desirable qualities and underestimate their undesirable qualities.
- **The illusion of manageability.** The tendency of individuals to attribute success to their past actions when, in fact, they were failures. In addition, this bias leads individuals to mistakenly think that should a problem arise, they would be able to fix it.
- **Groupthink bias.** The tendency of individuals to accept the opinions of other members of their group.
- **Naive realism.** The tendency to believe that one sees reality objectively and with no bias, while those who do not are either biased, irrational, or uninformed.
- **Social loafing bias.** The tendency of individuals to expend less effort to achieve a goal when undertaking a group effort than when working alone.

15.3.2.3 Memory Errors and Biases
These cognitive biases refer to errors that systematically distort individuals' memory recall.

- **Consistency bias.** The tendency to incorrectly remember one's past opinions and behavior as conforming to present attitudes and behavior.
- **Egocentric bias.** The tendency of an individual to recall their past actions in a self-serving manner.

- **False memory.** The tendency to form a misattribution where imagination is mistaken for an actual memory.
- **Generation effect.** The tendency for individuals to remember statements or actions that they have said or done in contrast with similar statements or actions uttered or performed by others.

15.4 Systems Failures

15.4.1 Cognitive Biases and Systems Failures

Based on analyses of past cases, it is easy to demonstrate how different cognitive biases distort logical decision-making processes. This distortion leads to human judgment errors, which could trigger the occurrence of incidents, crashes, collisions, and disasters.

Figure 15.2 depicts this process: Individuals develop their schema of the universe, which includes their unique cognitive biases. Sometimes, under specific circumstances like external pressure, uncertainty, or group expectations, these biases lead to decision-making failures that cause incidents, crashes, collisions, and disasters.

The following examples show how cognitive biases caused critical accidents by distorting decision-making: (1) the Bay of Pigs fiasco, (2) the 747 collision at Tenerife disaster, (3) the space shuttle *Columbia* disaster, (4) the *Deepwater Horizon* BP oil spill, and (5) the collapse of the Morandi Bridge in Genoa, Italy.

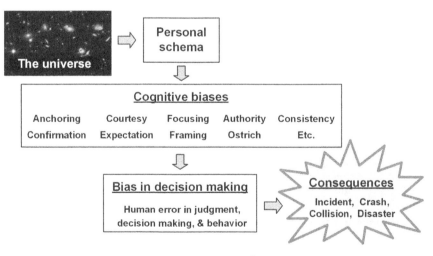

Figure 15.2 Model of cognitive biases and failures.[4]

---

4 Concept adapted from Murata et al. (2015).

15.4.2 The Bay of Pigs Fiasco (1961)

Fidel Castro came to power in 1958 and established a communist regime in Cuba. First, he nationalized American businesses, including banks, oil refineries, and sugar and coffee plantations. He then severed Cuba's formerly close relations with the United States and reached out to the United States' Cold War rival, the Soviet Union.

Three years later, in 1961, the United States attempted to overthrow Castro and establish a friendly, noncommunist regime in Cuba. The Bay of Pigs (BoP) invasion was a failed military landing action on the coast of Cuba by Cuban exiles who opposed Castro (Figure 15.3). The debacle was covertly financed and directed by the US Central Intelligence Agency (CIA) and approved by the recently installed US president, John Kennedy.

Figure 15.3 Cuban soldiers supported by T-34 tanks during the BoP operations.

The Bay of Pigs fiasco was a typical blander stemming from, among others, the following cognitive biases at the CIA and Kennedy's White House: anchoring bias, confirmation bias, expectation bias, focusing effect, and ostrich effect. However, most observers consider a groupthink bias to be the most dominant.

Consequently, US president John Kennedy attempted to avoid groupthink in his cabinet meetings. Instead, he encouraged cabinet members to discuss possible solutions within their departments and invited outside experts to present their opinions. Occasionally, Kennedy divided his cabinet into small units to break the group cohesion. Sometimes, he deliberately left the meeting room to allow open discussions.

Later, in 1962, the Soviet government placed nuclear weapons in Cuba, precipitating a crisis that came close to a nuclear war. However, the group that stumbled into the Bay of Pigs tackled this political and military challenge with wisdom and ingenuity.

15.4.3 The 747 Collision at Tenerife Disaster (1977)

In 1977, Boeing 747 KLM Flight 4805 at Tenerife Airport waited for clearance from the air traffic control (ATC) to take off, but because of reduced visibility due to fog at the airport, the takeoff clearance was delayed. The captain misunderstood a routine communication from the ATC and started the takeoff run while Pan Am 747 Flight 1736 was taxiing on the active runway. The underside of the KLM flight's fuselage ripped through the Pan Am plane, and both aircraft burst into a fiery explosion. All people aboard the KLM plane, as well as most of the passengers and crew aboard the Pan Am plane, some 583 souls, perished. Sixty-one passengers and crew, including the captain, first officer, and flight engineer aboard the Pan Am aircraft, survived. This disaster is the deadliest accident in aviation history (Figure 15.4).

The subsequent investigation concluded that the accident occurred because the KLM captain started the takeoff procedure without ATC permission. The disaster had a lasting influence on the industry, highlighting the importance of standardized phraseology in airport communications.

Regarding the captain of the KLM flight, researchers suggest that loss aversion bias may have contributed to the crash. This bias has probably been intensified due to (1) a reduction in the mandated rest period due to the flight delay, (2) the cost of accommodating the passengers at a hotel until the weather improves, and (3) stress due to a blot on the captain's reputation of being punctual. Presumably, the complicated interaction of these factors affected the decision-making skills of

Figure 15.4 Wreckage of one 747 aircraft involved in the Tenerife disaster.

a seasoned flight captain. As a result, the captain's loss aversion escalated, leading to a critical crash.

15.4.4 The Space Shuttle *Columbia* Disaster (2003)

Numerous investigations of incidents have determined that human error is central in highly adverse events or disasters, but few studies explicitly link cognitive biases to such occurrences. The space shuttle *Columbia* accident is an example of a significant catastrophe that was plausibly exasperated by multiple cognitive biases.[5]

On February 1, 2003, during reentry into Earth's atmosphere, the space shuttle *Columbia* disintegrated, and all seven crewmembers of flight STS-107 perished (Figure 15.5). During the early phase of *Columbia*'s launch, engineers observed a large piece of thermal insulation foam falling from the external tank and hitting the left wing's leading edge. Small foam debris dislodging from the external tank were a common sight during shuttle launches; however, with the *Columbia*, a relatively large piece hit a critical wing made of reinforced carbon–carbon composite material at a reasonably high speed.

NASA engineers analyzed the incident immediately after launch using a certified simulator called Crater, and, according to the Columbia Accident Investigation Board (CAIB F6.3-11, 2003) findings: "Crater initially predicted tile damage more serious than the actual tile depth. ... But engineers used their judgment to conclude that damage would not penetrate the dense tile layer." In other words, a certified

Figure 15.5 (L) Space shuttle Columbia and (R) flight STS-107 crew (left to right): Brown, Husband, Clark, Chawla, Anderson, McCool, and Ramon (Images: NASA).

---

5 Glamz, J. and Wong, E. (2003, February 4). Engineer's '97 report warned of damage to tiles by foam. *New York Times*. https://www.nytimes.com/2003/02/04/national/engineers-97-report-warned-of-damage-to-tiles-by-foam.html. Accessed: Jan. 2023.

tool (granted, with significant limitations) indicated a probable catastrophic failure, but this finding was overruled based on an engineering hunch.[6]

A physical test approximating the dynamic conditions of the actual event was conducted shortly after the accident. A similar piece of foam weighing approximately 0.5 kg was catapulted at a speed of roughly 230 m/sec onto a similar leading edge of a shuttle wing, creating a hole of about 20 cm. This experiment demonstrated that the "foam debris is the most probable cause creating the breach that led to the accident of the Columbia and the loss of the crew and vehicle."

Whether the crewmembers could have been saved even if NASA management had been fully aware of the actual situation on board flight STS-107 is debatable. But amazingly, no effort whatsoever was made to rescue the astronauts. One can plausibly hypothesize that many of NASA's organization-level cognitive biases contributed to this disaster.[7] Still, the author suspects that the framing effect, i.e., the tendency to react to how information is presented beyond its factual content, was at the heart of the problem.

The word *foam* gave engineers the comfortable feeling of the soft and fluffy foam used, for example, in household furniture. Such a substance can hardly damage a tile of carbon–carbon composite material. However, the foam covering the shuttle's external tank was made of relatively dense material. Weighing approximately 0.5 kg and moving at a relative speed of 230 m/sec, such debris posed a severe risk to any object it encountered.[8]

Confirmation bias (placing undue weight on data that supports the outcome one expects) also contributed to the disaster. For example, throughout the space shuttle program, NASA's engineers observed pieces of thermal insulation falling from the external tank during launches. As a result, they knew of the potential damage to the shuttle's thermal insulating tiles, classifying it as a risk that should be dealt with at every launch. However, over time, NASA gradually became accustomed to these phenomena, and, as the shuttle had flown successfully multiple times, the organization gradually accepted it as a normal and harmless event.

15.4.5 The Deepwater Horizon BP Oil Spill (2010)

The *Deepwater Horizon* was a mobile floating dynamically positioned drilling rig. The rig, operated by British Petroleum (BP), was located in the Gulf of Mexico, about 66 km off the Louisiana coast at a water depth of 1.6 km. During the accident, it was drilling a deep exploratory oil well 5.6 km below sea level.

---

6 This is not meant to denigrate engineering "gut feelings," which are essential tools in any engineer's arsenal. However, such feelings cannot be trusted when contrary data is presented.

7 For example, anchoring, bandwagon effect, confirmation bias, courtesy bias, expectation bias, neglect of probability, normalcy bias, ostrich effect, authority bias, in-group bias.

8 This debris packed a lot of kinetic energy, totaling 13,225 joules. When a smartphone (200 g) is falling vertically to the ground from a height of half a meter, 1 joule is the energy released.

On the morning of April 20, 2010, high-pressure methane gas from the well surged into the drilling rig, engulfed the platform, ignited, and exploded. Eleven missing workers are presumed to have died, and 94 crew members were rescued. The *Deepwater Horizon* collapsed and sank into the sea two days later. The accident occurred when the rig staff removed a 1.5 km drilling column without adequately confirming that the concrete seal blocked the opening of the crude oil well. The seal was not, in fact, secured, and removing the column resulted in a catastrophic blowout. This catastrophe is one of history's most significant environmental disasters.

A vast oil leak spread from the former rig site after the disaster. Despite extensive efforts to seal the oil well, crude oil continued to flow for 87 days at an approximate rate of 62,000 barrels per day. The estimated volume of leaked oil was approximately 5 million barrels, affecting 180,000 km^2 of the ocean. All in all, some 2000 km of coastline in Texas, Louisiana, Mississippi, Alabama, and Florida were contaminated by oil. Extensive damage to marine and wildlife habitats, fishing, and tourism industries was reported, making the *Deepwater Horizon* disaster the most extensive marine oil spill in history. Massive cleanup operations ensued using skimmer ships, floating booms, controlled burns (Figure 15.6), and some 7000 m^3 of oil dispersant.

Figure 15.6 A controlled fire near the *Deepwater Horizon* well (Image: US DoD).

After several failed efforts, the well was sealed on September 19, 2010. However, disclosures in 2012 indicated that the concrete seal on top of the well was still leaking. In addition, several investigations blamed BP and its partners for engaging in multiple cost-cutting measures and an inadequate safety culture. A US government report pointed to defective cement on the well, faulting mostly BP, the rig operator (Transocean), and the rig contractor (Halliburton). In 2014, the courts determined that "British Petroleum was primarily responsible for the oil spill because of its gross negligence and reckless conduct." As of 2018, the cleanup and penalties had cost BP more than $65 billion.

The *Deepwater Horizon* oil spill can be traced to several cognitive biases. These include biases related to sunk costs; availability heuristics; and, significantly, confirmation bias (placing undue weight on data that supports the outcome one expects). This expectation was derived from history related to some 4000 oil and gas platforms that had operated in the Gulf with no significant mishaps since 1979.

In low-risk situations, the availability heuristics bias is often substituted for intricate knowledge. However, ignoring such knowledge and skipping necessary procedures that organizations developed, tested, and trained people on can usher in risks and high-consequence catastrophes.

15.4.6 The Morandi Bridge Collapse in Genoa (2018)

On August 14, 2018, a 210-m portion of the Morandi Bridge in Genoa, Italy, collapsed, killing 43 people and leaving 600 homeless. This bridge was more than a kilometer long and rose to an average height of 45 m above the ground. It was the longest concrete bridge in the world. Constructed between 1963 and 1967, it crossed over the eponymous river, a railway depot, several large factories, and a densely populated area.

Named after Riccardo Morandi, the noted Italian engineer who designed it, the bridge boasted a unique design: a multispan, cable-stayed bridge characterized by a prestressed concrete structure for the piers, towers, and deck and only two stays per span (Figure 15.7).

As a result, the Morandi Bridge was more robust and lighter, with minimal use of steel, relative to other bridges of its era. In addition, the bridge exhibited a

Figure 15.7 The Morandi Bridge after the collapse of its central section.

clean, distinct design that quickly became an engineering and architectural landmark, a symbol of Italian engineering. However, the hybrid stays design, constructed from steel cables with prestressed concrete shells, made the stays susceptible to cracks, water intrusion, and corrosion of the internal steel. Another real risk associated with the Morandi Bridge was that each span was held by only two stays (in most bridges, multiple stays hold each span). Under this design, a failure of a single stay would cause the bridge to collapse.

Over the years, several inspections and analyses of the bridge, especially the stays, indicated an urgent need for the bridge's maintenance and overhaul. However, virtually nothing was done to maintain the bridge's safety. Consequently, two questions arise: (1) How did the Italian transportation authorities approve a fundamentally risky design? (2) Why had well-known bridge defects not been addressed for a long time?

One may speculate that the first answer emanates from cognitive biases like the bandwagon effect, courtesy bias, authority bias, and groupthink bias within the Italian transport authority vis-à-vis the celebrated bridge designer Riccardo Morandi. Similarly, one may speculate that the second answer emanates from cognitive biases like availability heuristics, confirmation bias, expectation bias, neglect of probability, ostrich effect, and social loafing.

15.5 Cognitive Debiasing

15.5.1 Abraham Lincoln's Legacy

Much evidence has been established that cognitive biases unconsciously affect a wide range of human behavior. Individuals are unaware of the phenomenon and cannot detect and mitigate it. Nevertheless, people who undertake cognitive debiasing training and play debiasing games that teach mitigating strategies have shown improved judgment and decision-making emanating from significant reductions in their cognitive biases.

So, any systems engineer should always adopt a healthy dose of suspicion regarding their own motives, opinions, and planned actions, since their mind is biased in one way or another. Therefore, systems engineers are advised to present their ideas to colleagues; friends; and, yes, rivals and then listen intently to their views. Their cognitive biases are invariably different, so their opinions could be priceless.

Finally, systems engineers should take an example from a distinguished political genius, Abraham Lincoln, the 16th president of the United States. Lincoln succeeded in cobbling together a cabinet that included three gifted rivals of national reputation (Figure 15.8) and "together, [they] created the most unusual cabinet in history, marshaling their talents to the task of preserving the Union and winning the war" (Goodwin, 2006).

Figure 15.8   Lincoln's Cabinet (1862).[9]

15.5.2   Cognitive Biases and Strategic Decisions

Cognitive biases are essential factors when making a strategic decision. Therefore, understanding how biases influence strategic decision processes will help engineers and scholars improve each process and make it more rational. Das and Teng (1999) proposed an intriguing integrative perspective for the relations between cognitive biases and strategic decision processes. They concluded that different cognitive biases affect decision processes differently. By examining these relationships, one can clarify the domain and the role of solid cognitive biases in strategic decision-making and better differentiate among various strategic decision processes.

15.5.3   Categories of Cognitive Biases

To simplify the process of associating cognitive biases with strategic decision processes, the authors used existing research to combine cognitive biases into four categories: (1) prior hypotheses and focusing on limited targets, (2) exposure to limited alternatives, (3) insensitivity to outcome probabilities, and (4) the illusion of manageability.

1. **Initial hypotheses and focusing on limited targets.** Research shows that decision-makers bring their previously formed beliefs or hypotheses into decision-making. As a result, they tend to overlook information and evidence that may prove the opposite.

---

9 Adapted from the first reading of the Emancipation Proclamation before the cabinet on July 22, 1862. Engraving by Alexander Hay Ritchie; painting by Francis Bicknell Carpenter, 1864.

2. **Exposure to limited alternatives.** Information is usually incomplete under most circumstances; therefore, decision-makers tend to focus on a relatively small number of options or use intuition to supplement rational analysis. As a result, decision-makers often specify only a subset of the decision spectrum, thus generating a limited number of alternative courses of action.

3. **Insensitivity to outcome probabilities.** Research has also shown that decision-makers do not trust and often do not understand and use estimates of outcome probabilities. One reason decision-makers do not use probability estimates is that they see each problem as a unique event rather than a single case out of multiple events. Furthermore, engineers and managers use a single or a few fundamental values rather than computing statistically based probabilities.

4. **The illusion of manageability.**[10] Another type of cognitive bias relates to engineers and managers who inappropriately perceive the success of a particular strategic decision when, in fact, it was a failure. In addition, they often mistakenly assume that should problems arise, they will be able to fix them. That is, they are convinced the outcomes of their decisions can be contained, corrected, or reversed, given sufficient efforts.

15.5.4 Strategic Decision Processes

Based on existing research, Das and Teng defined a set of strategic decision processes, which include (1) rational mode; (2) avoidance mode; (3) logical, incremental mode; (4) political mode; and (5) garbage can mode.

1. **Rational mode.** This strategic decision process is an ideal and theoretical benchmark against all other decision processes. It assumes that human behavior is rational and not affected by cognitive biases. Under rational mode, decision-makers are assumed to act with known objectives and diligently analyze the external environment and internal operations. Therefore, decision-making is a comprehensive, entirely rational process in which engineers and managers gather all relevant information, develop alternative decisions, and objectively select the optimal one.

2. **Avoidance mode.** This strategic decision process relates to the fact that strategic decision-making processes often incur organizations' tendency to resist changes. This phenomenon relates to the organization's tendency to avoid uncertainty and maintain the ongoing status quo.

3. **Logical, incremental mode.** In this process mode, strategic decision-making occurs incrementally or step by step. Since the overall environment is often either unknown or unstable and engineers' and managers' cognitive capabilities are limited, the desired strategy is to choose this mode to achieve

---

10 This cognitive bias has significant real-life implications. It is curious that this particular bias has not been sufficiently recognized in strategy research and practices.

optimal strategic objectives. Also, incrementally implementing strategic decisions allows organizations to move slowly to remain flexible as they gradually assimilate the impacts of new decisions.

4. **Political mode.** Under this strategic decision process, decision-makers often cannot reach a broad consensus on organizational objectives. More specifically, decision-makers must confront different groups within the organization, each of whom fights for a decision favorable to itself. Therefore, those who can form the most potent coalition decide the outcome. Thus, engineers and managers must deal with each party that perceives the problem in light of its sphere of interest.

5. **Garbage can mode.** This strategic decision process is the most uncertain and fluid mode. It has no inherent consistencies, and there is no particular rationale for making a strategic choice. Nevertheless, engineers and managers have little control over the process, but their cognitive biases are still prevalent in decision-making.

15.5.5 Cognitive Biases versus Strategic Decisions Processes

Das and Teng (1999) further analyzed relevant scientific literature and created a model depicting the type of strategic decision processes an engineer or a manager is likely to adopt. Here, each strategic decision is subject to the cognitive bias categories. In addition, the authors provide specific propositions (P1-P9) for each of the nine prevalent combinations of cognitive biases and strategic decision processes (Figure 15.9 and Table 15.1).

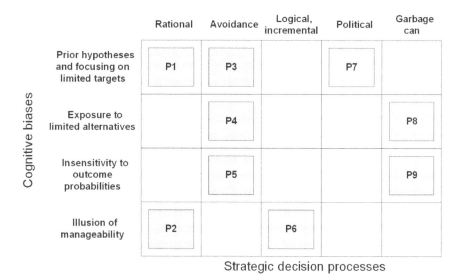

Figure 15.9 Cognitive biases versus strategic decision processes.

Table 15.1 Proposition Related to Strategic Decision processes.

Strategic Decision	#	Proposition
Rational mode	P1	The more rational and systematic the strategic decision process, the more likely the engineers and managers will bring prior hypotheses to their decision processes.
	P2	The more rational and systematic the strategic decision process is, the more likely the engineers and managers will have an illusion of manageability.
Avoidance mode	P3	The more emphasis on maintaining the status quo in a strategic decision-making process, the more likely the engineers and managers will bring prior hypotheses to their decision processes.
	P4	The more emphasis on maintaining the status quo in a strategic decision-making process, the more likely the engineers and managers will be exposed to limited alternatives.
	P5	The more emphasis on maintaining the status quo in a strategic decision-making process, the more likely engineers and managers will be insensitive to outcome probabilities.
Logical, incremental mode	P6	The more logically incremental the strategic decision-making process is, the more likely the engineers and managers will have an illusion of manageability.
Political mode	P7	The more political the strategic decision-making process is, the more likely the engineers and managers will bring prior hypotheses to their decision processes.
Garbage can mode	P8	The more disorderly and anarchical the strategic decision-making process is, the more likely the engineers and managers will consider limited alternatives.
	P9	The more disorderly and anarchical the strategic decision-making process is, the more likely the engineers and managers will be insensitive to outcome probabilities.

To summarize, Das and Teng show that combinations of four fundamental cognitive biases affect engineers and managers involved in different decision processes. As a result, distinct strategic decision processes can be better differentiated and understood by considering relevant cognitive biases. Furthermore, the proposed nine propositions can reveal the critical relationships between the four cognitive bias types and the five strategic decision process modes.

Thus, the integrative framework described above could be utilized to enhance strategic decisions, especially the ones that are highly uncertain and must be made promptly. Engineers and managers could become more aware of the assumptions, heuristics, and biases in their decision-making processes. This self-awareness of cognitive biases that are inherent in their decision-making should mitigate or reduce systematic errors arising from decision-makers' cognitive biases.

15.6   Bibliography

Das, T.K. and Teng B.S. (1999). Cognitive biases and strategic decision processes: An integrative perspective. *Journal of Management Studies* 36 (6): 757–778. https://faculty.baruch.cuny.edu/tkdas/publications/das-teng_jms99_cognitivebias_757-778.pdf. Accessed: Jan. 2023.

Engel, A. (2018). *Practical Creativity and Innovation in Systems Engineering* (Wiley Series in Systems Engineering and Management). Wiley.

Goodwin, D.K. (2005). *Team of Rivals: The Political Genius of Abraham Lincoln*, Simon & Schuster.

Kahneman, D. (2011). *Thinking, Fast and Slow*. Penguin Books.

Murata, A., Nakamura, T., and Karwowski, W. (2015, November 11). Influence of cognitive biases in distorting decision making and leading to critical unfavorable incidents. *Safety* 1 (1): 44–58. https://doi.org/10.3390/safety1010044. Accessed: Jan. 2023.

Pohl, R.F. (Ed.). (2022). Cognitive Illusions: Intriguing Phenomena in Thinking, Judgment, and Memory, Routledge; 3rd edition.

Schmidt, R.A. (1975). A schema theory of discrete motor skill learning. *Psychological review*, 82(4), 225.

16

Delivering Value and Resolving Conflicts

16.1 Introduction

Engineering processes are intended to build quality into systems. However, the goal is to deliver value to all stakeholders, which will correlate with the necessary quality factors. In addition, when designing systems, it is often difficult to understand and meet the expected values of different stakeholders. Along these lines, this chapter deals with two related topics: delivering systems value and conflict analysis and resolution.

The first part of this chapter presents a systematic approach to maximizing the delivery of systems value utilizing four concepts: (1) value understanding, (2) value characterization, (3) value proposition, and (4) value realization. Conflicts, or differences of viewpoints, inevitably arise whenever human beings interact with one another. For example, consider disputes among different units within a company when deciding to develop, manufacture, and market a new product. In this case, entities within the company will have to cooperate as much as possible within some group decision-making process to arrive at an agreeable action plan. This chapter discusses how to deliver value and resolve conflicts systemically. It includes the following elements:

- **Delivering systems value.** Including conceptual foundation, the notion of stakeholders' value, loss of value, value delivery framework, activities in the design world, activities in the operations world, and mapping and analysis of value.
- **Conflict analysis and resolution.** Including theoretical background, implementation procedure, and UAV design conflict example.

Systems Science for Engineers and Scholars, First Edition. Edited by Avner Engel.
© 2024 John Wiley & Sons, Ltd. Published 2024 by John Wiley & Sons, Ltd.

16.2 Delivering Systems Value[1]

16.2.1 Conceptual Foundation

For a system to be relevant to its stakeholders throughout its life, it must sustain its ability to deliver value to stakeholders. Therefore, delivering systems value requires identifying those things that enhance value to all stakeholders. In addition, it involves creating an original system whose fundamental concepts and properties must be well understood and established upfront. These requirements imply that three issues must be determined upfront: what will be the system's value for each stakeholder, how the system will produce value, and how the value degradation process over the system's life will be identified.

16.2.2 The Notion of Stakeholder Value

Value is often considered as it relates to the system's importance, usefulness, worth, or significance to stakeholders from their point of view. However, value is subjective and is relative to what the stakeholders believe they obtain from the system. As a result, every stakeholder has a different notion of what is of value to them at a particular time.

The determination of value considers various aspects like benefit, cost, meaning, profits, effects, aesthetics, social status, and so on. Moreover, this value must be provided over the system's useful life. In short, an awareness of stakeholders' values helps one to understand the expectations, belief systems, motivations, and boundaries within which the stakeholders can be engaged.

16.2.3 Loss of Value

Loss of value implies that the value obtained by stakeholders from a system degrades over time due to various factors, relationships, conditions, and other dynamics, thereby leading to adverse outcomes for stakeholders.

Even if the system of interest (SoI) continues to exhibit the same characteristics, the value desired by stakeholders often increases due to recent technological innovations and changes in market trends. Along this line, the actual value the system provides tends to decline due to an increased rate of system failures and parts obsolescence. In essence, the actual value of systems tends to decline over time, resulting in intangible or tangible losses to stakeholders. As a result, systems are upgraded or replaced (Figure 16.1).

---

1 This section was adapted with permission from Kumar (2021).

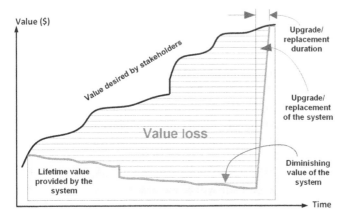

Figure 16.1   System's loss of value (Derived from Browning and Honour, 2005).

16.2.4   Value Delivery Framework

The value delivery framework utilizes four steps to capture the value dynamics of a system. These steps, shown in Figure 16.2, provide a sequence of activities that can be used to discover, diagnose, design, develop, and deliver systems value.

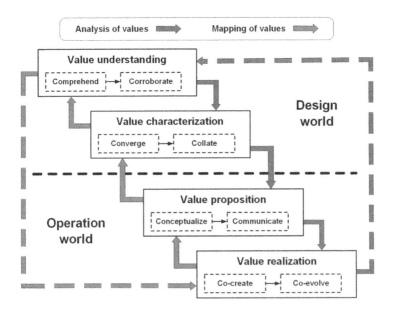

Figure 16.2   Value delivery framework.

In addition, this framework offers a set of guiding principles and beliefs that embody the basic idea of using value as the basis for engineering systems.

16.2.5 Activities in the Design World

The design world is where a given design can provide value to stakeholders in different situations and contexts. The two activities in the design world are value understanding and value characterization.

16.2.5.1 Value Understanding

The value understanding activity aims to uncover the different components that influence stakeholders. This activity involves two subactivities: (1) comprehending all possible scenarios of value creation and all possible means of creating this value and (2) corroborating all aspects of the value related to a particular situation context (Table 16.1).

Table 16.1 Expansion of Value Understanding Context.

Comprehend
- Understand stakeholders and their offerings
- Understand stakeholder concerns and how they are being addressed presently
- Understand what is essential to the various stakeholders
- Understand those things that are considered significant to stakeholders
- Understand concepts and resources that contribute to stakeholders' value
- Understand the cause-and-effect factors and their influences on value
- Understand the relevant economics and related dynamics

Corroborate
- Ascertain the core stakeholder activities and corresponding value
- Ascertain those things that are considered insignificant to stakeholders
- Ascertain what can be controlled and what cannot be controlled
- Ascertain the constraints that deter any change and impact progress
- Ascertain abnormal conditions and their impact on the stakeholders
- Ascertain circumstances and situations that impact value creation
- Ascertain possible risks to stakeholders and ways of mitigating them

16.2.5.2 Value Characterization

The value characterization activity aims to uncover the factors influencing value creation and reducing value destruction. This activity involves two subactivities: (1) converge, which seeks to identify and bring together common and specific ways, means, and influences, and (2) collate, which seeks to synthesize values using different value carriers (Table 16.2). In this chapter's context, value carriers are all those features and functions that are part of the system and can potentially contribute to stakeholder value.

Table 16.2 Expansion of Value Characterization Context.

Converge

- Identify different kinds of interactions between humans and machines to achieve value
- Validate whether these interactions between humans and machines can achieve value
- Identify system capabilities, processes, and qualities for achieving value
- Identify the boundary conditions, constraints, assumptions, and trade-offs for utilizing these capabilities, processes, and qualities
- Validate whether these capabilities, processes, and qualities can achieve value
- Identify the boundary conditions, constraints, assumptions, and trade-offs for utilizing these resources and functions
- Identify resources and functions necessary for achieving value
- Validate whether these resources and functions can gain value and refine them
- Identify the information requirements, structures, and flows that can enhance value
- Validate whether these information requirements, structures, and flows can enhance value

Collate

- Identify common patterns of interactions, capabilities, processes, qualities, resources, and functions that characterize stakeholder value
- Identify design decisions that ensure the achievement of the interactions, capabilities, processes, qualities, resources, and functions
- Identify constraints, strategic and tactical implications, and control and performance issues for the interactions, capabilities, processes, qualities, resources, and functions
- Identify strengths, weaknesses, opportunities, and threats (SWOT) for each interaction, capability, process, quality, resource, and function
- Formulate principles, guidelines, protocols, and standards for enabling the identified interactions
- Formulate principles, guidelines, protocols, and standards for utilizing the capabilities, processes, qualities, resources, and functions
- Identify what can or cannot be done based on principles, guidelines, protocols, and standards
- Develop a set of tactics to facilitate the achievement of the interactions, capabilities, processes, qualities, resources, and functions

---

16.2.6 Activities in the Operations World

The operation world synthesizes and implements a given design into a distinct system that provides a specific set of stakeholder values. The two activities in the operations world are value proposition and value realization.

16.2.6.1 Value Proposition

The value proposition activity aims to synthesize a collection of desired system behaviors that culminate in providing value to all stakeholders (i.e., rather than a few). This activity involves two subactivities: (1) conceptualize, which seeks to synthesize specific ideas related to the familiar and specific value propositions, and (2) communicate, which seeks to express the value propositions and system specifications that lead to these value propositions (Table 16.3).

Table 16.3 Expansion of Value Proposition Context.

Conceptualize

- Prepare a concise value definition and explain what exists versus what will be available
- Correlate this value definition to the sources and carriers of value
- Identify the relevant stakeholders of the value proposition
- Define measures to identify the impact of the value proposition on stakeholders
- Allocate the system elements, processes, and qualities into system components
- Prioritize system elements, processes, and qualities based on their importance in delivering value
- Synthesize a suitable structural relationship of system components
- Allocate concepts, qualities, behaviors, functions, and features to system components
- Identify rules governing elements, as well as their composition, interaction, and interdependence
- Identify the life cycle of system development and utilization processes
- Identify governance, management, and enablement processes that impact the system
- Identify key performance indicators through which the system performance can be managed
- Ensure that the system provides desired value propositions or enables them to be realizable

Communicate

- Document the context and value proposition of the system
- Document the sequence of activities to be fulfilled as part of the process
- Document the purpose, scope, breadth, and depth of the system
- Document design decisions and qualities of the system
- Document key concepts, properties, conditions, constraints, and assumptions
- Document guidelines, principles, protocols, and rationales of the system
- Document components, as well as their composition, interdependence, and interactions
- Document key performance indicators and how and when they should be measured
- Develop the specification consisting of relevant viewpoints, views, and models
- Document known limitations/constraints on system components, models, and processes

16.2.6.2 Value Realization

The value realization activity aims to implement the system and instantiate it for a specific situation faced by stakeholders so that they can experience their respective value propositions. This activity involves two subactivities: (1) co-create, which creates value by involving stakeholders, the system of interest, and other systems in the environment, and (2) co-evolve, which evolves co-creation of values and system design by understanding future stakeholder value expectations (Table 16.4).

Table 16.4 Expansion of Value Realization Context.

Co-Create

- Use appropriate technical disciplines to transform design description or system specification into actions that create a system
- Realize or adapt the system according to context, strategy, and constraints
- Maintain traceability of implemented system elements against the expected value
- Facilitate high-quality interactions among stakeholders that lead to value co-creation
- Adapt the system to suit the context in which the stakeholders operate
- Facilitate dialogue between stakeholders so that they can co-create personalized experiences at specific moments
- Reconfigure system resources dynamically in real time to accommodate stakeholder desires, intents, purposes, and personalization needs in line with their value propositions
- Facilitate heterogeneous interactions that lead to multiple value co-creation experiences

Co-Evolve

- Identify the situational/contextual factors in which the system is utilized
- Determine those value propositions that are found to be worthwhile to stakeholders
- Create observations and analyses on how the system can deliver an acceptable value
- Analyze the relationships between system inputs, contextual factors, and the stakeholder actions that generate stakeholder value
- Understand the interplay between system elements, the stakeholders, and the situation context
- Determine how value emerges from an understanding of successful stakeholder outcomes
- Analyze and synthesize a new configuration of system elements and the expected value from this new configuration
- Identify additional patterns of the interplay between system elements, stakeholders, and the situation context, which can aid in creating emergent value for stakeholders
- Build up knowledge about how a system behaves while delivering stakeholder value

---

16.2.7 Mapping and Analysis of Value

Inevitably, engineered systems exchange internal information between two or more activities. The forward-moving information is defined as mapping, and the feedback-moving information is defined as analysis. Mapping establishes the correlation between the carriers of value and the possible value outcomes. That is the mapping between the system elements, processes, human–machine interactions, and stakeholder value. The analysis examines the key attributes of the mapping along different dimensions, such as feasibility, viability, consistency, coherence, effort, cost, and time, to determine how the mapping impacts the system elements. That is, analysis verifies and validates the feasibility, viability, and effectiveness of the correlation between the carriers of value and the possible value outcomes. The general relationship between systems' life cycle and value delivery is depicted in Figure 16.3.

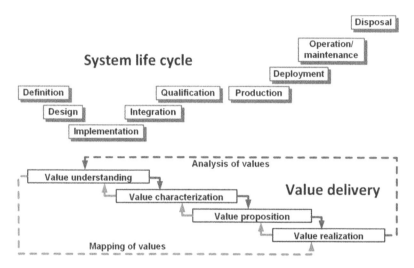

Figure 16.3 Temporal relationship between system life cycle and value delivery.

16.3 Conflict Analysis and Resolution[2]

16.3.1 Theoretical Background

Conflicts and their resolutions have been the subjects of many studies and much research.[3] For example, Ruble and Thomas (1976) proposed a two-dimensional model of conflicts and resolution strategies. They suggest that parties to a conflict (decision-makers [DMs]) make implicit trade-offs in their desire to seek gains versus their willingness to satisfy other DMs relevant to the conflict. On the one hand, DMs seek to maximize their advantages and, on the other hand, cooperate

---

2 This section was adapted with permission from: Engel (2018).

3 Originally, this section was inspired by Hipel and Obeidi's (2005) and Pinto and Kharbanda's (1995) papers.

with the other DMs to maintain good relationships. This two-dimensional model has five distinct, recognizable conflict-handling styles (Figure 16.4).

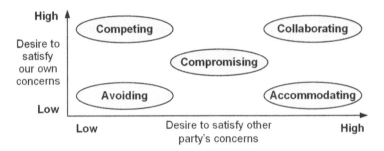

Figure 16.4 Conflicts and resolutions strategies (Ruble and Thomas, 1976).

These conflict-handling styles are described as follows.

16.3.1.1 Competing Behavior
This behavior emanates from an uncooperative attitude of the relevant DMs. By and large, such DM, be it a person or a group, have little regard for satisfying the other DMs' needs, viewing conflicts as challenging zero-sum game propositions. Competing behavior is often utilized by insecure DM who will use any device to get their way.

16.3.1.2 Accommodating Behavior
This behavior emanates from a spirit of passivity and amiability, usually to become a "team player." Accommodators usually approach conflicts to find ways to defuse the situation or allow other DMs' interests to be fulfilled. This behavior can be welcomed when resolving a conflict is more critical than letting it simmer and poison the operating dynamics among the DMs involved. On the other hand, disputes within reason tend to promote different opinions and viewpoints, enriching the overall process.

16.3.1.3 Avoiding Behavior
This behavior expresses disregard and, sometimes, actual disdain to satisfy the DM's objectives or the aims of other DMs in a conflict. In this respect, avoiding behavior is both apathetic and uncooperative. Avoiding behavior tends to be an effective method for sidestepping disputes the DM does not seek. However, if such a DM is in a position of responsibility, then this shirking of obligations could end badly for the individual, the group they lead, or the organization as a whole.

16.3.1.4 Compromising Behavior

This type of behavior combines assertiveness and cooperativeness. It represents a desire by one DM to satisfy his objectives while being willing to accept demands made by other DMs. Generally, compromisers consider conflicts as soft win–lose situations, realizing that obtaining some of their objectives necessitates yielding to other DMs' requirements. In other words, compromising behavior stems from the realization that, under most circumstances, making concessions is necessary to achieve particular objectives, especially in conflict situations.

16.3.1.5 Collaborating Behavior

This behavior is present where DMs exhibit strong tendencies for assertiveness and cooperativeness. Collaborators often seek win–win solutions by conducting negotiations among all the DMs, seeking to find agreements that, as much as possible, fully satisfy all DMs. Collaborating among several DMs under conflict situations requires a great deal of flexibility, creativity, and extensive communication channels amongst all concerned.

16.3.2 Graph Model for Conflict Resolution (GMCR)

The graph model for conflict resolution (GMCR) constitutes a formal (mathematical) and systematic approach to studying and resolving real-world conflicts. Under most circumstances, it is aligned with the compromising strategy for conflict resolution. The GMCR approach to conflict resolution is particularly suited to be implemented as a flexible tool for competitive environments.

The GMCR model is based on ideas from both graph and game theories, extending the realm of multiple objectives–multiple participants (MOMP) decision-making processes. Theoretically, any finite number of DMs may be defined, and each DM may control any finite number of conflict options. In addition, a particular DM can represent a person, a small group, or even a big organization or nation. Finally, the graph model can describe and distinguish between reversible and irreversible real-life actions. Implementing a basic GMCR methodology within an actual conflict entails the following steps.

- **Step 1: Identify the decision-makers (DMs).** Identify all the individuals or parties that are involved in the conflict.
- **Step 2: Identify options available to each DM.** Identify all relevant opportunities that each DM controls.
- **Step 3: Determine relative or specific preferences for options.** For each DM, determine each option's immediate or clear priorities under the said DM.
- **Step 4: Compute a set of possible conflict states.** Since an option can be taken or not by the DM who controls it, a collection of $2n$ possible conflict

states exists in the conflict space (where *n* represents the total number of options).

- **Step 5: Define option contradictions.** These may manifest within a specific DM's domain or several domains of different DMs.
- **Step 6: Compute a set of feasible conflict states.** Use the option contradictions data to identify infeasible conflict states and remove them from the result obtained in step 4, thus creating a set of feasible conflict states.
- **Step 7: Compute the preference ranking of states per each DMs.** For each DM, use their relative or specific option preference to compute the conflict states' preference ranking.
- **Step 8: Compute the preference ranking of states for all DMs.** Use the relative or specific preference of options to compute the combined preference ranking of conflict states for all DMs involved.
- **Step 9: Negotiate with all DMs on a reasonable compromise.** Based on the combined preference ranking of conflict states, negotiate with all DMs for an appropriate resolution through mutual concessions.

16.3.3 Example of System Design Conflict

16.3.3.1 UAV Project Background

The Pioneer (Figure 16.5) was an unmanned aerial vehicle (UAV) system that was initially developed and produced by the Israel Aerospace Industries (IAI). Since the early 1980s, various derivatives of these UAV systems have been purchased and used by several armed forces in Israel, the United States, and other nations.

Figure 16.5 The RQ-2B Pioneer (single-engine) UAV (Image: US DoD).

When the US Army issued its UAV short-range (SR) request for proposal (RFP) in 1988, IAI decided to participate in the UAV-SR project competition. Engineers within IAI argued about two very different UAV configurations. The more conservative engineering faction argued for a single-engine UAV similar in design and capabilities to the existing Pioneer UAV. The more radical and aggressive engineering faction argued for a completely new design based on a dual-engine UAV. Eventually, the latter prevailed, and the IAI's Hunter UAV system won the UAV-SR competition (Figure 16.6).

This example describes how to resolve individual or group conflicts using the GMCR methodology through compromises made by decision-makers (DMs).

Figure 16.6 The MQ-5B Hunter (dual-engine) UAV (Image: US DoD).

16.3.3.2 Initial System Design Strategies
Table 16.5 lists each of the two DMs, followed by a list of options under the control of each DM.

Table 16.5 Decision-Makers, Options Priorities, and Status Quo Conflict State.

DM	Options				Initial Management Preference
	#	Name	Description	Priority	
Single engine	1	U-cost	Minimal UAV unit cost	3	0
	2	D-cost	Minimal development cost	2	0
	3	Size	Minimal air vehicle size	1	0
Dual engine	4	Payload	Large payload	3	1
	5	Endurance	Long endurance	2	1
	6	Ceiling	High flight ceiling	1	1

The option priorities of each of the two DMs are defined in specific terms (1, 2, 3). Each DM generally defines their design strategy by assigning values to their options. A 1 means that a given DM desires a given option, and a 0 means that the said DM dislikes that option. As seen in this example, initially, management selected all the design options favored by the dual-engine faction. In contrast, none of the options the single-engine faction favored were selected. This result represents the existing design strategy that prevailed before the GMCR analysis.

16.3.3.3 The GMCR Analysis

Since each DM can take an option or not, a set of 2^6 or 64 possible conflict states exists in the UAV design conflict example. However, the collection of possible conflict states may contain some states that are unlikely to happen. In general, there are two main reasons for such infeasibilities. First, some options may be mutually exclusive for a given DM and cannot be selected simultaneously. Second, if one DM chooses one option, then, sometimes, another DM may be unable to select an option that directly contradicts the first selection. In this UAV design conflict example, all the contradictions belong to the second category and are shown in Table 16.6.

Table 16.6 Option Contradictions.

#	Single-Engine Options	Dual-Engine Options
1	Minimal UAV unit cost	Long endurance
2	Minimal air vehicle size	Large payload

All the infeasible conflict states are identified and removed from the set of possible conflict states, thus creating a new set of feasible conflict states. Figure 16.7 illustrates

DM	Options		Conflict States																	
	#	Names	1	2	3	4	5	6	7	8	9	10	11	12	17	19	21	23	25	27
Single engine	1	U-cost	0	1	0	1	0	1	0	1	0	1	0	1	0	0	0	0	0	0
	2	D-cost	0	0	1	1	0	0	1	1	0	0	1	1	0	1	0	1	0	1
	3	Size	0	0	0	0	1	1	1	1	0	0	0	0	0	0	1	1	0	0
	Ordinal ranking		0	3	2	5	1	4	3	6	0	3	2	5	0	2	1	3	0	2
Dual engine	4	Payload	0	0	0	0	0	0	0	0	1	1	1	1	0	0	0	0	1	1
	5	Endurance	0	0	0	0	0	0	0	0	0	0	0	0	1	1	1	1	1	1
	6	Ceiling	0	0	0	0	0	0	0	0	0	0	0	0	0	0	0	0	0	0
	Ordinal ranking		0	0	0	0	0	0	0	0	3	3	3	3	2	2	2	2	5	5

DM	Options		Conflict States																	
	#	Names	33	34	35	36	37	38	39	40	41	42	43	44	49	51	53	55	57	59
Single engine	1	U-cost	0	1	0	1	0	1	0	1	0	1	0	1	0	0	0	0	0	0
	2	D-cost	0	0	1	1	0	0	1	1	0	0	1	1	0	1	0	1	0	1
	3	Size	0	0	0	0	1	1	1	1	0	0	0	0	0	0	1	1	0	0
	Ordinal ranking		0	3	2	5	1	4	3	6	0	3	2	5	0	2	1	3	0	2
Dual engine	4	Payload	0	0	0	0	0	0	0	0	1	1	1	1	0	0	0	0	1	1
	5	Endurance	0	0	0	0	0	0	0	0	0	0	0	0	1	1	1	1	1	1
	6	Ceiling	1	1	1	1	1	1	1	1	1	1	1	1	1	1	1	1	1	1
	Ordinal ranking		1	1	1	1	1	1	1	1	4	4	4	4	3	3	3	3	6	6

Figure 16.7 Feasible conflict states in the UAV design conflict example.

the remaining 36 viable conflict states. The ordinal rankings (i.e., the sum of the fulfilled options times the priority of each option) of the conflict states for the single-engine and the dual-engine DMs are also shown. As can be seen, the single-engine DMs equally prefer the conflict states of 8 and 40. Similarly, conflict states 57 and 59 are selected solutions for the dual-engine DMs.

16.3.3.4   Final Compromised System Design

Typically, conflict evolution is conducted along with a compromising procedure, where each DM, in turn, is asked to make a small concession to the other DM. However, in the case of the UAV design conflict example, the initial management preference (conflict state 57) leaves no concession option for the single-engine DMs (Figure 16.8).

DM	Options		Conflict States			
	#	Names	57		59	44
Single engine	1	U-cost	0		0	1
	2	D-cost	0		1	1
	3	Size	0		0	0
Dual engine	4	Payload	1		1	1
	5	Endurance	1		1	0
	6	Ceiling	1		1	1

Figure 16.8   Evolution of the UAV design conflict example.

Therefore, the two DMs must pursue the collaborating procedure. First, the two DMs agree the project should adhere to a minimal development cost target. This agreement pushes the UAV design conflict example to conflict state 59. Next, the two DMs agree that the UAV design team should pursue a design leading to a minimal UAV unit cost. However, the upshot of this last decision means that the long endurance initially followed by the dual-engine DMs is not attainable. Therefore, these collaborating agreements push the UAV design conflict to conflict state 44, the most preferred solution for both DMs (ordinal ranking $= 5 + 4 = 9$).

To sum it up, engineering evaluation of the available options selected conflict with state 44, which favors a UAV design powered by two engines, which implements the following requirements: (1) minimal UAV unit cost, (2) minimal development cost, (3) carrying a large payload, and (4) achieving high flight altitude.

16.4   Bibliography

Browning, T.R. and Honour, E. (2005). Measuring the lifecycle value of a system. *Proceedings of the 15th Annual International Symposium of INCOSE, Rochester, NY.*

Engel A. (2018). *Practical Creativity and Innovation in Systems Engineering* (Wiley Series in Systems Engineering and Management). Wiley.

Hipel, K.W. and Obeidi, A. (2005). Trade versus the environment: Strategic settlement from a systems engineering perspective. *Systems Engineering* 8 (3).

Kumar A. (2021). Delivering system value: A systematic approach. In G.S.Metcalf, K.Kijima, and H.Deguchi (Eds.), *Handbook of Systems Sciences*. Springer.

Pinto, J.K. and Kharbanda, O.P. (1995). Project management and conflict resolution. *Project Management Journal* 26 (4): 45–54.

Ruble, T.L., and Thomas, K.W. (1976). Support for a two-dimensional model of conflict behavior. *Organizational Behavior and Human Performance* 16: 221–237.

17

Multi-objective Multi-agent Decision-Making

17.1 Introduction

There are many life and engineering situations where a decision must be made regarding several objectives rather than one. Furthermore, sometimes, decisions must be made by more than one person or a group of persons (henceforth, agents). Such situations are approached using multi-objective multi-agent (MOMA) decision-making theory. MOMA theory aims to find solutions that simultaneously optimize multiple conflicting or complementary objectives for each agent. It aims to achieve a balanced trade-off between these objectives.

In MOMA situations, information about individual agents' objectives, past actions, and interests is sometimes known to all and is sometimes concealed. Also, the MOMA theory incorporates uncertainty into the decision-making process. MOMA theory seeks to identify a set of Pareto-efficient solutions. Such solutions are considered Pareto efficient if no agent's objectives can be improved without worsening another agent's objectives. Finally, in MOMA systems, the reward for a group of agents as well as each agent is a vector, where each component represents performance related to a different objective. Finally, decisions should be analyzed based on the utility to be derived by the stakeholders of a system.

So, this chapter aims to describe a systemic approach to decision-making processes in multi-objective and, multi-agent environments. The chapter includes the following elements:

- **Multi-objective multi-agent.** Includes the MOMA dilemma, MOMA commuting example, utility-based rewards, and game theory.
- **Representation of systems decision processes.** Includes the simultaneous presentation form and sequential presentation form.

Systems Science for Engineers and Scholars, First Edition. Edited by Avner Engel.
© 2024 John Wiley & Sons, Ltd. Published 2024 by John Wiley & Sons, Ltd.

- **Key types of systems decision processes.** Includes cooperative and noncooperative, symmetric and asymmetric, zero-sum and non-zero-sum, simultaneous and sequential, perfect and imperfect information, and evolutionary system decision processes.
- **Example 1.** Wolves and sheep predation.
- **Example 2.** Cooperative target observation.
- **Example 3.** Seaport logistics and multi-objective optimization and solution domination.

17.2 Utility-Based Rewards

In multi-objective, multi-agent systems, the aim is to optimize the utility of the user(s). In single-agent, multi-objective problems, one seeks to maximize the utility of a single user with a single utility function.[1] The utility function can provide the optimal solution set that a multi-objective decision-theoretic algorithm could produce.

The situation is more complex in multi-agent settings because the utility function may vary per individual agent. For example, a group of engineers (agents) wishes to decide on key design parameters for a new aircraft. The objectives they agree on are (1) minimizing costs, (2) maximizing payload or passengers, (3) minimizing fuel consumption, (4) maximizing flight distance, and (5) maximizing flight safety. After a decision is reached, every agent will get the same return vector. However, each agent may have a different utility for each possible value in the agreed-upon return vector. This difference is the reason this decision problem may be challenging.

17.3 Representation of the Decision Process

Multi-objective, multi-agent (MOMA) decision-making entails making systems decisions involving two or more decision-makers (henceforth, agents), each seeking to achieve their objectives. Thus, the decision process must specify (1) the agents involved, (2) the information available to each agent, (3) the actions available to each agent at each decision point, and (4) the payoffs for each outcome. Two common representations of systems decision processes are the matrix and sequential forms.

17.3.1 Simultaneous Presentation Form

The simultaneous system decision processes representation uses a matrix that shows the agents, strategies, and payoffs associated with each agent, covering

---

1 An equivalent procedure may be used for multiple users whose utility functions are aggregated into a single utility function.

every possible combination of actions. Figure 17.1 depicts such a system decision processes matrix. Agent 1 chooses the rows, and agent 2 selects the columns. Each agent has two strategies, which lead to payoffs described in the interior of the matrix. The first value is the payoff received by agent 1, and the second is the payoff received by agent 2. For example, suppose agent 1 plays up, and agent 2 plays left. Then agent 1 gets a payoff of 4, and agent 2 gets a payoff of 3.

		Agent 2	
		(Left)	(Right)
Agent 1	(Up)	4, 3	-1, -1
	(Down)	0, 0	3, 4

Figure 17.1 Simultaneous system decision processes involving two agents and two strategies.

17.3.2 Sequential Presentation Form

The sequential system decision processes representation uses trees as a means of presentation. Each tree vertex represents an agent and a decision point for them. The arrows out of the vertex represent a possible action for each agent. The payoffs are stated at the bottom of the tree. The sequential system decision processes depicted in Figure 17.2 represent a system that is equivalent to the one presented in Figure 17.1.

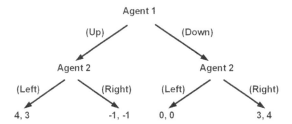

Figure 17.2 Sequential system decision processes involving two agents and two strategies.

17.3.3 MOMA Commuting Example[2]

By and large, MOMA decision-making is significantly more complex. The dependency among agents and the reward scheme is often complex. The following commuting example illustrates one type of multi-objective, multi-agent system

---

2 This commuting example was adapted from Radulescu et al. (2020).

decision process where the payoff received by the agents is a vector, and each element in the vector corresponds to the value of a different objective.

In this example, two agents wish to commute from a given origin to a destination. There are two transportation options available: taxi or train. Travel time by taxi is 10 minutes and by train is 30 minutes. If both agents choose to travel by taxi, they can split the cost equally between them. However, if they travel by train, each must purchase a train ticket. Finally, if one chooses to travel by taxi and the other by train, each must pay their fares individually. Figure 17.3 depicts the cost and travel time associated with each mode of transportation. Although a train ticket is cheaper than a taxi fare, a taxi journey takes less time than a train journey. So, depending on each agent's utility function, they will optimize their commuting actions. For example, travel costs may be paramount for one agent, whereas another may consider travel time crucial because they cannot afford to arrive late to work.

	(Time in minutes)	(Cost in $)
(Taxi)	10	20
(Train)	30	5

Figure 17.3 Travel time and cost for different modes of transportation.

The individual payoffs for each agent are shown in Figure 17.4. Note that the payoff values in this example represent a minimization problem for both objectives (i.e., cost, time). So, if both agents chose to commute by taxi (quarter A), they would arrive at their destination in 10 minutes, and each would pay $10. On the other hand, if agent 1 commutes by taxi and agent 2 commutes by train (quarter B), agent 1 will reach his destination in 10 minutes and pay $20, and agent 2 will reach his destination in 30 minutes and pay $5.

		Agent 2		Agent 2	
		(Taxi)		(Train)	
		[Time, Cost], [Time, Cost]		[Time, Cost], [Time, Cost]	
Agent 1	(Taxi)	A [10, 10],	[10, 10]	B [10, 20],	[30, 5]
	(Train)	C [30, 5],	[10, 20]	D [30, 5],	[30, 5]

Figure 17.4 Individual payoff matrix for each agent.

17.4 Key Types of Decision Processes

In general, each system decision process must specify the following elements: (1) the agents involved, (2) the information and actions available to each agent at each decision point, and (3) the payoffs for each outcome. The following is a short description of characteristic systems decision processes.

17.4.1 Cooperative and Noncooperative

Decision processes are cooperative if the decision-makers (agents) can form binding commitments. Decision processes are noncooperative if agents cannot form alliances. Collaborative decision processes are often analyzed through cooperative game theory, which predicts the coalitions that will form, the joint actions that groups will take, and the resulting collective payoffs. The opposite type is the noncooperative decision process, which focuses on predicting individual agents' actions and payoffs. Focusing on personal payoffs invariably leads to inferior results due to a lack of negotiation and agreement.

17.4.2 Symmetric and Asymmetric

Symmetric decision processes are situations where all agents' payoffs for performing specific strategies are the same. That is, symmetric decision processes offer payoffs depending only on the strategy employed and are not influenced by the agent. For example, many of the commonly studied 2×2 decision processes are symmetric. In addition, the standard representations of some decision processes (e.g., illustrated in game theory as chicken and prisoner's dilemma) are symmetric. Figure 17.5 depicts examples of symmetric and asymmetric system decision processes.

			Agent 2	
Symmetric decision processes	Agent 1		(Buy)	(Sell)
		(Buy)	4, 4	2, 6
		(Sell)	6, 2	3, 3

			Agent 2	
Asymmetric decision processes	Agent 1		(Opera)	(Concert)
		(Opera)	4, 5	0, 0
		(Concert)	0, 0	5, 4

Figure 17.5 Examples: symmetric and asymmetric decision processes.

17.4.3 Zero-sum and Non-Zero-Sum

Zero-sum decision processes are situations in which choices by agents cannot increase the overall available benefits. Instead, one agent's benefit equals other agents' losses for every combination of strategies. Poker, go, and chess games exemplify zero-sum decision processes. Non-zero-sum decision processes are situations where one agent's gain (or loss) does not necessarily lead to another agent's loss (or gain). In such cases, the total benefit gained by the agents increases relative to the actual situation (Figure 17.6).

		Agent 2	
		(Walk)	(Run)
Agent 1	(Walk)	2, -2	-2, 2
	(Run)	-2, 2	2, -2

Zero-sum decision processes

		Agent 2	
		(Attack)	(Defend)
Agent 1	(Attack)	0, 0	-2, 1
	(Defend)	1, -2	-6, -6

Non-zero-sum decision processes

Figure 17.6 Examples: zero-sum and non-zero-sum decision processes.

17.4.4 Simultaneous and Sequential

As mentioned above, in simultaneous decision processes, the agents move simultaneously or, sometimes, are unaware of each other's actions. Conversely, in sequential decision processes, later agents have some (but not necessarily all) information about earlier efforts. Therefore, the difference between sequential and simultaneous decision processes is embedded in the abovementioned representations. Finding an optimal strategy for many sequential decision processes is often difficult. This phenomenon is derived from the diversity of possible decisions available to the agents involved. Examples include chess, checkers, and go (Figure 17.7).

Figure 17.7 Garry Kasparov plays simultaneous chess, June 1985, Hamburg.

Beyond the above, real-life sequential decision processes may involve chance, making finding an optimal strategy even more difficult due to imperfect knowledge availability. Planning and executing an engineering project invariably belong to this category.

17.4.5   Perfect and Imperfect Information

One subset of sequential decision processes consists of a system whereby information is fully known to all agents at every step, including previous actions by all agents. For example, consumers may have complete information about the price and quality of all the available goods in a market. Examples of perfect information decision processes include checkers, chess, and go.

However, most decision processes are conducted under imperfect information availability. That is, most agents do not know all the moves and actions made by other agents. For example, many card games, such as poker and bridge, are grounded on imperfect information. Imperfect information situations are often represented by a dashed line uniting two nodes. This dashed line indicates that the relevant agent does not know which node they are in (Figure 17.8).

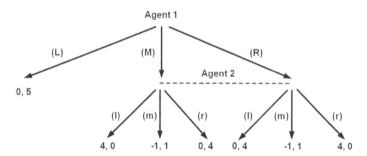

Figure 17.8   Example: Perfect and imperfect information in decision processes.

17.4.6   Evolutionary Decision Processes

Another subset of sequential decision processes consists of evolutionary decisions derived from Darwinian natural selection theory. Here, evolution represents a system whereby parents who practice more successful strategies have more surviving offspring, and, by and large, these offspring adopt their parents' survival strategies.

Biological evolutionary decision processes deal with populations $P(n)$ that exhibit variations among competing agents. During the ongoing decision processes, the strategies of individual agents are tested under existing rules. The mix of respective agents' strategies affects their survivability (fitness level). The original population produces a new cycle of population, P(*n* + 1), gradually replacing the old one. In the process, each new agent acquires a specific fitness level. Finally, the new generation replaces the original one, and the cycle repeats itself (Figure 17.9).

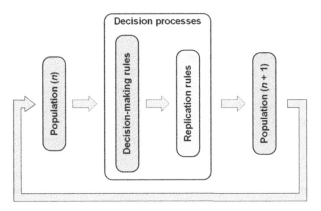

Figure 17.9 Evolutionary decision processes.[3]

Evolutionary decision processes have explicit biological roots and are attractive mainly to evolutionary scientists. However, social scientists (e.g., economists, sociologists, anthropologists, and philosophers) have also been attracted to this field (McKenzie, 2021). This attraction is due to the term *evolution*, which need not have only a biological connotation. Evolution may be understood as cultural evolution, which refers to changes in societal beliefs and norms over time.

17.5 Example 1: Wolves and Sheep Predation

The following wolves and sheep predation example is based on a mathematical model and software[4] that explores the stability of two agents, each with conflicting objectives. Such a predator–prey ecosystem is stable if it maintains itself over time, despite fluctuations in population sizes. Conversely, such a

---

3 Adapted from Evolutionary game theory. https://en.wikipedia.org/wiki/Evolutionary_game_theory. Accessed: Jan. 2023.
4 See NetLogo model and NetLogo software. https://ccl.northwestern.edu/netlogo/models/. Accessed: Jan. 2023.

system is unstable if it results in the elimination of one or more agents that are involved.

In this example, the primary objective of both agent groups is survival. In the case of the wolves, this means obtaining food and accomplishing reproduction. In the case of the sheep, it means avoiding predators, securing food, and accomplishing reproduction.

17.5.1   Wolves and Sheep Predation Model Parameters

The input for the wolves–sheep simulation with its nominal values is shown in Figure 17.10.

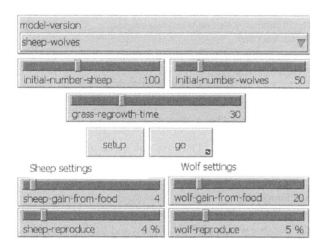

Figure 17.10   Wolves–sheep input simulation (Image – NetLogo).

The parameters of the wolves–sheep predation model and their nominal values are shown in Table 17.1.

The following are additional parameters of the wolves–sheep predation model:

1. One unit of energy is subtracted for every step a wolf takes.
2. One unit of energy is subtracted for every step a sheep takes.
3. Three monitors depict the populations of wolves, sheep, and grass during the simulation.
4. A population plot shows the dynamic population values.

Table 17.1 Wolves–Sheep Predation Model Nominal Parameters.

Name	Meaning	Nominal Value
Model-version	Model (a) involves sheep and wolves. Model (b) involves sheep, wolves, and grass.	
Initial-number-sheep	The initial size of the sheep population	100
Initial-number-wolves	The initial size of the wolf population	50
Grass-regrowth-time	The time it takes for grass to regrow once it is eaten	30
Sheep-gain-from-food	The number of energy units sheep get for every grass patch eaten	4
Wolf-gain-from-food	The number of energy units wolves get for every sheep eaten	20
Sheep-reproduce	The likelihood of a sheep producing offspring at each time step	4%
Wolf-reproduce	The likelihood of a wolf producing offspring at each time step	5%

17.5.2 Wolves and Sheep Predation Simulation Runs

The NetLogo software contains two models: (1) wolves and sheep simulations and (2) wolves, sheep, and grass simulations.

17.5.2.1 Wolves and Sheep Simulation
In the wolves–sheep model, the two agent groups, wolves and sheep, move randomly around the landscape while the sheep seek patches of grass and the wolves pursue the sheep to capture them. Each step costs the wolves energy, so they must eat sheep to replenish their energy. Otherwise, they run out of energy and die. On the other hand, sheep always have enough to eat. As such, sheep do not want to gain energy by eating or lose energy by moving. To allow the population to grow, each wolf or sheep has a fixed chance of reproduction within each simulated time step. This model version produces exciting population dynamics but is ultimately unstable.

Predation is a biological interaction among agents where one agent, the predator (wolves), kills and eats another agent, its prey (sheep). Figure 17.11 depicts two simulation runs of the wolves–sheep model embedded in the NetLogo software using the same nominal initial data. As the quantity of prey agents increases, so does the number of predator agents. Similarly, the quantity of prey agents declines as the quantity of predator agents increases. The three boxes at the top of each figure indicate the number of agents remaining at the end of the simulation run. For example, the figure on the left depicts a situation where both agents (predator and prey) die off. In contrast, the figure on the right indicates that one agent (predator) dies off, allowing the other agent (prey) to thrive and prosper. From a multi-agent, multi-objective perspective, this model produces exciting population dynamics but is ultimately unstable.

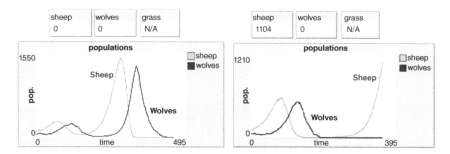

Figure 17.11 Nominal wolves and sheep predation simulation (two results).

17.5.2.2 Wolves, Sheep, and Grass simulations
In the wolves–sheep–grass model, a grass model is added to the wolves and sheep model. The grass model depicts a declining resource that is slowly restored. However, once the grass is eaten, it will grow only after a fixed amount of time. The disposition of the wolves is identical to the first model version; however, in this model, the sheep must eat grass to maintain their energy, and if they run out of energy, they die. This model version is more complex than the previous one but generally more factual.

Figure 17.12 depicts wolves, sheep, and nominal grass-growing simulation. Here, the limited amount of grass available to the prey agents (which takes 30 simulation

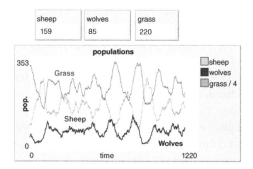

Figure 17.12 Wolves, sheep, and grass simulation (nominal grass-growing rate).

time-steps to regrow once eaten) constrains their long-term prosperity. In conjunction with the predator agents' effect, this makes the entire system stable.

Figure 17.13 depicts wolves, sheep, and a slow/very slow grass-growing simulation. Here, the slow grass takes 60 simulation time-steps to regrow, and the very slow grass takes 100 simulation time-steps to regrow once it is eaten. Under this circumstance, the predator agents die off after some time, and the number of prey agents and grass availability oscillate in a typical prey–predator manner.

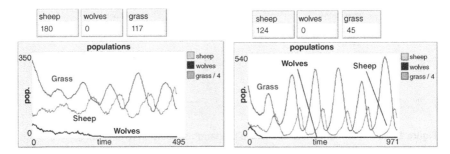

Figure 17.13   Wolves, sheep, and slow (L), very slow (R) grass-growing rate simulation.

17.6   Example 2: Cooperative Target Observation[5]

17.6.1   Background of the Example

Cooperative target observation (CTO) problems are interesting testbeds for studying multi-objective, multi-agent (MOMA) problems. These problems are significant because they are examples of dynamic multi-agent interactions and emergent behavior. In addition, there are many applicable motivations for studying CTO: unmanned vehicle control for security, survey, and surveillance tasks; tracking items in a warehouse or factory; tracking people in search and rescue; and so on.

Mobile observer agents and targets exist in this CMOMMT (cooperative multirobot observations of multiple moving targets) example. The objective of the observers is to collectively reach and stay within an "observation range" of a maximum number of targets. The observer agents move from one location to another along a planned path computed using one of several artificial intelligent (AI) algorithms. The targets wander randomly and, by definition, are slower than the observer agents. The field of operation is bounded and clear of obstacles. In this case, observers know the positions of all other observers and targets in the area. This knowledge is a realistic assumption for many real domains. Long-range radar and extensive communication among agents may provide bearings for all targets of interest, and vision or other short-range sensors may determine the observation range (Figure 17.14).

5 This section was adapted from Luke et al. (2005) with permission from: Prof. Sean Luke, Department of Computer Science, George Mason University.

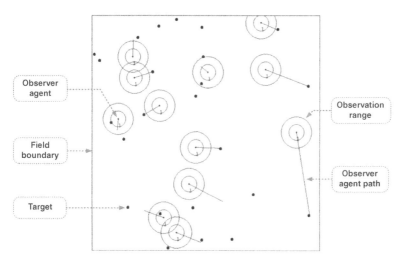

Figure 17.14 Cooperative target observation (screenshot and legends).

17.6.2 Example Details

1. **Rules of engagement.** In this cooperative target observation variation of CMOMMT, all observer agents know the locations and speeds of all targets and other observers in the field. However, each observer agent has a circular observation range centered at the agent, and the relevant agent observes any target within this circle. The field is a rectangular continuous two-dimensional area or three-dimensional volume that is free of obstacles. The CTO model contains n observer agents and m targets, where $n < m$.

2. **Observer agents' movements.** The movement of each observer agent is accomplished by computing a destination point and then having the agent travel toward this point. The destination point is determined using one of three cooperative target observation algorithms: (1) k-means clustering, (2) hill-climbing, and (3) k-means clustering followed by hill-climbing. Observer agents compute a new destination point every α time-steps. If an observer agent reaches its destination point in fewer steps, it waits until a unique destination point is calculated, and the process repeats itself.

3. **Target movements.** The movement of each target is done by computing a destination point and then moving each target toward its destination point. This process continues during $k < 100$ time-steps. When a given target reaches its destination, a new destination point is created randomly, and the cycle repeats itself.

4. **Example experiment.** All experiments were performed on the MASON simulation environment (Luke et al., 2003). The objective was to gather the time-steps of each simulation run and compute their overall mean. Although

many simulation parameters in MASON are tunable, the example depicted in Figure 17.14 uses the fixed parameters described in Table 17.2.

Table 17.2 Fixed Parameters for the MASON Simulator.

Parameter	Value
Width and height of the field	150×150 units
Time-steps per simulation run	1500
Number of simulations runs per data point	30
Number of targets	24
Number of observers	12
Speed of target	0.5 unit per time-step
Speed of observer agents	1 unit per time-step
Sensor range of each observer agent	15 units
AI algorithm update rate	10

5. **Example results.** Initial experiments compared k-means and hill climbing against random and stationary behaviors. It was found that the k-means and the hill climber are statistically better than the arbitrary and fixed algorithms over all combinations of target speed, subset size, range, and rate of updates. The results also verify that performance significantly decreases when either range decreases, target speed increases, or update rate decreases. For example, comparing subset sizes 1 and 12 indicated significant differences across all ranges, target speed, and update rate settings. Also, comparing extreme sets of the ranges, target speeds, and update rates for the same subset size yielded significant differences.

17.7 Example 3: Seaport Logistics[6]

17.7.1 Introduction

Recently, there has been a considerable increase in container transportation worldwide. Therefore, seaport terminals and operations are designed to maximize throughputs at minimum costs. These objectives are achieved by moving containers from ships to shore (i.e., seaport yard) and then from shore to trucks and rails, and vice versa, as optimally as possible.

The quayside operations of the system involve loading and unloading ships. The hinterland operations of the system involve loading and unloading trucks and

---

6 Example inspired by Pennada (2020). http://www.diva-portal.org/smash/get/diva2:1501741/FULLTEXT01.pdf. Accessed: Jan. 2023.

rails. However, because incoming and outgoing containers cannot be synchronized, a large volume of containers must be stored within the premises of the seaport terminal yard (import/export stock[7]). When containers are ready to leave the seaport terminal yard, they are moved to the appropriate operation area and loaded onto ships, trucks, or rails. Figure 17.15 depicts typical operational areas within a seaport terminal.

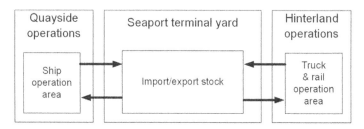

Figure 17.15 Typical operational areas inside a seaport terminal.

Virtually all seaport terminal yards are limited in space; therefore, containers must be stacked on top of one another (Figure 17.16). When a given container is scheduled for shipping, the seaport staff must extract it and move it to the ship or truck/rail operation area. However, removing the desired container from its current pile often necessitates moving other containers to different locations because only containers at the top of a given container pile are immediately available to the seaport crane. Since the seaport authorities attempt to maximize external containers' throughput, they naturally seek to minimize the number of internal containers moves as much as possible.

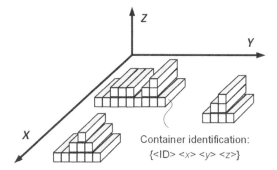

Figure 17.16 Container arrangement in a seaport terminal yard.

---

7 Exports are the goods and services a country produces domestically and sells to businesses or customers who reside in foreign countries. Imports are the goods and services domestic businesses or customers purchase from another country.

17.7.2 The Problem

An essential determinant of maritime transport costs is seaport efficiency. "Improving port efficiency from the 25th to 75th percentiles reduce[s] shipping costs by more than 12%" (Clark et al., 2004).

Therefore, for the sake of this example, we consider two agents. The first agent is the seaport authority. This agent's objectives are to (1) maximize the containers' throughput of the port and (2) maximize the customer-related profits of the port. The second agent is, in fact, a set of agents who are transportation customers of the seaport. The objectives of these agents are to (1) minimize the transportation time of their containers through the port and (2) minimize the transportation cost levied by the port. These objectives are typical multi-objective, multi-agent (MOMA) problems.

The above objectives are self-conflicting, as is common in MOMA problems. So, a single solution cannot satisfy all the stated goals. Therefore, an acceptable solution to such problems is to derive a set of solutions where each meets different objectives at some level without getting dominated by any other solution.

By definition, a port can deliver a limited number of containers per day, and minimizing the internal moves of containers is an essential factor in the overall port efficiency and minimization of cost. Here, internal container transport is defined as moving containers within the seaport terminal yard, and external container transport entails delivering them to the quayside or the hinterland operation areas.

Given the estimated arrival and departure dates of each container at/from the terminal yard as well as the average time and cost of internal and external container transports, the problem is to find the optimal placement position (x, y, and z coordinates) of each container within the seaport terminal yard.

17.7.3 Experiment

An experiment was conducted to find the containers' optimal placement position (x, y, and z coordinates) in the seaport terminal yard. There are 400 containers located in this area. Each has its identification number (ID), expected arrival and departure dates, and place within the import/export stockyard. This placement data is constrained to locations: $1 \leq x \leq 10$, $1 \leq y \leq 10$, and $1 \leq z \leq 5$. The problem, therefore, involved a search for optimal container positions in a seaport terminal yard under the following objectives:

- **Objective 1.** Minimize the time of internal and external containers transportation.
- **Objective 2.** Minimize the cost of internal and external containers transportation.

In this example, the expected internal cost/time of container transportation is $200 and 0.5 hour. The reciprocal external cost/time is $400 and 1.0 hour. This problem may be solved by using a genetic algorithm for multi-objective decision-making. Genetic algorithm (GA) is a meta-heuristic search technique based on the Darwinian concept whereby species adapting to the prevailing environment demonstrate a higher probability of surviving and producing offspring.

Figure 17.17 depicts an example of a genetic algorithm input and output. The input to the algorithm is the ID of each container in the seaport terminal yard as well as its expected arrival and departure dates. The output of the algorithm is (1) the optimal placement of each container, (2) the number of moves and the associated cost and time required for each internal and external container, and (3) the total cost and time associated with each container move.

Container number	Containers date		Container placement			Containers move						Total cost [$]	Total Time [Hr]
	Arrival	Departure	x	y	z	internal			External				
						#	Cost [$]	Time [Hr]	#	Cost [$]	Time [Hr]		
1	1	12	5	5	1	6	1,200	3.0	2	800	2.0	2,000	5.0
2	6	23	8	10	2	8	1,600	4.0	2	800	2.0	2,400	6.0
.....	.....	.....	.....	.....	.....	.....	.....	.....	.....	.....	.....	.....	.....
400	2	30	2	4	3	3	600	1.5	1	400	1.0	1,000	2.5
Total						17	3,400	8.5	5	2,000	5.0	5,400	13.5

Figure 17.17 Example of genetic algorithm input and output.

One way to apply a genetic algorithm to multi-objective optimization problems is to run a fixed number of iterations seeking to optimize one objective and then repeat the process, aiming to optimize each of the remaining objectives. This overall process is repeated many times to establish a set of optimal solutions, called the Pareto front. Figure 17.18 shows the establishment of the Pareto front in a two-objective optimization instance. Then the decision-makers must select the optimal combinations of these multi-objective solutions.

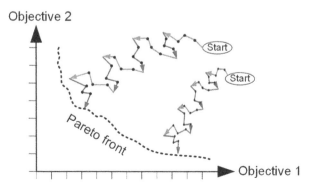

Figure 17.18 Establishing the Pareto front in a two-objective optimization instance.

17.7.4 More on Multi-objective Optimization and Solution Domination

Stated rigorously, the concepts of multi-objective optimization and solution domination may be as follows:

1. In multi-objective optimization problems with M objectives, each solution may be placed in an M-dimensional space based on its objective values.
2. A solution X1 dominates a solution X2 if all of X1's objective values are more desirable than the corresponding objective values of solution X2.
3. A solution X1 is dominated by a solution X3 if all of X3's objective values are more desirable than the corresponding objective values of X1.

These concepts may be clarified by way of an example.

Sometimes in multi-objective optimization, there is a single best solution for a subset or all the objective values. For example, Figure 17.19 depicts the results of several multi-objective optimization runs related to two objectives. Here, solution S3 is more desirable than solutions S1 and S2 relative to both objective 1 and objective 2. In other words, solution S3 dominates solutions S1 and S2 relative to both objectives.

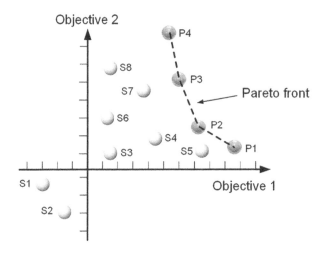

Figure 17.19 Pareto front and dominated solutions.

However, more often in multi-objective optimizations, there is a single best solution for each objective value. For example, solution P1 is more desirable than all other solutions vis-à-vis objective 1. In other words, solution P1 dominates all other solutions relative to objective 1. Similarly, solution P4 dominates all other solutions relative to objective 2.

Most often, however, in multi-objective optimization, nondominated solutions form a set of most desired solutions called the Pareto front. Each solution exhibits some trade-off, which cannot be decided a priori but needs to be explored posteriorly (based on other considerations).

17.8 Bibliography

Clark, X., Dollar, D., and Micco, A. (2004, Dec. 2). Port efficiency, maritime transport costs, and bilateral trade, Journal of Development Economics.https://www.sciencedirect.com/science/article/abs/pii/S0304387804000689#:~:text=In%20addition%2C%20we%20find%20that,markets%20for%20the%20average%20country. Accessed: Jan. 2023.

Evolutionary game theory. Wikipedia. https://en.wikipedia.org/wiki/Evolutionary_game_theory. Accessed: Jan. 2023.

Luke, S., Balan, G.C., Panait, L., Cioffi-Revilla, C., and Paus, S. (2003). MASON: A Java multi-agent simulation library. *Proceedings of Agent 2003 Conference on Challenges in Social Simulation* 9 (9).

Luke, S., Sullivan, K., Panait, L., and Balan, G. (2005). Tunably decentralized algorithms for cooperative target observation. *Proceedings of the Fourth International Joint Conference on Autonomous Agents and Multi-Agent Systems* (pp. 911–917).

McKenzie, A.J. (2021, Summer). Evolutionary game theory. In Zalta, E.N. (Ed.), *The Stanford Encyclopedia of Philosophy.*https://plato.stanford.edu/archives/sum2021/entries/game-evolutionary/. Accessed: Jan. 2023.

Pennada, V.S.T. (2020, June). Solving multiple objective optimization problem using multi-agent systems: A case in logistics management. MSc thesis, Faculty of Computing, Blekinge Institute of Technology, Karlskrona, Sweden. http://www.diva-portal.org/smash/get/diva2:1501741/FULLTEXT01.pdf. Last reviewed: July 2022.

Radulescu, R., Mannion, P., Roijers, D.M., and Nowe, A. (2020). Multi-objective multi-agent decision making: A utility-based analysis and survey. *Autonomous Agents and Multi-Agent Systems* 34 (1): 1–52.

Wilensky, U. (1997). NetLogo wolf sheep predation model. Center for Connected Learning and Computer-Based Modeling, Northwestern University, Evanston, IL. http://ccl.northwestern.edu/netlogo/models/WolfSheepPredation

Wilensky, U. (1999). NetLogo. Center for Connected Learning and Computer-Based Modeling, Northwestern University, Evanston, IL. http://ccl.northwestern.edu/netlogo/

18

Systems Engineering Using Category Theory[1]

Authors: Yaniv Mordecai, Avner Engel

18.1   Introduction

In all medium to large engineering projects, different systems engineers own different conceptual, logical, and physical components. Therefore, adopting a collaborative mindset is crucial since integration is first and foremost among people and only afterward among the systems and technologies they design or operate. This chapter uses category theory to enhance collaboration in systems engineering. The following aspects are discussed:

- **The problem of multidisciplinary collaborative design.** Collaboration is critical and challenging in processes such as (1) mapping solution architectures to requirements, (2) identifying emergent behaviors and higher-order interactions, (3) modifying the design and deriving variants of constantly evolving systems, and (4) coping with various concept representations.
- **Brief background on category theory and systems engineering.** The basic definitions of category theory and how these definitions help capture systems engineering concepts are presented.
- **Example: designing an electric vehicle.** The discussion begins with a historical perspective—the General Motors EV1 electric car and types of electric vehicles. Then, the main features of a battery electric vehicle (BEV) system, BEV key performance attributes (KPAs), BEV top-level functionality, BEV architecture, vehicle structure, electric propulsion, mechanical propulsion auxiliary systems functionality, BEV interfaces, and top-level BEV electric system diagram are explained.

---

1 The primary author of this chapter is Dr. Yaniv Mordecai.

Systems Science for Engineers and Scholars, First Edition. Edited by Avner Engel.
© 2024 John Wiley & Sons, Ltd. Published 2024 by John Wiley & Sons, Ltd.

- **Category theory (CT) as a system specification language.** A category with objects (types) and morphisms (mappings, compositions, isomorphism) is presented, including defining emergent mappings using compositions, isomorphisms, and abstractions, generalizing the definition of a category for system design, and integrating categories.
- **Categorical multidisciplinary collaborative design (C-MCD).** The following are specified: C-MCD categories, central knowledge base (CKB), expert knowledge base (EKB), expert models (EMs), integrated design graphs (IDGs), and integrated design views (IDVs).
- **The categorical design processes.** A process that consists of five steps (0–4) is introduced: (0) formalizing the C-MCD environment and process, (1) creating categories for design disciplines and areas of expertise, (2) building expert models following the categorical structuring of each model, (3) capturing dependencies among design categories through functorial mappings, and (4) disseminating new design knowledge to the design categories.

18.2 The Problem of Multidisciplinary, Collaborative Design

Many systems problems are multidisciplinary and include mechanical, electrical, computational, ergonomic, and operational aspects. The design of such systems under such conditions is referred to as a multidisciplinary, collaborative design (MCD). Systems engineers face four critical challenges in MCD projects: (1) mapping solution architectures to requirements, (2) identifying emergent behaviors and higher-order interactions, (3) modifying the design and deriving variants of constantly evolving systems, and (4) coping with a variety of concept representations and terminologies.

18.2.1 Mapping Solution Architectures to Requirements

Systems engineers own requirement specifications and allocate them to system elements: components, functions, input/output flows, interfaces, and their relations. Systems engineers must collaborate with the disciplinary design experts when specifying requirements and allocating them to system elements to ensure that the best approach is taken. Requirements must be identified and allocated such that the solution design adheres to the problem statements at any abstraction level, which is often challenging. Solution architectures encompass many micro-architectures that act as integrated solutions for high-level requirements. Isolating each micro-architecture with the individual elements that play a role in the solution is complex. For example, providing energy to a vehicle control system requires multiple elements to play a role and perform some function. The capability to derive the solution architecture across all the subsystems and components is not apparent.

18.2.2   Identifying Emergent Behaviors and Higher-Order Interactions

Systems engineers are trusted to see the big picture, the end-to-end flow, and the checks and balances across the system. Managing direct interactions and interfaces is relatively trivial, and it may be easy to capture one-hop or two-hop interactions and illustrate them in diagrams. However, it is impossible to map all these interactions without well-defined methods and the ability to derive indirect mappings. The problem intensifies in siloed design spaces, where one subsystem's components, functions, and internal interfaces are not necessarily visible to the other subsystems. Systems engineers should derive such interactions even when they are not clearly illustrated.

18.2.3   Modifying the Design and Deriving Variants of Constantly Evolving Systems

Systems engineers oversee the evolving integrated design modifications across the system. Design modifications require version and configuration control, particularly in ceaselessly evolving systems, and they may result in variant designs and different products. For example, an automotive product manager may define a requirement to monitor battery temperature and display it to the driver. This feature may be released in the following product model or with some premium products. Systems engineers may want to use the core system design as the baseline for a product line or design modification, with various products and components that fit diverse customer and stakeholder needs. Each variant may modify a subset of elements in the baseline design. Systems engineers must oversee the derivation and modification process to ensure that variant designs remain modular, reusable, and cost-efficient.

18.2.4   Coping with a Variety of Concept Representations

Systems engineers should adapt to various concept representation methods and languages, speak the language of the experts they work with, show sufficient understanding of the subject matter, and ask tough questions. To that end, systems engineers should master multiple tools, read various diagrams, analyze different datasets, and learn various operational and technological terminologies. These tools, methods, and datasets often change from project to project, sometimes even during a single project. Systems engineers should be proficient enough to understand and explain an electrical wiring diagram to a software engineer, an interface specification to a hardware designer, and a simulation report to a customer. Therefore, systems engineers should facilitate quick and efficient concept and relation abstraction, generalization, translation, and projection from one domain to another.

18.3 Category Theory in Systems Engineering: A Brief Background

Sharing and capitalizing on design-related knowledge has become a significant challenge in modern systems design. Such design has evolved and become more concurrent, multidisciplinary, and collaborative. The breadth of disciplines, concurrent design activities, stakeholder perspectives, and synergetic actions often introduce significant complications, risks, and delays rather than enhance productivity, creativity, and delivery of results.

Most engineers utilize their domain knowledge, know-how, and perspectives during concurrent design. Knowledge is the ability to use information in a particular context based on stakeholder interpretation. Know-how is the knowledge required to perform a task, create a design or aspect of a design, analyze, develop, operate, and so on. Know-how is often its owner's trade secret and strategic asset, leading to the concealment of such knowledge from collaborators. Tacit knowledge and know-how are personal and usually not documented, shared, or transferred. They consist of experiences and broad subject matter understanding and can be acquired through practice. Conversely, explicit knowledge is intended to be publicly available, accessible, and sharable in libraries and databases.

Capitalizing on knowledge—implicit and explicit, private and shared alike—is a crucial success factor in collaborative design. Nevertheless, capitalizing on all the knowledge requires significant time, human effort, and monetary resources. Therefore, systems engineers may have to capitalize only on the most valuable knowledge, which calls for methods to identify critical knowledge and focus on capturing, communicating, and utilizing those knowledge artifacts.

Parametric design (PD) enhances knowledge sharing and arguably reduces the downside of contemporary design. The PD methodology consistently maintains fine data granularity (i.e., constraints and parameters). However, PD approaches are limited because they are based on informal practices. Identifying multidomain knowledge to be capitalized upon is becoming increasingly complex. Relying on formal methods, models, and mathematical techniques is desired (Camba et al., 2016).

Category theory (CT) is a branch of mathematics that formalizes mathematical concepts, structures, and relations. It captures *objects* and relations between objects, which are called *morphisms*. A collection of objects and morphisms among them can be packed into a *category* and visualized as a labeled directed graph whose nodes are the objects and whose labeled directed edges are the morphisms (Spivak and Kent, 2012). The category-theoretic object concept applies to types or classes of items, not specific items.

A *morphism* is any arbitrary mapping or relation between types, not only a mathematical or algebraic expression. *Functors* are transformations of knowledge from one category to another. These structure-preserving operators act on categories much like functions act on sets. CT has been applied as a unified, comprehensive formalism and common language for capturing relations among different system concept representations (Mordecai et al., 2021; Mordecai et al., 2022) and stakeholder knowledge bases (Fradi et al., 2022). CT can formalize concepts by defining knowledge bases as categories and mapping, translating, or connecting them through *functors*. CT can be applied to design knowledge orchestration, thus formally enabling the identification and sharing of knowledge artifacts in systems design and furthering the efficiency and usability of contemporary parametric design approaches.

The following sections present a conceptual automotive system design using conventional systems engineering terms. The basic definitions and tenets of CT are then introduced and demonstrated through the perspective of this example. After that, a scenario for applying CT in conjunction with parametric design knowledge orchestration is described. This approach is called categorical multidisciplinary collaborative design (C-MCD).

18.4   Example: Designing an Electric Vehicle

18.4.1   Historical Perspective: The General Motors EV1 Electric Car

The General Motors (GM) EV1 was a battery electric vehicle produced and leased from 1996 to 1999 (Figure 18.1). It was a major automaker's first mass-produced and purpose-designed electric vehicle of the modern era. The EV1 was made available through limited lease agreements, initially to residents of the states of California and Arizona and, later, Georgia. The EV1 cars were unavailable for purchase and could be serviced only at designated dealerships. While customer reactions to the EV1 were positive, GM management believed that electric

Figure 18.1   The General Motors EV1 electric car. (Image: GM)

vehicles occupied an unprofitable segment of the automobile market and destroyed virtually all the EV1, ignoring customer protests. Nowadays, as EVs are gaining popularity, one must wonder if that was a wise business decision.

18.4.2 Types of Electric Vehicles

Electric vehicles (EVs) can be classified into two main concepts: hybrid electric vehicles (HEV) and battery electric vehicles (BEV). First, the differences between hybrid and battery will be illustrated in Figure 18.2. Then, each concept will be briefly explained, with a focus on the system architecture of BEV.

HEV (Figure 18.2a) is based on an internal combustion engine (ICE) and one electric motor that uses energy stored in its battery. Therefore, HEVs combine the benefits of low emissions and fuel economy, maintaining the power and range of conventional vehicles. A wide variety of HEV models are available. Although HEVs are often more expensive than comparable conventional vehicles, fuel savings may recover some costs. By and large, HEVs are not designed to obtain electricity from the electrical grid. Instead, the combustion engine charges the battery. In addition, the vehicle captures energy during braking operations by utilizing the motor as a generator and capturing the created energy in the battery.

BEV (Figure 18.2b) uses a battery to store the electrical energy that powers the motor. Electric vehicle batteries are charged by connecting the vehicle to an electric power source. Both heavy-duty and light-duty electric vehicles are commercially available. Electric vehicles are typically more expensive than similar conventional vehicles. However, some costs can be recovered through fuel savings. Generally, BEVs have a shorter electric charge range than conventional vehicles. However, city driving has more stops, which maximizes the benefits of idling and regenerative braking. At the same time, highway travel requires more energy to overcome the increased air drag at higher speeds.

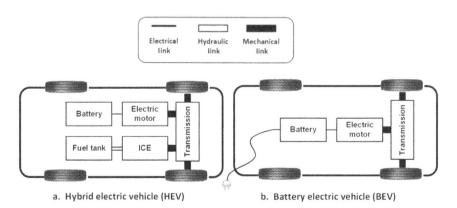

a. Hybrid electric vehicle (HEV)   b. Battery electric vehicle (BEV)

Figure 18.2 Two types of electric vehicles.

18.4.3 The BEV System

The battery electric vehicle (BEV) passenger car system is the running example in this chapter. The BEV uses an electric motor and energy stored in an onboard battery. While moving, the BEV system is quieter than ordinary automobiles and has no exhaust emissions. While at rest, the battery within the BEV system can be charged using standard or specially designed electrical outlets. The BEV system in its environment is depicted in Figure 18.3.

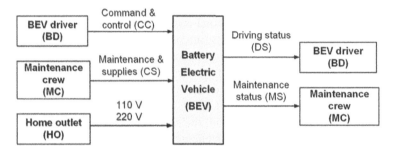

Figure 18.3 The battery electric vehicle (BEV) system in its environment.

18.4.4 BEV Key Performance Attributes

Automotive power electronics should typically live about 15 years, support 12,000 operating hours and 54,000 engines on/off cycles, and qualify on rigorous pressure, shock, vibration, and temperature tests (Scheuermann, 2009). In addition, typical physical performance attributes must be on par with or better than conventional combustion engine vehicles. Table 18.1 summarizes the BEV's key performance attributes (KPAs).

Table 18.1 BEV Key Performance Attributes (KPA).

KPA	Specified Value	Dimension	Maximize Goal	Minimize Goal
Electric range	380	Kilometers (km)	✓	
Maximal speed	225	Kilometers per hour (km/h)	✓	
Acceleration 0–100 km/h	6.1	Seconds (sec)		✓
Total power	239	Kilowatts (kW)	✓	
Total torque	420	Newton-meter (Nm)	✓	
Useable battery	57	Kilowatt-hours (kWh)	✓	

Table 18.1 (Continued)

KPA	Specified Value	Dimension	Maximize Goal	Minimize Goal
Vehicle efficiency	150	Watt-hours per kilometer (Wh/km)		✓
Vehicle life span	15	Years (yr)	✓	
Operating hours (OpHrs)	12,000	Hours (hr)	✓	
Engine on/off cycles	54,000	Cycles (cy)	✓	

18.4.5 BEV Top-Level Functionality

The BEV's primary function is to transport the driver and passengers with their belongings safely and efficiently. The benefits may include comfort, speed, safety, availability, operating expenses, and other attributes. Defining the most comprehensive collection of features and the combination scheme that best reflects the needs and requirements of all stakeholders is beyond the scope of the current chapter. Still, it is undoubtedly a critical factor in the solution design process.

18.4.6 BEV Architecture

The BEV architecture (Figure 18.4) consists of four primary subsystems: vehicle structure (VS), electric propulsion (EP), mechanical propulsion (MP), and auxiliary systems (AS). The subsystems and their primary functions are described in the following subsections. An attempt has been made to ascribe a primary role to each component. Although this may not be a comprehensive and complete specification, it is a good starting point and a common ground for standard vehicle design.

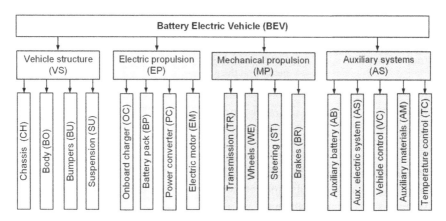

Figure 18.4 The battery electric vehicle (BEV) top-level architecture.

Vehicle structure (VS) includes a chassis, a body, bumpers, and suspension. The functionalities that these components provide are described below.

Component	Functionality
Chassis (CH)	Provides a structural and mechanical basis for the BEV system
Body (BO)	Provides housing and access into and out of the vehicle
Bumpers (BU)	Protect against front and rear collisions
Suspension (SU)	Connects the chassis to the wheels

Electric propulsion (EP) subsystem consists of an onboard charger, a battery pack, a power converter, and an electric motor. Their functionalities are listed below.

Component	Functionality
Onboard charger (OC)	Receives household electrical power (110 to 220 V AC) and converts it to high-voltage electrical DC energy
Battery pack (BP)	Receives, stores, and discharges high-voltage electrical DC energy
Power converter (PC)	Converts high-voltage electrical DC energy into usable electrical power
Electric motor (EM)	Receives and converts electric energy from the power converter into mechanical torque

Mechanical propulsion (MP) components are the transmission, wheels, steering, and brakes.

Component	Functionality
Transmission (TR)	Connects and synchronizes rotation between the electric motor and the wheels
Wheels (WE)	Provide rotary motion to propel the vehicle
Steering (ST)	Controls the direction of the BEV system
Brakes (BR)	Slow or stop the BEV system

Auxiliary systems (AS) include an auxiliary battery, electric system, vehicle control, auxiliary materials, and temperature control, among other subsystems that are not elaborated upon here.

Component	Functionality
Auxiliary battery (AB)	Provides standard electrical energy (12 V) DC to the auxiliary electric system
Operating system (OS)	Collects and provides information to the driver, receives commands from the driver, and transfers commands to the vehicle's central control system
Vehicle control (VC)	Collects, disseminates, and controls system status and command data
Auxiliary materials (AM)	Ensure continuous and reliable vehicle operation (e.g., lubrication between moving parts, hydraulic pressure control, air condition cooling/heating means, auxiliary battery operation)
Temperature control (TC)	Senses and controls the temperature and airflow in the system

18.4.7   BEV Interfaces

The BEV system interface types and descriptions are listed in Table 18.2.

Table 18.2   The Battery Electric Vehicle (BEV) Types of Interfaces.

Interface ID	Interface Type	Interface Description
1	Force/position	Mechanical (fixed interface)
2	Force/position	Mechanical (moving interface)
3	Energy	Electrical (low voltage: 12 V)
4	Energy	Electrical (high voltage: 100 to 800 V)
5	Information	Status data
6	Information	Command data
7	Manual operation	Maintenance crew
8	Manual operation	Driving operations
9	Material	Auxiliary material
10	Material/energy	Cooling/heating

A dependency structure matrix (DSM) captures the interfaces among system components. The kernel of the DSM is a square matrix where the gray squares along the diagonal represent the systemic and environmental elements. Each column element may receive inputs from row elements. Similarly, each row element may transmit output to column elements. Cells at intersections between rows and columns specify the interface type between the row and column elements. The DSM in Figure 18.5 maps subsystems and system components to one another using interface types listed in Table 18.2. The DSM also captures interactions with environmental entities: the driver, maintenance crew, and power outlet.

The DSM shows that the onboard charger (OC) has a fixed mechanical interface (1) with the chassis (CH). The OC receives low voltage (3) from the auxiliary electric system (AS), command data (6) from the vehicle control (VC), and high-voltage electricity (4) from the home outlet (HO). In addition, the OC provides high-voltage electricity (4) to the battery pack (BP) and status data (5) to the vehicle control (VC). Like all other components, the OC undergoes maintenance (7) by the maintenance crew (MC).

Group	Component	CH	BO	BU	SU	OC	BP	PC	EM	TR	WE	ST	BR	AB	AS	VC	AM	TC	BD	MC	HO
Vehicle Structure (VS)	Chassis (CH)		1	1	1	1	1	1	1	1	2	2	2	1	1	1		1		7	
	Body (BO)	1					*Output*									5	1	5	2	7	
	Bumpers (BU)	1																		7	
	Suspension (SU)	1									2	1	1							7	
Electric Propulsion (EP)	Onboard charger (OC)	1		*Input*			4									5				7	
	Battery pack (BP)	1						4								5				7	
	Power converter (PC)	1							4						3	5				7	
	Electric motor (EM)	1								2						5				7	
Mechanical Propulsion (MP)	Transmission (TR)	1									2					5				7	
	Wheels (WE)	2			2								3			5				7	
	Steering (ST)	2			1						2					5			8	7	
	Brakes (BR)	2			1						2					5			8	7	
Auxiliary Systems (AS)	Auxiliary battery (AB)	1													3	5				7	
	Aux. electric system (AS)	1	3			3	3	3	3	3	3	3	3			5		3		7	
	Vehicle control (VC)	1				6	6	6	6	6	6	6	6		6			6	5	7	
	Auxiliary materials (AM)		9						9					9	9	5			5	7	
	Temperature control (TC)	1	10													5				7	
Vehicle IO (VIO)	BEV driver in (BD)		2									8	8			8					
	Maintenance crew in (MC)	7	7	7	7	7	7	7	7	7	7	7	7	7	7	7	7	7			
	Home outlet (HO)					4															

Figure 18.5 The BEV internal and external interfaces.

18.4.8 Top-Level BEV Electric System Diagram

The BEV's electrical flow is depicted in Figure 18.6. It shows high-voltage current flow from a home outlet into the onboard charger (OC) and thence to the battery pack (BP) and power converter (PC). High-voltage electricity then flows to the electric motor (EM), and low-voltage flows into the auxiliary battery (AB). Finally, the auxiliary battery provides low-voltage energy to the auxiliary system (AS).

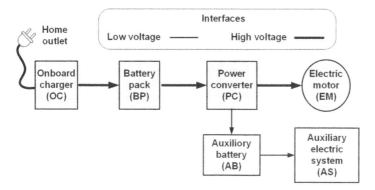

Figure 18.6 Top-level BEV electric system diagram.

18.5 Category Theory (CT) as a System Specification Language

The discussion now turns to an explanation of how CT can serve as a system specification language using the concepts, constructs, and rules that apply to categories. Recall that *objects* and *morphisms* are the building blocks of categories. A *morphism* is any arbitrary mapping or relation between types, not only a mathematical or algebraic expression. The identity morphism maps every object to itself such that $id(X) = X$ for any object X. Identity morphism is a critical building block of CT, as it facilitates deep mathematical underpinnings for CT. In the category-theoretic sense, the object concept defines a type or class of items, not a specific item. The *type* and *mapping* concepts, which are synonymous with *object* and *morphism*, respectively, are used. Each mapping has a domain (dom) and a codomain (cod), such that for any $m_{12} : T_1 \rightarrow T_2$, $dom(m_{12}) = T_1$ and $cod(m_{12}) = T_2$. Consider each mapping as a function that receives its input from the domain type and returns its output to the codomain type. It does not necessarily mean that the domain or codomain types are the inputs and outputs themselves, but they can be.

18.5.1 Defining a Category with Objects (Types) and Morphisms (Mappings)

Consider, for instance, a category of vehicles in the context of the example presented here. One prominent *type* is *Vehicle*. Some more helpful types represent systems or subsystems, for example, *PowerSystem*. Before going further, this category of vehicles and power systems should be defined. The identity mapping is defined for each type: $id(Vehicle) = Vehicle$, $id(PowerSystem) = PowerSystem$. It can be referred to as an object definition statement (Figure 18.7).

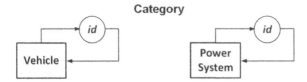

Figure 18.7 A category with two types in the Automotive domain and their identity morphisms.

Types without relations are not very useful. A trivial mapping *Vehicle* → *PowerSystem* can be defined using the verb *has*. It is specified as *has: Vehicle* → *PowerSystem*, and it can be pronounced that (any) vehicle *has (a)* Power System. Likewise, an *Energy* type can be defined, and the *PowerSystem* can be mapped to *Energy*with a second mapping, *uses*: (any) Power System *uses* energy. Thus, our category consists of vehicles, power systems, and energy. Two mappings connect the types *has* and *uses*. In our case, *dom(has)* = *Vehicle*, *cod(has)* = *PowerSystem*, *dom(uses)* = *PowerSystem*, and *cod(uses)* = *Energy*. Note that *cod(has)* = *dom(uses)* = *PowerSystem*. This category is illustrated in Figure 18.8.

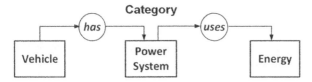

Figure 18.8 A category with three types and two mappings in the Automotive domain.[2]

A category of natural language types and relations is known as an OLOG (Spivak and Kent, 2012). Categories represent universal sets of arguments. Hence, per our category, *any* Vehicle has a Power System, and *any* Power System uses energy. These statements may be considered hypotheses, requirements, constraints, theorems, facts, or assertions. Typically, many systems design statements are assertions because they capture the desired scope of a system under design. This notion of the categorization of systemic relations is a fundamental one.

Our category is still very abstract: It contains generic types but does not include anything specific. The category can be enhanced with two types of Energy: Mechanical and Electrical Energy. *Energy*is mapped to both*MechanicalEnergy*and *ElectricalEnergy* with a third mapping that represents specialization: *canBe*. The two Energy types can

---

2 These illustrations may seem alien to category theory experts. This example adopts a modular view, which resembles logical block diagrams, to appeal to the design thinkers and architects who read this work.

be used to define three *PowerSystem* types: *CombustionPowerSystem*, *BatteryPowerSystem*, and *HybridPowerSystem*. The mapping from *PowerSystem* to each one of these is also *canBe*. The mapping of the specialized *PowerSystem* types can be completed to the specialized *Energy* types with the existing *uses* mapping:

$$uses: \begin{cases} CombustionPowerSystem \rightarrow MechanicalEnergy \\ BatteryPowerSystem \rightarrow ElectricalEnergy \\ HybridPowerSystem \rightarrow \{MechanicalEnergy, ElectricalEnergy\} \end{cases}$$

Similarly, the mapping *canBe* is used to derive specialized Vehicle types: *CombustionEngine*, *BatteryElectric*, and *HybridElectric*. These types are related to *PowerSystem* subtypes using the *has* mapping. Our category can now be referred to as a **Vehicle Power System Classification Category**. The category is illustrated in Figure 18.9.

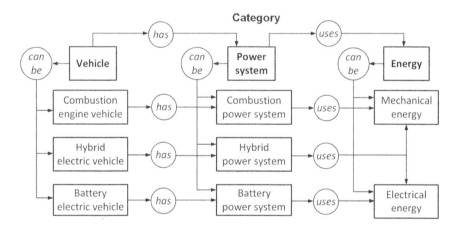

Figure 18.9 Classification categories of a vehicle power system.

Our additional relations extended the domains of the has and uses mappings:

- *dom(has)* = {*Vehicle, CombustionEngineVehicle, HybridElectricVehicleBattery ElectricVehicle*}
- *cod(has)* = {*PowerSystem, CombustionPowerSystem, HybridPowerSystem, BatteryPowerSystem*}
- *dom(uses)* = {*Power System, Combustion Power System, Hybrid Power System, Battery Power System*}
- *cod(uses)* = {*Enegy, MechanicalEnergy, ElectricalEnergy*}

18.5.2 Compositions

The composition theorem in category theory asserts that two morphisms' composition or sequential operation equals an operation from the first morphism's domain to the second morphism's codomain. The composition of the two morphisms $m_{12}: O_1 \rightarrow O_2$ and $m_{23}: O_2 \rightarrow O_3$ emerges as $m_{13}: O_1 \rightarrow O_3$. Driving home from work can be considered a complex process. Still, it can also emerge as a composition of simpler processes of passing through primary road segments between two junctions/interchanges.

Accordingly, the composition of *has(Vehicle, PowerSystem)* and *uses(Power-System, Energy)* emerges as a third mapping from *dom(has)* to *cod(uses)*, that is, from *Vehicle* to *Energy*. The composed mapping can be explicitly referred to as *has · uses*. Semantically, one can say that if a subsystem uses some resource, the system also uses that resource. The direct *has* mapping can be distinguished from the indirect *has'* mapping. Hence, *BatteryElectricVehicleuses' ElectricalEnergy* and *HybridElectricVehicleuses' ElectricalEnergy and MechanicalEnergy*. This intuitive notion emerges from the category without defining it explicitly in the category. This fundamental concept allows us to derive many indirect compositional mappings from direct ones.

Compositions are essential for deriving indirect mappings from basic ones. The derivation of indirect mappings for specialized types like *BatteryElectricVehicle* and *HybridElectricVehicle* is also related to composition. A complete directed path of mappings is needed through any series of types to let composite, indirect mappings emerge. For example, a composition from *BatteryElectricVehicle* and *HybridElectricVehicle* to *ElectricalEnergy, MechanicalEnergy* requires a mediating type. However, our category does not define such a path. Note that the mapping *canBe:Vehicle* → {*BatteryElectricVehicle, HybridElectricVehicle*} is defined such that *Vehicle* is in *dom(canBe)*—not the other way around.

18.5.3 Isomorphism

An isomorphism is a pair of morphisms m_{12}, m_{21} such that for a pair of objects O_1, $O_2, m_{12}: O_1 \rightarrow O_2$ and $m_{21}: O_2 \rightarrow O_1$. This equation means that there is a capability to return from O_1 to O_1 through O_2 and from O_2 to O_2 through O_1 by composing the two morphisms: $m_{12} \cdot m_{21}: O_1 \rightarrow O_1, m_{21} \cdot m_{12}: O_2 \rightarrow O_2$. This vital concept facilitates equivalence, substitutability, and reversibility. The three mappings *canBe*, *has*, and *uses*, and their respective reciprocal mappings *are*, *in*, and *serves*, are shown in Figure 18.10. Due to isomorphism, it can be asserted that in our category, every mapping m_{ij} from any type T_i to any type T_j has an isomorphism, such that a reciprocal mapping m_{ji} exists.

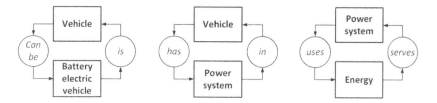

Figure 18.10 Isomorphisms: left (*canBe, is*); center: (*has, in*); right: (*uses, serves*).

18.5.4 Defining and Deriving Emergent Mappings

Similarly, mappings with emergent semantics among types based on any explicitly defined mappings can be derived by combining abstraction, composition, and isomorphism. This powerful capability of category theory enables simplification of our categories without losing the ability to cope with the typical degrees of systems complexity. An entirely directed isomorphic path from any specialized vehicle type to any specialized energy type can now be seen: Since *is: BEV → Vehicle, has: Vehicle → PowerSystem, uses: PowerSystem → Energy, canBe: Energy → ElectricalEnergy*} is a series of mappings where each mapping's codomain is the following mapping's domain, then the sequence (*is · has · uses · canBe*) is a composition that abstracts simply as *uses*": *BEVuses"ElectricalEnergy*. Also, consider *BEVuses"ElectricalEnergy* as an instantiation of the pattern defined in Figure 18.8. Therefore, statements such as the following can also be made:

- *BEV is a Vehicle that uses' ElectricalEnergy*
- *BEV is a Vehicle that has a PowerSystem that uses ElectricalEnergy*
- *BEV has a PowerSystem that uses' ElectricalEnergy*

No statement is objectively more helpful or relevant than another: They are all based on suitable compositions. However, subjectively, one may be preferred over another. High semantic value—significant meaning—is typically attributed to longer chains.

BEV, BPS, and ElectricalEnergy are specific *objects* that represent *instances* rather than *types*. Instances implement the properties of the type (or class) they are molded from. The compositional mappings among the various types and instance objects are illustrated in Figure 18.11. The indirect mappings are shown in dashed lines, the instance objects are labeled in bold text, while the type objects are marked in italics.

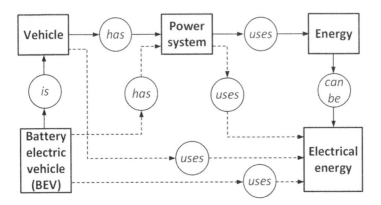

Figure 18.11 Composition and abstraction of BEV *is · has · uses · can Be* Electrical Energy.

18.5.5 A Generalized Definition of a Category for System Design

Category theory's powerful capability to define systems generally or, specifically, at any level of abstraction facilitates definitions of abstract interactions with system constructs. Abstraction conceals the internal structure or workings of a system. Any system or subsystem has or can have smaller subsystems or components, and any system can use various resources. Abstract categories capture a broad class of interactions among components and resources. Our abstract category includes the *System* and *Resource* types and generalizes the relations *has* and *uses* to these types. This generalized category of systems and resources is illustrated in Figure 18.12. *System* is shadowed only for visual distinction. Any subsystem and resource can be encoded in the BEV architecture as instances of generic types. The specialized types and instances implement the mappings that apply to the generic types.

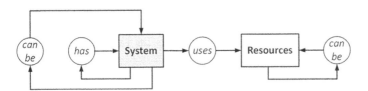

Figure 18.12 A generalized category of systems and resources.

18.5.6 Integrating Categories

How a category can capture direct and indirect mappings among various system concepts has been discussed. As systems become complex and multifaceted, capturing everything in a single category is impossible. However, a combination of categories can capture the system's full scope. The following presents an approach to integrate two categories: boundary objects and full-category mappings.

Boundary Objects. Boundary objects are objects in one category that may appear in other categories. Each boundary object has a 1:1 equivalence mapping to a twin object in another category. Resources are intuitive boundary objects. For example, the low-voltage current flowing from the power converter through the auxiliary battery to the auxiliary systems is a boundary object. It appears in the electrical propulsion and auxiliary systems categories, as shown in Figure 18.13. The boundary objects are depicted with a thick contour line to indicate their role as boundary objects. Another example of a boundary object is the torque the electric motor provides to the transmission in the electrical propulsion and mechanical propulsion categories.

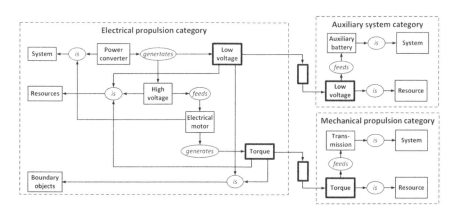

Figure 18.13 Boundary objects between categories.

Boundary objects may not necessarily be resources, inputs, or outputs. Components can also be boundary objects. For example, a steering wheel is a boundary object in a direct mechanical interface with the driver. The wheels are also boundary objects in direct contact with the road. The notion that the physical touch or friction between the surfaces is the boundary object is also a valid argument. Category theory accommodates any level of abstraction that is desired or needed. There may not need to be a focus on the friction between the hands of the driver and the steering wheel, but there may be a desire to model and understand the friction between the wheel and the road. Each problem has a suitable abstraction level.

Design parameters (DPs) are attributes that impact the design, structure, and behavior of the system or specific components. DPs are also boundary objects. Parametric design (PD) captures these critical attributes and articulates the design using relations among DPs. For example, the electrical charge that can be stored in the batteries affects the vehicle's driving range. CT allows us to define critical attributes as DPs and compositional algebraic formulations of behavior, performance, and dependent attributes.

Integrating design paradigms and spaces through categories is as simple as coordinating the boundary objects. The set of boundary objects shared by two categories comprises the interface between these categories. The boundary objects inside each category can be classified as a boundary to or from other categories. Digital engineering environments may help us coordinate the representations of the boundary objects to prevent misalignment. For example, suppose the electrical propulsion system designer updates the low-voltage current specification to include the magnitude of the current in ampere units. In that case, it can automatically appear in the auxiliary systems category.

Functor. A functor is a mapping between two or more categories. It maps the objects and morphisms of one category to the objects and morphisms of the other. The functor maps everything from one category to another, while a morphism maps inside a category. Mathematically, a functor is a morphism in the category of categories, where categories are the objects, and functors are the morphisms. Due to their unique role in mapping whole categories to each other, functors have been branded with a separate term. In addition, the idea of a functor (between categories) closely resembles a function between sets. Sets and functions make the objects and morphisms in the category of sets.

Various categories can be mapped to each other—not only subsystem design categories. For example, systems engineers often need to maintain a bill of materials (BOM) and an interface control document (ICD). A BOM is a list or hierarchy of the system's components. An ICD is a list of all the flows in the system, into and out of each subsystem. These two lists should be defined as design categories, and mappings from each disciplinary design category should be defined to these categories.

Defining cross-cutting BOM and ICD categories requires abstracting the design categories. The generic systems and resources category (*SRCat*) that was previously defined can be beneficial here. Suppose a mapping from *SRCat* to a BOM category (*BOM*) and an ICD category (*ICD*) is defined. This mapping applies to all the design categories based on *SRCat*, thanks to the composability attribute.

A functor from *SRCat* to the ICD category $F1: SRCat \rightarrow ICD$ maps the boundary resources in *SRCat* to boundary objects in *ICD*. Internal resources are not exported to ICD. Instead, the ICD's boundary object is associated with the subsystem's blackbox object, concealing internal details. As a result, component design experts can modify the internal design and add or replace components to the boundary object generation pipeline without changing the ICD (at least not the boundary object). Conversely, a functor from *SRCat* to *BOM*, *F2*: *SRCat* → *BOM* maps internal subsystems as components of a blackbox object that represents the entire subsystem. The functors that map *SRCat* to *BOM* and *ICD*—*F1* and *F2*, respectively—are illustrated in Figure 18.14.

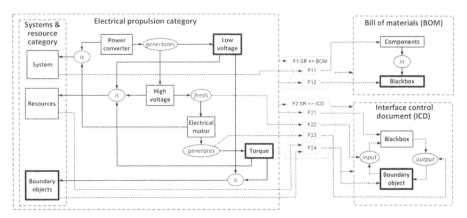

Figure 18.14   Functors that map component design categories to system design categories.

The electrical propulsion category is an instance of *SRCat* that contains the types defined in *SRCat*. Accordingly, any functor that applies to *SRCat* applies to the electrical propulsion category. The result is that the functors *F1* and *F2* apply to the objects and morphisms in the electrical propulsion category. In our case, *F2*: *SRCat* → *ICD* is defined as follows:

1. *SRCat* → *Blackbox*. This mapping projects the category into a blackbox type in the *ICD* category.
2. $O_i|\{O_i \in SRCat, O_i \in Dom(is \mid cod(is) = Resource), O_i \in B(SRCat)\}$ → *Boundary Object*. This covers any object that meets these criteria:
   a. The object O_i is an object in a category *SRCat*.
   b. The object O_i is a resource: It is in the domain of the *is* mapping whose codomain is *Resource*, representing the resource type. Note that subsystems are also in the domain of *is*, but the codomain is *System*. Hence, they are not considered resources.
   c. The object O_i is a boundary object: It is in the set of boundary objects of the *SRCat*.
3. $feeds|O_i \in cod(feeds)$ → $to(BoundaryObject, Blackbox)$. This mapping projects the feeds morphism itself as an input morphism between the *BoundaryObject* and the *Blackbox*. Note that in our example, no object qualifies as an input flow. The boundary object for the home outlet power can be defined as an input flow.
4. $generates|O_i \in dom(generates)$ → $from(BoundaryObject, Blackbox)$. This mapping projects the generated morphism as an output morphism between

the *BoundaryObject* and the *Blackbox*. In our example, *LowVolumeCurrent* and *Torque* qualify as output flows.

The mapping to *ICD* enables tracking and monitoring changes to the category, and any change to these four rules entails an ICD change. An automated verification can be easily implemented here and help raise flags or issue updates regarding projected modifications in other categories. Simple representations of transformations using categorical logic are extremely helpful in facilitating integration among categories. This case highlights transitions to a conceptual or integrative category, such as *ICD* or *BOM*, rather than a logical subsystem category. This example demonstrates how design categories can focus on any vertical or horizontal aspect of the system.

18.6 Categorical Multidisciplinary Collaborative Design (C-MCD)

This section presents a categorical multidisciplinary collaborative design (C-MCD) framework based on category theory. C-MCD integrates inputs from various stakeholders, perspectives, disciplines, and knowledge bases. Essentially, C-MCD synthesizes knowledge formalisms, represented as expert models. An expert model (EM) is a formal specification that contains two different sets of objects: (1) generic disciplinary expertise, knowledge, and know-how and (2) design specifications for the particular problem, system of interest, and solution, including design assumptions, constraints, and requirements. In addition, the output of the EM includes expertise-based design guidance.

EMs can be generated as, with, or from computer-aided design (CAD) models, wiring diagrams, systems modeling language (SysML) models, object-process methodology (OPM) models, Simulink models, analytical models, data spreadsheets, and so on. In order to serve and function as an EM, a design model has to (1) receive and maintain generic streams of reference data, (2) receive and maintain case-specific streams of reference data, and (3) fuse the streams and generate a common set of reference data, which semantically represents a design. A requirement is several knowledge representations that complement the EM and comprise a holistic iterative design process that accommodates and facilitates collaboration among multiple design disciplines. As a categorical framework, C-MCD consists of the following categories:

1. A central knowledge base (CKB), denoted as C1, that includes a formal reference to the problem and solution as they evolve throughout the system's life cycle
2. A collection of expert knowledge bases (EKB), denoted as C2x (where each x represents a single field of expertise), that specify disciplinary expertise that informs and affects EM

3. A collection of expert models (EM), denoted as C3x (where x represents a single discipline), that specify disciplinary design guidance based on the standard reference and disciplinary expertise
4. A semantic integration model (SIM), denoted as C4, defines a set of rules that map disciplinary constructs in expert models into a common system language
5. An integrated design graph (IDG), denoted as C5, fuses information from all the expert models into a unified view according to rules defined in the semantic integration model
6. A collection of integrated design views (IDV), denoted as C6v (where v represents a single view), that derive information from the IDG and present it to stakeholders in various visualization formats and methods (e.g., diagrams, matrices, simulations)

Following category theory, the mappings among the categories are specified as functors. The functor names are encoded as follows: F_SN_TN: $SC \rightarrow TC$, where:

- SN is the number of the source category (1.6 as defined above, where some categories are also denoted by a serial number like 2x, 3x, and 6v).
- TN is the number of the target category.
- SC is the acronym of the source category: CKB, EM, IDG, and so on.
- TC is the acronym of the target category.

The categories and functors are depicted in directed graphs (Figure 18.15) and are defined below.

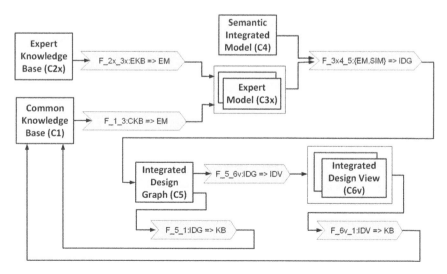

Figure 18.15 Categorical multidisciplinary collaborative design (C-MCD) framework.

1. A functor from the CKB (C1) to each EM (C3x), denoted F_1_3, is a singular functor that provides the entire knowledge base in a standard form to any consumer.
2. A functor set from each EKB (C2x) to its EMs (C3x), denoted F_2x_3x, populates a problem-oriented EM with disciplinary tenets and generic design expertise.
3. A functor set from each EM (C3x) in conjunction with the SIM (C4) into the IDG (C5), denoted F_3x4_5 (where the first item represents a combination of each EM category with the SIM category).
4. A functor set from the integrated design graph (C5) into each IDV (C6v), denoted F_5_6v.
5. A feedback functor from the interface design graph (C5) into the CKB (C1), denoted F_5_1.
6. A feedback functor set from each IDV (C6v) into the CKB (C1), denoted F_6v_1.

18.7 The C-MCD Categories

C-MCD uses representations of categories as directed graphs. These graphs specify any category as tuples comprising the (c, r, s, t, u, v) components, where c is the name/identifier of the category, r is the name/identifier of the relation/morphism/mapping, s is the source/domain object, t is the target/codomain object, u is a unique identifier of the mapping, and v is a version identifier. This single tuple structure can encode and represent any category. In addition, combining categories is as simple and trivial as vertically concatenating the first category's tuple set with the second category's tuple set. As a result, all the C-MCD categories can be represented as the tuple set of a directed graph. The graph stores tuples in a way that is indifferent to their consumption, utilization, and analysis. This graph arrangement allows for separating syntax from semantics. The category can be analyzed with many graph-theoretic methods, techniques, tools, and algorithms.

18.7.1 Central Knowledge Base (CKB)

The central knowledge base is a shared repository of requirements, constraints, and general design guidelines that refer to the system as a whole, not necessarily to specific design disciplines. Initially, the CKB includes stakeholder requirements and system requirements. As the solution architecture evolves, it will also have the reviewed and approved parts of the architecture.

Figure 18.16 depicts a simple central knowledge graph defining cost requirements for the power system. The figure and text show two cost requirements for an electric vehicle using the object process methodology (OPM) language (Dori, 2016). The visual part on the left-hand side is a conceptual model that defines a structure with attributes, functions, and outputs. OPM represents objects with rectangles, states, or values within this rectangle and processes or functions within ovals. OPM uses special graphic symbols for common generic relations such as aggregation (black triangle), exhibition (triangle-wrapping triangle), and generalization (blank triangle). OPM also includes a formal, automatically generated textual specification of the diagram in natural language, as shown on the right-hand side of the figure.

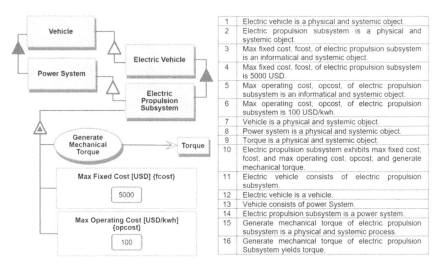

1	Electric vehicle is a physical and systemic object.
2	Electric propulsion subsystem is a physical and systemic object.
3	Max fixed cost, fcost, of electric propulsion subsystem is an informatical and systemic object.
4	Max fixed cost, fcost, of electric propulsion subsystem is 5000 USD.
5	Max operating cost, opcost, of electric propulsion subsystem is an informatical and systemic object.
6	Max operating cost, opcost, of electric propulsion subsystem is 100 USD/kwh.
7	Vehicle is a physical and systemic object.
8	Power system is a physical and systemic object.
9	Torque is a physical and systemic object.
10	Electric propulsion subsystem exhibits max fixed cost, fcost, and max operating cost, opcost, and generate mechanical torque.
11	Electric vehicle consists of electric propulsion subsystem.
12	Electric vehicle is a vehicle.
13	Vehicle consists of power System.
14	Electric propulsion subsystem is a power system.
15	Generate mechanical torque of electric propulsion subsystem is a physical and systemic process.
16	Generate mechanical torque of electric propulsion Subsystem yields torque.

Figure 18.16 Central knowledge graph defining cost requirements for the power system.[3]

The two cost requirements specified in the OPM model—maximum fixed cost and maximum operating cost—apply at least three different expert models: (1) the electric propulsion design model; (2) the cost breakdown model; and (3) the reliability, availability, maintainability, and safety (RAMS) model. In addition, the third model includes artifacts that may impact or be impacted by cost constraints,

---

3 Created using OPCloud (https://opcloud.systems/).

such as the cost of maintaining the battery, which affects the operating cost. Moreover, other subsystems may need this information for their calculations or decisions.

The CKB is distributed to all design experts regardless of their role or discipline. Each design expert may decide to adopt, refine, adjust, or even ignore some parts of the central model. Once the knowledge is delivered to a design expert, it is within the expert's discretion to determine how to use it as part of the model they own and maintain. This is also an example of the transferability of categorically representable knowledge from one EM with its modeling language and design domain to another EM, which may use different representation and design paradigms. Finally, Table 18.3 translates the specification of the OPM diagram into a set of category statements.

Table 18.3 Categorical Representation in the OPM Model.

Category	Domain	Morphism	Codomain
C11_EP	Vehicle	generalizes	Electric Vehicle
C11_EP	Vehicle	aggregates	Power System
C11_EP	Power System	generalizes	Electric Propulsion Subsystem
C11_EP	Electric Vehicle	aggregates	Electric Propulsion Subsystem
C11_EP	Electric Propulsion Subsystem	exhibits	Max Fixed Cost [USD] {fcost}
C11_EP	Electric Propulsion Subsystem	exhibits	Max Operating Cost [USD/kwh] {opcost}
C11_EP	Electric Propulsion Subsystem	exhibits	Generate Mechanical Torque
C11_EP	Generate Mechanical Torque	outputs	Torque
C11_EP	Max Fixed Cost [USD] {fcost}	hasState	5000
C11_EP	Max Operating Cost [USD/kwh] {opcost}	hasState	100

18.7.2 Expert Knowledge Base (EKB)

An expert knowledge base is a category of design rules or patterns encoded as graph tuples. Nodes can be design elements in EMs, and relations can be valid design morphisms among those design elements. Indeed, the purpose of EKB is to define subsets of relationship patterns that together represent some integrated perspective on the design. Some examples discussed in Section 18.5 qualify as design rules or patterns. For example, while it is evident and trivial that any vehicle should have a power system (whether a combustion engine or a battery), power system designers may have more design guidelines to encode and utilize when considering a power system design problem, for instance, automotive power electronics should typically live about 15 years; support 12,000 operating hours and 54,000 engines on/off cycles; and qualify on rigorous pressure, shock, vibration, and temperature tests (Scheuermann, 2009).

An EKB graph that defines two of the above standard requirements—a 15-year life span and 12,000-hour operational time—is illustrated both in graphical form (Figure 18.17) and in tabular form (Table 18.4). This design pattern constrains any power system (PS) component to meet these design requirements. The composition can be seen [PS exhibits OpHrs/Lifespan, OpHrs/Lifespan is an Attribute, Attribute applies_to Component]. Design rules also imply a reciprocal path using isomorphism.

Note that all its components must also exhibit the same attribute the PS exhibits. Therefore, if a component exhibits Attribute, Attribute canBe OpHrs/ LifeSpan, OpHrs is greater than or equal to (gteq) 12000hr / Lifespan gteq 15yr]. If this design pattern is imported into a case-specific PS expert model, these design rules can be applied as case-specific design specifications. These values may also be traded against other factors, such as the cost or weight dictated by the KB.

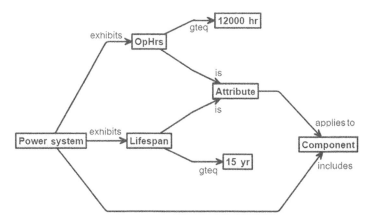

Figure 18.17 Expert knowledge graph defining power system life span and operational hours.[4]

___

4 Created using online diagram editing tool (https://nomnoml.com/).

Table 18.4 Categorical Representation of Power System Life Span and Operation Hours.

Category	Domain	Morphism	Codomain	Nomnoml Statement
C21_PS	Power System	exhibits	OpHrs	[Power System] → exhibits [OpHrs]
C21_PS	Power System	exhibits	Lifespan	[Power System] → exhibits [Lifespan]
C21_PS	OpHrs	gteq	12000hr	[OpHrs] → gteq [12000hr]
C21_PS	Lifespan	gteq	15yr	[Lifespan] → gteq [15yr]
C21_PS	OpHrs	is	Attribute	[OpHrs] → is [Attribute]
C21_PS	Lifespan	is	Attribute	[Lifespan] → is [Attribute]
C21_PS	Power System	includes	Component	[Power System] → includes [Component]
C21_PS	Attribute	applies_to	Component	[Attribute] → applies_to [Component]

Note: OpHrs = operational hours; gteq = greater than or equal to

18.7.3 Expert Models (EM)

An expert model (EM) is a category in which design elements are the objects, and design relations are the morphisms. EMs encode specific knowledge about designing and about designs. It may be generic, domain-specific, or solution-specific. An example EM that draws on the expert knowledge graph presented above is illustrated in Figure 18.18 and Table 18.5. This EM applies the design rules from the expert graph to a specific solution component—in this case, the charger, which is part of a battery PS. Notice that the model does not necessarily adhere to the guidance. In this case, the PS is electrical, has no moving parts, and can be active for more operational hours. OpHrs, which is an inherited OpHrs attribute for a specific instance of the type Component, equals 18,000, whereas the baseline design guidance is 12,000 hours. However, its actual life span of 12 years is shorter than the required life span of 15 years due to the degradation in the battery capacity over time.

The information in the EM may affect the vehicle's life cycle cost since it will require replacing the battery after 12 years on average. It may also result in excess annualized cost over an equivalent period of the 15 years the car is active. The second battery may be salvaged when the vehicle reaches 15 years and gets scrapped, but it probably will not compensate for the additional cost. These considerations directly impact the cost structure and maintenance models. They may also have an impact on other subsystem design models. This information can serve as a revised reference for the other EM and affect their design decisions by being fed into the IDG and, from there, back into the CKB.

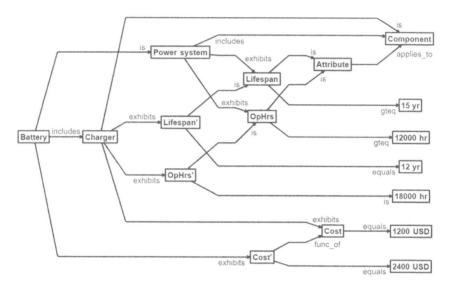

Figure 18.18 Battery-powered system expert model applying design rules to components.[5]

Table 18.5 Categorical Representation of Onboard Charger Life Span and Operation Hours.

Category	Domain	Morphism	Codomain	Nomnoml Statement
C31_OC	OpHrs	gteq	12000hr	[OpHrs] → gteq [12000hr]
C31_OC	Lifespan	gteq	15yr	[Lifespan] → gteq [15yr]
C31_OC	Lifespan'	equals	12yr	[Lifespan'] → equals [12yr]
C31_OC	Lifespan'	is	Lifespan	[Lifespan'] → is [Lifespan]
C31_OC	OpHrs	is	Attribute	[OpHrs] → is [Attribute]
C31_OC	Lifespan	is	Attribute	[Lifespan] → is [Attribute]
C31_OC	Power System	includes	Component	[Power System] → includes [Component]

(Continued)

_____
5 Created using online diagram editing tool (https://nomnoml.com/).

Table 18.5 (Continued)

Category	Domain	Morphism	Codomain	Nomnoml Statement
C31_OC	Attribute	applies_to	Component	[Attribute] → applies_to [Component]
C31_OC	Battery	is	Power System	[Battery] → is [Power System]
C31_OC	Battery	includes	Charger	[Battery] → includes [Charger]
C31_OC	Charger	exhibits	OpHrs'	[Charger] → exhibits [OpHrs']
C31_OC	Charger	exhibits	Lifespan'	[Charger] → exhibits [Lifespan']
C31_OC	OpHrs'	is	OpHrs	[OpHrs'] → is [OpHrs]
C31_OC	OpHrs'	is	18000hr	[OpHrs'] → is [18000hr]
C31_OC	Charger	is	Component	[Charger] → is [Component]
C31_OC	Charger	exhibits	Cost	[Charger] → exhibits [Cost]
C31_OC	Cost	equals	1200USD	[Cost] → equals [1200USD]
C31_OC	Cost'	func_of	Cost	[Cost'] → func_of [Cost]
C31_OC	Cost'	equals	2400USD	[Cost'] → equals [2400USD]
C31_OC	Battery	exhibits	Cost'	[Battery] → exhibits [Cost']
C31_OC	Power System	exhibits	OpHrs	[Power System] → exhibits [OpHrs]

EMs may require some transformation into a categorical structure. The simplicity of the data structure is its most potent advantage—the ability to represent any artifact or relation makes it incredibly easy to perform this transformation. The ontological classification of design objects is more challenging, particularly regarding boundary objects. General-purpose systems ontologies, enterprise or domain terminologies, or recognized international standards may provide the necessary information.

Many organizations follow an evolutionary ontology approach—they train systems designers to reason about classifying elements, particularly abstractions. Then, when a new term is necessary, they determine where it fits in the terminology or add it. For example, terms like *redundancy* or *low-energy device* may emerge during the design and make their way into the terminology on first use. Others may consider or be expected to utilize them as part of their work.

The proposed approach is a powerful enabler of parametric design (PD). As explained, PD defines and utilizes standard design parameters in formulating the design concept and guidance for various system components and aspects. The performance and quality attributes presented above may constitute design parameters. Defining and utilizing these attributes as design parameters is supported by referring to them as boundary objects that permeate the design space through their sharing and dissemination. The transformation of EM primarily supports this into an integrated design graph (IDG), as is described next.

18.7.4 Integrated Design Graphs (IDG)

Integrated design graphs (IDG) integrate knowledge from disparate EM and represent specific aspects. The IDG consumes EM statements as domain-morphism-codomain triplets, with boundary objects of the individual EM categories as domain/codomain members. IDG can draw from the subset of shareable artifacts each EM exposes as visible artifacts that affect the integrated design. This may be the entire scope of an EM or a subset the design expert decides to expose. Each IDG can represent several aspects. The IDG in Figure 18.19 shows a joint view of the EMs, primary subsystems, components, and their relations.

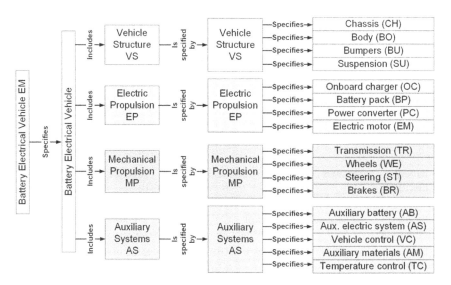

Figure 18.19 Integrated design graph mapping attributes to system attributes.

This IDG resembles the system architecture breakdown diagram in Figure 18.4. However, the IDG combines EM categories and boundary objects—the BEV system, subsystems, and components. The set of triplets in Table 18.6 is derived from the joint set of public triplets of all the design categories. It shows the relations among EMs, the system of interest, subsystems, and components. The architecture can be modified by updating the set of triplets and re-rendering the diagram from the updated set.

Table 18.6 Categorical Statements of an Integrated Design Graph.

Domain	Morphism	Codomain	NomnoML.com
Auxiliary Systems	isSpecifiedBy	Auxiliary Systems EM	[<cat> Battery Electrical Vehicle EM] → specifies [Battery Electrical Vehicle]
Auxiliary Systems EM	specifies	Auxiliary battery (AB)	[Battery Electrical Vehicle] → includes [Vehicle Structure]
		Auxiliary materials (AM)	[Battery Electrical Vehicle] → includes [Electrical Propulsion]
		Operating system (OS)	[Battery Electrical Vehicle] → includes [Mechanical propulsion]
		Temperature control (TC)	[Battery Electrical Vehicle] → includes [Auxiliary Systems]
		Vehicle control (VC)	[Vehicle Structure] → is specified by [<cat> Vehicle Structure EM]
Battery Electrical Vehicle	includes	Auxiliary Systems	[Electrical Propulsion] → is specified by [<cat> Electrical Propulsion EM]
		Electrical Propulsion	[Mechanical Propulsion] → is specified by [<cat> Mechanical Propulsion EM]
		Mechanical Propulsion	[Auxiliary Systems] → is specified by [<cat> Auxiliary Systems EM]
		Vehicle Structure	[Vehicle Structure EM] → specifies [Chassis (CH)]
Battery Electrical Vehicle EM	specifies	Battery Electrical Vehicle	[Vehicle Structure EM] → specifies [Body (BO)]
Electrical Propulsion	isSpecifiedBy	Electrical Propulsion EM	[Vehicle Structure EM] → specifies [Bumpers (BU)]
Electrical Propulsion EM	specifies	Battery pack (BP)	[Vehicle Structure EM] → specifies [Suspension (SU)]
		Electric motor (EM)	[Electrical Propulsion EM] → specifies [Onboard charger (OC)]
		Onboard charger (OC)	[Electrical Propulsion EM] → specifies [Battery pack (BP)]
		Power converter (PC)	[Electrical Propulsion EM] → specifies [Power converter (PC)]
Low Voltage Current	flowsTo	Auxiliary battery (AB)	[Electrical Propulsion EM] → specifies [Electric motor (EM)]

Table 18.6 (Continued)

Domain	Morphism	Codomain	NomnoML.com
Mechanical Propulsion	isSpecifiedBy	Mechanical Propulsion EM	[Mechanical Propulsion EM] → specifies [Transmission (TR)]
Mechanical Propulsion EM	specifies	Brakes (BR)	[Mechanical Propulsion EM] → specifies [Wheels (WE)]
		Steering (ST)	[Mechanical Propulsion EM] → specifies [Steering (ST)]
		Transmission (TR)	[Mechanical Propulsion EM] → specifies [Brakes (BR)]
		Wheels (WE)	[Auxiliary Systems EM] → specifies [Auxiliary battery (AB)]
Power Converter (PC)	generates	Low Voltage Current	[Auxiliary Systems EM] → specifies [Operating system (OS)]
Vehicle Structure	isSpecifiedBy	Vehicle Structure EM	[Auxiliary Systems EM] → specifies [Vehicle control (VC)]
Vehicle Structure EM	specifies	Body (BO)	[Auxiliary Systems EM] → specifies [Auxiliary materials (AM)]
		Bumpers (BU)	[Auxiliary Systems EM] → specifies [Temperature control (TC)]
		Chassis (CH)	[Power converter (PC)] → generates [Low Voltage Current]
		Suspension (SU)	[Low Voltage Current] → feeds [Auxiliary battery (AB)]

Various IDG may now be created to aggregate system component attributes, such as costs, masses, volumes, power consumptions, or operating hours. Each of these may have a separate IDG with its aggregation function—a simple sum or a more complex calculation. For example, the number of vehicle operating hours is determined as $MIN(OpHrs_1, .., OpHrs_i, .., OpHrs_N)$ of all the components. The system initialization time will be calculated as $MAX(T_1, .., T_i, .., T_N)$, where T_i is the initialization time of component i. Some abstract combination schemes may be captured only as complex functions, requiring elaborate algebraic, logical, or textual aggregations behind the scenes.

IDG may be visually similar, where the difference is primarily in (1) types that are imported into the IDG (mainly boundary objects) and (2) mappings among the design attributes and the system attributes. The semantic integration model (SIM) maps boundary objects' names, types, and values to integrated design model values. The SIM is used to determine the semantics of IDG constructs during the construction of the IDG from the boundary objects of the EMs. The SIM can convert names, types, and units of measurement; it can merge and combine artifacts, filter out artifacts that should not be included in the IDG, and so on. The SIM is the codex that affects how the functor from EM to IDG will behave.

The IDG shown here is only a small-scale visualization, which may not necessarily scale up very well when the integrated design consists of dozens of aspects, hundreds of components, functions, and so on. Moreover, the actual value of information is not in the illustrative visualization of the graph. However, experts may quickly detect anomalies and make various inferences by looking at the graph. The tabular [C, R, S, T] structure of relations represents the graph more robustly. Moreover, it is amenable to various analyses, including multiple cross-products of this table, to infer higher-order compositions.

18.7.5 Integrated Design Views (IDV)

There is no limit to the types of visualizations and representations that can be applied to the IDG. Some practical examples include design structure matrices (DSM), inputs to system simulations, aggregations over common attributes in the IDG, point-to-point connectivity analyses, and so on. Stakeholder need is the primary driver of view generation. Therefore, design experts should specify visualizations and representations that improve their capability to deliver better designs. Many compositions represent interpretations or additional considerations with advanced semantics. Several examples are reviewed next.

Design Structure Matrices. The DSM in Figure 18.5 is obtained by creating compositions of the *generates* morphism with the *feeds* morphism, defined syntactically as *generates · flowsTo* and semantically as *feeds*. The *feeds* composition's domain, *dom(generates)*, is the output provider, while the morphism is specified through *cod(generates)* = *dom(flowsTo)* as the specific I/O resource. The construct's codomain, which is *cod(flowsTo)*, is the input receiver. A composition triplet in which the I/O resource acts as a morphism is created by mapping the output provider to the input receiver. The kernel of the DSM shown in Figure 18.5 is created by placing the domain objects of the I/O composition in the rows and the codomain objects in the columns. The row structure can be built as a hierarchy of subsystems and output-providing components using the immediately available *aggregates/includes* morphism (depending on the representation language). *aggregates · generates · flowsTo · composes* can be composed to obtain a subsystem-I/O-subsystem composition, abstract the components, and keep only the subsystems as black boxes.

Flow Abstraction. The level of abstraction in I/O flow representation depends on our goal and perspective and on the design problem whose solution is sought. I/O mappings are often represented directly. For example, the flow item or signal labels the flow arrows between pairs of subsystems or components in informal wiring diagrams. Significant information about the I/O resource is abstracted (or ignored) by not capturing it as an object. Moreover, the composition that starts at the output provider and ends at the input receiver is an abstraction and perception of a series of steps that may not necessarily be strongly coupled. Generators that emit output *regardless of* the action of reception or consumption by input receivers include broadcasting devices; sources that emit light that an observer may pick up; commands or messages that are sent over a network and may be read by a listening port; and mechanical force generated by the rotation of wheels and tires, which can happen while the vehicle is on the road, but also when it is on a lift, where no external surface interfaces with the tires.

Neighbor Detection. The composition *neighbors = composes · includes*, which is defined such that $dom(composes)! = cod(includes)$ is defined; that is, each system component can potentially neighbor all other system components except itself. This appraisal may seem like a trivial graph theory exercise. However, design knowledge discovery in the form of neighboring component detection may be valuable for any design team working on a specific component in a large-scale complex system with a growing number of components when one design team is not necessarily aware of the other teams. Various compositions of such a nature can be defined and sought with a generic, abstract approach.

Emergent Patterns. Experts may define new and meaningful semantics for compositions. These new semantics give rise to emergent, indirect, and nontrivial design patterns. For example, the composition *specifies · composes* means *refines*: Each EM refines the system with a specialized component design model. Similarly, *includes · performs* means abstracts: The system abstracts the functions that are performed by the subsystems.

Anomaly Detection. Sets of morphisms can be analyzed and searched for cases of empty rows or empty columns. Blank rows in an I/O matrix indicate design entities with no outbound mapping—they never provide output. An empty column indicates design entities with no inbound mapping—they never receive any input. Such a finding may suggest that the design is partial, requiring additional work, or that some components are unnecessary or redundant.

Inference of Isomorphisms. Designers should not have to specify reciprocal morphisms for each morphism. For example, the *generates* morphism is reciprocated by an *isGeneratedBy* morphism from the resource to the output generator. Reciprocal morphisms may have various uses. A categorical analysis algorithm can complement these morphisms. Design teams can utilize reciprocal morphisms without the elaborate and cumbersome effort of specifying them explicitly.

18.8 The Categorical Design Process

We advocate for a comprehensive adoption and implementation process that constitutes a critical enabler of our categorical multimodal collaborative design (C-MCD) approach. The process enables stakeholders to generate the formal artifacts described and demonstrated in the previous sections of this chapter. Essentially, the proposed process is a method for identifying crucial relevant knowledge for capitalization during collaborative systems design. The method formalizes the knowledge extraction task, allows upscaling to accommodate various needs, and reduces execution time. This method is derived from the method presented by Fradi and colleagues (2022). Figure 18.20 illustrates an overview of the process.

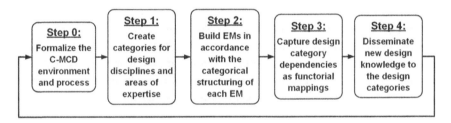

Figure 18.20 The categorical design process.

18.8.1 Step 0: Formalize the C-MCD Environment and Process

A design process expert (DPE)—a person or a team—shall oversee the entire C-MCD process. The DPE shall own and specify the process, train, and mentor designers on working effectively within the process context, and build or acquire tools and techniques that allow designers and design stakeholders to interact with the process and collaborate. The DPE shall create a list of subject matter experts (SME) and design stakeholders as well as acquire information regarding their expertise, work methods, tools, and know-how. This list shall be the first knowledge artifact all design teams should know. As a design expert for the design process, the DPE shall create and maintain an expert model (EM) of the relevant design disciplines for the system of interest. This EM is not necessarily an organizational chart, but it can help drive managerial decisions, outsourcing, insourcing decisions, and so on.

18.8.2 Step 1: Create Categories for Design Disciplines and Areas of Expertise

The DPE shall create categories for disciplines and aspects of the design. Typically, these categories correspond to the responsibility areas of the SME and should be defined in collaboration with the SME. Accordingly, each EM shall be an implementation of a particular category. For example, a thermal design category generalizes all the EM that deal with the thermal aspects of the system. Therefore, it is necessary to define the boundary objects of each category and, consequently, the boundary objects of the EM. The boundary objects are the objects that act as the interfaces of the category—the inputs and outputs, the operators and operands, and the design attributes or parameters. These objects must be public and shared, whereas the internal workings of the category may not necessarily be further elaborated.

18.8.3 Step 2: Build EMs in accordance with the Categorical Structuring of Each EM

Each SME shall build a collection of EMs according to the definition of the category. The EM will likely require or provide additional boundary objects. Each boundary object that the EM requires as an input must be defined in the model. The DPE must determine the object's origin and, accordingly, verify the availability of the object as an outbound boundary object of the originating category or EM. Similarly, when a boundary object is provided, it should be shared with the other design disciplines so that they may consider its relevance to their design process or solution. In that case, they must define corresponding boundary objects in their category/EM and find the appropriate way to utilize them.

18.8.4 Step 3: Capture Design Category Dependencies as Functorial Mappings

The PDE and SME shall build functors that map design categories to each other and generate representations of relations among categories as mappings in the category of design categories. Each design category and EM will likely include multiple objects and morphisms. However, they may be unable to capture dependencies and interactions with external design categories, EM, and design artifacts. The PDE should capture each boundary object of each design category in the integrated design category so that the integrated category may serve as a mediator and integrator of interfaces and interactions among design categories. The PDE should capture mappings representing dependencies among parameters, attributes, and functions in the integrated design category.

18.8.5   Step 4: Disseminate New Design Knowledge to the Design Categories

The PDE shall share design knowledge across design categories and EMs, a holistic view of the dependencies, and relationships among categories. Decision-makers shall determine the depth level of dependencies necessary and valuable for external design experts to be informed about. Accordingly, the team should specify compositions of two, three, four, or even more morphisms with emergent semantics and explain how any two objects are related. The team shall construct and generate the dependencies and indirect relations that may be critical and useful for the various design experts.

18.9   Conclusion

Considering the increased complexity of engineered systems, systems engineers should adopt formal, reliable, and collaborative design methods. The formal framework proposed in this chapter enables crucial knowledge identification and utilization during the multidisciplinary collaborative design process. This framework is based on the category theory called categorical multidisciplinary collaborative design (C-MCD). A categorical approach to knowledge transformation and the recording of design knowledge is critical in enabling evolving system design in a multidisciplinary environment.

Four critical challenges that systems engineers face in such environments have been discussed—tracing requirements to the design, integrating design decisions, tracking design evolution, and "speaking" diverse design languages. It has been shown how the categorical approach empowers system designers to tackle these challenges by formally representing systems concepts as objects (types and instances) and mappings within and between categories (morphisms and functors, respectively). The chapter has demonstrated each definition and step of the process through a notional battery electric vehicle design problem and the consideration of various system aspects.

The categorical approach does not materially change the MCD process. However, this is desired since systems engineers should be allowed to continue working similarly, delivering the same outcomes and artifacts in a more rigorous, robust, scalable, and coordinated manner. Readers should feel comfortable immediately putting the C-MCD approach to the test, as few preconditions are needed for adoption, and categorical thinking can be quickly taught and explained. This chapter has demonstrated every concept and step in our method with simple desktop tools like drawing software, free online graph editing tools, and spreadsheets.

18.10   Acknowledgment

Dr. Yaniv Mordecai wrote the category theory portion of this chapter. The author of this book is deeply indebted to Dr. Mordecai for contributing to this book.

18.11   Bibliography

Camba, J.D., Contero, M., and Company, P. (2016). Parametric CAD modeling: An analysis of strategies for design reusability. *CAD Computer Aided Design* 74: 18–31. https://doi.org/10.1016/j.cad.2016.01.003.

Dori, D. (2016). *Model-Based Systems Engineering with OPM and SysML* (Vol. 15). Springer.

Fradi, M., Gaha, R., Mhenni, F., Mlika, A., & Choley, J. Y. (2022). Knowledge capitalization in mechatronic collaborative design. *Concurrent Engineering Research and Applications* 30 (1): 32–45. https://doi.org/10.1177/10632 93X211050438.

Mordecai, Y. and Engel A. (2023, April). Multimodal system design integration using category theory. The 17th annual IEEE International Systems Conference (SysCon2023), April 17–20, 2023, Vancouver, Canada.

Mordecai, Y., Fairbanks, J.P., and Crawley, E.F. (2021). Category-theoretic formulation of the model-based systems architecting cognitive-computational cycle. *Applied Sciences* 11 (4): 1945. https://doi.org.10.3390/app11041945.

Mordecai, Y., Markina-Khusid, A., Quinn, G., and Crawley, E.F. (2022). Applying model-based ontology coverage analysis to mission architectures. *IEEE Aerospace Conference*, 1–18.

Scheuermann, U. (2009). Reliability challenges of automotive power electronics. *Microelectronics Reliability* 49 (9–11): 1319–1325.

Spivak, D.I., and Kent, R.E. (2012). Ologs: A categorical framework for knowledge representation. *PLoS ONE* 7 (1). https://doi.org/10.1371/journal.pone.0024274.

19

Holistic Risk Management Using SOSF Methodology

Authors: Takafumi Nakamura[1], Avner Engel

19.1   Introduction

The predominant worldview on risk management in current engineering practice is that the risk of systems failure can be prevented or significantly mitigated at the design phase. This worldview is evident if we realize that mainstream methodologies use a reductionist approach based on a static model. However, most such methods should be augmented to cope with emergent properties, thus ignoring side effects from quick fixes, which often leads to repeated failures.

For example, introducing redundant safety mechanisms does little to reduce human errors. The more redundancy is used to eliminate risk, the greater the chance of spurious actuation. While the instrumentation is being improved to enable users to run their operations more efficiently and quickly, the risk remains unchanged (Perrow, 1999). This risk is due to current methodologies that tend to identify a system failure as a single, static event. Therefore, organizational learning tends to be limited to a simple rectifying process (single-loop learning model). Thus, in this chapter, we extend the scope of the conventional risk management process using the systems of systems failures (SOSF) methodology (Nakamura and Kijima, 2012). This chapter includes the following elements:

- **Limitations of current risk management practices.**
- **Features of SOSF.** Including multiloop learning, failure classes, failure types, failure owners, and failure dynamics.
- **Top level SOSF actions.** Including failure resolution procedure and risk management principles.

---

1 Adapted with permission from Nakamura and Kijima (2012) and Nakamura (2022).

Systems Science for Engineers and Scholars, First Edition. Edited by Avner Engel.

- **Example 1: holistic risk management and failure classes.** Including phase 1: becoming fully aware of a system failure breadth; phase 2: identifying the stakeholders; phase 3: identifying the relevant system failure model; phase 4: selecting methodology using SOSF; phase 5: implementing a corrective intervention; and phase 6: obtaining new learning using SOSF.
- **Example 2: synthetic SOSF risk management.** Including failure scenarios of artificial cardiac pacemaker (ACP) systems, systems incidents and failures, stakeholders, components, and failure statistics of ACP systems.
- **Description of a typical ACP system.** Including a description of the functionality and structure of a typical ACP system.

19.2 Limitations of Current Risk Management Practices

The main shortcomings of current risk management practices are derived from the tendency of engineers to look for causes of risks within the system boundaries. The common rationale of system preservation and stability tends to justify systems as ends without considering that a system exists only to satisfy the requirements of larger systems in which it is embedded. More specifically, current risk management methodologies are technically well-established.[2] Still, they are undertaken mainly during the design phase and are often not helpful for understanding the real implications of risks and whether they provide real solutions or merely tentative fixes. Most methodologies are based on a reductionist worldview, which may be summarized as follows:

- Current mainstream troubleshooting is often based on cause–effect analysis to find out natural root causes. Forward sequences (as in failure modes and effects analysis [FMEA] or event trees) or backward sequences (as in fault trees) are often employed (IEC 60812).
- The enormous speed of technological advances causes various misunderstandings among systems stakeholders. This responsibility disjunction is often managed improperly within current methodologies.
- The basic assumption of systems risk management is that the goal and operating norm of the system are static and predetermined at the design phase and are based on complex systems thinking.

The above precepts hinder the examination of systems failures from a holistic viewpoint, making it impossible to manage the soft, systemic, emergent, and dynamic aspects of systems failures.

---

2 International Organization for Standardization (ISO) and International Electrotechnical Commission (IEC) standards.

19.3   Features of SOSF

This section describes the main features of systems of systems failures (SOSF) methodology. In particular, SOSF deals with multidimensional holistic risk management to govern the dynamic aspects of systems failures and thereby overcome the current methodology's shortcomings. This approach includes consideration of (1) multiloop learning, (2) failure classes, (3) failure types, (4) failure owners, and (5) failure dynamics (Figure 19.1).

Figure 19.1   Multidimensional holistic risk management.

19.3.1   Multiloop Learning

The basic premise of SOSF is that more than one stakeholder (e.g., project manager, customer, regulator) alone is needed to overcome current methodological shortcomings. We should thus expand our view on systems failures to multistakeholder situations. Under this concept, several critical success factors for overcoming present methodological flaws exist. First, there should be a meta-methodology (i.e., the meta-model box in Figure) to promote the multiloop process. This meta-methodology should be adapted by stakeholders to collectively and exhaustively deal with the nature of risk management. Second, each stakeholder should recognize its unique mental model of the failure's root cause and all its relevant ingredients (i.e., the mental model box in each stakeholder's domain in Figure 19.2). Otherwise, the failures caused by stakeholders' mental model gaps will not be resolved effectively. Third, there should be failure classes based on the origin of the failure. These failure classes are essential to ensure the adequacy of the entire process.

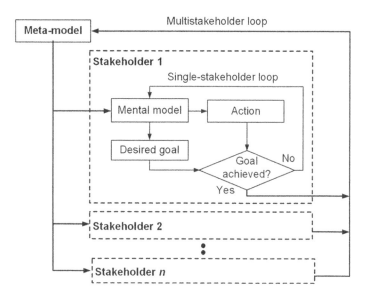

Figure 19.2 Multistakeholder environment.

There are three origins of systems failures: (1) the meta-model, (2) the mental model of each stakeholder, and (3) a mental model gap between stakeholders.

The stakeholders should first agree on a common meta-model to ensure that risk management is correct and essential rather than being fulfilled with quick fixes that introduce long-term side effects. After that, each stakeholder should establish a mental model associated with the specific individual system failure event. Once these two steps have been taken, all the stakeholders should discuss the system failure model to investigate why the failure happened, what should be done about it, and what should be learned in the organizational process to avoid further occurrence of the failure.

19.3.2 Failure Classes

Another SOSF dimension is the relevant failure classes: (1) failure of deviance, (2) failure of the interface, and (3) failure of foresight. Identifying the relevant failure class clarifies the system boundary and the nature of a problem (i.e., predictable or unpredictable). The failure classes are logically identified according to the following criteria:

- **Class 1 (failure of deviance).** The root cause of failures is within the system boundary, and conventional troubleshooting techniques are applicable and practical.

- **Class 2 (failure of interface).** The root failure causes are outside the system boundary but are predictable at the design phase.
- **Class 3 (failure of foresight).** The root failure causes are outside the system boundary and are unpredictable during the design phase.

The failure classes thus depend on whether the root causes are inside or outside the system boundary. However, note that several stakeholders may identify the same failure as belonging to different failure classes. Therefore, a failure class definition is relative and recursive. Figure 19.3 expands the two-dimensional SOSF into a three-dimensional SOSF space, adding the system failure dimension.

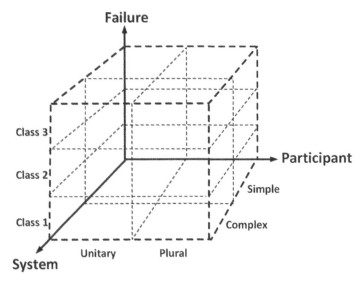

Figure 19.3 Three-dimensional SOSF space.

19.3.3 Failure Types

Systems of systems failures (SOSF) promote multiloop learning. This learning process is essential for determining whether operating norms (i.e., stakeholders' mental models) are appropriate.[3] SOSF also provides a meta-methodology for changing mental models to overcome system improvement shortcomings. In particular, SOSF is designed by allocating each type of failure from a taxonomy of systems failures (van Gigch, 1986) into two dimensions, systems versus participant failures space.

In SOSF, the type of system failure is divided into simple and complex. In general, simple systems failures result from the linear propagation of causes and effects. The underlying assumption is that system failure development is

---

3 Based on Jackson. (2003). *System Thinking: Creative Holism for Managers.*

deterministic, and there must be cause-and-effect links to these failures. Generally, complex systems failures arise from various factors and combinations of those factors. Such factors often have a far-reaching qualitative–quantitative nature and require a holistic approach to mitigate their effect on the system.

Similarly, the stakeholders involved in systems failures are divided into unitary and plural. In general, system failure that has minimal side effects, affecting— more or less—a single stakeholder, is defined as unitary failure. In contrast, a system failure that generates multiple side effects, requiring discussions and debates among different system levels of stakeholders, is defined as plural failure (Figure 19.4).

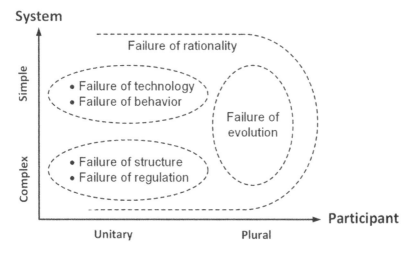

Figure 19.4 Types of failures in a system versus participant space.

19.3.4 Failure Owners

Another aspect of SOSF is identifying the problem owner in terms of its stakeholders' group and the organization that should assume responsibility for handling and rectifying any problem associated with the system. For example, Beer (1984) defined a viable system model (VSM) depicting the organizational processes related to risk management.

- Organizational levels 1, 2, and 3 are the operational levels that ensure internal harmony and maintain internal systems' homeostasis. They define when operations should be done, how these operations are coordinated, and how to keep corporate management involved.
- Organizational level 4 ensures strategic corporate management involvement in the integration of internal and external inputs to chart enterprise

strategies (i.e., external homeostasis). In addition, it clarifies who should be responsible for those strategies.

- Organizational level 5 ensures normative corporate management involving the formulation of long-term policies (i.e., planning and foresight) and deciding what should be done.

19.3.5 Failure Dynamics

As a part of SOSF, the system failure dynamic model is a nonlinear systemic model depicting systems failures caused by environmental changes through time. The model encourages stakeholders to focus on the dynamic aspects of the causes and effects of systems failures rather than the static aspects. It is applicable in all technology areas, including high-risk technology domains.

Turner and Pidgeon (1997) found that organizations that are responsible for failures and disasters commonly encounter "failure of foresight." Such events have a long incubation period characterized by several discrepant events that signaled potential danger. However, these events were typically overlooked or misinterpreted, and they accumulated unnoticed. To clarify that mechanism, Turner and Pidgeon decomposed the system life cycle into six stages, from initial development to cultural readjustment to catastrophic disasters. According to Ramesh (2014), these stages are (1) initial beliefs and norms, (2) incubation period, (3) precipitating event, (4) onset, (5) rescue and salvage, and (6) full cultural readjustment.

Identifying the incubation stage is challenging due to the multiple side effects of quick fixes. Therefore, this stage plays a crucial role in the lead-up to catastrophic disasters. Systems failures have specific features corresponding to these six stages. Class 1 failures occur early, while class 2 and 3 failures often emerge gradually. If we can identify the failure class, doing so can prolong the system life cycle by introducing countermeasures. The system failure dynamic model should be used periodically to ensure that the system behaves as expected and that side effects due to quick fixes are prevented.

19.4 Top-Level SOSF Actions

This section describes the top-level SOSF actions, which include (1) the failure resolution procedure and (2) risk management principles.

19.4.1 Failures Resolution Procedure

Multiple stakeholders arriving at an agreed-upon mental model (as shown in Figure) is a complex process that emanates from various factors and combinations thereof. A holistic and effective procedure that can analyze complex systems failures to rectify the problem at hand is shown in Figure 19.5. It promotes practical decision-making using holistic means of double-loop learning.

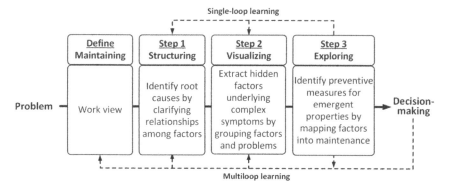

Figure 19.5 Overview of failure resolution procedure.

19.4.2 Risk Management Principles

Another aspect adopted by SOSF relates to the principles of risk management. For example, Flood and Jackson (1991) identified seven principles of holistic risk management (Table 19.1).

Table 19.1 Seven Principles of Holistic Risk Management.

#	Principle
1	Appreciating the full breadth of problem situations from one perspective is too complex to tackle with quick fixes.
2	Therefore, problem situations and their relevant issues should be investigated from various perspectives.
3	Once the major issues and problems have been highlighted, a suitable system methodology must be identified to guide the intervention process.
4	The relative strengths and weaknesses of different system methodologies should be analyzed, and this knowledge should guide the choice of appropriate response.
5	Different perspectives and system methodologies should be complementary to highlight and address various aspects of organizations and their issues and problems.
6	The total system intervention sets out a systemic inquiry cycle, with back-and-forth interaction between its three phases.
7	Facilitators and participants should be engaged at all stages of the system intervention process.

19.5   Example 1: Holistic Risk Management and Failure Classes

This section describes an example of applying the holistic risk management methodology under SOSF. In this example, a user of the XYZ product encounters a problem and reports it to the help desk of the XYZ system provider (Figure 19.6).

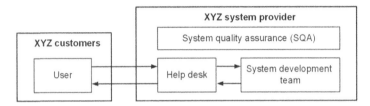

Figure 19.6   Risk management example.

The help desk concludes that the problem may emanate from one of two sources: (1) a user error resulting from a misunderstanding of the product specifications or (2) an existing system problem. The help desk then identifies the cause of the incident, and if a faulty product has caused it, they escalate the problem to the system development team for further investigation.

The system development team updates the products based on data from the escalated incident that the help desk believes was due to a product defect. This procedure is mainly because user-related incidents are screened at the help desk so the system development team can concentrate on product-related issues. There are six phases in the application of holistic risk management. These phases are discussed below in the context of this example.

19.5.1   Phase 1: Becoming Fully Aware of the Breadth of a System Failure

In this phase, owners of issues and problems should act according to the first risk management principle. They should understand that issues are invariably too complicated to understand from one perspective and cannot be resolved by quick fixes.

In this example, the system development team believes, based on internal benchmarking, that their product quality is superior to that of their competitors. However, a third-party customer survey reveals that customers judge the quality as less important than what the internal benchmarking indicates. Upon learning of this discrepancy, the system quality assurance (SQA) section of the XYZ system provider set up a working group to identify product-related problems.

19.5.2 Phase 2: Identifying the Stakeholders

In this phase, owners of issues and problems should act according to the second risk management principle. First, they should identify all the stakeholders related to the problems or concerns from phase 1. In this example, the SQA section will identify three relevant stakeholders: the user of the XYZ product, the help desk, and the system developers of the XYZ system provider.

19.5.3 Phase 3: Identifying the Relevant System Failure Model

In this phase, the relevant stakeholders should act according to the third and sixth risk management principles. They should identify the system failure model appropriate to their issues or problems. The following are three standard system failure models.

19.5.3.1 The Simple Linear System Failure Model

A simple linear model explains system failure as a "linear propagation of a chain of causes and effects" (Heinrich et al., 1980). The underlying principle is that system failures are deterministic and must have cause–effect links. Fault tree analysis (FTA) and failure mode and effects analysis (FMEA) are representative methodologies.[4] They follow backward and forward chains, respectively.

19.5.3.2 The Complex Linear System Failure Model

A complex linear model explains system failure as latent events caused by earlier operations. In other words, system failures surface at a given time due to hidden (latent) suppressed deviations.

19.5.3.3 The Nonlinear or Systemic Model

The nonlinear or systemic model explains system failures as being due to the complexity of systems in terms of the number of elements, interactions, feedback loops, and the like. For example, Perrow (1999) argues that the conventional engineering approach to ensuring safety—building more warnings and safeguards—fails because system complexity makes failures inevitable.

In this example, the SQA section identifies the initial difference in the mental models between the help desk and the system development team. However, the help desk is incentivized by political motives to increase the user responsible incident (URI) statistics. Similarly, political reasons incentivize the system development team to decrease the product responsible incident (PRI) statistics.

---

4 See: IEC 61025:2006 and IEC 60812:2006.

This tendency is because, in both cases, the XYZ company does not have to bear the cost of fixing the problem. Instead, the user should be instructed on operating the system, and the system stays intact. There may be better ways to handle incidents because both organizations are not user oriented. The SQA section identifies this situation as an opportunity to resolve the issue and push for organizational improvements.

19.5.3.4 Phase 4: Select Methodology Using SOSF

In this phase, all the stakeholders should act according to the fourth risk management principle. They should assess different system methodologies' relative strengths and weaknesses and select the most appropriate one. In SOSF meta-methodology, problem situations should be mapped using three axes: (1) complex/straightforward, (2) unitary/plural, and (3) class 1/2/3, following the level of agreement or disagreement among the participants.

In this example, the initial stakeholder opinions have opposing views: (1) The user of the XYZ claims that the problem is a product-related issue that the system development team must correct; (2) the help desk disagrees, claiming that the problem is not a product-related issue and that the user made an error in operation; and finally, (3) the system development team agrees with the user. At this stage, the SQA section identified three possible archetypes of failures.

19.5.3.5 Misunderstanding Class 2 or 3 Failure as Class 1 Failure

In this system failure scenario, the source of the failure is inside the help desk system boundary (i.e., a class 1 failure), although the actual cause is outside this boundary. This archetype (Figure 19.7) represents a single-loop learning scenario explaining why system failures reoccur following a quick or inappropriate fix. Such quick fixes might reduce the number of system failures in the short term, but their accumulation gradually becomes saturated at a level exceeding the organization's goal level. The balancing intended consequence (BIC) loop opens, so quick fixes have no further effect. The balancing unintended consequence (BUC) loop also becomes open due to misunderstanding the system failure class and not providing an effective solution.

The traditional sequence of this archetype is as follows. Arrow 1+ indicates that an increase in the number of class 1 failures causes an increase in corrective actions. Arrow 2+ shows that the number of activities increases the number of quick fixes. Dotted arrow 3- indicates that the rise in quick fixes contributes slightly to reducing the number of class 1 failures. The root cause is outside the system boundary and is unaffected by dotted arrow 4. Finally, arrow 5+ indicates that the root cause will increase the number of class 1 failures.

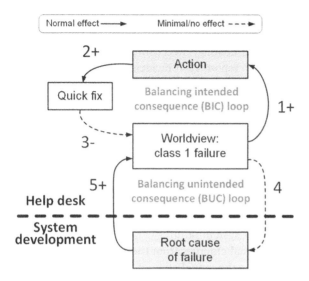

Figure 19.7 Misunderstanding class 2 or 3 failure as class 1 failure (phase 1).

The reinforcing intended consequences (RIC) action to improve the situation (Figure 19.8) leads to the introduction of additional quick fixes, which leads to the repetition of a similar scenario. Arrow 6+ indicates that an increase in class 1

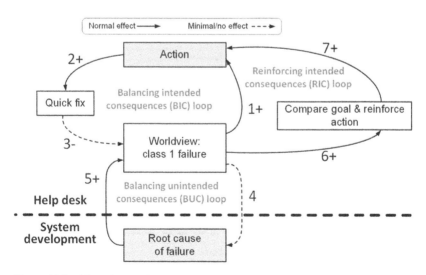

Figure 19.8 Misunderstanding class 2 or 3 failure as class 1 failure (phase 2).

failures reinforces the compare goal and reinforces action. Arrow 7+ shows that supporting the compare goal and adjusting action increases the number of activities. Thus, this action causes various side effects, including erosion of safety goals accompanied by an incentive to report fewer incidents.

These side effects are hard to detect because the performance malfunction alarm is muted, and management can identify these effects only by quantitatively measuring performance. This mechanism explains why a single-loop learning solution for improving system performance is bound to fail.

19.5.3.6 Erosion of Safety Goals Accompanied by the Incentive to Report Fewer Incidents

This side effect is introduced when the RIC loop becomes tighter without a further reduction in the number of system failures (Figure 19.9). As a result, increased pressure to achieve the goal emerges from the BUC loop by shifting the plan (i.e., lowering it) or hiding the actual state of quality or safety from management. In this scenario, managers who stay within the system boundary have difficulty detecting the actual quality status within the organization.

Arrow 8+ indicates that an increase in class 1 failures causes pressure to adjust the goal or creates an incentive to report fewer incidents. Arrow 9- shows an increase in the number of class 1 failures that are hidden.

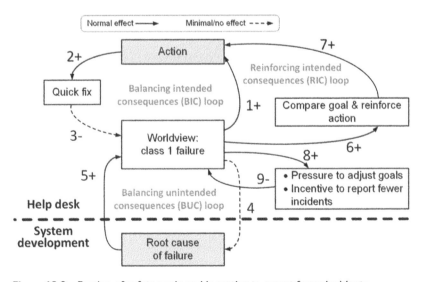

Figure 19.9 Erosion of safety goals and incentive to report fewer incidents.

19.5.3.7 Fix That Fails Archetype (Side Effect)

In this system failure scenario, the source of the failure is outside the help desk's system boundary. Figure 19.10 shows a typical example of local optimization. The action taken vis-à-vis the root cause is a short-term solution to the problem. However, it introduces delayed, unintended consequences outside the system boundary, resulting from class 2 or 3 failures. For example, an operations manager might shift resources from a proactive task team to a reactive task team because of a rapid increase in system failures. This action would only stmulate the reinforcing unintended consequences (RUC) loop, further increasing system failures.

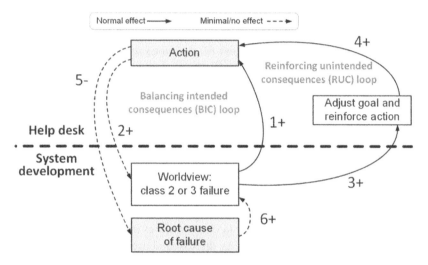

Figure 19.10   Fix that fails archetype (side effect).

This out-of-control situation can damage the organization in the long term. Arrow 1+ indicates that an increase in class 2 or 3 failures increases the number of actions within the system boundary. These actions do not attack the root cause. Therefore, dotted arrow 2+ does not reduce the number of class 2 or 3 failures. This arrow might increase the number of class 2 or 3 failures because of local optimization side effects. Arrows 3+ and 4+ introduce an adjusted goal and reinforce action without reducing the number of class 2 or 3 failures. Dotted arrows 5- and 6+ are not in effect during this phase of the archetype.

19.5.4   Phase 5: Implementing a Corrective Intervention

In this phase, relating to the fifth and sixth risk management principles, methodologies are applied to produce change. The methods should be complementary to highlight and address different aspects of organizations and their issues and problems.

In this example, the help desk and the system development team concluded that the problem stems from a genuine system problem. As a result, all the stakeholders, namely, the user as well as the XYZ system's quality assurance, help desk, and system development team, agreed upon the selected resolution method. After that, the system development team was responsible for fixing the problem.

19.5.5 Phase 6: Obtaining New Learning Using SOSF

In this phase, the intervention should be evaluated to learn about the problem situation, the meta-methodology, the generic system methodologies, and the specific methods used. As discussed in this example, overcoming the misunderstanding of class 2 or 3 failure as a class 1 failure may be achieved in three ways: (1) introduce an absolute goal, (2) close the gap between stakeholders, or (3) enlarge the system boundary. All three actions promote double-loop learning by altering the process design to improve system quality or safety. In contrast, single-loop learning leads to side effects, as explained above.

19.5.5.1 Multiloop Learning for Class 2 Failure Archetype (Solution)
In this system failure scenario, we focus on the possibilities of relative achievement or the side effects of a quick fix. In addition, an implicit assumption of a gap between stakeholders should surface throughout the discussion and debate to close the responsibility gap. The application of this misunderstanding system failure archetype is illustrated in Figure 19.11.

Arrow 1+ indicates that an increase in class 2 failures increases the number of actions within the system boundary. As discussed above, these actions induce

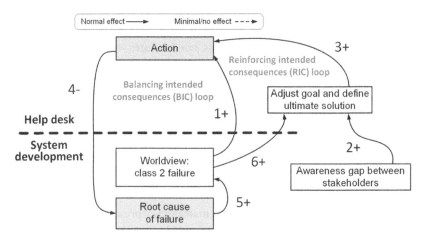

Figure 19.11 Multiloop learning for class 2 failure (solution).

various side effects (erosion of safety goals or reporting fewer incidents). Arrow 2+ indicates reviewing the stakeholders' mental model gap and redefining or adjusting the ultimate goal. Arrow 3+ indicates provoking a new action. Arrow 4- suggests that the further action attacks the root cause, which resides outside the system boundary. Arrow 5+ indicates eventually reducing the number of class 2 failures. Finally, arrow 6+ suggests adjusting the goal and defining the ultimate solution.

19.5.5.2 Multiloop Learning for Class 3 Failure Archetype (Solution)
In this system failure scenario, the current goal becomes obsolete due to the speed of technological advancement and the growth of complexities (Figure 19.12). These phenomena are the root cause of a system failure, with no party responsible. In other words, the system failure emerges through no one's fault. This kind of failure can be avoided by monitoring goal achievement and benchmarking competitors.

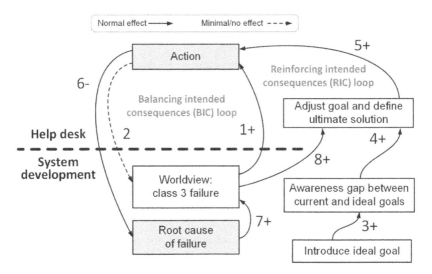

Figure 19.12 Multiloop learning for class 3 failure (solution).

Arrow 1+ indicates that an increase in class 3 failures increases the number of actions within the system boundary. These actions do not attack the root cause, so there is no effect on reducing the number of class 3 failures, as indicated by arrow 2. Arrows 3+ and 4+ lead to the introduction of an ideal goal. This goal creates awareness of the gap between the current and ideal goals. This ideal goal is then altered to define the ultimate solution. Arrow 5+ indicates introducing a new action, and arrow 6- indicates attacking the root cause, which reduces the number of class 3 failures, as arrow 7+ indicates. Finally, arrow 8+ indicates further enhancement to adjust the goal and define the ultimate solution.

19.5.5.3 Double-Loop Learning for a Fix That Fails Archetype (Solution)

In this system failure scenario, the solution for this archetype is to raise the viewpoint of the problem (Figure 19.13). Class 2 and 3 failures become class 1 if the presumed system boundary is enlarged.

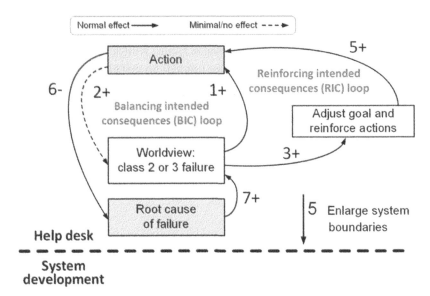

Figure 19.13 Multiloop learning for a fix that fails archetype (solution).

Arrow 5 indicates enlarging the system boundary to incorporate the root cause. This dynamic converts Class 2 and 3 failures into class 1 failures. Finally, arrow 6- indicates attacking the root cause and reducing the number of class 2 or 3 failures, as indicated by arrow 7+.

19.6 Example 2: Synthetic SOSF Risk Management

19.6.1 Failure Scenarios of ACP Systems

In this example, the risk management process that uses SOSF is demonstrated with synthetic data. The example is based on an earlier paper (Engel et al., 2021) involving an artificial pacemaker. The example depicts a scenario where the

ABC company develops, manufactures, and maintains artificial cardiac pacemakers (ACP). In addition, the company collected failure statistics associated with each of these activities for eight years to utilize the SOSF methodology (Figure 19.14).

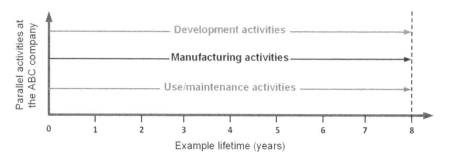

Figure 19.14 Lifetime duration of the example.

19.6.2 Systems Incidents and Failures

Sophisticated electronic devices and pacemakers may be affected by many failure mechanisms. In such cases, failure events may impact the system throughout its lifetime, that is, from the development and manufacturing stages to the use/maintenance activities. In particular, during use and maintenance, electromagnetic interference (EMI) sources may affect the appropriate function of an implanted device.[5] For example, a pacemaker may respond by delaying or stopping its pacing, as intense EMI may cause transitory or permanent damage to device electronics (Erdogan, 2002).

Short transitory events and an infrequent need to perform minor adjustments of internal parameters are often considered "incidents." In general, no statistics are collected regarding their occurrence. Figure 19.15 presents an example of a conventional pacemaker's dynamic output pulse frequency variations, incident, and failure. Note that the error in the pacemaker performance example in year 3 is a typical helpful life failure (in this case, a temporary failure), which may occur randomly—often due to unexpected electrical, thermal, mechanical, radiative, and so on transient overload.

---

5 Susceptibility to EMI is just a proxy for a host of noise factor sources, for example, flawed design, defective manufacturing, cosmic radiation–induced soft errors, inappropriate device and electrical leads implantation by the surgeon, improper device tuning by the cardiologist, physical impact due to a patient falling or being involved in a mild car crash, and so forth.

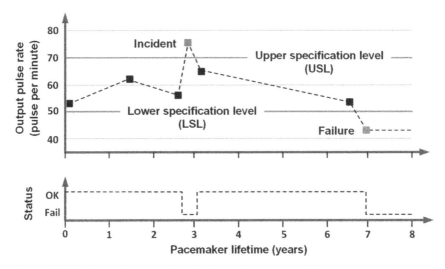

Figure 19.15 Pacemaker dynamic output pulse frequency variations.

The author used Ghosh and Sharma's (2022) classification of key failure categories and causes of pacing system malfunctions, as presented in Table 19.2.

Table 19.2 Typical ACP Failures.

Failure ID	Nature of Failure
1	Undersensing or oversensing heart signals
2	Loss of ACP output
3	Wrong ACP pulse rate, shape, or intensity
4	Shifting sense or impulse lead positions within the heart
5	Inappropriate cardiac stimulation
6	Pulse generator failure within the ACP
7	Pacemaker inappropriate adjustments

19.6.3 Stakeholders

The individuals or groups who constitute the stakeholders involved in various ACP failures are presented in Table 19.3.

Table 19.3 Stakeholders Involved in ACP Failures.

Stakeholder ID	Characteristic of Stakeholders
1	Development team
2	Manufacturing team
3	Management team
4	FDA[6] medical devices
5	Heart surgeons
6	Cardiologists
7	Patients

19.6.4 Components of ACP

Typical ACP systems are composed of six top-level subsystems. These subsystems are presented in Table 19.4.

Table 19.4 ACP Subsystems.

Subsystem ID	Description of Subsystem
1	Pulse generator
2	Sense leads
3	Impulse leads
4	Receiver
5	Transmitter
6	Battery

19.6.5 Synthetic ACP Failure Statistics

The following sections describe synthetic ACP failure statistics collected by the ABC company over eight years, covering the company's development, manufacturing, and maintenance operations.

19.6.5.1 Synthetic Failure Statistics During Development

Table 19.5 presents synthetic ACP failure statistics during eight years of development activities. This data includes 200 failure events of new and modified ACP systems. Of the stakeholders, the development team was the most affected by failures in the system. Inappropriate cardiac stimulation was the most prevalent subsystem failure, and interface failures were the dominant failure class.

---

6 US Food and Drug Administration (FDA).

Table 19.5 Synthetic Failure Statistics During the Development Activities.

Phase	Failures affecting stakeholders							Failing pacemakers' subsystems							Failure classes		
	1. Development team	2. Manufacturing team	3. Management team	4. FDA Medical Devices	5. Heart surgeons	6. Cardiologists	7. Patients	1. Under-sensing	2. Loss of output	3. Wrong pulse parameters	4. Shifting sense/impulse leads	5. Inappropriate cardiac stimulation	6. Pulse generator failure	7. Pacemaker inappropriate adjustment	1. Failure of deviance	2. Failure of interface	3. Failure of foresight
Development	180	10	2	4	1	1	2	50	26	8	14	60	22	20	80	100	20
Total	200							200							200		

19.6.5.2 Synthetic Failure Statistics During Manufacturing

Table 19.6 presents synthetic ACP failure statistics during eight years of manufacturing activities. This data includes 60 failure events of new and modified ACP systems. Of the stakeholders, the manufacturing team was the most affected by failures in the system. Inappropriate cardiac stimulation was also the most prevalent subsystem failure, and interface failures were the dominant failure class.

Table 19.6 Synthetic Failure Statistics During the Manufacturing Activities.

Phase	Failures affecting stakeholders							Failing pacemakers' subsystems							Failure classes		
	1. Development team	2. Manufacturing team	3. Management team	4. FDA Medical Devices	5. Heart surgeons	6. Cardiologists	7. Patients	1. Under-sensing	2. Loss of output	3. Wrong pulse parameters	4. Shifting sense/impulse leads	5. Inappropriate cardiac stimulation	6. Pulse generator failure	7. Pacemaker inappropriate adjustment	1. Failure of deviance	2. Failure of interface	3. Failure of foresight
Manufacturing	6	40	2	4	2	2	4	12	10	4	6	16	8	4	12	44	4
Total	60							60							60		

19.6.5.3 Synthetic Failure Statistics During Use-Maintenance

Table 19.7 presents synthetic ACP failure statistics during eight years of use-maintenance activities. This data includes 600 failure events of new and modified ACP systems. Of the stakeholders, the ACP patients were the most affected by failures in the system. The pulse generator was the most prevalent subsystem failure, and failure of foresight was the most dominant failure class.

Table 19.7 Synthetic Failure Statistics During the Use-Maintenance Activities.

Phase	Failures affecting stakeholders							Failing pacemakers' subsystems							Failure classes		
	1. Development team	2. Manufacturing team	3. Management team	4. FDA Medical Devices	5. Heart surgeons	6. Cardiologists	7. Patients	1. Under-sensing	2. Loss of output	3. Wrong pulse parameters	4. Shifting sense/impulse leads	5. Inappropriate cardiac stimulation	6. Pulse generator failure	7. Pacemaker inappropriate adjustment	1. Failure of deviance	2. Failure of interface	3. Failure of foresight
Use-Maintenance	172	68	44	12	26	38	240	58	88	74	68	110	136	66	202	148	250
Total	600							600							600		

19.7   Description of Typical ACP Systems

This section describes artificial cardiac pacemaker (ACP) systems. Pacemakers are small medical devices that generate and deliver electrical pulses to the heart muscles of individuals suffering from various heart diseases . These pulses trigger and regulate the heart's beating (Figure 19.16).

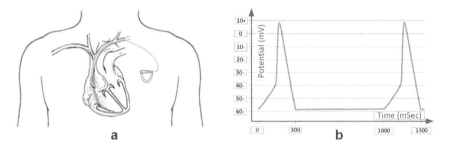

Figure 19.16   (a) Pacemaker embedded in the body and (b) pacemaker pulse shape.

Therefore, a pacemaker's primary purpose is to maintain an adequate heart rate in patients with various heart diseases. An irregular heart rhythm disorder may induce fatigue, dizziness, and fainting in a patient. The power source for a pacemaker is usually a lithium–iodine battery that lasts for more than eight years in a state-of-the-art pacemaker. An average pacemaker uses about half its battery power for cardiac stimulation. The other half is used for housekeeping tasks such as device control and data monitoring (Mallela et al., 2004).

Figure 19.17 presents a top-level block diagram of a pacemaker system within its environment. The system consists of six subsystems: (1) a pulse generator, (2) sense leads, (3) impulse leads, (4) a receiver, (5) a transmitter, and (6) a battery.

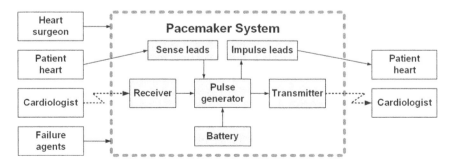

Figure 19.17   Pacemaker block diagram system and environment.

The system delivers electrical pulses to the patient's heart according to its continual behavior. A heart surgeon installs the system in the patient's body, and a cardiologist provides lifelong maintenance service.

19.8 Conclusion

In the engineering arena, the principal methodologies for risk management (i.e., ensuring system quality and safety) are rooted in complex systems thinking. Furthermore, engineers in the development sections see systems as a combination of components whose quality determines the system's quality. Therefore, their key performance indicators for daily routine processes are drawn only from within their defined systems. Under this thinking paradigm, the approach to ensure systems' quality is to identify all deviances from the internal systems' goals and rectify them. This technique and methodology are pertinent to the simple unitary domain of the meta-methodology systems of systems failures (SOSF).

However, more than the general simple risk management approach is needed in complex systems and pluralistic stakeholder environments, which can lead to many problems and systems failures. Therefore, holistic risk management using SOSF methodology examines system quality and safety using these dimensions: (1) life cycle vision, (2) multiloop learning, (3) multistakeholder considerations, and (4) types of systems and failures classes.

The chapter describes a typical example of six phases characterizing holistic risk management and failure classes: (1) becoming fully aware of a system failure breadth, (2) identifying the stakeholders, (3) identifying the relevant system failure model, (4) selecting methodology using SOSF, (5) implementing a corrective intervention, and (6) acquiring new learning using SOSF.

19.9 Acknowledgment

This chapter is based on Nakamura and Kijima's (2012) and Nakamura's (2022) papers. The author of this book is deeply indebted to Dr. Nakamura and Dr. Kijima for their permission to embed texts and graphics from the said papers in this chapter.

19.10 Bibliography

Beer, S. (1984, Jan.). The viable system model: Its provenance, development, methodology and pathology. *Journal of the Operational Research Society (JORS)* 35, 7–25.

Engel, A., Teller, A., Shachar, S., and Reich Y. (2021, June). Robust design under cumulative damage due to dynamic failure mechanisms, *Systems Engineering* 24 (5): 322–338.

Erdogan, O. (2002). Electromagnetic interference on pacemakers. *Indian Pacing Electrophysiology Journal* 2 (3): 74–78.

Flood, R.L. and Jackson, M.C. (1991). Total systems intervention: A practical face to critical systems thinking. *Systems Practice* 4, 197–213.

Heinrich, H.W., Peterson, D., and Roos, N. (1980). *Industrial Accident Prevention*, fifth edition. McGraw Hill.

IEC 60812. (2006). Procedure for failure mode and effect analysis (FMEA), 4.05.2011. http://webstore.iec.ch/webstore/webstore.nsf/artnum/035494/

IEC 61025. (2006). Fault tree analysis (FTA), 4.05.2011. http://webstore.iec.ch/webstore/webstore.nsf/artnum/037347/

Jackson, M.C. (2003). *Systems Thinking: Creative Holism for Managers*. John Wiley & Sons. https://citeseerx.ist.psu.edu/document?repid=rep1&type=pdf&doi=7aa3919 3789328d14f1125834834d9ccd4f92a31. Accessed: Jan. 2023.

Maisel, W.H., Sweeney, M.O., Stevenson, W.G., Ellison, K.E., and Epstein, L.M. (2001). Recalls and safety alerts involving pacemakers and implantable cardioverter-defibrillator generators. *Journal of the American Medical Association (JAMA)* 286 (7): 793–799.

Mallela, S.V., Ilankumaran, V., and Srinivasan N. (2004). Trends in cardiac pacemaker batteries. *Indian Pacing Electrophysiology Journal* 4 (4): 201–212.

Nakamura, T. (2022). Promoting system safety and reliability through risk quantification/visualisation methodology. *WIT Transactions on the Built Environment* 214: 149–160.

Nakamura, T. and Kijima, K. (2012). System of system failure: Meta methodology to prevent system failures. *System of Systems* 31, 10-5772.

Perrow, C. (1999). *Normal Accidents: Living with High Risk Technologies*. Princeton University Press.

Ramesh, G. (2014). Escalating crisis and lagged response: Perspectives from the Mumbai terrorist attack. *South Asian Journal of Management* 21 (3): 167.

Turner, B.A. and Pidgeon, N.F. (1997). *Man-Made Disasters*, second edition. Butterworth-Heinemann.

van Gigch, J.P. (1986, June). Modeling, metamodeling, and taxonomy of system failures. *IEEE Transactions on Reliability* R-35 (2): 131–136.

Ghosh, P. and Sharma, S. (June 21, 2022). Pacemaker Malfunction. *Medscape Reference*. http://emedicine.medscape.com/article/156583. Accessed: Jan. 2023.

20

Systemic Accidents and Mishaps Analyses

20.1 Introduction to Accident Causation Models

Different accident causation models explain how accidents happen. However, few consider the significant changes that have occurred in modern times, and they do not reflect the current complex sociotechnical environment. Consequently, new accident models based on systems theory have been introduced. This chapter concentrates on one systemic accident model, the systems-theoretic accident model and process (STAMP) in some detail. The chapter includes the following elements:

- **Basic accidents, incidents, and mishaps concepts.** Including hazard, risk, and loss events.
- **Classification of accident causation models.**
- **Systems theoretic accident model and process (STAMP).** Including STAMP background, STAMP sociotechnical failure mechanisms, and STAMP procedure.
- **Introduction to CAST.** Including causal analysis system theory (CAST) procedure and an example of CAST analysis involving an accident involving two CH-53 helicopters.

20.2 Basic Accident, Incidents, and Mishap Concepts

As terminology goes, accidents are events that happen unintentionally, resulting in damage to property, the environment or injury to humans or animals. Incidents are also events that occur unintentionally but do not result in damage or injury. Finally, mishaps are minor incidents.

Accidents usually occur due to a chain of events resulting from inadequate risk control or the lack of application of safety constraints that ultimately harm people,

Systems Science for Engineers and Scholars, First Edition. Edited by Avner Engel.
© 2024 John Wiley & Sons, Ltd. Published 2024 by John Wiley & Sons, Ltd.

property, and the environment. So, people in general and engineers in particular attempt to design, build, and maintain safe systems that protect human resources and habitats as well as reduce the risk of losses. In other words, the ultimate goal of safety engineering is to prevent accidents and mishaps.

One way to reduce the number of accidents and their severity is to use various accident causation models. Such models clarify the cause, processes, and consequences of accidents, incidents, and mishaps, providing tools for precise analysis of the occurrence and development of accidents. More specifically, causal incident models produce a path to analyze an incident and identify the various causes and shortcomings that led to its occurrence. Using incident causation models is essential in implementing postaccident investigations and preventing future accidents.

This chapter presents a top-level classification of incident causation models. Then it concentrates on one systemic incident model: the systems theoretic accident model and process (STAMP), which was developed by Prof. Nancy Leveson of the Massachusetts Institute of Technology (MIT) and her colleagues (Leveson, 2016, Leveson, 2023).

Figure 20.1 depicts an example of a generic mishap event chain. Some basic terms related to mishap analyses (i.e., *hazards*, *risks*, and *loss events*) are discussed below.

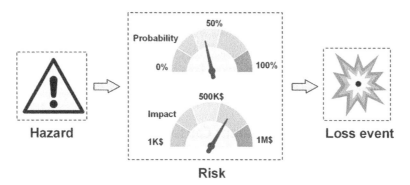

Figure 20.1 Example of generic accident event chain.

20.2.1 Hazard

There are many definitions for *hazard*, but one definition is "A hazard is any object, situation, or behavior that can cause injury, ill health, or damage to property or the environment".[1] Hazards may be classified into one or more of the following categories:

1. **Physical hazards.** These hazards are the most common causes of accidents, including extremes of temperature, excessive noise, electrical exposure, high elevation, unguarded machinery, and ionizing or nonionizing radiation.

---

1 See https://www.safeopedia.com/definition/152/hazard. Accessed Jan. 2023.

2. **Mechanical hazards.** These hazards are usually created by machinery, often with protruding and moving parts.
3. **Chemical hazards.** These hazards appear when persons are exposed to chemicals. Some chemicals are safer than others, but even standard compounds can cause illness, skin irritation, or breathing problems for sensitive individuals.
4. **Biological hazards.** These hazards include viruses, bacteria, fungi, parasites, and any living organism that can infect or transmit diseases to human beings.
5. **Ergonomic hazards.** These hazards include the physiological demands of any activity upon people. This type of hazard considers issues beyond productivity, health, and safety.
6. **Psychosocial hazards.** These hazards may arise from various psychosocial factors that persons may find unsatisfactory, frustrating, or demoralizing.

20.2.2 Risk

Risk is the possibility that an object (e.g., a person, a system, the environment) will be harmed or induce an adverse effect due to a hazard. Risk is expressed as the likelihood of a loss event occurring multiplied by the damage caused by that event.

20.2.3 Loss Event

A loss event is an unexpected physical event that, causes harm to people, organizations, the environment, and so on. Loss events may result from control failure or a lack of control of identified or unidentified hazards/risks.

20.3 Classification of Accident Causation Models

There are many classification methods for accident causal models. Gui et al. (2019) propose an accident classification model divided into linear and nonlinear models. Linear accident causation models usually examine the causes of various stages of an accident and identify a chain according to the logical sequence so that examiners can observe the multiple causes of the accident and the relationships between them. Nonlinear accident causation models generally focus on analyzing critical factors of accidents. Such models may be classified into four categories: human-based models, statistics-based models, energy-based models, and system-based models (Figure 20.2).

1. Human-based accident models are concerned with the human factors of an accident.
2. Statistics-based accident models apply accident statistics data to study the relationships between the number and severity of accidents. Such models reveal the proportional relationship between accidents of different severity.
3. Energy-based accident models mainly consider energy release and transfer before, during, and after accidents.

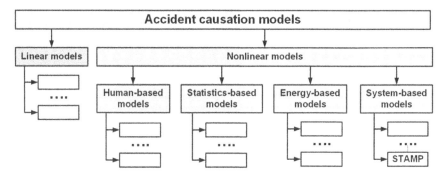

Figure 20.2 Top-level classification of accident causation models.[2]

4. System-based accident models bring the object, human, and management factors into the accident analysis. Currently, these models are the most frequently used in accident investigations.

20.4 Systems Theoretic Accident Model and Process (STAMP)[3]

20.4.1 STAMP Background

As mentioned, Leveson developed the systems theoretic accident model and process (STAMP). STAMP is based on systems and control theory. It suggests that adverse events occur when interactions between system components are not controlled through managerial, organizational, physical, operational, and manufacturing-based controls. According to Leveson, safety risks are managed through a hierarchy of controls and feedback mechanisms, and adverse events emerge when systems' behavior and emergent properties are not adequately controlled. Therefore, STAMP is a systemic accident analysis method used to identify the control and feedback failures that enabled the accident or mishap under analysis to occur. An example of a generic functional safety control loop is shown in Figure 20.3.

Accordingly, in STAMP, systems are viewed as interrelated components that maintain a state of dynamic equilibrium through feedback loops of control and information across all levels. Each level, therefore, includes a description of the relevant agents and organizations that play a role in system design or operation. In addition, control and feedback mechanisms are included to show what controls are enacted down the hierarchy. Finally, the specific information about the system's status that must be returned up the hierarchy should be included.

---

2 Top-level classification derived from Gui et al. (2019).

3 Figures, tables, and texts adapted with permission from Leveson (2016).

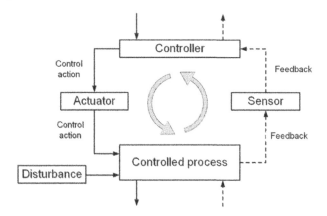

Figure 20.3 Example of a generic functional safety control loop.

The arrows flowing down the hierarchy represent controls, and the arrows flowing up the hierarchy represent feedback loops. In other words, each entity has control and authority over the entities immediately below it, and each entity is likewise subject to control and management from the entities immediately above it.

As mentioned, the STAMP model has two basic hierarchical control structures: one for system development and one for system operation, with interactions between them. Similarly, information is communicated between the layers of the control structure. For example, the downward channel provides constraint information for the next layer, and the upward channel reports feedback information for the constraint.

A top-level STAMP model of sociotechnical controls and feedback is depicted in Figure 20.4. A detailed level of a STAMP model of sociotechnical controls and feedback, considering both the system development and system operation, is shown in Figure 20.5.

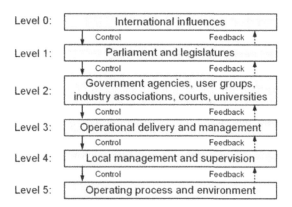

Figure 20.4 STAMP top-level model of sociotechnical control.

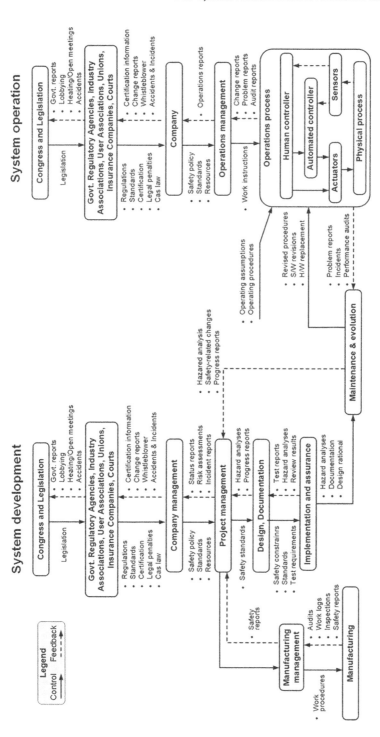

Figure 20.5 STAMP detailed model of sociotechnical control (Image: Leveson, 2016).

20.4.2 STAMP Sociotechnical Failure Mechanisms

STAMP is a nonlinear system-based accident theory. According to this model, system components are interrelated and enforced by specific safety constraints. This theory allows for determining the dynamics of the interrelationships between system components. STAMP works by identifying where control and feedback mechanisms fail. One may use the STAMP failure taxonomy (Table 20.1) to classify each contributory factor into specific control and feedback failures.

Table 20.1 Classification of Accident Contributory Factors.

Inadequate enforcement of constraints	Unidentified hazards
	Inappropriate, ineffective, or missing control actions for identified hazards
	• The design of the control process does not enforce constraints
	■ Flaws in the creation process
	■ Process changes without an appropriate change in the control process
	■ Incorrect modification or adaptation
	• The process model is inconsistent, incomplete, or incorrect
	■ Flaws in the creation process
	■ Flaws in the updating process
	■ Time lags and measurement inaccuracies or not accounted for
	Inadequate coordination among controllers and the decision-makers
Inadequate execution of control actions	Communication flaw
	Inadequate actuator operation
	Time lag
Inadequate or missing feedback	Not provided in system design
	Communication flaw
	Time lag
	Inadequate sensor operation

STAMP general factors leading to unsafe systems controls are depicted in Figure 20.6.

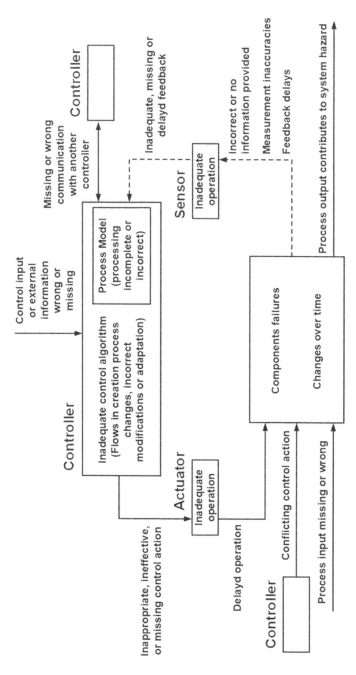

Figure 20.6 STAMP general factors leading to unsafe systems controls (Image: Leveson, 2016).

20.5   Causal Analysis System Theory (CAST)

CAST[4] (Leveson, 2019) is an accident analysis technique that considers all causes of a given accident and optimizes learning from it to improve the system as a whole. It reduces hindsight bias, takes a system's view of human behavior, and provides a blame-free explanation of why the accident occurred.

CAST uses a comprehensive accident causality model that concentrates on the sets of control and feedback created to prevent this type of accident but failed. In addition, CAST suggests ways to strengthen safety control and feedback structures to prevent similar accidents in the future.

20.6   CAST Procedure

The CAST procedure generally involves five steps, as shown in Figure 20.7 and elaborated below.

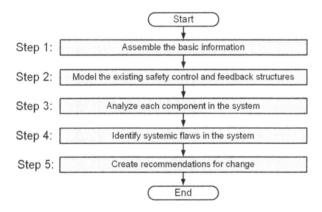

Figure 20.7   Typical CAST accident investigation procedure.

20.6.1   Step 1: Assemble the Basic Information

This step includes the collection of basic information needed for the analysis. It may include the following components:

- Define the system involved and the boundary of the analysis

---

4 Adapted from: Nancy Leveson. MIT Partnership for Systems Approaches to Safety and Security (PSASS). See: MIT Partnership for Systems Approaches to Safety and Security (PSASS) and Joel Parker Henderson, See http://www.joelparkerhenderson.com.

- Describe the physical loss and hazardous state that led to it regarding the equipment, people, controls, and feedback
- Describe the system states and environmental conditions that led to the accident
- From the hazard, identify the system-level safety constraints required to prevent the hazard
- Describe what happened (the events) without conclusions or blame
- Analyze the design to prevent this type of accident, as well as the missing or inadequate physical controls that might have prevented the accident and any contextual factors that influenced the events

20.6.2 Step 2: Model the Existing Safety Control and Feedback Structures

The goal of this and the following steps is to identify the limitations of the safety control structure that allowed the loss and how to strengthen it in the future. This step involves the creation of models depicting the existing safety control and feedback structures. Typical models could be:

- Development and operations safety control structure
- Management-level safety control structure
- Physical-level safety control structure

20.6.3 Step 3: Analyze Each Component in the System

This step examines the components of the safety control and feedback structures to determine why they were not effective in preventing the relevant accident. In addition, it shows the role each component played in the accident and the explanation for the behavior. The analysis should identify all the contributory factors that played a causal role in the accident, including factors across all levels of the control and feedback structures. This analysis may include the following elements:

- Contributions to the accident
- Mental model
- Flaws
- Context

20.6.4 Step 4: Identify Systemic Flaws in the System

This step identifies systemic flaws that contributed to the loss. The systemic factors span the individual system control and feedback structure components, including:

- Communication and coordination
- Safety information system (SIS)

- Design of the safety management system
- Culture
- Changes and dynamics in the system and its environment
- Economics
- System environment

20.6.5   Step 5: Create Recommendations for Change

This step creates recommendations for changes to the safety control and feedback structures to prevent a similar accident in the future. Such recommendations may include:

- Assigning responsibilities, priority, scheduling, and budgeting for implementing the recommendations
- Establishing a feedback system to determine whether the recommendations and implementation effectively strengthened the control and feedback structures
- Follow up

20.7   CAST Example: CH-53 Helicopters Mid-Air Collision

20.7.1   Background

On February 4, 1997, two Israeli Air Force (IAF) CH-53 Sea Stallion Sikorsky helicopters collided in mid-flight during an operational mission of transferring Israeli Defense Force (IDF) soldiers to their posts in Lebanon. All aboard—73 crew, officers, and soldiers—perished as these helicopters plunged to the earth. This investigation aims to identify the system-wide control and feedback failures that interacted to create this disaster. In addition, the scope of a typical accident investigation includes both the developer of the helicopter and especially the chain of operators of the system from IDF headquarters down to the pilots operating the two helicopters.

20.7.2   Step 1: Assemble the Basic Information

1. CH-53 Accident Overall System

The overall system involved in the two CH-53 helicopters accident is described below. Any component outside the marked boundary is considered the context (environment) of the system.

- Israeli Defense Force (IDF)
- Israeli Air Force (IAF)
- IAF headquarters
- IAF Material Directorate
- Air Directorate
- IAF Department of Safety & Quality Control
- CH-53 Squadron
- CH-53 Helicopter, tail number (TN) 357
- CH-53 Helicopter, tail number (TN) 903

2. CH-53 Helicopter History

CH-53 Sea Stallion was manufactured by the Sikorsky Aircraft Company (SAC). It is one of the oldest and most reliable air traffic helicopters ever. Two older models of the Sikorsky helicopters (CH-53A and CH-53D) have been in the IAF service since 1969 (Figure 20.8). However, they have become obsolete in the rest of the world. The US Navy operates the E model, an aircraft that is different from the Israeli model, in most of its dynamic and electronic systems.

Figure 20.8 Sikorsky helicopter CH-53.

3. Accident Overview

On February 4, 1997, two Israeli Air Force (IAF) CH-53 Sea Stallion Sikorsky helicopters were on a routine mission to transport Israeli Defense Force (IDF) soldiers to their posts in Lebanon. The two helicopters, tail numbers TN 903 and TN 357, left Mahanayim Airbase at night. Then, eight minutes after departure, the TN 903 main rotor hit the TN 357 tail rotor. Both helicopters crashed in the vicinity of the She'ar Yashuv village. As these helicopters plunged to earth, they were destroyed, and all aboard, a total of 73 officers and soldiers, perished (Figure 20.9).

Figure 20.9 Map of helicopters' flights and part of one CH-53 remains.

4. The Flow of Immediate Accident Events

Figure 20.10 depicts the flow of immediate events at the operating level. This sequence was generated at NASA's lab, simulating the last 60 seconds before the accident. As can be seen, NT 903 lost its leading position in the two-aircraft flying formation and eventually collided with NT 357.

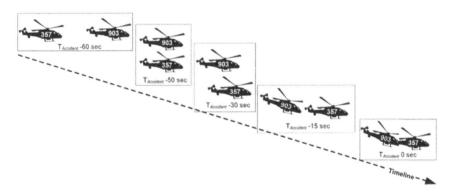

Figure 20.10 NASA lab simulation of the last minute before the accident.

20.7.3 Step 2: Model the Existing Safety Control and Feedback Structures

Three models depicting the existing safety control and feedback structures of the CH-53 system were created. They include the following: (1) development and operations safety control structure, (2) management-level safety control structure, and (3) physical-level safety control structure.

a) Development and Operations Safety Control Structure

The overall development and operations safety control structure associated with this accident is shown in Figure 20.11.

b) Management-Level Safety Control Structure

The expansion of Figure 20.11 regarding the management-level safety control structure is shown in Figure 20.12.

c) Physical-Level Safety Control Structure

The physical-level safety control structure is shown in Figure 20.13. This mapping represents critical decisions and actions made by the TN 903 and the TN 357 immediately before the accident. It helps in identifying broader systemic contributory factors.

20.7.4   Step 3: Analyze Each Component in the System

a) Hazards and Safety Constraints

The hazards and safety constraints associated with this accident were examined and are presented in Table 20.2.

Table 20.2   Hazards and Safety Constraints.

Hazard (H)	Safety Constraint (SC)
H1: Helicopter (one or both) can break a minimal positive separation between them.	SC1: Both helicopters must keep a minimal positive distance between each other (either on flight path or height).
H2: Helicopter (one or both) can break a minimal positive separation between aircraft and terrain.	SC2: Both helicopters must keep a minimal positive distance from the terrain.
H3: One or both helicopters can enter an uncontrolled maneuver into the ground.	SC3: Flight regimes must follow the helicopter manufacturer's limits (regarding velocity, maneuvers, and allowable carriage weight definitions).
H4: Helicopter (one or both) can break flying formation.	SC4: Verbal communication and coordination must exist during flight time to keep formation.
	SC5: Crew assignments must follow the single-pilot training, qualification, and health state.

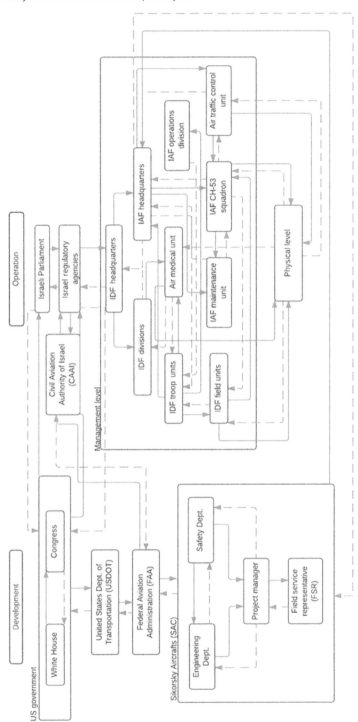

Figure 20.11 Development and operations safety control (Image: Baktare and Hartmann, 2016).

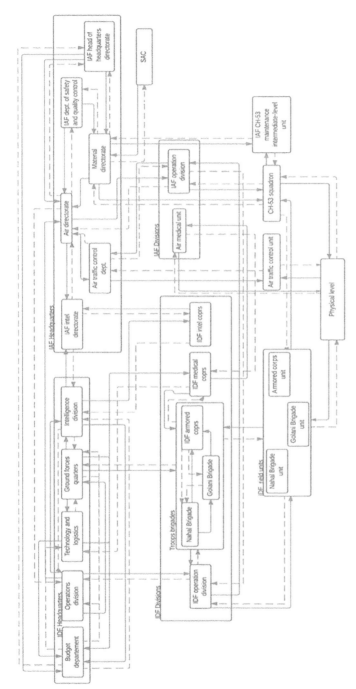

Figure 20.12 Management-level safety control (Image: Baktare and Hartmann, 2016).

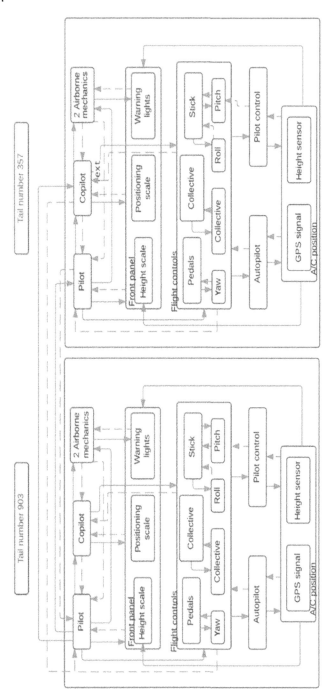

Figure 20.13 Physical-level safety control (Image: Baktare and Hartmann, 2016).

b) Main Findings: Heritage Devices

H2: Minimal safety distance between both aircraft

H3: Aircraft can enter uncontrolled maneuver into the ground

Three options:

- Pilots didn't know about an inherent limit of the night sight device from the squadron management.
- Pilots never complained about the 40° limited field of view.
- Pilots complained, but no action was taken (by the squadron leadership or headquarters personnel).

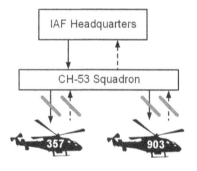

c) Findings: Training and Allocation Flaws 1

H1: Minimal positive separation between aircrafts (A/Cs)

H2: Minimal safety distance between both A/Cs and the terrain

Mutual light inspection training.

- The squadron commanders did not provide training, and none of the crew had undertaken such training.
- No evidence of training protocol for such inspection was mentioned or investigated.

d) Findings: Training and Allocation Flaws 2

H4: Helicopter can foil formation flying

- No evidence of formation flying training protocol was mentioned or identified.
- If there was a protocol:
  - Was it up to date and precise?
  - Were all squadron pilots familiar with the procedure?
  - Did it define the flying limits to keep the safety constraints?
  - Did it define the pilot's training procedure?

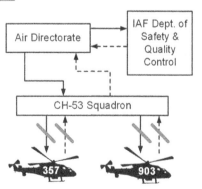

- Did it take into consideration the manufacturer's limits? Other operators' definitions?

e) Findings: Training and Allocation Flaws 3

H4: Helicopter can foil formation flying
If there was no protocol:

- How does the IAF define a formation flying leader?
- Was the need for such a protocol raised by the squadron to the air directorate?
- Did the air directorate raise it to the safety and quality control department?

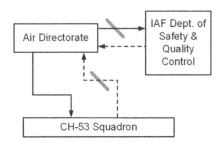

f) Findings: Warning Devices

H1: Minimal positive separation between A/Cs
H2: Minimal safety distance between both A/Cs

- Neither aircraft was equipped with a cockpit voice recorder (CVR), black box, or proximity warning system (PWS).
- Two options:
  - The need for such devices was never raised to the headquarters
  - No headquarter approval for equipping (no funds, low risk, prioritization, etc.)

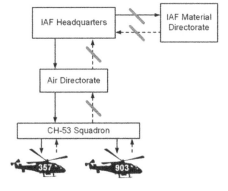

20.7.5 Step 4: Identify Systemic Flaws in the Overall System

a) Accident Investigation's Main Findings

- The TN 903 pilot was responsible for the accident due to a lack of visual contact with TN 357.
- Neither pilot qualified as a formation flying leader.
- Night vision devices limited the visual angle. This limitation contributed to the accident by significantly restricting sight coverage.

- Behavioral analysis suggests that no signs of competition were found between the two pilots.
- There was no evidence of any technical malfunction within the two aircraft.
- Both aircrafts' take-off weights exceeded the maximum limit.
- No cockpit voice recorder or black box was available to understand the accident circumstances fully.

b) Systemic Hazards in IAF

- Safety culture mission-oriented behavior context: "Mission comes above safety"
- Basic nonroutine procedures missing (e.g., formation flying definitions and qualification procedures)
- IAF air directorate and material directorate is recognized as most vulnerable part of the system due to (1) too many spans of control and (2) too many feedback loops
- IAF's risk analysis and assessments are not suitable for nonroutine flight regimens
- Active communication between the IAF and the Israeli Aviation Authority needed

20.7.6 Step 5: Create Recommendations for Change

The following is a top-level recommendation for change within the IAF:

- The STAMP model and CAST analysis revealed more profound and systematic weaknesses of the IAF hierarchical structure.
- Most of the findings showed a lack of communication between the hierarchical levels and/or a lack of feedback.
- Formation flying matter was never discussed.
- After the 1997 accident, the air directorate was declared a weak point and divided into two different authorities for a long-term training agenda. The IAF separated training authorities between fighter jets and helicopters due to the significant difference between their missions and training protocols.

20.8 Bibliography

Baktare, K. and Hartmann, D. (2016). System theoretic safety analysis of Israeli Air Force (IAF) CH-53 1977 and CH-53 1997 aviation disasters. 4th European STAMP Workshop, *Zurich, Switzerland*, September 2016.

Delikhoon, M., Zarei, E., Banda, O.V., Faridan, M., and Habibi, E. (2022). Systems thinking accident analysis models: A systematic review for sustainable safety management. *Sustainability* 14 (10): 5869.

Gui, F., Xuecai, X., Qingsong, J., Zonghan, L., Ping, C., and Ying, G. (2019). The development history of accident causation models in the past 100 years: 24Model, a more modern accident causation model. *Process Safety and Environmental Protection* 134.

Henderson, J.P. (n.d.). Causal analysis based on system theory. GitHub. joelparkerhenderson/causal-analysis-based-on-system-theory. Accessed: Jan. 2023.

Leveson, N.G. (2023, Nov. 14). *An Introduction to System Safety Engineering*. MIT Press.

Leveson, N.G. (2019). CAST handbook: How to learn more from incidents and accidents. See https://psas.scripts.mit.edu/home/get_file4.php?name=CAST_handbook.pdf. *Accessed: Jan.2023.*

Leveson, N.G. (n.d.). MIT Partnership for Systems Approaches to Safety and Security (PSASS). https://psas.scripts.mit.edu/home/. Accessed: Jan. 2023.

Leveson, N.G. (2016). *Engineering a Safer World: Systems Thinking Applied to Safety (Engineering Systems)*, reprint edition. MIT Press.

Salmon, P.M., Stanton, N.A., Walker, G.H., Hulme, A., Goode, N., Thompson, J., and Read, G.J. (2022). The systems theoretic accident model and process-causal analysis based on systems theory (STAMP) method. In *Handbook of Systems Thinking Methods* (pp. 229–250). CRC Press.

Straker, D. (n.d.). CAST: Causal analysis using system theory (CAST): Implementation and integration http://psas.scripts.mit.edu/home/wp-content/uploads/2020/08/CAST-Implementation-and-Integration.pdf. Accessed: Jan. 2023.

Appendix A

Distinguished Systems Science Researchers

As mentioned before, systems science research covers many topics in many domains. Therefore, readers are advised to explore relevant information on distinguished systems scientists and their specializations listed below. This table was derived with permission from an initial list of distinguished systems scientists from Professor Len Troncale and others (Troncale, 2018).

Distinguished Systems Science Individuals and Their Specializations[1]

Researcher	Specialization
Abraham Ralph	Chaos math
Allen Timothy	Hierarchies
Auyung Sunny	Complex systems
Bak Per	Self-criticality
Bar-Yam Yaneer	Complex systems
Barabasi Albert-Laszlo	Network theory
Barrow John	Physics
Bertalanffy Ludwig von	General systems theory
Boulding Kenneth	General systems theory, economy
Corning Peter	Synergy, biology
Cowan George	Complex systems
Doxiadis Constantinos	Human settlements
Eigen Manfred	Hypercycles
Gel Mann Murray	Flexions

(Continued)

---

1 Derived with permission from: L. Troncale (2018).

Systems Science for Engineers and Scholars, First Edition. Edited by Avner Engel.
© 2024 John Wiley & Sons, Ltd. Published 2024 by John Wiley & Sons, Ltd.

Researcher	Specialization
Haken Herbert	Synergy, physics
Holland John	Agent-based modeling
Hood Lee	Systems biology
Iberall Arthur	Viable systems
Karplus Martin	System chemistry
Kauffman Stuart	Emergence
Klir George	Systems math, fuzzy sets
Langton Christopher	Artificial life
Latour Bruno	Actor net theory
Leontief Wassily	Systems economics
Lorenz Konrad	Chaos
Mandelbrot Benoit	Fractals
Mesarovic Mihalo	Systems biology
Miller James	Living systems
Mitchell Melanie	Complex systems
Odum Howard	Systems ecology
Pattee Howard	Hierarchy theory
Prigogine Ilya	Thermodynamics
Rapoport Anatol	Game theory
Randall Lisa	Physics
Salthe Stan	Hierarchies
Shannon Claude	Information theory
Simms Jim	Quantitative living systems
Simons Herbert	Computer science, economics
Thom Rene	Catastrophe theory
Troncale Len	System process theory
Von Foerster Heinz	Cybernetics
Weinberg Gerald	Systems engineering
Weiner Norbert	Feedback
West Gregory	Systems allometry
Whiteside George	Systems chemistry
Wilson Albert	Hierarchies
Wolfram Stephen	System math

Researcher	Specialization
Wymore Wayne	Systems engineering
Zadeh Lofti	Fuzzy math
Zeeman Erik	Catastrophe theory

Bibliography

Troncale L. (2018). *On the Nature of Systems Thinking and Systems Science: Similarities, Differences, and Potential Synergies, Disciplinary Convergence in Systems Engineering Research* (pp. 647–663). Springer International Publishing.

Appendix B

Distinguished Systems Thinking Researchers

As mentioned before, systems thinking research covers many topics in many domains. Therefore, readers are advised to explore relevant information on distinguished systems thinking scientists and their specializations listed below. This table was derived with permission from an initial list of distinguished systems scientists from Professor Len Troncale and others (Troncale, 2018).

Distinguished Systems Thinking Individuals and Their Specializations

Name	Specialization
Ackoff Russell	Systems management
Axelrod Robert	Cooperation
Bahm Archie	Systems philosophy
Banathy Bela	Systems education
Bateson Gregory	Systems philosophy
Beer Stafford	Systems management
Bogdanov Alexander	Organization
Bosch Ockie	Bayesian applications
Bunge Mario	Systems philosophy
Cabrera Derek	Systems dynamics
Callon Michel	Actor-network theory
Checkland Peter	Soft systems
Chomsky Noam	Systems linguistics
Churchman Charles	Systems management
Corning Peter	Synergy bio

1 Derived with permission from: L. Troncale (2018).

Systems Science for Engineers and Scholars, First Edition. Edited by Avner Engel.
© 2024 John Wiley & Sons, Ltd. Published 2024 by John Wiley & Sons, Ltd.

Name	Specialization
Doxiadis Constantinos	Human settlements
Forrester Jay	Systems dynamics
Francois Charles	Encyclopedia
Fuller Buckminster	Systems architectures
Gerard Ralph	Systems neuroscience
Hall Arthur	Meta systems
Hammond Debora	Systems history
Jackson Michael	Critical systems thinking
Jantsch Erich	Systems philosophy
Laszlo Ervin	Systems philosophy
Maturana Humberto	Self-creation
Mead Margaret	Systems anthropology
Meadows Donella	Systems dynamics
Midgley Gerald	Interventions
Mitroff Ian	Systems management
Richmond Barry	Systems dynamics
Ring Jack	Systems engineering
Rousseau David	Systems philosophy
Senge Peter	Systems management
Skyttner Lars	General systems theory
Starkerman Rudolf	Systems dynamics
Sterman John	Systems dynamics
Strogatz Steven	Systems math
Varella Francisco	Self-creation
Vesterby Vincent	General systems theory
Vickers Geoffrey	Systems management
Von Foerster Heinz	Cybernetics
Warfield John	Systems modeling

Bibliography

Troncale L. (2018). *On the Nature of Systems Thinking and Systems Science: Similarities, Differences, and Potential Synergies, Disciplinary Convergence in Systems Engineering Research* (pp. 647–663). Springer International Publishing.

Appendix C

Permissions to Use Third-Party Copyright Material

0. Book Front Cover and Dedication Page

Book front cover	• Image created by the NIRCam instrument onboard NASA's (National Aeronautics and Space Administration) James Webb Space Telescope in 2022. Image available in the public domain (NASA).
Book dedication page	• Image obtained from: Albert Einstein, 1947. Reproduced with Wikimedia Commons permission (work is in the public domain because it was published in the United States between 1928 and 1963, and the copyright was not renewed). Photograph by Orren Jack Turner, Princeton, N.J. Modified with Photoshop by PM_Poon and later by Dantadd.

1. Chapter 1: Introduction to Systems Science

Figure 1.3	• Image concept adapted from: Rockstrom et al. (2009).
Figure 1.6	• Image concept adapted from: Prof. Len Troncale's writings.
Figure 1.7	• Sub-image obtained from: Concrete staves are prefabricated parts of equal strength regardless of silo size. Reproduced with Wikimedia Commons permission. Author: DMahalko, Dale Mahalko, Gilman, WI, USA -- Email: dmahalko@gmail.com.
Figure 1.9	• Image obtained with author permission from: Rafols et al. (2010).
Table 1.2	• Concept adapted with modifications from: Mobus and Kalton (2015).
Section 1.4.1	• Image obtained from: Belarussian writer Alexander A Bogdanov. Reproduced with Wikimedia Commons permission. Author: Unknown author
Section 1.4.2	• Image obtained from: The young Ludwig von Bertalanffy in 1926. Reproduced with Wikimedia Commons permission. Author: Unknown photographer.
Section 1.4.3	• Image obtained from: Kenneth E. Boulding. Reproduced from: Wikimedia. Author: unknown.

Systems Science for Engineers and Scholars, First Edition. Edited by Avner Engel.
© 2024 John Wiley & Sons, Ltd. Published 2024 by John Wiley & Sons, Ltd.

- Note: This photograph is copyrighted and is not under a free license. However, it is believed that using this work in this chapter to provide visual identification of this specific individual qualifies as fair use under United States copyright law.

Section 1.4.4 Section 1.4.5 Section 1.4.6	Reproduced with permission obtained from: the Michigan Neuroscience Institute, University of Michigan Medical School for the following images:

- James Grier Miller
- Ralph Waldo Gerard
- Anatol Rapoport

Section 1.4.7	Image obtained from: Professor George Klir at the IEEE Conference "Intelligent Systems" 2008. Varna, Bulgaria. Reproduced with Wikimedia Commons permission. Author: Vassia Atanassova – Spiritia.

Section 1.5 (1)	Reproduced with permission obtained from: Prof. George Mobus for the following images:

- Principles of systems science (book cover image)
- George Mobus
- Michael Kalton

Section 1.5 (2)	Reproduced with permission obtained from: Prof. Gary Metcalf for the following images:

- Handbook of Systems Science (book cover image)
- Gary Metcalf
- Kyoichi Kijima
- Hiroshi Deguchi

Permission to adapt text and ideas.	• Prof. Eberhard Umbach. Criticism of systems science.

2. Chapter 2: Principles of Systems Science (Part I)

Figure 2.1	• Sub-image adapted from: Milky Way Galaxy. Image in the public domain. Author: Jet Propulsion Laboratory (JPL), NASA: Caltech/R. Hurt (SSC/Caltech).
	• Sub-image adapted from: View of the universe captured by the Hubble Space Telescope. Reproduced with Wikimedia Commons permission. Author: NASA, ESA, H. Teplitz and M. Rafelski (IPAC/Caltech), A. Koekemoer (STScI), R. Windhorst (Arizona State University), and Z. Levay (STScI).
Figure 2.3	• Image adapted from: The Great Wall of China at Mutianyu, near Beijing. Reproduced with Wikimedia Commons permission. Author: Nicolas Perrault III.
Figure 2.12	• Sub-image adapted from: Structure of DNA. Reproduced with Wikimedia Commons permission. Author: Zephyris.

- Sub-image adapted from: Plant t cell type collenchyma. Reproduced with Wikimedia Commons permission. Author: Carl Szczerski.
- Sub-image adapted from: Red fox. Reproduced with Wikimedia Commons permission. Author: Shiretoko-Shari Tourist Association.
- Sub-image adapted from: Actiniaria. Reproduced with Wikimedia Commons permission. Author: Giacomo Merculiano (1859–1935).
- Sub-image adapted from: Annual mean sea surface. Reproduced with Wikimedia Commons permission. Author: Plumbago.
- Sub-image adapted from: Baja California Desert in the Catavina region, south of Ensenada, Mexico. Reproduced with Wikimedia Commons permission. Author: Tomas Castelazo.
- Sub-image adapted from: Emperor penguins with young. Reproduced with Wikimedia Commons permission. Photographer: Giuseppe Zibordi (NOAA image – public domain).
- Sub-image adapted from: the Human eye. Reproduced with Wikimedia Commons permission. Author: che.
- Sub-image adapted from: Cell of eukaryotes. Reproduced with Wikimedia Commons permission. Vectorized by: Mortadelo2005.
- Sub-image adapted from: Molecule of water. Reproduced with Wikimedia Commons permission. Author: Dbc334 / Jynto.

Figure 2.13	• Image adapted from: Scene at the Signing of the Constitution of the United States. Reproduced with Wikimedia Commons permission. Artist: Howard Chandler Christy (1873–1952. Source: The Indian Reporter.
Figure 2.15	• Image adapted from: A Blue Starfish (Linckia laevigata) resting on hard Acropora and Porites corals. Reproduced with Wikimedia Commons permission. Author: Richard Ling <wikipedia@rling.com>.
Figure 2.17	• Sub-image adapted from: Red deer (Cervus elaphus) young stag, Glen Garry, Highland. Reproduced with Wikimedia Commons permission. Author: Charles J Sharp.
	• Sub-image adapted from: Wolf in the Kolmarden Zoo (Sweden). Reproduced with Wikimedia Commons permission. Author: Daniel Mott from: Stockholm, Sweden.
	• Sub-image adapted from: Wolves' impact on red deer in the Voronezhsky reserve. Graph used with permission of Prof. Boris Romashov and Dr. Aleksandr Mishin from: Voronezhsky State Nature Biosphere Reserve in Russia.
Figure 2.21	• Image adapted from: Timeline of the Universe. Reproduced with Wikimedia Commons permission. Author: NASA/WMAP Science Team.
Figure 2.22	• Image adapted from: The Solar System. Image in the public domain. Author: Jet Propulsion Laboratory (JPL), NASA.

Figure 2.24	• Image adapted from: Stromatolites growing in Hamelin Pool Marine Nature Reserve, Shark Bay in Western Australia. Reproduced with Wikimedia Commons permission. Author: Paul Harrison.
Figure 2.26	• Image adapted from: State of matter: phase transition. Reproduced with Wikimedia Commons permission. Author: ElfQrin.
Figure 2.27	• Image adapted from: Heavy rust on the links of a chain near the Golden Gate Bridge in San Francisco. Reproduced with Wikimedia Commons permission. Author: Marlith.
Permission to adapt text and ideas.	• Prof. Boris Romashov and Dr. Aleksandr Mishin. Red deer and wolves' interactions.

3. Chapter 3: Principles of Systems Science (Part II)

Figure 3.9	• Sub-images adapted from: Electrical handheld drill (made by DeWalt). Reproduced by Van Wie et al. (2001).
Figure 3.10	• Sub-image adapted from: Illustration of the Ørsted spacecraft in orbit. Image in the public domain. Image credit: DRSI, European Space Agency (ESA).
	• Sub-image adapted from: The Ørsted satellite mounted for vibration tester. Image in the public domain. Image credit: Per Thomsen, European Space Agency (ESA).
Figure 3.21	• Sub-image adapted from: tap mechanism. Reproduced with Wikimedia Commons permission. Author: Chabacano.
Figure 3.22	• Sub-image adapted from: MQ-9 Reaper flies above Creech AFB during a local training mission. Reproduced with Wikimedia Commons permission. Author: U.S. Air Force photo by Paul Ridgeway.
Figure 3.23	• Image adapted from: PID controller overview. Reproduced with Wikimedia Commons permission. Author: Arturo Urquizo.
Figure 3.24	• Image adapted from: Tuning PID controller showing effect of P, I, and D on response. Reproduced with Wikimedia Commons permission. Author: Physicsch.
Figure 3.25	• Sub-images adapted from: Human Body. Reproduced with Wikimedia Commons permission. Author: Mikael Haggstrom.
Figure 3.27	• Sub-image adapted from: a Scanning electron micrograph of Escherichia coli. Reproduced with Wikimedia Commons permission. Author: Rocky Mountain Laboratories, NIAID, NIH.
	• Sub-image adapted from: Acanthamoeba trophozoites with the characteristic acanthopodia. Reproduced with Wikimedia Commons permission. Author: Jacob Lorenzo-Morales, Naveed A. Khan, and Julia Walochnik.

- Sub-image adapted from: Fly Agaric (Amanita muscaria) near Tyndrum, Scotland. Reproduced with Wikimedia Commons permission. Author: Tim Bekaert.
- Sub-image adapted from: A Wild Cherry in flower. Reproduced with Wikimedia Commons permission. Author: Benjamin Gimmel, BenHur.
- Sub-image adapted from: Plains zebra in Etosha National Park, Namibia. Reproduced with Wikimedia Commons permission. Author: Yathin S Krishnappa.

Figure 3.29	• Image adapted from: Primate skeletons. Reproduced with Wikimedia Commons permission. Author: Unknown author.
Figure 3.30	• Image adapted from: Biological derivation relationship of the various bones in the forelimbs of four vertebrates. Reproduced with Wikimedia Commons permission. Author: Volkov Vladislav Petrovich.
Figure 3.32	• Image adapted from: Bee swarm on a tree, Victoria, Australia. Reproduced with Wikimedia Commons permission. Author: Fir0002/Flagstaffotos [at] gmail.com.
Figure 3.33	• Image adapted from: The flock of starlings acting as a swarm. Reproduced with Wikimedia Commons permission. Author: John Holmes.
Figure 3.34	• Image adapted from: Wildebeests engage in the annual great African migration. Reproduced with: Free Images & Free stock photos – PxHere permission.
Figure 3.35	• Image adapted from: Prey fish schooling or shoaling forming a circular bait ball in a defensive move against predation flanked by two larger butterfly fish. Reproduced with Wikimedia Commons permission. Author: lifefish.
Figure 3.36	• Image adapted from: Cathedral Termite Mounds in the Northern Territory. Reproduced with Wikimedia Commons permission. Author: Brian Voon Yee Yap: w: User:Yewenyi.
Section 3.3.4.3	• Image obtained from: Sir William Rowan Hamilton. Reproduced with Wikimedia Commons permission. Author: Unknown.
Permission to adapt text and ideas.	• Dr. Louise Kjaer. Environmental input-output analysis related to corporations and products.
	• Prof. Steven Frank. Input-output relations in biological systems.
	• Prof. Olivier de Weck and Dr. Kaushik Sinha. Structural complexity.

4. Chapter 4: Systems Thinking

Figure 4.1 Figure 4.7	• Sub-image adapted from: Part of a printing press in the Musee des Arts et Metiers in Paris. Reproduced with Free Images & Free stock photos – PxHere permission.
Figure 4.2	• Image adapted from: Bicycle diagram-en.svg. Reproduced with Wikimedia Commons permission. Author: A12.

Figure 4.4	Image created from: photomontage of:
	• Sub-image adapted from: South Shetland-2016-Southern Ocean. Reproduced with Wikimedia Commons permission. Author: Godot13
	• Sub-image adapted from: Iceberg.jpg. Reproduced with Wikimedia Commons permission. Author: Uwe Kils (iceberg) and Wiska Bodo (sky).
Figure 4.6	• Image adapted from: 1511 The Limbic Lobe. Reproduced with Wikimedia Commons permission. Author: OpenStax College.
Section 4.6.1	• Image obtained from: Norbert Wiener, American mathematician. Reproduced with Wikimedia Commons permission. Author: Konrad Jacobs.
Section 4.6.2	• Image obtained from: Talcott Parsons (1902-1979). Reproduced with Wikimedia Commons permission. Author: Tonnies.
Section 4.6.3	• Image obtained from: W. Ross Ashby (1948). Reproduced with Wikimedia Commons permission. Author: Unknown.

5. Chapter 5: Systems Engineering

Figure 5.1	• Image adapted from: Viaduc de Millau, France, seen from: the air. Reproduced with Wikimedia Commons permission. Author: Mike Lehmann, Mike Switzerland.
Figure 5.2	• Sub-image adapted from: Qantas Boeing 747-400ER; VH-OEI@LAX;18.04.2007/463fi. Reproduced with Wikimedia Commons permission. Author: Aero Icarus from: Zürich, Switzerland.
Figure 5.3	• Image adapted from: The Millennium Dome, London, UK. Reproduced with Wikimedia Commons permission. Author: https://www.flickr.com/photos/jamesjin/.
Figure 5.7	• Image adapted from: Simulation of the Space Launch System (SLS) rocket during liftoff as it clears the launch tower during future missions. The Image is in the public domain. Author: NASA Langley Research Center engineer, Hampton, Virginia.
Figure 5.10	• Sub-image adapted from: Visual of how the law of conservation of mass means that there must be the same number of atoms of each element for the reactants and the products. Reproduced with Wikimedia Commons permission. Authors: Jynto, Robert A. Rohde, Jacek FH, Jynto.
Figure 5.13	• Image adapted from: Titanic sinking. The image is in the public domain. Artist: Willy Stower (died in May 1931).
Figure 5.14	• Sub-image adapted from: Side plan of the RMS Titanic. Reproduced with Wikimedia Commons permission. Author: Anonymous.
Figure 5.15	• Image adapted from: The Tacoma Narrows Bridge Collapsing. Reproduced with Wikimedia Commons permission (Work is in the public domain).

Figure 5.16	• Image adapted from: The Forgotten Legacy of the Banqiao Dam Collapse, The Economic Observer, Feb. 8, 2013. Author: Eric Fish.
Figure 5.17	• Image adapted from: Exterior view of the Union Carbide pesticide factory in Bhopal, India, scene of the world's worst industrial disaster in 1985. Reproduced with Wikimedia Commons permission. Author: Bhopal Medical Appeal.
Figure 5.18	• Image adapted from: Icicles formed on the launch pad and service tower in the evening and early morning hours on January 28, 1986. Reproduced with Wikimedia Commons permission. Author: NASA.
Figure 5.19	• Image adapted from: Historical collections of the Chernobyl accident. Reproduced with Wikimedia Commons permission. Author: Ukrainian Society for Friendship and Cultural Relations with Foreign Countries (USFCRFC).
Figure 5.20	• Sub-image adapted from: Hubble Space Telescope Primary Mirror. Reproduced with Wikimedia Commons permission. Author: NASA Marshall Space Flight Center.
	• Sub-image adapted from: The Hubble Space Telescope as seen from: the departing Space Shuttle Atlantis, flying STS-125, HST Servicing Mission 4. Reproduced with Wikimedia Commons permission. Author: Ruffnax (Crew of STS-125).
Figure 5.21	• Sub-images adapted from: New Orleans Elevations. Reproduced with Wikimedia Commons permission. Author: Alexdi at English Wikipedia.
Figure 5.23	• Image adapted from: Diagram of the Fukushima Nuclear Power plant accident. Reproduced with Wikimedia Commons permission. Author: Sodacan.
Section 5.2.6.2	• Failed engineering project. Image adapted from: Tory_II-C_ reactor. Reproduced with Wikimedia Commons permission. Author: US Department of Energy.
Permission to adapt text and ideas.	• The Royal Academy of Engineering, London, United Kingdom. Philosophy of Engineering, Proceedings of a series of seminars, Volume 1. The authors of the original papers are Lipton P., Hoare T., Turnbull J., Franssen M., and Elliott C. Reproduced with permission of the Royal Academy of Engineering, London, UK.
	• Prof. Len Troncale. Data on recurring systems engineering human-systems problems.

6. Chapter 6: Comparative Analysis - Two Domains

Figure 6.1	• Image adapted from: Inner view of a Seagate 3.5-inch hard disk drive. Reproduced with Wikimedia Commons permission. Author: Eric Gaba (Sting-fr:Sting).
Figure 6.4	• Image adapted from: Diagram of DNA in a eukaryotic cell. Reproduced with Wikimedia Commons permission. Authors: Sponk, Tryphon, Magnus Manske, User: Dietzel65, LadyofHats (Mariana Ruiz), Radio89.

| Figure 6.6
Figure 6.7 | • Images adapted with permission from: Prof. David D'Onofrio (D'Onofrio and an 2010). |
| Permission to adapt text and ideas. | • Prof. David D'Onofrio. Comparative analysis between the structure and function of computer hard drives and DNA. |

7. Chapter 7: Holistic Systems Context

Figure 7.2	• Image adapted from: Bernese Oberland, Switzerland. Reproduced with Wikimedia Commons permission. Author: Ryan Gsell.
Figure 7.3	• Image adapted from: Poster showing a pyramid that symbolizes class society. At the top we can see Leopold II (King of the Belgians). Reproduced with Wikimedia Commons permission. Author: Parti ouvrier belge (POB).
Figure 7.8	• Image adapted from: Production line for C-10 personal computer at Cromemco factory in Mountain View, California. Reproduced with Wikimedia Commons permission. Author: Cromemco.
Figure 7.9	• Image adapted from: A scenario of how society reacts to a stock market bubble. Reproduced with Wikimedia Commons permission. Author: Wikimedia Commons.
Figure 7.10	• Image adapted from: The Plumb-pudding in danger, or, State epicures taking un petit souper. Reproduced with Wikimedia Commons permission. Author: James Gillray (1756–1815).
Figure 7.11	• Image adapted from: Code of Hammurabi. Reproduced with Wikimedia Commons permission. Author: N/A.
Figure 7.12	• Image adapted from: Sociocultural system diagram. Reproduced with Wikimedia Commons permission. Author: Jason Cupertino.

8. Chapter 8: Example: UAV System of Interest (SoI)

Figure 8.1	• Sub-image adapted from: RQ-2B Pioneer (drawing). Reproduced with Wikimedia Commons permission. Author: Information not available.
Figure 8.2	• Image adapted from: U.S. Navy RQ-2B Pioneer Unmanned Aerial Vehicle. Reproduced with Wikimedia Commons permission. Photographer: Mate 2nd Class Daniel J. McLain.
Figure 8.7 Figure 8.9	• Sub-image adapted from: RQ-2B Pioneer (drawing). Reproduced with Wikimedia Commons permission. Author: Information not available.

9. Chapter 9: Example: UAV Context (Part I)

| Figure 9.1 | • Image adapted from: A young man is pictured burning electrical wires to recover copper at Agbogbloshie, Ghana. Reproduced with Wikimedia Commons permission. Author: Muntaka Chasant. |

Figure 9.3	• Image adapted with permission from: Mr. Eric Freeman, CEO of Alpha Unmanned Systems.
Figure 9.4	• Image adapted from: Ten-engine electric remotely piloted aircraft completes successful Flight test. Image in the public domain (NASA). Photograph: NASA Langley/David C. Bowman.
Figure 9.5	• Image adapted from: OnyxStar XENA-8F coax foldable and pliable drone. Reproduced with Wikimedia Commons permission. Author: ZullyC3P.
Figure 9.6	• Image adapted from: U.S. Air Force researchers needed distributing airborne tactical beamforming capabilities to enable future generations of aerial swarming drones. Image in the public domain (U.S. Air Force). Author: U.S. Air Force Research Lab Information Directorate.
Figure 9.7	• Sub-image adapted from: Drawing of the X-ray space telescope Uhuru of NASA. Reproduced with Wikimedia Commons permission. Author: NASA.
	• Sub-image adapted from: RQ-2B Pioneer (drawing). Reproduced with Wikimedia Commons permission. Author: Information not available.
Figure 9.8	• Sub-image 21OTL – Permission to include an image from the manufacturer: Avidrone Aerospace, Canada.
	• Sub-image Draganfly – Permission to include an image from the manufacturer: Draganfly, Canada, US.
	• Sub-image Ehang EH216-S – Permission to include an image from the manufacturer: Ehang H.L Limited, China.
	• Sub-image GRIFF 300 – Permission to include an image from the manufacturer: Griff Aviation, Norway.
	• Sub-image APT 70 – Permission to include an image from the manufacturer: Bell-APT, US.
Figure 9.13	• Sub-image adapted from: Looking south above Interstate 80, the east shore freeway, near Berkeley, California. Reproduced with Wikimedia Commons permission. Author: User Minesweeper on en. Wikipedia.
	• Sub-image adapted from: Station Flight Control Room Monitors Spacewalk. Image in the public domain (NASA). Photo credit: NASA.
	• Sub-image adapted from: The first 100% Brazilian oil platform, the P-51. Reproduced with Wikimedia Commons permission. Author: Divulgacao Petrobras / ABr.
	• Sub-image adapted from: Grafenrheinfeld Nuclear Power Plant: 2013. Reproduced with Wikimedia Commons permission. Author: Avda.
	• Sub-image adapted from: the Control room for MSG (Meteosat Second Generation) satellites, Darmstadt, Germany. Reproduced with Wikimedia Commons permission. Author: No machine-readable author provided. Ysangkok assumed (based on copyright claims).

	• Sub-image adapted from: Mumbai Airport New ATC Tower. Reproduced with Wikimedia Commons permission. Author: Yatrik Sheth.
	• Sub-image adapted from: A simulation of the original design of the GPS space segment, with 24 GPS satellites (4 satellites in each of 6 orbits). Reproduced with Wikimedia Commons permission. Author: El pak at English Wikipedia.
Figure 9.16	• Image adapted from: The Honeywell RQ-16 T-Hawk Micro Air Vehicle (MAV) flies over a simulated combat area during an operational test flight. Reproduced with Wikimedia Commons permission. Author: Photo by Mass Communication Specialist 3rd Class Kenneth G. Takada.
Figure 9.17	• Image adapted from: A drone intended for agricultural use can carry 25 kg. Reproduced with Wikimedia Commons permission. Author: Agridrones Solutions Israel.
Figure 9.18	• Image adapted from: Windmills and Sailboats on the Ocean. Reproduced with Wikimedia Commons permission. Author: CGP Grey.

10. Chapter 10: Example: UAV Context (Part II)

Figure 10.2	• Sub-image adapted from: MQ-1 Predator armed with AGM-114 Hellfire missile. Reproduced with Wikimedia Commons permission. Author: information not available.
	• Sub-image adapted from: An RQ-4 Global Hawk unmanned aircraft. Reproduced with Wikimedia Commons permission. Author: U.S. Air Force photo by Bobbi Zapka.

11. Chapter 11: Global Environment Crisis

Figure 11.1	• Image adapted from: Planetary Boundaries status in the 2023 updated. Reproduced with Wikimedia Commons permission. Author: Richardson, K. et al.
Figure 11.2	• Image adapted from: Environmental doughnut infographic. Reproduced with Wikimedia Commons permission. Author: DoughnutEconomics.
Figure 11.4	• Image adapted from: Temperature changes have been most pronounced in northern latitudes and over land masses. Reproduced with Wikimedia Commons permission. Author: NASA's Scientific Visualization Studio, Key and Title by the uploader (Eric Fisk).
Figure 11.5	• Image adapted from: Changes in global surface temperature over the past 170 years (black line). Reproduced with Wikimedia Commons permission. Author: Efbrazil.
Figure 11.6	• Image adapted from: CO_2 emissions per capita vs. GDP per capita, 2018. Image in the public domain. Author: Our World in Data, a project of the Global Change Data Lab, a registered charity in England and Wales.

Figure 11.7	• Image adapted from: Nitrogen fertilizer consumption. Total nitrogenous fertilizer consumption measured in tons of total nutrients per year. Reproduced with Wikimedia Commons permission. Author: Our World In Data.
Figure 11.8	• Image adapted from: the Burning Rainforest in Brazil. Reproduced with Wikimedia Commons permission. Author: w: NASA.
Figure 11.9	• Image adapted from: Clearcutting in Southern Finland. Reproduced with Wikimedia Commons permission. Author: Tero Laakso.
Figure 11.10	• Image adapted from: Stacked column chart showing annual loss of tree cover globally, based on World Resources Institute data published on Mongabay. Reproduced with Wikimedia Commons permission. Author: RCraig09.
Figure 11.11	• Image adapted from: Cutaway views showing the internal structure of the Earth. Image in the public domain (United States Geological Survey: USGS). Author: USGS.
Figure 11.12	• Sub-image adapted from: A wildfire on the East Fork of the Bitterroot River on the Sula Complex in the Bitterroot National Forest in Montana, United States. Reproduced with Wikimedia Commons permission. Author: Cbrittain10 (talk contribs).
	• Sub-image adapted from: Flood protection. Image in the public domain (U.S. Department of Homeland Security). Author: DHS.
Figure 11.13	• Image adapted from: 2000 Years of Greenhouse Gas Concentrations. Reproduced with Image in the public domain (U.S. Global Change Research Program, Global Climate Change Impact in the United States – 2009 Report). Image References: Forster et al. (2007); Blasing (2008).
Figure 11.14	• Sub-image adapted from: Wolfsburg, Germany: VW-Werk. Reproduced with Wikimedia Commons permission. Author: Andreas Praefcke.
	• Sub-image adapted from: Daniel and Esther Bartlett House. The upper door is for ventilation, typifying old barns used when winnowing grain. Reproduced with Wikimedia Commons permission. Author: Swroche.
Figure 11.15	• Image adapted from: Observed and projected changes in global mean sea level for 1800–2100. Reproduced with Wikimedia Commons permission. Author: Efbrazil.
Figure 11.18	• Image adapted from: Gordon Dam, Southwest National Park, Tasmania, Australia. Reproduced with Wikimedia Commons permission. Author: JJ Harrison.
Figure 11.19	• Image adapted from: Effects of acid rain, woods, Jizera Mountains, Czech Republic. Reproduced with Wikimedia Commons permission. Author: Lovecz.

Figure 11.20	• Sub-image adapted from: A large blank world map with oceans marked in blue (Robinson projection). Reproduced with Wikimedia Commons permission. Author: John McColgan, Bureau of Land Management, Alaska Fire Service. – Alaskan Type I Incident Management Team.
	• Sub-image adapted from: Showing off a docile Anaconda at the ophiological center, Leticia, Colombia. Reproduced with Wikimedia Commons permission. Author: Dick Culbert from: Gibsons, B.C., Canada.
Section 11.3.4.1	• Image adapted from: Giant cuttlefish annual breeding cycle in the shallow waters off Whyalla, South Australia. Reproduced with Wikimedia Commons permission. Author: Yvonne.
Section 11.3.4.2	• Image adapted from: Proterorhinus tataricus from the Chornaya River, Ukraine. Reproduced with Wikimedia Commons permission. Author: Jorg Freyhof.
Section 11.3.4.3	• Image adapted from: Achatinella fuscobasis. Reproduced with Wikimedia Commons permission. Author: Brenden Holland.
Section 11.3.4.4	• Image adapted from: A full length parrot portrait. Sirocco, the kakapo, poses for the camera. Reproduced with Wikimedia Commons permission. Author: Photo: Mike Bodie, Department of Conservation.
Section 11.3.4.5	• Image adapted from: Lord Howe Island stick insect (Dryococelus australis) at Melbourne Museum. Reproduced with Wikimedia Commons permission. Author: Dryococelus_australis_02_Pengo.jpg: Peter Halasz. (User: Pengo).
Section 11.3.4.6	• Image adapted from: Male Calumma Tarzan from Tarzanville, Eastern Madagascar. Reproduced with Wikimedia Commons permission. Author: Sebastian Gehring.
Section 11.3.4.7	• Image adapted from: Kahuzi-Biega National Park silverback gorilla and child. Reproduced with Wikimedia Commons permission. Author: Kbnp.
Section 11.3.4.8	• Image adapted from: Triops cancriformis Beni-Kabuto Ebi Albino. closeup showing how transparent the carapace. Reproduced with Wikimedia Commons permission. Author: John Alan Elson.
Section 11.3.4.9	• Image adapted from: Wakehurst Place woodland Wollemi pine. Reproduced with Wikimedia Commons permission. Author: AndyScott.
Section 11.3.4.10	• Image adapted from: Staghorn Coral. Reproduced with Wikimedia Commons permission. Author: public domain.
Section 11.3.4.11	• Image adapted from: Green sawfish (Pristis zijsron) at the Genova Aquarium. Reproduced with Wikimedia Commons permission. Author: Flavio Ferrari.

Section 11.3.4.12	• Image adapted from: Golden Barrel (Echinocactus grusonii). Reproduced with Wikimedia Commons permission. Author: Andre Karwath aka.
Section 11.3.4.13	• Image adapted from: Ecnomiohyla rabborum (Rabb's Fringe-limbed Treefrog). Reproduced with Wikimedia Commons permission. Author: Brian Gratwicke from DC, USA.
Section 11.3.4.14	• Image adapted from: Zamia inermis cone. Reproduced with Wikimedia Commons permission. Author: Robtalbert23.

12. Chapter 12: Systemic Environment Action Plan

Figure 12.1	• Image adapted from: Wolfsburg, Germany: VW-Werk. Reproduced with Wikimedia Commons permission. Author: Andreas Praefcke.
Figure 12.2	• Image adapted from: Aerial view of the William H. Zimmer Power Station on the Ohio River in 2017. Reproduced with Wikimedia Commons permission. Author: Antony-22.
Figure 12.3	• Image adapted from: Ibama and the Brazil Federal Police are fighting a criminal group responsible for illegally extracting and trading wood from: the Gurupi Biological Reserve and the Caru and Alto Turiaçu Indigenous Lands in Maranhão. Reproduced with Wikimedia Commons permission. Author: Ibama from: Brazil.
Figure 12.5	• Image adapted from: Carbon Storage at Sea. Reproduced with Wikimedia Commons permission. Author: The joy of all things.
Figure 12.6	• Image adapted from: Column chart showing annual CO_2 sequestration. Reproduced with Wikimedia Commons permission. Author: RCraig09.
Figure 12.7	• Image adapted from: Global Water Consumption 1900-2025, by region, in billions m3 per year. Reproduced with Wikimedia Commons permission. Author: Sampa.
Figure 12.8	• Image adapted from: Drip Irrigation Layout and its parts. Reproduced with Wikimedia Commons permission. Author: Jisl at English Wikipedia.
Figure 12.9	• Image adapted from: Collapse of Atlantic cod landings off the East Coast of Newfoundland in 1992. Reproduced with Wikimedia Commons permission. Author: Lamiot.
Figure 12.10	• Image adapted from: Terraces near the village of Písac in the Sacred Valley on the Urubamba River, Peru. Reproduced with Wikimedia Commons permission. Author: Alexson Scheppa Peisino (AlexSP).
Figure 12.12	• Image adapted from: The estimates and probabilistic projections of the total population of the world. Reproduced with Wikimedia Commons permission. Author: United Nations, DESA, Population Division.

13. Chapter 13: Global Energy Crisis

Figure 13.1	• Image adapted from: Global sources for energy from: 2000 to 2020. Reproduced with Wikimedia Commons permission. Author: Efbrazil.
Figure 13.2	• Image concept and data created from: Energy Return on Investment (EROI), Written by Corporate Finance Institute (CFI), Published August 24, 2020, Updated June 28, 2023.
Figure 13.5	• Image adapted from: Ashalim is a solar power station in Israel. Reproduced with Wikimedia Commons permission. Author: Michael.vainshtein.
Figure 13.6	• Image adapted from: Perovo Solar Park, Crimea. Reproduced with Wikimedia Commons permission. Author: Activ Solar.
Figure 13.7	• Image adapted from: Wind turbines in southern California 2016. Reproduced with Wikimedia Commons permission. Author: Erik Wilde from: Berkeley, CA, USA.
Figure 13.8	• Image adapted from: World energy consumption. Reproduced with Wikimedia Commons permission. Author: Con-struct.
Figure 13.9	• Image adapted from: Boiling water reactor system diagram. Reproduced with Wikimedia Commons permission. Authors: Robert Steffens (alias RobbyBer 8 November 2004), SVG: Marlus_Gancher, Antonsusi (talk) using a file from: Marlus_Gancher. See File talk: Schema Siedewasserreaktor.svg#License history.

14. Chapter 14: Systemic Energy Action Plan

Figure 14.1	• Sub-image adapted from: Transformer at the Limestone Generating Station in Manitoba, Canada. Reproduced with Wikimedia Commons permission. Author: Jasonbook99.
	• Sub-image adapted from: 2011 Toyota Corolla photographed in the USA. Reproduced with Wikimedia Commons permission. Author: U.S. National Highway Traffic Safety Administration.
Figure 14.2	• Sub-image adapted from: U.S. GAO report: Technology Assessment: Nuclear Reactors: Status and Challenges in Development and Deployment of New Commercial Concepts. Reproduced with Wikimedia Commons permission. Author: U.S. Government Accountability Office from: Washington, DC, United States.
	• Sub-image adapted from: Transformer at the Limestone Generating Station in Manitoba, Canada. Reproduced with Wikimedia Commons permission. Author: Jasonbook99.
Figure 14.3	• Image used is based on a copyright license made on November 4, 2022, between NuScale Power, LLC, and Dr. Avner Engel. "Various images, text, or other works included in this material are copyright © 2007 or later by NuScale Power, LLC. All rights reserved. The works owned by NuScale Power, LLC may not be copied or used to create derivative works without NuScale's express permission."

Figure 14.4	• Image adapted from: The first Russian floating nuclear power station transported from: Murmansk. Reproduced with Wikimedia Commons permission. Author: Elena Dide.
Figure 14.5	• Image adapted from: The reactor pit of the ACP100 multi-purpose small modular reactor (SMR) within the containment building. Image in the public domain. Author: China National Nuclear Corporation (CNNC).
Figure 14.6	• Image adapted from: ITER exhibits at the International Fusion Energy Days 2013. Monaco. 2 December 2013. Reproduced with Wikimedia Commons permission. Author: IAEA Imagebank, (Photo Credit: Conleth Brady / IAEA).
Figure 14.8	• Image adapted from: Figure 1 in "JT-60SA Construction"—a paper updated on Dec. 22, 2020, available on Japan's National Institutes for Quantum Science and Technology (QST) website. Reproduced with formal QST permission granted to Dr. Avner Engel (License number: F-23-046).
Permission to adapt text and ideas.	• Mr. David Climenhaga. Small Modular Nuclear Reactors (SMRs), their advantages, and disadvantages.

15. Chapter 15: Engineering and Systemic Psychology

Figure 15.1	• Sub-image adapted from: Cerebrospinal System. See a full animation of this medical topic. Reproduced with Wikimedia Commons permission. Author: BruceBlaus. • Sub-image adapted from: Hubble Captures a Cluster in the Heart of the Milky Way. Image in the public domain (NASA/ESA). Author: NASA/ESA.
Figure 15.2	• Sub-image adapted from: The Hubble Ultra Deep Field is an image of a small region of space in the constellation Fornax. Image in the public domain (NASA/ESA). Author: NASA and the European Space Agency.
Figure 15.3	• Image adapted from: Counter-attack by Cuban Revolutionary Armed Forces supported by T-34 tanks near Playa Giron during the Bay of Pigs invasion, 19 April 1961. Reproduced with Wikimedia Commons permission. Author: Rumlin.
Figure 15.4	• Image adapted from: One of the two crashed aircraft, Component No. 929-1006. Reproduced with Wikimedia Commons permission. Author: onbekend.
Figure 15.5	• Sub-image adapted from: A close-up camera view shows Space Shuttle Columbia as it lifts off from: Launch Pad 39A on mission STS-107. Launch occurred on 16th of January, 2003. Reproduced with Wikimedia Commons permission. Author: NASA. • Sub-image adapted from: STS-107 on the Space Shuttle Columbia. Launch occurred on 16th of January, 2003. Reproduced with Wikimedia Commons permission. Author: NASA.

Figure 15.6	• Image adapted from: Dark clouds of smoke and fire emerge as oil burns during a controlled fire in the Gulf of Mexico, May 6, 2010. Reproduced with Wikimedia Commons permission. Author: Petty Officer 2nd Class Justin Stumberg.
Figure 15.7	• Image adapted from: View of the collapsed Morandi bridge over the Polcevera Valley near Genoa. Reproduced with Wikimedia Commons permission. Author: Salvatore1991.
Figure 15.8	• Image adapted from: The First Reading of the Emancipation Proclamation before the Cabinet. Reproduced with Wikimedia Commons permission (Image is in the public domain). Source: United States Senate (http://www.senate.gov).
Permission to adapt text and ideas.	• Prof. T.K. DAS. Cognitive biases.

16. Chapter 16: Delivering Value and Resolving Conflicts

Figure 16.5	• Image adapted from: U.S. Navy RQ-2B Pioneer Unmanned Aerial Vehicle in a flight demonstration at the 2005 Naval UAV Air Demo held at the Naval Air Station, Patuxent River. Reproduced with Wikimedia Commons permission. Author: Mate 2nd Class Daniel J. McLain.
Figure 16.6	• Image adapted from: MQ-5B-Hunter (US Army). Image in the public domain (US Army. Image credit: US Army. See: https://search.usa.gov/search/images?affiliate=www.army.mil&query=MQ+5B.
Permission to adapt text and ideas.	• Dr. Anand Kumar. A systematic approach to deliver system value.

17. Chapter 17: Multi-objective, Multi-agent Decision-Making

Figure 17.7	• Image adapted from: Garry Kasparov plays simultaneously against Felix Magath and other celebrities, an event organized by Spiegel magazine in June 1985 in Hamburg. Reproduced with Wikimedia Commons permission. Author: Kasparov Magath 1985 Hamburg. jpg: GFHund.
Figure 17.10 to Figure 17.13	• Image extracted from: The NetLogo software simulator with author permission. Author: Prof. Uri Wilensky.
Figure 17.14	• Image extracted from: The MASON software simulator with author permission. Author: Prof. Luke Sean.
Permission to adapt text, software, and ideas.	• Prof. Uri Wilensky. The NetLogo software simulator executes the "Wolf-Sheep predation" model. • Prof. Luke Sean. The MASON software simulator executes the "Cooperative Multi-robot Observation of Multiple Moving Targets" model. • Teja Pennada. Containers' optimal positions in a seaport terminal yard.

18. Chapter 18: Systems Engineering Using Category Theory

Figure 18.1	• Image of adapted with permission from: General Motors EV1 Records, Archives Center, National Museum of American History, Smithsonian Institution. Author: General Motors.
Author of category theory section.	• Dr. Yaniv Mordecai. Using category theory in systems engineering.

19. Chapter 19: Holistic Risk Management Using SOSF Methodology

Figure 19.2 to Figure 19.13	• Images adapted from: Nakamura and Kijima, 2012, with author permission.
Permission to adapt text and ideas.	• Prof. Takafumi Nakamura. Holistic risk management using SOSF methodology.

20. Chapter 20: Systemic Accidents and Mishaps Analyses

Figure 20.5	• Image adapted from: STAMP detailed model of socio-technical control (Leveson, 2016). Author: Nancy Leveson.
Figure 20.6	• Image adapted from: STAMP general factors leading to unsafe systems controls (Leveson, 2016). Author: Nancy Leveson.
Figure 20.8	• Image adapted from: CH-53 Sea Stallion "Yas'ur" heavy transport helicopter of the Israeli Air Force, Independence Day 2017. Reproduced with Wikimedia Commons permission. Author: MathKnight and Zachi Evenor.
Figure 20.9	• Sub-image adapted from: Wreckage of a Yasur chopper near the crash site. Reproduced with Wikimedia Commons permission. Author: IDF Spokesperson's Unit / Gil Pasternak.
Figures 20.10, 20.11, 20.12, 20.13.	• Image adapted with permission from: Baktare K. and Hartmann D., System Theoretic Safety Analysis of Israeli Air Force (IAF) CH-53 1977 and CH-53 1997 Aviation Disasters, 4th European STAMP Workshop, Zurich, Switzerland, September, 2016.
Permission to adapt text and ideas.	• Prof. Nancy Leveson. Engineering a Safer World, CAST Handbook. • Joel Parker Henderson. Causal Analysis Based on System Theory. • Baktare Kanarit & Dr. Hartmann Daniel. CH-53 1997 Aviation Disasters, CAST example.

21. Appendix A: Distinguished Systems Science Researchers

Permission to adapt text and ideas.	• Prof. Len Troncale. Distinguished systems science researchers

22. Appendix B: Distinguished Systems Thinking Researchers

Permission to adapt text and ideas.	• Prof. Len Troncale. Distinguished systems science researchers

Appendix D

List of Acronyms

2D	Two Dimensional
3D	Three Dimensional
A/C	Aircraft
AASHTO	American Association of State Highway and Transportation
ABS	Acrylonitrile, Butadiene, and Styrene
ACE	Army Corps of Engineers
ACP	Artificial Cardiac Pacemakers
ADC	Analog-to-Digital Converters
AI	Artificial Intelligent
AMS	Analog and Mixed Signal
APAC	Asia Pacific
API	Application Program Interface
ARC	Affordable, Robust, Compact
AS	Air System
AS	Auxiliary Systems
ATC	Air Traffic Control
AUVSI	Association for Uncrewed Vehicle Systems International
BEV	Battery Electric Vehicle
BFA	Biodiversity for Food and Agriculture
BFAT	Biological equivalent FAT
BFR	Brominated Flame Retardant
BIC	Balancing Intended Consequence

Systems Science for Engineers and Scholars, First Edition. Edited by Avner Engel.
© 2024 John Wiley & Sons, Ltd. Published 2024 by John Wiley & Sons, Ltd.

Bio-OS	Biological Operating System
BIOS	Basic Input/Output System
BOM	Bill of Materials
BoP	Bay of Pigs
BP	British Petroleum
BTC	Basil Transcription Complex
BTI	Bias Temperature Instability
BUC	Balancing Unintended Consequence
BWR	Boiling Water Reactor
C3	Command, Control, and Communication
CAD	Computer-Aided Design
CAIB	Columbia Accident Investigation Board
CAS	Collision Avoidance System
CAST	Causal Analysis System Theory
CBD	Convention on Biological Diversity
CCS	Carbon Capture and Sequestration
CDC	Center for Disease Control
CE	Circular Economy
CERN	Council for Nuclear Research
CFI	Corporate Finance Institute
CFS	Commonwealth Fusion Systems
CHD	Computer Hard Drive
CIA	Central Intelligence Agency
CKB	Central Knowledge Base
CLD	Causal Loop Diagram
C-MCD	Categorical multidisciplinary collaborative design
CMOMMT	Cooperative Multi-robot Observations of Multiple Moving Targets
CMOS	Complementary Metal Oxide Semiconductor
CNNC	China National Nuclear Corporation
CPU	Central Processing Unit
CRT	Cathode Ray Tubes
CT	Category Theory
CT	Chromosome Territory
CT	Computerized tomography

CTO	Cooperative Target Observation
CVR	Cockpit Voice Recorder
DESA	Department of Economic and Social Affairs
DfD	Design for Disposal
DfE	Design for the Environment
DHD	DNA Hard Drive
DIS	Safety Information System
DKK	Danish Krone
DM	Decision-Maker
DNA	Deoxyribonucleic Acid
DoD	Department of Defense
DoJ	Department of Justice
DOS	Disk Operating System
DPE	Design Process Expert
DSM	Dependency Structure Matrix
E&F	Electricity and Fuel
EAST	Experimental Advanced Superconducting Tokamak
EIA	Energy Information Administration
EKB	Expert Knowledge Base
EM	Expert Models
EMI	Electromagnetic Interference
EP	Electric Propulsion
EPA	Environmental Protection Agency
EROI	Energy Return On Investment
ESA	European Space Agency
EV	Electric Vehicle
FAA	Federal Aviation Administration
FAO	Food and Agriculture Organization of the United Nations
FAT	File Allocation Table
FDA	Food and Drug Administration
FMEA	Modes and Effects Analysis
FRC	Field Reversed Configuration
FWC	Florida Fish and Wildlife Conservation Commission

GA	Genetic algorithm
GAO	Government Accountability Office
GCO	Ground Communication
GCS	Ground Control Station
GDP	Gross domestic product
GF	General Fusion
GHG	Greenhouse Gas
GIS	Geographic Information Systems
GM	General Motors
GMCR	Graph Model for Conflict Resolution
GOV	Government
GPS	Global Positioning System
GRS	Gamma-Ray Spectrometer
GST	General Systems Theory
HCI	Hot Carrier Injection
HEV	Hybrid Electric Vehicle
HFC	Hydrofluorocarbon
HGP	Human Genome Project
HR	Human Resources
HS	Hyperspectral
HST	Hubble Space Telescope
IAEA	International Atomic Energy Agency
IAF	Israel Air Force
IAI	Israel Aerospace Industries
ICAO	International Civil Aviation Organization
ICBM	InterContinental Ballistic Missile
ICD	Interface Control Document
ICE	Internal Combustion Engine
ICF	Inertial Confinement Fusion
IDF	Israeli Defense Force
IDG	Integrated Design Graphs
IDV	Integrated Design Views
IEC	International Electrotechnical Commission

IFSR	International Federation for Systems Research
INCOSE	International Council on Systems Engineering
IO	Input/Output
IPBES	Intergovernmental Science-Policy Platform on Biodiversity and Ecosystem Services
IPCC	Intergovernmental Panel on Climate Change
IR	Infrared
ISA	Instruction Set Architecture
IT	Information technology
ITER	International Thermonuclear Experimental Reactor
IUCN	International Union for Conservation of Nature
IV	Intravenous
IW	International Workshop
JASS	Japan Association for Social and Economic Systems Studies
JET	Joint European Torus
JPL	Jet Propulsion Laboratory
KPA	Key Performance Attributes
LHC	Large Hadron Collider
LI	Laser Illumination
LIDAR	Light Detection and Ranging
LNCR	UAV Launcher
LRF	Laser Range Finder
LST	Living Systems Theory
MAR	Matrix Attachment Regions
MASON	Multi-agent Simulation Environment
MCD	Multidisciplinary, Collaborative Design
MIMO	Multiple Input Multiple Output
MIT	Massachusetts Institute of Technology
MOMA	Multiobjective Multiagent
MOMP	Multiple Objectives Multiple Participants
MP	Mechanical Propulsion

MRI	Magnetic resonance imaging
MS	Multispectral
MTF	Magnetized Target Fusion
NAS	Nuclear Attachment Substrate
NASA	National Aeronautics and Space Administration
NCJ	National Institute of Justice
NETL	National Energy Technology Laboratory
NGO	Nongovernmental Organization
NIF	National Ignition Facility
NIR	Near Infrared
NIRCam	Near Infrared Camera
Nm	Nanometer
NOAA	National Oceanic and Atmospheric Administration
NSWG	Natural Science Working Group
O&G	Oil and Gas
O&U	Operators and Users
OA	Operational Amplifiers
OPM	Object-Process Methodology
OS	Operating System
PC	Personal Computer
PD	Parametric Design
PFC	Perfluorocarbon
PID	Proportional Integral and Derivative
PRI	Product Responsible Incidents
PV	Photovoltaic
PVC	Poly Vinyl Chloride
PWS	Proximity Warning System
Qbits	Quad Bits
QHC	Quantum Hamiltonian Complexity
QST	National Institutes for Quantum Science and Technology

R&D	Research and Development
RAM	Random Access Memory
RE	Renewable Energy
RFP	Request for Proposal
RIC	Reinforcing Intended Consequences
RMS	Royal Mail Steamer
RNA	Ribonucleic Acid
RO	Ring Oscillators
ROI	Return on Investment
ROM	Read Only Memory
RT	Remote Terminals
RUC	Reinforcing Unintended Consequence
RVM	Requirement Verification Matrix
SAC	Sikorsky Aircraft Company
SAR	Scaffold Attachment Regions
SAR	Successive Approximation Registers
SAR	Synthetic Aperture Radar
SC	Safety Constraint
SC	Switched Capacitors
SE	Support Equipment
SE	Systems Engineering
SEBoK	Systems Engineering Body of Knowledge
SEMP	System Engineering Management Plan
SIL	System Integration Laboratory
SIM	Semantic Integration Model
SIP	System Integration Plan
SISO	Single Input Single Output
SLS	Space Launch System
SME	Subject Matter Expert
SMR	Small Modular Reactors
SoI	System of Interest
SOS	Systems of Systems
SOSF	Systems Of Systems Failures
SQA	System Quality Assurance

SR	Short Range
SRR	System Requirements Review
SRS	System Requirements Specification
SSDD	System/Subsystem Design Document
SSDR	System/Subsystem Design Review
SSWG	Systems Science Working Group
ST	Systems Thinking
STAMP	Systems-Theoretic Accident Model and Processes
STD	System Test Description
STP	System Test Plan
STR	System Test Results
STS	Space Transportation System
SWOT	Strengths, Weaknesses, Opportunities, and Threats
SysML	Systems Modeling Language
TAE	Tri Alpha Energy
TE	Tokamak Energy
TENS	Transcutaneous Electrical Nerve Stimulation
TEPCO	Tokyo Electric Power Company
TFR	Thick-Film Resistors
TN	Tail Number
TNT	Trinitrotoluene
TRL	Technology Readiness Level
TS	Training Simulator
UAS	Unmanned Aircraft System
UAV	Unmanned Air Vehicle
UK	United Kingdom
UMA	UAV Mission Authority
UN	United Nation
UNEP	United Nations Environment Program
UNESCO	United Nations Educational, Scientific and Cultural Organization
UPS	United Parcel Service
URI	User Responsible Incidents
US	United States

USA	United States of America
USAF	US Air Force
USGS	US Geological Survey
USN	US Navy
UV	Ultraviolet
VAFB	Vandenberg Air Force Base
VL	Visible Light
VS	Vehicle Structure
VSM	Viable System Model
VTOL	Vertical Take-Off and Landing
VVT	Verification, Validation, and Testing
VVT-MP	VVT Management Plan
WBS	Work Breakdown Structure
WEEE	Waste Electrical and Electronic Equipment
WHO	World Health Organization
WMO	World Meteorological Organization
WWF	World Wildlife Fund

Index

Systems Science for Engineers and Scholars, First Edition. Edited by Avner Engel.
© 2024 John Wiley & Sons, Ltd. Published 2024 by John Wiley & Sons, Ltd.

Printed and bound by CPI Group (UK) Ltd, Croydon, CR0 4YY

27/10/2024

14580668-0004